# Teaching and Training in Post-Compulsory Education

Third edition

# Teaching and Training in Post-Compulsory Education

## Third edition

*Andy Armitage, Robin Bryant, Richard Dunnill, Karen Flanagan, Dennis Hayes, Alan Hudson, Janis Kent, Shirley Lawes and Mandy Renwick*

Open University Press

Open University Press
McGraw-Hill Education
McGraw-Hill House
Shoppenhangers Road
Maidenhead
Berkshire
England
SL6 2QL

email: enquiries@openup.co.uk
world wide web: www.openup.co.uk

and
Two Penn Plaza
New York, NY 10121–2289, USA

First edition published 1999
First published in the third edition 2007

A catalogue record of this book is available from the British Library

ISBN10: 0 335 22267 6 (pb)    0 335 22268 4 (hb)
ISBN13: 978 0 335 22267 4 (pb)    978 0 335 22268 1 (hb)

Library of Congress Cataloging-in-Publication Data
CIP data has been applied for

Typeset by RefineCatch Limited, Bungay, Suffolk
Printed in Poland by OZGraf S.A.
www.polskabook.pl

The McGraw·Hill Companies

# Contents

# Acknowledgements

The authors and publisher are grateful to the following: Lifelong Learning UK for its cooperation in the use of the new professional standards in relation to each chapter (although the selection of these standards was made by the authors); Nathan Wells of Orpington College for the lesson plan and evaluation in Chapter 2; Mary Garland, Canterbury Christ Church University PGCE (Post-Compulsory) student, for the extract from her reflective journal in Chapter 2; Katrina McIntyre and Maria Gurrin of Sheppey College for the Temporary Record of Practical Assessment in Chapter 6; Anita Goymer of Sheppey College for the Working With Others and ILP/Tutorial Record Sheet pro-formas in Chapter 6; the Assessment and Qualifications Alliance for permission to reproduce material from Teachers' Guide to GCSE AS and A Health and Social Care in Chapter 6.

The publisher is very grateful to the following universities for permission to reproduce photographs on the cover: UCE Birmingham, University of Brighton, Bristol UWE and Loughborough University.

In addition, the authors would like to thank our colleagues at Canterbury Christ Church University and our colleagues and many students throughout the Canterbury Christ Church University Certificate in Education (Post-Compulsory) Consortium, without whose practice and experience this book would not have been possible.

Although this book has been a joint venture by the central team of the Canterbury Christ Church University College Department of Post-Compulsory Education and associated colleagues, individuals took responsibility for the following: Andy Armitage for overall editorial control and Chapter 6; Robin Bryant and Karen Flanagan for Chapter 5; Richard Dunnill for Chapters 7 and 8; Dennis Hayes for Chapter 1; Dennis Hayes and Alan Hudson for Chapter 9; Andy Armitage and Janis Kent for Chapter 2; Shirley Lawes for Chapter 3; and Mandy Renwick for Chapter 4.

# Abbreviations

| | |
|---|---|
| ACL | Adult and Community Learning |
| AE | adult education |
| ALI | Adult Learning Inspectorate |
| AoC | Association of Colleges |
| AP(E)L | Accreditation of prior (experiential) learning |
| AQA | Assessment and Qualifications Alliance |
| AUT | Association of University Teachers |
| AVCE | Advanced Vocational Certificate of Education |
| BEC | Business Education Council |
| BTEC | Business and Technology Education Council |
| C&G | City & Guilds |
| CAL | computer-aided learning |
| CAT | college of advanced technology |
| CBET | competence-based education and training |
| CBI | Confederation of British Industry |
| CBL | computer-based learning |
| CEF | Colleges' Employers' Forum |
| CEL | Centre for Excellence in Leadership |
| CETT | Centre for Excellence in Teacher Training |
| CGLI | City & Guilds London Institute |
| CLA | Copyright Licensing Authority |
| CNAA | Council for National Academic Awards |
| CPD | continuing professional development |
| CPVE | Certificate of Pre-vocational Education |
| CSE | Certificate of Secondary Education |
| CSJ | Commission on Social Justice |
| DCSF | Department for Children, Schools and Families |
| DDP | 14–19 Diploma Development Partnership |
| DES | Department of Education and Science |
| DfE | Department for Education |
| DfEE | Department for Education and Employment |

| | |
|---|---|
| DfES | Department for Education and Skills |
| DIUS | Department for Innovation, Universities and Skills |
| DoE | Department of Employment |
| DWP | Department for Work and Pensions |
| ECDL | European Computer Driving Licence |
| ECM | Every Child Matters |
| EEC | European Economic Community |
| EHEI | Enterprise in Higher Education Initiative |
| EQ | emotional intelligence quotient |
| ERA | Education Reform Act 1988 |
| ESOL | English as a second or other language |
| FAQ | frequently asked questions |
| FE | further education |
| FEDA | Further Education Development Agency |
| FEFC | Further Education Funding Council |
| FENTO | Further Education National Training Organisation |
| FEU | Further Education Unit |
| FHE | further and higher education |
| GCE | General Certificate of Education |
| GCSE | General Certificate of Secondary Education |
| GNVQ | General National Vocational Qualification |
| GTC | General Teaching Council |
| HE | higher education |
| HEA | Higher Education Academy |
| HEFCE | Higher Education Funding Council for England |
| iWB | Interactive Whiteboard |
| IAP | Individual Action Plan |
| IfL | Institute for Learning |
| IiP | Investors in People |
| ILA | Individual Learning Account |
| ILP | individual learning plan |
| ILT | Institute for Learning and Teaching in Higher Education |
| IPPR | Institute for Public Policy Research |
| IQ | intelligence quotient |
| ISP | Internet service provider |
| IT | information technology |
| ITALS | Initial Teaching Award Learning and Skills |
| ITB | Industrial Training Board |
| LA | local authority |
| LLL | lifelong learning |
| LLUK | Lifelong Learning UK |
| LSC | Learning and Skills Council |
| LSN | Learning and Skills Network |
| LSRN | Learning Skills Research Network |
| MSC | Manpower Services Commission |
| NATFHE | National Association of Teachers in Further and Higher Education |

| | |
|---|---|
| NCC | National Curriculum Council |
| NCLB | No Child Left Behind (US) |
| NCVQ | National Council for Vocational Qualifications |
| NEDO | National Economic Development Office |
| NHS | National Health Service |
| NIACE | National Institute of Adult Continuing Education |
| NTI | New Training Initiative |
| NTO | National Training Organization |
| NVQ | National Vocational Qualification |
| OFL | open and flexible learning |
| Ofsted | Office for Standards in Education, Children's Services and Skills |
| OHP | overhead projector |
| OHT | overhead transparency |
| OVAE | Office of Vocational and Adult Education (US) |
| PCE | post-compulsory education |
| PCET | post-compulsory education and training |
| PGCE | Postgraduate Certificate of Education |
| PTLLS | Preparing to Teach in the Lifelong Learning Sector |
| QCA | Qualifications and Curriculum Authority |
| QIA | Quality Improvement Agency |
| QTLS | Qualified Teacher Learning and Skills |
| RAE | Research Assessment Exercise |
| RBL | resource-based learning |
| RSA | Royal Society of Arts |
| RSI | repetitive strain injury |
| SATs | Standard Assessment Tasks |
| SCAA | School Curriculum and Assessment Authority |
| SEAC | School Examinations and Assessment Council |
| SSC | Sector Skills Council |
| SSDA | Sector Skills Development Agency |
| T2G | Train to Gain |
| TA | Training Agency |
| TDLB | Training and Development Lead Body |
| TEC | Training and Enterprise Council/Technician Education Council |
| *TES* | *Times Educational Supplement* |
| TILT | Teaching with Independent Learning Technologies |
| TOPS | Training Opportunities Scheme |
| TTA | Teacher Training Agency |
| TTRB | Teacher Training Resource Bank |
| TUC | Trades Union Congress |
| TVEI | Technical and Vocational Education Initiative |
| VLE | virtual learning environment |
| UCU | University and College Union |
| WEA | Workers' Educational Association |
| YOP | Youth Opportunities Programme |
| YTS | Youth Training Scheme |

# Introduction

This book is chiefly a resource for students following courses such as 'Preparing to Teach in the Lifelong Learning Sector' (PTLLS) and Certificate (CTLLS) or Diploma (DTLLS) in Teaching in the Lifelong Learning Sector or Certificate in Education in Post-Compulsory Education (PCE), or in what may variously be termed 'further education' (FE), 'adult and further education' or similar, which all have in common a concern with students post-14 offered by National Awarding Bodies or higher education institutions. While directed primarily at such students, this book will also prove useful to students training to teach in the secondary, FE and HE sectors on Professional or Postgraduate Certificate of Education (PGCE) courses. In addition, those intending to gain and retain Qualified Teacher Learning and Skills status (QTLS) will need to engage annually in 30 hours' continuing professional development. CPD will be central to the delivery of the 14–19 curriculum, particularly the specialist diplomas, so that teachers of post-14 students involved in staff development in schools, sixth-form, tertiary or FE colleges, or in the adult education sector will find this book a helpful resource. Finally, the book will be useful in relation to a wide range of development activities for those involved in training in industry and commerce, in both the public and the private sectors.

*Teaching and Training in Post-Compulsory Education* is not intended as a textbook to be read from cover to cover. Its purpose is more practical and dynamic. It assumes that its users are engaged in a programme of training or staff development and that they are either teaching/training or engaged in teaching practice. It makes teachers' professional contexts the focus for their development and each section therefore contains a series of practical tasks which, in all cases, are based on those contexts. However, since the emphasis of courses such as the PTLLS and CTLLS is on the acquisition of basic teaching skills and we feel the Diploma in TLLS should build on this foundation by developing the capacities to analyse critically and reflect, the practical tasks are stimulated or complemented by theory, analysis, information, discussion or examples of student work.

Although this book does have a developmental structure (outlined below), users can dip into chapters as they wish. Each chapter is divided into self-contained subsections with their own key issues and can be used separately.

Since PCE tutors teach in such a range of isolated contexts, often with little experience of the sector as a whole, Chapter 1 looks at the breadth of the sector. It questions whether PCE teachers are united by a common concept of professionalism, traces the ideas underpinning some key PCE issues to the work of three educational thinkers and ends with a consideration of the current dominance of vocationalism in PCE. This chapter encourages students to take stock of their own professional/ideological stance which we regard as either an implicit or explicit feature of every teacher's work.

Chapter 2 looks at the central learning processes a PCET teacher training course is likely to involve. Our experience has been that many students have not been engaged in systematic study for many years and the chapter therefore acts as an introduction to the skills required for using such learning processes. It should be particularly valuable at the beginning of a course when students may be arriving from a variety of course types with a range of curriculum models.

With the 'learning society' and 'lifelong learning' (LLL) high on the national political agenda, Chapter 3 considers what this can mean for learning in PCE. The major learning theories are examined to see what they can offer to a sector where breaking down learning barriers is a priority and which is very rapidly moving along the road to learning autonomy.

Chapter 4 focuses on the growing range of teaching skills needed in the increasing variety of roles PCE tutors are being required to play, from instructor, lecturer and coach to counsellor, adviser, enabler and facilitator.

At the same time as giving users a very practical guide to the main teaching and learning resources, Chapter 5 develops Chapter 3's concern with learning autonomy by considering the resource implications of the expansion of information technology (IT) and the increasing reliance on open, flexible, resource-based approaches.

Although Chapter 6 looks closely at competence-based assessment, now dominant in the sector, and offers support to those engaged in assessor awards, it recognizes that the expertise of many in PCE may be limited to such an approach, and so offers a wider view of the basic concepts, principles and practice of assessing students.

Chapters 7 and 8 recognize not only the increasing importance in PCE of teachers' capacity to reflect on and evaluate the courses they teach but also the vital role many may now have to play in designing and developing courses to meet students' changing needs.

Chapter 9 offers a detailed chronology of PCE as a resource for supporting a research-based project students may wish to undertake into an aspect of PCE, drawing on their work related to previous chapters. In addition, there is a section on comparative chronologies.

## Introduction to the third edition

The four years since the publication of the second edition this book have seen the extension and development of many of the themes, policies, initiatives and innovations affecting the professional practice of both new and experienced teachers both first and second editions attempted to address. In such a rapidly developing sector, however, there are major changes in policy and practice which now require consideration.

All of these are noted, explained or discussed in Chapters 1 and 9 which offer an overview of the sector. In addition, specific developments are dealt with as follows. Those LLUK standards which we feel are relevant to the content of chapters are set out at the end of each one. From September 2007, all new teachers, trainers and lecturers who successfully complete their initial teacher training will be awarded Qualified Teacher Learning and Skills (QTLS) status and will be registered with the Institute for Learning (IfL) as holding a full licence to practise. However, in order to maintain this licence, each teacher must renew their licence annually by completing 30 hours of suitable continuing professional development (CPD) each year. The impact of such changes on the profession is considered in Chapter 2. The importance of personalized learning and of assessment for learning have been at the centre of a range of policy initiatives which will make demands on teachers' pedagogical and assessment capabilities (Chapters 3, 4 and 6). A range of resources, particularly ICT resources, have become available to teachers in the sector and these are considered in Chapter 5. Arguably, the most important changes affecting the sector relate to the 14–19 age phase (Chapter 7). Broadly, they can be described as follows: a greater focus on the 3Rs – the functional skills needed for everyday life, demonstrated through real-life application; stronger vocational routes, where young people develop in part through practical experience, with qualifications that give them a broad enough education to progress further in learning as well as into employment; more stretching options on both general and applied routes and activities which extend young people, backed by greater flexibility for young people to accelerate through the system, or to take longer in order to achieve higher standards; new ways to tackle disengagement and to ensure that those in danger of dropping out can be motivated to stay in learning. In curriculum terms, the major development involves 14 lines of specialized diplomas which are to be phased in from 2008.

# 1

# Working in post-compulsory education

## 1.1 What is Chapter 1 about?

This chapter will set out a series of problems and choices which face all teachers and trainers in PCE. Section 1.2 attempts to define what 'post-compulsory education' means and raises the problem of what, if anything, can be understood by talk of teacher professionalism in the ever-expanding PCE sector. The notion of 'professionalism' is related to different discussions of the nature and importance of knowledge. A discussion of the knowledge base of PCE then leads us to examine the relationship between 'education' and 'training', and 'teaching' and 'training' in PCE, and their relation to a new professionalism based on the notions of responsibility and duty. Section 1.3 examines the views of three educational philosophers whose ideas are central to thinking about PCE today and invites the post-compulsory teacher to consider their own philosophical standpoint. Section 1.4 discusses how forms of 'vocationalism' have come to dominate thinking across the post-compulsory sector and the challenges this poses for the PCE teacher or trainer.

---

**Task 1.1: Preliminary reading**

Our assumption is that the reader will already know something of the changing nature of further, adult and higher education, such as:

- The role of government quangos such as the Learning and Skills Councils (LSCs); Higher Education Funding Council for England (HEFCE); and Lifelong Learning UK (LLUK).

- The range of qualifications from National Vocational Qualifications (NVQs) at various levels and the structure of GCSEs and A levels (including 'vocational' A levels) to new initiatives such as Foundation Degrees.

- The role of professional bodies such as the University and College Union; the Association of Colleges (AoC); the Quality Improvement Agency (QIA); the Learning and Skills Network (LSN) and the Institute for Learning (IfL).

However, if you are unfamiliar with this field, we would particularly recommend the

Chronology of PCE in Chapter 9 of this book as a very useful starting point and reference work. Other than this, there is a range of introductory books. For example, Vince Hall's *Further Education in the UK* (1994) is a standard work, and Prue Huddleston and Lorna Unwin's *Teaching and Learning in Further Education*, first published in 1997, gives basic information in a straightforward way. With the introduction of mandatory teaching qualifications for lecturers working in further and adult education settings a range of introductory books has come onto the market that provide an introduction to the PCE sector and what is currently required of teachers (see Hayes et al. 2007: chapter 8, for a discussion of these). The issues discussed throughout this book are of a universal character, dealing with topics such as the nature of professionalism and the conflict between education and practicality.

## 1.2  Contested concepts of professionalism in PCE

**KEY ISSUES**

PCE implies a notion of professionalism that is grounded in paid employment. This is the first and most minimal definition of professionalism.

This professionalism is a broad notion but one which implies subject expertise.

Educational thought of the 1960s and 1970s led to theoretical subjects achieving primacy in the curriculum. Does this create a gap between the academic and vocational which excludes a great deal of what happens in PCE?

Is there a permanent *deprofessionalization* of PCE teachers and trainers or is there a *reprofessionalization* around new concepts of responsibility, being promoted by the IfL?

What does the popular phrase the 'new' professionalism mean?

The term PCE is often no more than an alternative for FE. However, this is to forget or ignore the 'training' dimension of PCE, and as a result PCE is sometimes referred to as post-compulsory education and training (PCET). Then there is adult education (AE), further and higher education (FHE), higher education (HE), university education, training in industry and commerce, and informal teaching and training situations. There have been recent government-inspired attempts to define aspects of PCE policy such as the attempt to redesignate PCE as the 'learning and skills sector'. This is too narrow a definition although it should forewarn us of the future trend of policy (see Chapter 9). We could attempt to cover all these areas of PCE with the term 'lifelong learning' (LLL) but this is more of a slogan to be defined than a catch-all. Where do we begin the process of defining PCE? Helena Kennedy starts her report, *Learning Works: Widening Participation in Further Education* with the throwaway definition 'Further Education is everything that does not happen in schools or universities' (Kennedy 1997b: 1). Likewise, we could define PCE as everything that does not happen in schools up to the age of 16. This is a general and not very useful definition. (It is not even true, as it ignores the range of vocational and academic courses provided for 14–19-year-olds in schools and colleges.) The field is obviously vast and it is becoming commonplace to talk as if PCE was about any learning that takes place outside compulsory schooling. But this is a dangerous and misleading perspective. A good and proper starting point is to say that we are only talking about learning in which there is normally a 'cash nexus': someone is paying or being paid for the learning that goes on, or someone is being trained to enter paid employment. There are many marginal cases that might be raised in objection. For example: Percy has retired but still teaches his daughter-in-law German in his home; Alan provides a group of interested young students with an introduction to history outside of their formal programme. These unpaid or informal learning sessions do not differ in any way that matters from 'paid' sessions. They are simply imitations of them that become less and less recognizable as they become less formal. This distinction is very crude but it has its point. An idealistic colleague recently declared that she would go on teaching even if she wasn't paid. Advocates of the 'learning society' or 'learning organization' often promote learning, with an evangelical fervour, as the responsibility of all, in a way reminiscent of the 'de-schoolers' and certain adult educationalists. We will return to these views later. What they represent here is an elementary attack on professionalism. The sort of learning we are talking about is the learning that is brought about by an individual or individuals who see themselves as professional teachers or trainers who are paid for what they do. In the LLL literature there is a tendency to discuss other sorts of learning than formal learning. This can even include such concepts as 'family learning' which we might think has gone on for centuries (Alexander and Clyne 1995; Alexander 1997). We argue that this is to elevate less important forms of knowledge as equivalent to serious forms of study. Rhetorical talk about 'the information society', the 'knowledge economy' or 'the learning society' often fosters the acceptance of a very wide definition of knowledge that also encourages a lack of discrimination about different sorts of knowledge. This must necessarily diminish the worth of the paid professional. Issues about professionalism, therefore, are closely connected with a PCE teacher or trainer's view of knowledge and its worth.

---

**Task 1.2: Identifying elements of professionalism in PCE**

Do you consider yourself to be a professional? Try to identify what makes you a professional. If you do not describe your role as 'professional', how do you describe it?

---

Apart from being paid, are there other elements to the professional role within PCE? The traditional discussion has always looked at two other criteria of professionalism: 'knowledge', which we have already touched on, and 'responsibility' (Langford 1985: 52–3). The debates of the 1970s and 1980s were concerned with whether teaching was a 'profession' or a 'job'. Issues such as status and salary were crucial. The legacy of this historical discussion of professionalism is a focus on the teaching and personal style of individuals. In this light you might have thought of 'professionalism' as a mode of presentation of self or of subject: sharply dressed, perhaps, with a 'PowerPoint' presentation and a study pack for your audience! Alternatively, you might have listed activities in your wider role: serving on committees, undertaking quality audits, designing courses and distance learning packs, recruitment and marketing. Most of this is managerial and administrative work that will often be included as part of a 'wider' understanding of the professional role. The requirement to undertake such wider roles is an element of the 'managerialism' that has become part and parcel of PCE today. What we want to examine here is a more narrow 'professionalism' which we could describe as 'subject professionalism'.

It is an assumption throughout this book that there can be both professional teachers and professional trainers. To establish this we need to explore the distinction between the two. This will require further discussion of the sort of knowledge that is being passed on. It might be thought that what 'teaching' and 'training' mean will depend to some extent on what individuals teach and how they go about it. As this book is addressed to a wide audience, we will sketch a general picture to illustrate the problems that this approach would present us with. Consider the following typical teaching and training activities:

- a university lecturer giving lectures based on his or her research into 'learning styles';
- a researcher giving seminar papers on her or his research into 'bullying';
- an AE tutor teaching A level English literature;
- an FE lecturer teaching art and design;
- a practitioner giving talks on his or her research findings in chiropody;
- a lecturer teaching a motor vehicle NVQ;
- a hairdresser teaching trainees within a private scheme;
- a police officer teaching crime-scene management;
- a human resources manager disseminating her or his firm's equal opportunities policy;
- an instructor teaching social and life skills to adults with learning difficulties.
- a counsellor teaching basic counselling skills (awareness) to teachers;
- a tutor facilitating a discussion of citizenship with play workers;
- a part-time (sessional) lecturer teaching parenting skills to a group of young mothers;
- a mother talking to her children about their family history and the forms of their extended family;
- a personal adviser talking about a student's Individual Learning Plan (ILP);
- students taking emotional intelligence quotient (EQ) tests.

These teaching and training activities are varieties of 'subject' teaching in a very ordinary sense of the word. But there is another sense in which some are 'theoretical' or knowledge-based subjects, some are 'practical' subjects and others are more difficult to classify but could be important to the college or in wider social life (e.g., the ILP).

---

**Task 1.3**

Review the list of 'subjects' above and divide them into 'practical' and 'theoretical' subjects. Are there any subjects that are difficult to place?

---

In a paper written in 1965, 'Liberal education and the nature of knowledge', Paul Hirst gave a famous description of liberal education as being 'determined in scope and content by knowledge itself' (Hirst [1965] 1973: 99). He further classified knowledge as follows: '(1) Distinct disciplines or forms of knowledge (subdivisible): mathematics, physical sciences, human sciences, history, religion, literature and the fine arts, philosophy. (2) Fields of Knowledge: theoretical, practical (these may or may not include elements of moral knowledge)' (p. 105). In this catalogue, if a subject was 'practical' it was not part of a 'liberal education' as defined. This is not to say that it was not of use – the utility of the practical cannot be denied – but it had no logical connection with the forms of human knowledge. Using this description, very few of the activities above would be part of a liberal education. They might be part of a 'general education' but this means something like 'schooling' or 'the college curriculum'.

---

**Task 1.4**

Consider the list of teaching sessions given above in the light of Hirst's distinction between 'forms' and 'fields' of knowledge. Do you now look at it differently?

---

A parallel distinction to that between liberal education and the practical fields of knowledge is that between teaching and training. Making the latter distinction is straightforward if we base it on the former. But it must not be held to undervalue the role of the trainer in society. This would not be a wise move as the teacher and trainer may be the same person in different contexts. Both the teacher and the trainer aim at getting a student or trainee to think or act for themselves. Gilbert Ryle has examined in some depth the differences between teaching and training and notions such as 'drilling' or the formation of 'habits' and 'rote' learning (Ryle 1973: 108–10). When we talk of training we do not mean to reduce it to this limited caricature which, Ryle comments, comes from memories of the nursery. Teaching and training involve teaching and training *how to do something*. They are not 'gate shutting' but 'gate opening' activities (Ryle 1973: 119). We would see the trainer with specialist knowledge and a set of practical skills as equally 'professional' as the teacher of academic subjects. We would add that recent developments, to be discussed below, threaten the professional 'gate opening' activities of both the teacher and the trainer.

**Task 1.5**

Do you see yourself as primarily a 'teacher' or a 'trainer'? What would you see as the essential difference between the two?

In the 1960s and early 1970s, educational thought was dominated by rationalist principles. Human beings were characterized by their cognitive capacities. A powerful and positive concept of human rationality dominated educational thought. Judgements about objective truth could be made. Human beliefs, actions and emotions could be guided by reason. Hirst has come to see his earlier view to be a 'hard rationalism' (Hirst 1993: 184) and says of his previous position, 'I now consider practical knowledge to be more fundamental than theoretical knowledge, the former being basic to any clear grasp of any proper significance of the latter' (p. 197). Hirst now sees education as primarily concerned with social practices. More specifically, he prioritizes 'personal development by initiation into a complex of specific, substantive social practices with all the knowledge, attitudes, feelings, virtues, skills, dispositions and relationships that it involves' (p. 197).

Underpinning the rationalism of the 1960s described above was the thinking of the early Enlightenment philosophers of the seventeenth century, such as Newton, Locke, Pascal and Descartes, who established modern intellectual values such as a belief in knowledge, objective truth, reason, science, progress, experimentation and the universal applicability of these to all of mankind's ability to control nature. It has to be said about Hirst's explanation of forms and fields of knowledge that he in some ways merely reflected the current thinking of his time (see Chapter 9 – the 1960s was the decade of the space race and the first moon landing). This does not make his educational epistemology false, but it does mean that as times have changed and people have become less confident about science and knowledge. Hirst has begun to reflect this in his thinking.

There have also been attacks on such confident views of the importance of knowledge by postmodernists (Usher and Edwards 1994) and seemingly radical thinkers (Bloomer 1996, 1997; Harkin et al. 2001). Postmodernists will ask 'Whose knowledge?', stress a variety of truths and distrust reason. They further distrust science and the notion of progress and question the damage done by attempting to control nature. They seek to emphasize different and particular views rather than universal 'theories' which attempt to explain how the world or society works. It is better to see such views as a reflection of less confident times rather than as a serious contribution to educational thought, although like all extreme and distorted philosophies they are not without their insights. As far as the relativity of knowledge – the notion that there are different 'truths' – is concerned, postmodernists have to answer a fatal critique first made by Socrates in Plato's *Theaetetus* (Burnyeat 1990) over 2000 years ago. A simple formulation of this critique is to express the postmodern viewpoint in a simple statement – 'All truths are relative' – and to ask 'Is this statement true?' The consequences of the question are that either the statement is true or its negation is true. Therefore there is a true statement that is not relative. This simply shows that the more facile forms of relativism that some postmodernists desire are contradictory if they are articulated. Fortunately, postmodernist thought has had little impact on the PCE sector other than, and most worryingly, in some sectors of HE.

This is not the case with the increasing numbers of PCE teacher-educators and trainers influenced by 'critical theory'. Critical theorists and their followers see the challenge of PCE teaching and training as making 'classrooms more open in language practices', which means that 'Differences of gender, culture and outlook should be celebrated as part of a democratic endeavour' (Harkin et al. 2001: 135). Martin Bloomer's somewhat artificial notion of 'studenthood' comes out of this school of thought. He notes that 'studenthood' conceptualizes the ways in which students can begin to learn independently and recognize 'the problematic nature of knowledge' (Bloomer 1996: 140) through reflection on their own learning experiences. The consequence is that they can begin to 'exert influence over the curriculum' in 'the creation and confirmation of their own personal learning careers' (p. 140). Bloomer's conceptualization of PCE teaching situations might be an example of what is often called 'praxis' or 'practical wisdom'. The result of these individualistic applications of what were originally Marxist ideas is not radical because it leaves students engaging in a critical self-reflection that is a sort of therapy (see Therborn 1978: 125–8). The appeal of this to some PCE teachers and trainers is a false sense of being able to solve social problems through 'the enlightened efforts of critical students and scholars' (Therborn 1978: 139).

This radical view of the potential of teachers, trainers and students has a parallel in a more conservative view of PCE and one that is widespread. Radical teacher-trainers may see education as transformative for individuals, but managers and government policymakers are more likely to promote the idea that FE, in particular, can regenerate the economy. We can call this the Bilston College Fallacy as that college did much to promote this view in a series of publications (see Reeves 1997 and, for a critical assessment, Bryan 1998). (Ironically, Bilston College experienced severe financial difficulties shortly after the publication of its well-known book.) Both the radical and conservative views of FE overestimate the role of education in, respectively, politics and the economy (see Section 1.4).

**Task 1.6**

Consider the knowledge content in your subject or area of practical expertise and how you present this to students. Do you see yourself as having the traditional role of initiating students into worthwhile forms or fields of knowledge, or areas of practical knowledge; or are you inclined towards the postmodern or relativist school of thought that sees education as something particular and of many varieties; or do you see it in the more radical way as transformative in terms of communication or through 'praxis'? If you see yourself as primarily a trainer, do you consider any of these approaches to knowledge relevant?

It can be argued, however, that such challenges to Enlightenment thinking open the door to at least two factors which could seriously undermine the status of knowledge. The first is the introduction of the concept of competence into discussions of education and training. Hyland has made three general criticisms of competence-based education. These are that it is no more than a confused slogan, that it has foundations in behaviourist theories which ignore human understanding, and that there is no coherent account of knowledge in the competence literature (Hyland 1994: chs. 2, 4, 5). Hyland has made some excellent criticisms of various writers on the nature of competence as having a crude understanding of know-how, of skill and of the complexities of judgements required in making a knowledge claim. All that is held to be required are certain stipulated outcomes that we can pick out. This is linked with a 'tendency to reduce all talk of knowledge, skills, competence, and the like, to talk about "evidence"' (Hyland 1994: 74). This gives some competence statements a spurious and vague meaning. However it provides us with a very impoverished concept of what it is to 'know' something, that relates only to the performance of work functions.

---

**Task 1.7**

Competence and knowledge: find examples of competence statements from your own or another subject, or from a teacher training course. Consider what concept of knowledge they embody, and see if it makes sense. Do they refer to narrow skills or dispositions or to broad general capacities? Do they adequately take account of the nature of judgement? You might like to review Hyland's criticisms (1994: chs. 5, 8) and how far the introduction of General National Vocational Qualifications (GNVQs) and subsequent changes has gone to meet them.

---

There is a hint of paradox in that competence-based training schemes are often couched in the empowering 'student-centred' language of progressive or humanistic education. But by emphasizing learning by doing, rather than becoming critical thinkers, competence-based programmes require students to be both intellectually passive and yet very busy. Keeping students working at gathering evidence to establish competence seems to many critics to be the introduction of the discipline of the workplace in the interest of any future employer.

---

**Task 1.8**

To what extent have you observed the conjunction of competence-based training programmes and humanistic or student-centred philosophies? Try to find a clear example of such a conjunction in a course document or handbook.

---

The second way in which knowledge could be seen to be devalued concerns the introduction of competence-based programmes of teacher training. The absence of theory and academic knowledge in teacher training programmes is a result of many years of government spokespeople blaming theory, particularly that of the 1960s, for all the problems in education, if not all the ills of society! It is hardly surprising, therefore, that we find competence-based schemes predominating in teacher education. In FE the early 1990s saw the introduction of the competence-based vocational assessor qualifications (D32 and D33) by the Training and Development Lead Body (TDLB), the launch of a competence-based C&G Further and Adult Education Teacher's Certificate and the start of many competence-based Certificate in Education (FE) courses. The outcome of many of these courses could be said to be the deprofessionalization of the post-compulsory teacher (Hyland 1994: 93). The replication in teacher training, at all levels, of the competence-based model means that the model of control applied to students could also operate with staff. It would be a work-related, operational form of discipline that would be adopted, but it would be self-imposed. Many staff who have been working in PCE for some time will have obtained D32 and D33 and other competence-based qualifications. Despite some early cynicism, these programmes are now universally accepted. The consequence of all this is that teachers and trainers in AE and FE have come to see themselves as assessors, checking portfolios to see if there is evidence that student learning has occurred. It is difficult to find ways of opposing these schemes when not only your own subject knowledge but academic knowledge itself is being challenged. The shift in terminology from 'competences' to 'standards' is an example of a simple change of label and should not be seen as of any importance, except that 'standards' seems to be less obviously work-related. It is, of course, much harder to object to 'standards' than 'competences', which are obviously work-based. There is a danger of this approach to teacher education spreading to HE through the implementation of recommendations from the Dearing Report *Higher Education in the Learning Society* (Dearing 1997). Dearing's report led to the formation of the Institute for Learning and Teaching in Higher Education (ILT), now absorbed into the Higher Education Academy (HEA), that has rapidly expanded teacher training in HE with the specific aim of redressing the balance between teaching and research. The most likely outcome of this development will be a competence-based scheme similar to those found in FE. The crucial difference here is that the business of HE is knowledge and research, not competence or skills. It is the ethos created by this focus on advancing knowledge that makes teaching so exciting for many at this level. Dearing's proposals to make HE teaching more learner-centred will not necessarily help students. The idea is that the student is not to be passive but must actively engage in the learning process. At HE level this is to turn the focus of education away from the knowledge and understanding needed to ultimately engage in research, to playing with methods of learning, something that could turn the academy into a mere centre of 'edutainment'. But, crucially, Dearing's general view of knowledge is as a commodity that can be delivered by teachers or through IT. His report reveals no clear understanding of what a university is. This failing could reduce all teachers in HE to the position that many FE teachers now find themselves in: as assessors checking off whether they have evidence that learning has occurred. The engagement and interaction with research-based knowledge could become a rare experience (see Hayes 2002).

**Task 1.9: Teaching, assessing or guiding?**

The argument we have put forward is that there is a danger that in devaluing knowledge and critical thinking we necessarily turn from being teachers to being assessors. However, the latest shift is for staff in PCE to take upon themselves the role of educational guidance workers, assisted by personal advisers from the Connexions Service (the service intended to provide a single point of contact, offering advice to all young people). Although this may seem to be a shift away from assessing, it is a complementary activity that requires that teachers and trainers now assess more and more aspects of a student's life rather than theoretical or practical learning. The emphasis now being placed on individual guidance is more the formalization of an existing change than something qualitatively different. Many PCE teachers will say that although their formal job is to assess learning, much of their time is taken up with coaching, advising and getting students to reflect and explore their ideas, and that therefore the assessment part of their work has become a formality. Consider whether this is true by reflecting upon how much of your own teaching involves imparting knowledge and developing critical thinking, or involves personal (and educational) guidance.

It may be thought that the notion of the post-compulsory teacher or trainer as a 'reflective practitioner' could be a way out of the teacher or assessor dilemma. There are problems in understanding what the phrase 'reflective practitioner' means to most people and even of making sense of the most careful expositions (see Gilroy 1993). The term appears to replicate the use of humanistic, student-centred rationales for competence-based programmes for students and trainees. It confines the teacher or trainer to their particular concerns in the classroom and redefines 'theory' to mean the systematic restructuring of the teacher's own experience and ideas. In this way, the model rejects a rationalist model of objective truth (see Elliott 1993). In the context of a general attack on academic knowledge and critical thinking, the term 'reflective practitioner' might not, as we may be tempted to think, allow us to subvert the competence-based curriculum. The theorists of reflective practice could be involved in an implicit attack on just this possibility, however much they dislike the competence-based approach. Some of them would respond that they do offer a sort of theory: critical theory. 'Critical theory', which is the product of former Marxists of the 'Frankfurt School' is essentially a politicization of PCE that works through an emphasis on questioning all assumptions (Hillier 2005). The aim is a critical consciousness to promote positive or even revolutionary social change but the practical result, in what are far from revolutionary times, is to leave PCE teachers and trainers confused and uncertain, even anxious about what they are doing, as too much has been questioned (Hayes 2005). Others have abandoned any meaningful notion of theory and celebrate a totally subjective 'I Theory' (McNiff and Whitehead 2002; McNiff 2003).

The force of this criticism of reflective practice can be understood by considering the traditional way in which academic studies, such as some of those on any Certificate of Education (post-compulsory) programme, relate to professional practice. This was often posed as the question of the relationship of theory to practice. The attempt to link the two produced perspectives such as those involving a notion of 'praxis' (see above) but once this becomes more than an attempt to relate theory to practice and slides into talk about 'practical wisdom' or 'reflective practice', the traditional question has been turned on its head and *practice* is re-presented, however subtly, *as theory*. Tutors and students then begin to systematize and elaborate a description of their practice and call it 'theory'. This is a very special use of the term 'theory' and we would argue that the traditional way of looking at the relationship of theory to practice is still important, if only in that it reminds us that much of the work that has been done in psychology, sociology, philosophy and other disciplines is still important for the teacher to know as it is a part of the framework through which we understand the world, whether or not it is of immediate practical use.

The debate about the behaviourist philosophy of competence-based education and training (CBET) and the seeming paradox of humanistic delivery of CBET through the PCE curriculum is almost historical. This is in part because of the understanding made possible by the recent popularizing in Britain of the work of the French academic and political propagandist Pierre Bourdieu. As a result of Bourdieu's work and his discussion of what he calls 'cultural capital' it is possible to see that a different notion of 'competence' is developing that resolves this seeming paradox. There is also a more important shift in the nature of this seeming paradox which gives more attention to process – the humanistic delivery – and less to content – competence based or content based – because of what has been called by Dennis Hayes, the 'therapeutic turn' in PCE (see Hayes 2003b, 2004; Hyland 2005, 2006).

However, this needs some contextualizing and we have deferred a discussion of this new notion of competence to Section 1.4 (see p. 29).

However, at this stage it might be useful to consider the concept of 'guidance' a little further. This is the third of our three criteria of professionalism, in addition to our being paid for what we do and, most importantly, that we possess knowledge of a specialized sort. The notion of guidance we want to consider in the final part of this section is not restricted to the tutorial, personal or career guidance provided by teachers, trainers or personal advisers but 'guidance' related to the concept of making students aware of their *duties*. Increasingly, teachers and trainers find themselves dealing with cross-curricular themes rather than subjects. Key skills have already made inroads into subject-based teaching and it is possible to find whole degree programmes written in terms of the development of key skills, now that these are a required element in all HE programmes. Key skills are content-free. This is not true of other 'neglected' cross-curricular themes such as 'citizenship' and the 'environment'. It is guidance in these issues that is new. These topics are part of a new professional ethic that stresses the importance of 'duties' within an emerging 'global conception' of citizenship and the 'public good' (Bottery 2000: 235).

What is important to note about the new professionalism is how far the idea of being a professional has moved from someone being paid, or having expert knowledge, to the concept of the professional who is the vehicle for giving students a particular (and contestable) set of moral and political ideas.

With the establishment of a professional body, the Institute for Learning (IfL), there is, on its website and in its publications, evidence of the conscious working out of a notion of professionalism for PCE that reflects the above discussion. The IfL has drawn on discussions of professionalism in teacher education and is tending to adopt an external concept of professionalism that requires PCE teachers to commit to certain values, including those of environmentalism (IfL 2006a), and to a code that is, at the time of writing, tending towards the authoritarian and, it has to be said, that presents a somewhat paternalistic set of criteria for professionalism in its 'code of professional practice' (Ifl 2006b, c). Whether this will develop into a more open idea of professionalism that is grounded in subject knowledge and allows a freer, if contested, moral space depends on the IfL engaging in further debate around the issues in this chapter.

---

**Task 1.10**

Which model(s) of teacher education does your Certificate of Education course presuppose? Do you consider any of the dangers of competence-based or reflective practitioner approaches outlined above have the potential to affect you? Do you think that part of a professional role is to ensure that your students have certain sets of values?

---

## 1.3 Three educational thinkers

We have selected three educational thinkers to illustrate the philosophical basis of contemporary, if theoretically underdeveloped, ways of thinking about PCE. Following our discussion of the 'new professionalism' above, the inclusion of Socrates will be obvious. There are other reasons related to the discussion of professionalism as to why we have picked Rousseau as he is the first significant thinker to stress personal growth as an educational goal and all the problems and difficulties of sustaining such a view are apparent in his work. Our third choice of John Dewey is now a necessity. His thinking dominates all recent work in the area of PCE and, arguably, other areas of education (see Pring 1995). Every contemporary idea from 'relevance' and 'building on experience' to 'democratic' education and the possibility of a 'vocational education' that is not merely training for a job are to be found in his first major work (see Dewey [1916] 1966 and below). A case could be made for the inclusion of other thinkers. The British empiricist philosopher John Locke has been influential with a commonsensical approach to education that was intended for the English gentleman. Aristotle is in vogue with philosophers and a case could be made for including him because of his historical influence. But our selection is not meant to cover historically or fashionably influential thinkers. Our intention is to stimulate some philosophical thinking about education so that the PCE student can put contemporary thinking into perspective and not be restricted to the eclectic thinking provided in policy documents or, indeed, in books such as this.

We may never think to formulate our educational philosophy, but the terms in which we describe our professional practice will nevertheless indicate a leaning towards some form of articulated philosophy. Our argument is that we all have a 'philosophical style' as much as we have a 'teaching and learning style'.

**Task 1.11: Identifying your educational philosophy**

Consider the three groups of ideas below and select that which best describes your idea of what education should be about.

1    Critical thinking, the development of knowledge, the search for objective truth, with the teacher having authority about these matters (Socrates).

2    Personal development, autonomy in learning, growth to reach natural potential, the teacher as the facilitator of learning (Rousseau).

3    Knowledge should be useful, socially relevant, involve problem solving and be taught through practical activities; teaching should be cooperative and democratic (Dewey).

Each of these sets of ideas reflects the views of one of the philosophers we discuss below. You might have found it difficult to choose just one view and this is understandable but, in the end, we argue that they are largely incompatible. Review your choice after reading this section.

## Socrates

Socrates (469–399BC): Athenian philosopher, whose ideas come to us from Plato (429–347BC). In 387BC Plato founded a school in a grove in Athens that became known as the 'Academy', which existed for over 900 years. Plato's major educational works are the *Republic* (366BC) and the *Meno* (387BC). Another work referred to below, the *Apology*, was written in the decade after Socrates' death.

'The Socratic education begins . . . with the awakening of the mind to the need for criticism, to the uncertainty of the principles by which it supposed itself to be guided' (Anderson 1980a: 69). Criticism is at the heart of the Socratic philosophical method, but it is a criticism that seeks to show that wisdom is 'not thinking that you know what you do not know'. Socrates is wise to the extent that he does not claim to have knowledge but nevertheless seeks knowledge by a ruthless examination of the claims of individuals to have knowledge or wisdom. It is not an empirical method proceeding by reference to facts but a rationalist approach that works through the exposure of contradictions and absurdities in someone's thinking. This method can be irritating for the modern reader of the Platonic dialogues who sees his or her opinions and beliefs subjected to it (Buchanan 1982: 21). Something of the impact of this method on individuals can be gleaned from Socrates' cross-examination of Meletus at his trial, recounted in the *Apology*. Here Meletus is forced into a contradiction by being made to claim that Socrates believes in no gods and yet to see that his charge against Socrates could only be made against someone who believed in gods (Plato, *Apology*: 37–67). This is a method of teaching through which the teacher reveals a person's ignorance to them through the dialectic of discussion and the questioning of answers. Although there is a debate about this, the term 'philosophy' originally meant not 'love of wisdom' but 'love of a wise friend'. It is a wise teacher who shows you your ignorance and education thus requires a teacher to be in an entirely superior position to the pupil. An example of this method is given in the celebrated passages in the *Meno* (Plato, *Meno*: 82a–85e) where Socrates questions a slave boy about geometry. The slave boy responds confidently to the early questions but ultimately recognizes his ignorance: 'It's no use Socrates, I just don't know' (84a). This 'numbing' and 'perplexing' part of the Socratic process, or the *elenchus*, does away with false knowledge and instils the desire to learn. We are not concerned here with this proof of the theory of anamnesis, or the remembering of the immortal soul in its contemporary state, but with Socrates' methodology. For Socrates, unlike Plato, there is no end to the process of critical questioning.

It is a common mistake to confuse the views of Plato and Socrates because almost all of what we know of Socrates' teaching comes from Plato's dialogues. Some commentators make excellent distinctions between the two thinkers (Holland 1980: 18; Perkinson 1980: 14–30; Tarrant 1993: xv–xxii). We will only make the broad distinction that for Socrates education was solely about learning to be critical whereas for Plato education led, by the process of criticism, to truth. The view that education is fundamentally about criticism, however, does not require us to accept the Socratic view of wisdom or the metaphysic of Platonism.

Most discussions of the Socratic idea of education in colleges and in educational textbooks look at the system of schooling set out in the *Republic*, ignoring the discussion of the dialectic in Book VII (Plato, *Republic*: 546–84) and in the earlier dialogues. This gives undue emphasis to what Plato would consider the lower processes of education, which are really forms of training and habit formation (see Holland 1980: 18–21). In our short discussion we have tried to give an indication of the power and value of what is now dismissed by the proponents of reflective practice as 'theory-based and impractical' rationalism (Elliott 1993: 1).

In summary, the Socratic education is about the need for criticism. To overcome ignorance it utilizes a certain method: the dialectic of questioning and testing ideas. In turn, this demands that the teacher guide the pupil through a process of learning to be critical which may be perplexing and numbing. Finally, the process may or may not lead to knowledge in the form of objective truth, but that is always the goal.

---

### Task 1.12: Education as critical thinking

Is the development of critical thinking at the heart of your concept of education? If not, what role has criticism in your idea of education? Consider how important the element of critical thinking is in your particular subject area. If you are a trainer, are there ways in which you encourage a critical approach?

*Further reading*: Plato's works are accessible and easy to read. The *Apology* and *Meno* are good starting points. Both are short and relevant to contemporary educational debates about the role of the teacher. There are many editions but it is an advantage to have one with a commentary.

## Rousseau

Jean Jacques Rousseau (1712–78): essayist and philosopher of the Enlightenment period. Major educational work: *Émile* (1762).

Rousseau is a thinker of the Enlightenment period but stands in romantic reaction to it. In Section 1.2 we have already considered criticism of the Enlightenment tradition, but it may be helpful to state once again the basic principle of the Enlightenment as: a belief in the universal applicability and value to humanity in overcoming our dependence on nature by means of science, reason, progress and experimentation. Rousseau's work is not aimed at defending the *ancien régime*. He believes in the revolution that is sweeping it away but is concerned at what it is creating, the new enemy, the 'bourgeois'. He is a man who thinks only of himself and whose prime motivation is fear of his own death (Bloom 1991: 3–28). Rousseau's model of the bourgeois is based upon the pre-revolutionary bourgeois he saw growing up around him in France but also on the English gentleman whose education is described in John Locke's ([1693] 1989) *Some Thoughts Concerning Education*.

It is surprising that Rousseau has not been adopted as the educational thinker of the so-called 'postmodern age' or of 'new age thinking'. *Émile* begins with the declaration: 'Everything is good as it leaves the hands of the Author of things; everything degenerates in the hands of man' (Rousseau [1762] 1991: 37). Society, even living in small groups, corrupts man's nature. It is to nature that we must turn to save us from disfiguring everything. Rousseau describes the child as a plant, and organic and growth metaphors abound. 'Plants are shaped by cultivation, and men by education' (p. 38).

Rousseau uses a wide definition of education to mean any change brought about after our birth. It is, therefore, threefold and comes from nature, men and things. It is only the education by men that we have entire control of so we must use it to ensure that education from nature is the dominant form. Nature is defined as a state in which our dispositions are uncorrupted by opinion (Rousseau [1762] 1991: 39). Rousseau enjoins mothers to 'Observe nature and follow the path it maps out for you' (p. 41). In thinking to correct or change that path we do more harm than good.

Man in his natural state is entirely for himself. Both Locke and Rousseau held this opinion. In Locke's view the adult knows best and denies the child all his wants while giving reasons that are appropriate to the age of the child (Locke [1693] 1989: sections 39 and 44). The adult dominates and only looks for the man in the child. But Locke seeks to limit impositions and restrictions on freedom only to those that are absolutely necessary. Rousseau believes that if a child is educated by nature and things as described in the story of Émile's education, he will come to accept restrictions as legitimate rather than necessary. He will then impose them on himself. This is the essence of the good citizen. Of course, adults are active in the education of the child but only to ensure that nature takes its course. The child or young person must find out for themselves but their tutor arranges things so that certain results will follow.

In the natural order, all men are equal (Rousseau [1762] 1991: 41) so Rousseau considers only the education of the individual into man's estate. Although he was a primitivist to a certain extent, he wants men to live in society and not return to the condition of some mythical 'noble savage'. He praises Plato's *Republic* as 'the most beautiful educational treatise ever written' (p. 40). Yet he believes its vision of public education can no longer exist. His concerns are not with any particular educational institution or arrangement. He is setting out the methodology of a new form of education. In Rousseau's work we see that education has a social aim. This is to produce the citizen who will voluntarily act in accordance with the civil or 'general will'. They will do this in the same way that individuals in a state of nature act in their own self-interest (Perkinson 1980: 145). Pupils or students must learn from nature or things. The teacher must facilitate learning so that pupils or students learn for themselves.

---

### Task 1.13: Learning from nature

Is learning best undertaken by learning for oneself? How far is your own practice governed by concepts that might be compatible with Rousseau's idea of not interfering directly in the educational process for fear of corrupting learning?

*Further reading*: the clearest statement of Rousseau's philosophy is given in Books I–III of *Émile*. Book V which covers the 'last act in the drama of youth' might be of more interest to the teacher in PCE.

---

## Dewey

John Dewey (1859–1952): Professor of Philosophy at the University of Chicago from 1894. Major educational works: *Democracy and Education* (1916) and *Experience and Education* (1938).

'If in our own time the distinction between education in the traditional sense and vocational training, as increasingly demanded by a technological society, has become somewhat blurred, this is in part due to the influence of Dewey's work' (Russell [1959] 1989: 296). In the four decades since Russell asserted this balanced judgement, Dewey's work has remained a subject for fierce criticism and passionate praise. For example, journalist Melanie Phillips criticized Dewey's emphasis on process over product (knowledge) and argued that his influence on education has been 'malign, revolutionary and destructive' (Phillips 1996: 210), while Professor Frank Coffield claims that Phillips has misunderstood Dewey and agrees with him that education is the 'fundamental method of social progress' and is about 'the formation of proper social life' (Coffield 1997).

Dewey's writings encourage such different interpretations. They are written with a radical reforming zeal that often masks the kernel of what he is saying. For teachers in PCE the key element of interest in Dewey's work is his concern with vocational education and with using this to make education more relevant to students. It is important to understand what Dewey actually said because he is the most influential and frequently quoted philosopher in the PCE field, and because his work is subject to various interpretations. (It would also be useful before tackling the discussion of vocationalism in Section 1.4.)

In *Democracy and Education* (1916) Dewey warns against the separation in modern society between the capacities of the young and the concerns of the adult. Direct sharing in the pursuits of adults becomes increasingly difficult. Therefore teaching in formal institutions becomes necessary. This teaching is less personal and vital, and formal instruction 'easily becomes remote and dead – abstract and bookish' (Dewey [1916] 1966: 8).

The teaching of subjects is held to be 'specialist' teaching. The 'technical philosopher' could be 'ill advised in his actions and judgement outside of his speciality': 'Isolation of subject matter from a social context is the chief obstruction in current practice to securing a general training of mind. Literature, art, religion, when thus disassociated, are just as narrowing as the technical things which the professional upholders of general education strenuously oppose' (Dewey [1916] 1966: 67). One of the ways of overcoming this is to ensure that the child's native experience is not undervalued and that 'active occupations' form the basis of all teaching. This is the nearest Dewey comes to being 'child-centred'. What his injunction intends is obviously achieved by the introduction of subjects such as gardening, woodwork and cooking, but for mathematics and science: 'Even for older students the social sciences would be less abstract and formal if they were dealt with less as sciences (less as formulated bodies of knowledge) and more in their direct subject-matter as that is found in the daily life of the social groups in which the student shares' (Dewey [1916] 1966: 201).

Dewey criticizes the individualism of Rousseau and sees 'natural development' as an aim of education, but one only partially stated if it refers only to our primitive powers. He sees nurture not as corrupting but as the development of those natural powers ([1916] 1966: 111–18, 123). There is, however, a particularly American form of individualism in Dewey, who accepted the myth of the frontier as something that had elevated American society above the worst features of the development of European capitalism. In this sense, he looks back to a pre-industrial world in which there is a harmony between learning and adult life. This leaves him closer to Rousseau than he thinks. The difference is that he believes that industrialization has created the possibility for a truly democratic society which can be achieved through education.

Ryan is correct to point out, in opposition to Dewey's cruder critics, that he was not arguing that 'the point of industrial training was to produce a docile workforce adapted to the needs of capitalist employers' (Ryan 1995: 177). Dewey thought that capitalism was at best a semi-ambulant corpse but rejected the revolutionary route (Ryan 1995: 178). The central chapter in Dewey's book is Chapter 7, 'The Democratic Conception in Education' (Dewey [1916] 1966: 81–99). He sets out a vision for education in terms of an end to the separation into classes by ending the division between 'mental' and 'manual' labour. This is experienced as the division between those who receive a 'liberal education' and those who receive something poorer, or mere training for work. He envisages an education that reflects the democratic ideal. Democracy is a form of associated living, with numerous and varied points of contact with a plurality of social groups, which in itself will perpetuate democracy (Dewey

[1916] 1966: 86–8). Education shares these ideals and is therefore essential to democratic society.

Some writers have held Dewey's chapter on vocationalism to be the poorest in the book. It is, however, Dewey's clearest attempt to spell out the implications of his earlier chapters. Dewey defines vocationalism as 'such a direction of life activities as renders them perceptibly significant to a person because of the consequences they accomplish, and also useful to his associates' (Dewey [1916] 1966: 307) It is neither 'narrowly practical' nor 'merely pecuniary'. A later summary adds a temporal requirement: 'A vocation is any form of continuous activity which renders service to others and engages personal powers on behalf of the accomplishment of results' (Dewey [1916] 1966: 319). There is a clear emphasis here on the utility of what is undertaken to 'others' or society. The definition is also so general it covers activities we would not normally call vocational. For example it includes academic study and scholarship as a vocation, as training for an academic 'career'. But here the question of 'utility', especially to society, makes no sense and can only be destructive of the quest for knowledge by subjecting it to the requirement of producing results or being useful to society (Anderson 1980b: 139–40).

Dewey claims that 'the only adequate training for occupations is in training *through* occupations' (Dewey [1916] 1966: 310, original emphasis). He argues that industrial society has created the necessity and possibility for educational reorganization but 'there is a danger that vocational education will be interpreted in theory and practice as trade education' ([1916] 1966: 316). The only way of avoiding this is the methodological one of producing in schools 'a projection of the type of society we should like to realise, and by forming minds in accord with it gradually modify the larger and more recalcitrant features of adult society' ([1916] 1966: 317).

Dewey sees education as essential to the achievement of a democratic society. By reflecting that society in its organization it will ensure that democracy comes into being or continues to develop and change. He stresses the importance of the pupil's or student's experience and of socially relevant activities or 'occupations' in the classroom. Dewey recognizes the dangers in how people may take his suggestions and rejects narrow training for work as a definition of 'vocational education'.

---

**Task 1.14: Dewey: for or against?**

Dewey sets education the project of building a democratic society. How far are you in sympathy with this aim? Consider how it differs from the aim of education for Socrates and Rousseau.

---

These three philosophies of education will appear in discussions of curriculum ideology in broad categories such as classical humanism, humanism and social reconstructionism (Chapter 7) and in learning theory (Chapter 3) when cognitive, humanistic and empirical theories are discussed (behaviourism is merely an example of the latter). When working through these discussions, relate them to the philosophical positions outlined here. Remember that they may not always be distinct.

## 1.4 The 'triumph' of vocationalism

**KEY ISSUES**

'Vocational education' is understood in a variety of ways.

According to one particular view, questions of value and value judgement are outside its sphere.

Many have sought to reconcile vocational and liberal education.

The essential elements of the new educational initiatives of the 1980s could be said to fit a special needs deficit model.

The potential of technology to transform lives is the subject of a wide range of views from those of a variety of political persuasions.

**Task 1.15**

Try to describe what you understand by 'vocational education'. Review your statement when you have finished reading this section.

The aim of this section is to examine how 'vocationalism' has come to dominate thinking across the whole of PCE. It is related to the general themes we have discussed in the two previous sections: the attack upon 'academic' or subject-based knowledge and Dewey's criticism of the arid and dry nature of formal education. It is our contention that vocationalism has triumphed in the sense that it dominates our thinking and that Tony Blair's three priorities for Britain, 'education, education, education', could refer to an impoverished notion of education dominated by vocationalism.

Vocationalism is a term used to refer to various theories, ideological positions and some simplistic attitudes that have attempted to link the world of work to a greater or lesser degree with education. Such approaches often suggest that, as work is an important part of life, we should find a place for it in schools and colleges (Lewis 1997). But the variety of these theories and the unanalysed popular usage of terms can seem confusing or, worse still, simply unproblematic. The situation is so chronic that one set of academics has been led to declare that 'No single characteristic defines this new vocationalism. It is marked by a variety of policies and programmes and diversity of action and actors. But it is guided, if not propelled, by a determination to establish closer and better interrelationships between the experience of both formative education and preparatory training and the working world' (Skilbeck et al. 1994: 2).

A general trend we can identify at the outset is for vocationalist initiatives to be presented as part of a package of a supposedly radical rethinking of the aims of education, or providing the basis for reforms leading to a more relevant or modern, technologically based education. They often claim to be more democratic, offering a better education for the masses rather than a pale shadow of the elitist education offered to the better-off or to specific social groups. The terminology of the theorists of vocationalism can be particularly confusing. For example, we come across one theorist arguing for a 'critical vocationalism' (Donald 1992). Intellectual acrobatics are required even to attempt to understand what this could possibly mean. On a more everyday level, we find teachers using the phrase 'vocational education' in relation to a variety of courses, which may have some educational element, or may simply be training courses. Either way, there is no doubt that the advocates of the priority of practice over knowledge have triumphed. Frequent references to the 'vocational element in education' are seen as unremarkable. It is, however, possible to argue for an education that is entirely theoretical and to see it as a duty to combat those who would promote an education that is in any way practical. This would be the traditional position of the liberal educator. However extreme this view may seem, it is coherent and deserves attention (Anderson 1980c: 157).

There does seem to be a consistent refusal by participants in debates about vocationalism to recognize important conceptual distinctions. The Kennedy Report, *Learning Works* (Kennedy 1997b), talks throughout in an undiscriminating way about 'learning'. Kennedy makes no attempt to analyse what we mean by 'learning' in different contexts. Thus learning to use a lathe, to chop vegetables, learning citizenship, mathematics and ancient languages are given a spurious equality. The treatment of complex philosophical distinctions and debates as easily resolved or as semantic questions reaches its apogee in the introduction to the third Dearing Report (Dearing 1997). Here we find Dearing declaring with unmasked enthusiasm that the near future will see the *'historic boundaries between vocational and academic education breaking down*, with increasingly active partnerships between higher education institutions and the worlds of industry, commerce and public service' (p. 8, emphasis added). Dearing writes as if the 'academic' and 'vocational' divide was something totally unproblematic to be resolved through the mutual respect of the partners as they work together.

The recognition of an academic and vocational divide has been part of the debate about the nature of education for over 2000 years. Aristotle in the *Politics* notes that in his own day 'nobody knows' whether the young should be trained in studies that are useful 'as a means of livelihood' or to 'promote virtue' or in the 'higher studies' (discussed in Lester Smith 1957: 11). The point is not that nothing changes; this would be ahistorical, as ancient Greek society and Britain today bear no comparison. But at least it is apparent from Aristotle that the Greeks felt that there was a real and important problem here. Contemporary discussions are simply trivial and sanguine by comparison.

It is the intention in this section to provide an introduction to what should be a real debate by providing a critical guide to the discussions of the various types of vocationalism that have manifested themselves since James Callaghan (the Labour prime minister 1976–79) launched the 'Great Debate'. We deliberately restrict our use of the label 'new' vocationalism because, if it has any meaning, it applies only to one very particular post-war period.

## The way we think now

To understand the sense in which vocationalism is triumphant, it is worthwhile locating it within a more general intellectual malaise. This has been well described by writer and critic Richard Hoggart, who sees contemporary Britain as being swamped by a tidal wave of relativism, which he defines as 'the obsessive avoidance of judgements of quality or moral judgement' (Hoggart 1996: 3). One element of this dominant mood is the acceptance of vocationalism at all levels of the educational system. Arguments about improving the quality of life, or turning around Britain's economic performance, are often supported by talk of the need for skills training, or of the promotion of some form of vocational education or training. This is apparently a 'classless impulse' (Hoggart 1996: 220), but, Hoggart argues, only to those who oppose the traditional notion of education being a good in itself, whatever its practical benefits. It does seem to be true that vocationalism, as a standpoint which avoids debate and discussion about important differences of value, is widespread. A glimpse of the extent of the obsession with the vocational is apparent from the following passage from the *Economist* (1996):

> On the face of it, the case for generous public support for training is strong. Unskilled people are much more likely to be out of work than skilled ones; if only their qualifications could be improved, they might find jobs more readily. Not only would they benefit, but so would the economy as a whole. A better-trained productive workforce would be a more productive one; so more training ought to mean not just lower unemployment but faster growth and higher living standards. Unions like training programmes because they can use them to push up wages. Academics like them because they increase demand for education. Parents like them because they give out-of-work, out-of-school youths something to do. Prophets of a postmodern society praise them as part of an ethic of lifelong learning. And employers don't mind because the public pays the bill.

Everyone is in favour of training. A recent study showed that a massive 66 per cent of workers thought that education and training were the means of progressing their careers (Hudson et al. 1996). There is constant discussion in the media about a 'skills gap' (IRDAC 1990) to be filled by training. But the *Economist* simply refers to training for work rather than vocational education. This is sometimes referred to as 'vocationalism' in its old or traditional sense of training to do a job. The argument of the article is that the most successful training takes place in the workplace and is provided by employers, as opposed to training provided by the state or its quangos. This may be true but it is dynamic economies which are referred to to illustrate the argument. There is a chicken and egg question to be resolved here. Is the problem identified as a 'skills gap' a result of relative economic decline or its cause? Any skills gap which does exist must surely be resolved at the political or economic level and not by scapegoating the employed and unemployed as unskilled. It could, indeed, be seen as a 'jobs gap'. In fact the debate about a 'skills gap' is one-sided, being largely promoted by employers' organizations. When asked to specify skills needed, most employers provide answers in terms of moral or personal qualities that have little to do with 'skills' in the sense that most people understand the term. We think of a skill in a traditional way as relating to, say, carpentry, engineering or IT. However, the skills needed at work are usually those that can be learned in a few weeks with minimal difficulty. The dynamic of industry is to reduce, diminish or replace such skills (Marx [1867] 1974: 407–8, 457–8; Korndörffer 1991: 222–3). Even in the case of IT, it is far from certain that we are at the dawn of a 'new era' or 'knowledge age' (Woudhuysen 1997). It is important to recognize that there is a debate here that is closely related to our assumptions about whether we face a 'skills gap' or a 'jobs gap'.

**Task 1.16**

Looking at your own area of expertise, identify any 'skills' that are in short supply. Are the skills you identified technical, educational or personal? Could they be met within PCE?

## Liberal education (early twentieth century)

There have been many attempts to analyse various forms of vocationalism, and most of these attempt to reconcile 'vocational' and 'liberal' education (e.g. Williams 1994: 97–8). In Britain, the traditional or 'narrow view' of vocationalism as 'training for a job' was mostly rejected by educational reformers. R.H. Tawney was perhaps the best-known writer whom we associate with this line of thinking (Tawney [1922] 1988). Not only conservatives or traditionalists but also most socialists and radicals sought a decent liberal education in traditional and modern subjects for everyone. Access to the whole of humanity's cultural inheritance was the demand that was made. What was good enough for the sons of the masters was good enough for the workers. Vocational training was held to be entirely a matter for employers. This does not mean that individuals did not seek vocational training, but the traditional position was against vocationalism. This must be stressed as it is now almost forgotten, particularly by proponents of a 'democratic' education. According to this view, there is simply no connection between 'education' and 'training'. It could be argued that work-related training does go on in schools and colleges, but this does not establish anything other than an organizational connection between the two.

## Training for jobs (the 1960s)

In the 1960s, employers relied upon the state to provide training in technical colleges but the employer was responsible for the day release of young employees. The lack of system in this method of training led to its being called 'stop gap' or 'gap filling' by many critics (Hall 1994: 43–5), but whatever its faults it was clearly related to training for jobs. When Harold Wilson spoke to the 1962 Labour Party conference of forging a new Britain in the 'white heat of the technological revolution' there was no other conception in anyone's mind but real training for real jobs. The main debates were about 'upskilling' the workforce. This is a reminder that talk of technological revolution is not new and in the 1960s the technological revolution put man on the moon (compare Ainley 1988: 143 who argues 'technological change is developing exponentially'). We can consider vocationalism as training for jobs as the major form of training up to the mid-1970s.

## Training without jobs (the 1970s)

In the 1970s, economic crisis and rising youth unemployment changed things. One clear consequence of James Callaghan's 'Great Debate' was the systematic involvement of industry in the planning of the educational process. There were other elements too. The increasing role of the state in directing vocational training in a time of financial cutback has been well discussed (Benn and Fairley 1986; Finn 1987; Ainley 1988, 1990). The training on offer was still largely related to jobs. It is important to remember the general antagonism and resistance there was to the various adult and youth training initiatives. There were youth protests and opposition from the trade unions, trades councils and political groups. The main criticisms were of 'slave labour' schemes or the use of 'cheap labour' to replace existing jobs. Out of this grew an emphasis on pre-vocational and basic skills training. This transitional period is one in which the concept of 'vocationalism' starts to shift in meaning from 'day release' or 'stop gap' provision towards 'pre-vocational provision'. We could date it as beginning in 1976 but its fullest flowering is in the period of the Youth Training Scheme (YTS) from 1983 to 1989. Most analyses focus on the increasing or changed form of state involvement with the training of young people (see Hickox 1995). While these discussions are important it is our argument that the curriculum developments proposed help us understand the long-term impact of these changes rather than simply seeing them as a matter of the state crudely forcing young people into years of slave labour.

## The 'new' vocationalism (the 1980s)

Employers in this crisis situation were asking: why should we be training young workers who cannot benefit from work because of their attitudes, lack of basic skills or poor discipline? Although this attitude ran counter to the facts, it became the basis of the Manpower Services Commission's (MSC) development of a range of training initiatives, culminating in the YTS, which were available to all unemployed young people. This pre-vocationalism is the basis of what came to be called the 'new' vocationalism. What was on offer was a curriculum derived from special needs programmes based on the sort of personal and social training necessary to prepare youngsters with learning difficulties for the world of work. The limitations of these pre-vocational courses and initiatives did not stop them being successful as a stage in the development of vocationalism.

YTS can be seen as a failure if judged by comparison with earlier vocational training in the narrow sense, and as a pre-vocational scheme. It provided employment for only two-thirds of the trainees who completed the courses and this employment was often short term. The only vocational element in these courses was an increasingly tenuous belief on the part of the providers that young people could get a job. However, there were wider forces influencing young people and their teachers. This was the decade in which the Further Education Unit (FEU) produced its influential documents winning over the newer college lecturer with curriculum-based papers. Lower-level technical college courses and private training courses sprang up all over the country funded by the MSC. The Technical and Vocational Education Initiative (TVEI) gave educational developments and experiment a free rein. The labour market reality of the time was that there was no work in the traditional sense of a job for life. Employment was going to be intermittent and temporary, and life at college was better than unemployment. A traditional life pattern of the time was for young people to move from a YTS to employment, then on to a college course or evening class, then into a period of unemployment and than back into another, adult, training scheme. Many of those who worked in colleges or were real or potential trainees were totally sceptical about the value of these courses. But a lumpen scepticism is entirely passive: the pragmatic lessons of unemployment had been learned, and youth rebellion did not materialize. The unions and the Trades Union Congress (TUC) came back on-side to discuss training. A credit-led boom brought the yuppie into temporary being, and in this climate there was the expectation that you could make it and find a job but you were on your own.

The new vocationalism is often seen as a Thatcherite victory in creating an employer-dominated training scheme for young people. The early opposition to the Youth Opportunities Programme (YOP) and YTS faded away leaving only a few radical educationalists arguing for something better. However, many of those opposing YTS schemes did not see them as a betrayal of the ideal of a liberal education for all, but the failure to provide something different. These writers were influenced by Marx and Engels' occasional comments on education (Marx [1867] 1974: 453–4, [1875] 1968: 329; Engels [1878] 1975: 378–82) and generally promote technological education. For example, Willis (1987) and Ainley (1990, 1993) argue that the working classes need to improve their skills for sale on the market and radical thinkers do them a disservice by not arguing for a form of vocational education that will meet their needs as a class. Willis (1987: xvii) puts this case well: 'how is it, and is it, possible to reconcile the tensions between training as class reproduction and training as working-class interest more in the favour of the working class?' Ainley (1993: 93) sees technological advance as the answer:

> In a modernising economy, education and training must raise the skills of all workers from the bottom up . . . Education and training will then integrate rather than separate mental and manual labour . . . New technology provides the potential to enable all working people to become multiskilled and flexible in a true sense . . .

Precursors of these views include Harold Wilson's populist technological revolution in the 1960s and the 'post-Fordist' utopian visions of the 1980s. Such arguments have been savagely attacked as being unrelated to the reality of contemporary capitalism (Roberts et al. 1994), as this level of training would simply make employment too expensive. With an eye on profits there is no possibility that employers or the state would promote such training and the result would be redundancy for the mass of workers who would be too expensive to employ (see Yaffe 1978: 12–13). The illusion lies in a belief in the power of technology to transform people's lives rather than a political movement doing so, which has been a popular view since the end of the cold war. But such views are not necessarily implied by a Marxist analysis as Brian Simon proved in his defence of liberal education in response to the 'Great Debate' (Simon 1985). The consequence of arguments about the possibility of a new industrial revolution which will benefit workers is a convergence of the views of the 'left' and of the 'right', represented by employers. There is therefore no real opposition to vocationalism, only opposition to its crudest forms.

## Education without jobs (the 1990s)

The period from 1989 to the present can be seen as one of containment. The number of young people staying on in FE increased dramatically to 89 per cent of all 16-year-olds, and led Nick Tate, the head of the School Curriculum and Assessment Authority (SCAA), to comment in the summer of 1997 that the effective school leaving age was now 18. With 30 per cent of all young people going on to HE and many into other training schemes, we might make the effective leaving age 21 or even higher. The mass expansion of FE and HE has few critics, and even they see some basis to be positive about aspects of the work of the new universities (Ainley 1994). This period of containment is also the period of the qualification explosion. Demand for NVQs, GNVQs, GCSEs, A levels, degrees, credit-bearing courses and in-service qualifications seems never ending. The expansion of qualifications available and the apparent improvement in their attainment by young people has been questioned, and one writer is notorious for calling the whole thing a sham (Phillips 1996). Certainly, qualifications are now required for jobs that were previously thought to be unskilled, such as classroom assistants. We need to ask if there is any element of vocationalism here. Perhaps only in the residual sense of 'employability' which was a theme that grew out of government papers and reports in the mid-1990s (DfEE 1995a) and is highlighted in the Report of the Commission on Social Justice (CSJ 1994: 175–6). Employability is divorced from vocational skills or even from pre-vocational skills, so why even refer to 'employability' as having to do with jobs at all? Why not just talk of 'learning' and 'education'? This is certainly a popular move with politicians, and educationalists are also seeking a move away from vocationalism: 'Serious attention now needs to be given to educating as opposed to training a majority of the population hitherto denied access to further and higher education' (Avis et al. 1996: 180).

So, is vocationalism defeated? The answer is 'no'. Mainstream education is dominated by the vocational themes of a work-related, often competence-based curriculum, the introduction of pre-vocational or personal and social development under the guise of 'employability' and above all by the supposed need to adapt to a life in a new 'communication' or 'technological' age. Education as a whole has become vocationalized in the sense that the connection between the worlds of work and education is seen as necessary rather than contingent. What this means is that, whereas people once thought that the knowledge gained in getting an education was not irrelevant to the workplace, now the sort of knowledge that is on offer seems to be only that which is relevant to work. Even to lecturers in vocational areas this must be seen as a complete debasement of knowledge. As mentioned above, the Dearing Report

(Dearing 1997) sets out exactly this model for the development of HE. Even if we call for a return to 'educating' rather than 'training', what is likely to be provided is not a liberal education but a poor vocationalized replacement. The same can be said of the Kennedy Report (Kennedy 1997b) with its promotion of LLL. What is being offered is an 'education' that amounts to learning up to NVQ Level 3 – a vocational standard, and one that is set *very* low. This has parallels with the 'back to basics' drives promoted by some ministers that make Britain sound like a Third World country. Standards are being set but set much lower than they were at the time of the Robbins Report (Robbins 1963). Vocationalism is triumphant but it appears disguised as education – 'education' of a debased kind.

There is a major difficulty with this new focus on education, although it is almost self-contradictory for educationalists, professionally and philosophically, to oppose 'education'. There are also other difficulties in making education a political priority. Education is a personal or individual matter. But individual aspirations and achievements cannot be a replacement for the vision of a society actually going somewhere. Even the narrowly work-related vocationalism that Dewey objected to and the socially divisive 'new vocationalism' had some sort of economic or political vision behind them. The new individualized educational curriculum that begins with key skills initiatives, extends through Curriculum 2000 and may become a reality with the introduction of personal advisers and the new Matriculation Diploma may leave people isolated and socially disconnected (see Chapter 9 for an introduction to these developments). A PCE system made up of isolated individuals, like a society of isolated individuals, can easily become fractious and discontented. This will not be the sort of discontent predicted by some writers (Bloomer 1996; Harkin et al. 2001; Tomlinson 2001) but a much more personal affair based on individual rather than social conflict. What explains this state of affairs – which reminds us of Margaret Thatcher's assertion that 'there is no such thing as society only individuals and their families' – is the unpredicted and huge expansion of service industries (see Poynter 2000).

## Cultural capital and the 'therapeutic turn' in PCE

The key asset that individuals now have in the labour market is not their specific vocational (or even academic) knowledge and skills but what Bourdieu (1986) calls their 'cultural capital'. Cultural capital takes three forms: 'connected to individuals in their general educated character – accent, dispositions, learning, etc.; connected to objects – books, qualifications, machines, dictionaries etc.; and connected to institutions – places of learning, universities, libraries, etc.' (Grenfell and James 1998: 21). Having cultural capital ensures success in education and at work – particularly in gaining access to employment. It was once thought that the more qualifications people had the more productive they would be (sometimes called an increase in human capital), but at a time of credential inflation when qualifications are universal (there are even those which recognize common sense or forms of unskilled work such as many forms of domestic or caring work), other factors come into play in the job market (compare Young 1998: 152). From the period of the economic recession of the late 1980s the situation was unclear as to what was the major factor at play (see Bills 1988), but now it is fairly clear that the crucial factor is 'cultural capital'. It is the cultural capital that you have that makes you 'competent' in the modern work environment and this is a new interpretation of 'competence'. This sense of competence cannot be acquired in the way that NVQ competences can. It would be wrong to consider this as the ever present 'networking' or 'it depends on who you are or know' emphasized by cynics and theorists of 'social capital'. It is something qualitatively different. If PCE is still to keep a nexus between the curriculum on offer and the new service work it will – consciously or unconsciously – have to adapt to develop cultural capital. This is already happening in what is called 'emotion work', the 'Have a nice day!' training for McDonald's and call centres.

There has been a growing debate as to whether the new work requires a different workforce more orientated around 'emotion work' or 'aesthetic labour' which requires a different sort of training that is shifting towards a concern with 'emotional literacy' and 'emotional intelligence' (Mortiboys 2005). The obsessive concern with young people's self-esteem is well known and there is a growing concern with 'emotional well-being' and even 'happiness' as educational goals (Ecclestone and Hayes 2007). There are sociological explanations as to why this has happened. The argument is that there is a general loss of confidence in the possibility of human progress that has led to a downplaying of the intellectual in favour of the emotional (Furedi 2004; Hayes 2006). In PCE the humanistic aspect of training is now dominant but has taken on a specific aspect which ignores the normal content of humanistic approaches, a liberal education or real skills involving the training of judgement, whether or not in the distorted form of CBET, and concentrates instead on ways of approaching the inner emotional life (Hayes 2003a, b, c, 2004). This a contested view, and Hyland, for example, still argues that it is the commodified form of CBET that is the major threat to proper education and training and that therapeutic elements in PCET are marginal (Hyland 2005, 2006). The debate continues.

The illusion that this provision of cultural capital, in therapeutic forms or not, will be 'education' rather than a different sort of preparation for work is contestable. The abstract notion of 'cultural capital' adopted by policymakers and academics, often merely reflects the views of what government and employers think people need to be employable in a changing world (Hayes 2003b). Thinking of 'education' as merely a preparation for work is now an almost universal assumption, as is thinking that education is all about the acquisition of 'skills'. This functional view of education restricts and limits students, denying them the opportunity to achieve their potential. The difficulty for all those interested in the direction of PCE is what sort of education to propose in its place. A return to subject-based teaching and training grounded in knowledge – education for its own sake – seems impossible to argue for, either pragmatically or (for some) philosophically (Ainley 1999; Waugh 2000). But what is the alternative?

### Task 1.17

We have looked at vocationalism in several forms, as narrow training, as pre-vocational training, as being concerned with employability, and in a 'back to basics' or 'educational' manifestation. We have also seen how the contemporary obsession with 'education,

education, education' meets changing workplace needs. We have outlined our belief that this new curriculum does not unlock human potential but restricts it to the needs of the workplace. What role do you consider that PCE has in unlocking human potential and do you think that, if there is an increasingly therapeutic aspect to PCE, that this hinders or fosters student achievement?

## Related new professional standards for teachers and trainers in the lifelong learning sector

### Domain A: professional values and practice

| PROFESSIONAL KNOWLEDGE AND UNDERSTANDING | PROFESSIONAL PRACTICE |
|---|---|
| *Teachers in the lifelong learning sector know and understand:* | *Teachers in the lifelong learning sector:* |
| AK 2.1  Ways in which learning has the potential to change lives. | AP 2.1  Use opportunities to highlight the potential for learning to positively transform lives and contribute to effective citizenship. |
| AK 2.2  Ways in which learning promotes the emotional, intellectual, social and economic well-being of individuals and the population as a whole. | AP 2.2  Encourage learners to recognize and reflect on ways in which learning can empower them as individuals and make a difference in their communities. |
| AK 4.1  Principles, frameworks and theories which underpin good practice in learning and teaching. | AP 4.1  Use relevant theories of learning to support the development of practice in learning and teaching. |
| AK 4.3  Ways to reflect, evaluate and use research to develop own practice, and to share good practice with others. | AP 4.3  Share good practice with others and engage in continuing professional development through reflection, evaluation and the appropriate use of research. |

## Domain C: specialist learning and teaching

| PROFESSIONAL KNOWLEDGE AND UNDERSTANDING | PROFESSIONAL PRACTICE |
|---|---|
| *Teachers in the lifelong learning sector know and understand:* | *Teachers in the lifelong learning sector:* |
| CK 1.2 Ways in which own specialism relates to the wider social, economic and environmental context. | CP 1.2 Provide opportunities for learners to understand how the specialist area relates to the wider social, economic and environmental context. |
| CK 4.2 Potential transferable skills and employment opportunities relating to own specialist area. | CP 4.2 Work with learners to identify the transferable skills they are developing, and how these might relate to employment opportunities. |

# 2

# The lifelong learning teacher: learning and developing

## 2.1 What is Chapter 2 about?

It is assumed that readers of this book will be engaged in a programme of training or continuous personal development and be teaching or on teaching practice. Chapter 2 will therefore consider ways in which teachers or trainers can build on their professional profile and support their development. It will reflect upon the various mechanisms available to teachers and trainers in ensuring their learning is effective, giving an introduction to skills that many practitioners, while knowledgeable and expert in their own fields, may need to cultivate in order to develop practices that embody their own professional values and principles and focuses on their professional context.

This is of particular importance in the light of the changes introduced in *Equipping Our Teachers for the Future* (DfES 2004) in which the Government outlined its proposal to introduce a 'licence to practise' for all teachers and lecturers in the lifelong learning sector. All new teachers, trainers and lecturers who successfully complete their initial teacher training will be awarded Qualified Teacher Learning and Skills (QTLS) status and will be registered with the Institute for Learning (IfL) as holding a full licence to practise. However, in order to maintain this licence, each teacher must renew their licence annually by completing a set number of hours[1] of suitable continuing professional development (CPD)[2] each year. It is essential that the CPD is appropriate to the individual practitioner and therefore this chapter is designed to encourage you to reflect upon staff development and how it can be used to enhance your practice and improve your performance.

Section 2.2 considers different notions of 'the good teacher'. You should be clear about what you understand by this as a basis for your development, as well as examining how your professional context may help or hinder this. Section 2.3 will concentrate on continuing professional development and its importance to you as a practitioner in enhancing pedagogical practice, while Section 2.4 outlines some initiatives implemented to support CPD in lifelong learning education. Section 2.5 offers a range of strategies that can be used in planning and meeting your learning and development needs.

## 2.2 Teacher learning and development

| KEY ISSUES |
| --- |
| Effective teacher development assumes a model of 'the good teacher'. |
| Notions of the good teacher vary in what features they emphasize. |
| Professional development cannot take place unless learning is applied to the teacher's own professional context. |

Your ideas about how you can effectively learn and develop must be connected with your notion of what makes a good teacher.

### Task 2.1: Your own experience

2.1(a)   Consider your experiences as a learner when at school and since then. What qualities did good teachers have? What qualities did bad teachers lack?

2.1(b)   Share these views with the rest of the group.

Figure 2.1 shows the responses of a group of AE teachers to Task 2.1. Responses such as those shown in Figure 2.1 tend to focus of three aspects of teaching and these are defined in Figure 2.2. You may notice that the three aspects broadly correspond with Bloom's (1964) classification of educational objectives into

**Figure 2.1** AE teachers' responses to Task 2.1

'I remember getting interested in history for the first time when I did an evening course. The tutor had a passion for it.'

'He was clearly a brilliant physicist but he couldn't get his ideas over.'

'However frustrated you became, this teacher had limitless patience.'

'She seemed to be able to help you because she'd experienced the same difficulties herself.'

'We never learned anything because we didn't listen to him. And we didn't listen to him because we didn't respect him.'

'She seemed to make learning even the most routine things fun.'

'He had the ability to bring the subject to life.'

'He couldn't control our class. We soon found he couldn't control any class.'

'She could always explain even the most difficult things in terms you could understand.'

'He didn't seem to enjoy being with students.'

**Figure 2.2** Three key aspects of teaching

---

*Subject knowledge and expertise*
Those thought of as good teachers tend to know their subjects, either through study or experience or both. But this is no guarantee of effectiveness: a very common experience is of the knowledgeable teacher who can't communicate.

*Skills and abilities*
Whether controlling a class, communicating or understanding learning difficulties, the good teacher is seen as one who demonstrates skills and abilities to a high degree.

*Commitment and emotions*
This third aspect is wide-ranging but includes references to 'enthusiasm', 'passion', 'caring' and 'patience' – all qualities to do with emotions, attitudes and dispositions.

---

cognitive, psychomotor and affective domains. The kind of learning that you feel would make you a better teacher will depend upon the value you place on each aspect. Nationally, policy has swung between all three aspects. In the 1960s there was a move away from 'teacher training' to 'teacher education', a desire to emphasize the knowledge-based academic content of the then new BEd degree in contrast to previous skill-orientated programmes. But in the past fifteen years, teacher education, along with training across many vocational areas, has moved towards learning in the second and third aspects, which can be broadly termed a 'competence-based approach'.

**Task 2.2: Your own priorities**

2.2(a)   Looking at the three aspects in Figure 2.2, which aspects of teaching do you feel you need to focus on to make you a better teacher?

2.2(b)   Share your thoughts with the group. Where the emphasis differs, how do you account for this? Contrasting subjects taught? Differing institutions? Variety in personal and professional background and experience?

You should now have a clearer notion of your own learning priorities and will need to consider how you wish to develop them. However, before doing so, you will need to reflect upon the current context within which you teach. It will have a number of important features, shown in Figure 2.3 overleaf.

**Task 2.3: Your professional context**

2.3(a)   Describe your own professional context in the light of the features in Figure 2.3.

2.3(b)   Given your context, what aspects of it might help or hinder your professional development? Share this with the group. How might common barriers to development be overcome?

**Figure 2.3**  Contexts in which teaching takes place

*Your institution*
Is it a large college, a small adult centre, the training section of a public service or industrial/commercial organization? How do you fit into it? What resources and support are available to you?

*The extent to which you work with others*
Do you work closely with colleagues as part of a course team for example, or do you attend an evening centre once a week, meeting only your students? Do you have a line manager? If not, to whom are you accountable?

*Degree of professional autonomy*
Who decides what you teach? Is there a detailed syllabus? Can you determine content and sequence?

*Student targeting and recruitment*
Do you control this or does the institution?

## 2.3  Continuing professional development

| KEY ISSUES |
| --- |
| A commitment to continuing professional development is an essential part of being a professional. |
| The aim of continuing professional development is to raise student achievement. |
| Continuing professional development must be considered on an individual basis as experience and circumstances dictate. |

The acquisition of an initial teaching training qualification is just the first step towards becoming a 'professional' teacher or trainer. It is important to understand that belonging to a 'profession' does not simply mean membership of a 'club', it means embracing the criteria that ensures a particular job is seen as a profession rather than an occupation, even though the term 'professional' is contestable. The definition proposed by the functional sociologists (Millerson 1964) is broadly useful because, while recognizing the necessity for a profession to insist that a certain standard of skill be demonstrated by means of some kind of examination, it also acknowledges that 'professionalism' goes beyond an initial body of knowledge and skills. It demands that those practising within the profession be given education and training in relevant skills, and that good practice should be promoted; in other words a commitment to continuing professional development is an essential part of being a 'professional'.

The purpose of continuing professional development (CPD), for those in post-compulsory education, is to improve student achievement. This might include building on your skills and supporting career progression, but it must remain focused on the raising standards and improving student learning. CPD demands that you keep learning in order to enable you to play an informed role in the delivery of a curriculum and influence developments inside and outside your own institution. This is particularly pertinent in terms of the Government's notion of a learning society. The post-compulsory sector is playing a crucial role in the development of lifelong learning, and therefore it is essential that post-compulsory institutions be seen as active learning organizations themselves.

It is with the improvement in the rates of student achievement in mind that the Government has introduced the licence to practise and its requirement for compulsory continuing professional development. There are no 'hard and fast' identified 'routes' laid down for this professional development; the complexity of roles and responsibilities of the lifelong learning practitioner means that any continuing education must take account of individual experience and circumstances. However, professional standards have been identified (described as the skills, knowledge and attributes required by teachers, trainers and lecturers in the lifelong learning sector) and these standards are a good place to start when considering your own CPD.

---

**Task 2.4: Professional needs analysis**

Think about your professional practice and identify what you consider to be your strengths and your areas of weakness. Do not simply reflect on your performance in the classroom, but look at your wider responsibilities (e.g., course planning and development or contributions to meetings). You might like to discuss this with a colleague.

---

## 2.4 Initiatives supporting CPD

| KEY ISSUES |
| --- |
| Nationally recognized standards are being used to raise the quality of post-compulsory provision. |
| There are various initiatives that are designed to support continuing professional development. |

### Lifelong Learning UK (LLUK) standards

Lifelong Learning UK (LLUK) is the national leadership body responsible for the development, quality assurance and promotion of national standards for the lifelong learning sector. It replaced the Further Education National Training Organisation (FENTO) in January 2005, and aims to provide a range of occupational standards relevant to those working in the lifelong learning sector.

In 2000, the Minister of State for Higher Education introduced the framework for FE teaching and principals' qualifications. In the 'New Policy on Qualifications and Development for Further Education Teachers and College Principals', guidelines were laid down to enable practitioners to obtain appropriate professional, academic and vocational qualifications and to undertake continuing professional development. The policy focused heavily on the introduction of qualifications based on FENTO standards, with the aim of ensuring that all those employed in the FE sector hold a recognized teaching qualification appropriate to their role. However, the FENTO standards applied only to colleges and were not really appropriate for initial teacher training. Therefore, in 2004, LLUK was asked to develop standards and specifications that could be used across the whole of the lifelong learning sector.

## LLUK professional standards for teachers, tutors and trainers in the lifelong learning sector

LLUK published the new overarching professional standards for teachers, tutors and trainers in the lifelong learning sector in December 2006 and it is likely that you are already familiar with them. They were developed specifically in response to Ofsted's call for clearer standards for new entrants to the lifelong learning sector and for more emphasis to be placed on competence in the practitioner's own particular area of specialism. New qualifications for all new entrants to the profession based on the standards were introduced in September 2007.

The standards are a crucial element of any teacher-training programme and are broken down into six main domains: professional values and practice, learning and teaching, specialist learning and teaching, planning for learning, assessment for learning and access and progression. These are underpinned by a set of professional values within which all professional activity must sit, one of which is AS4 'Reflection and evaluation of their own practice and their continuing professional development as teachers'. It is likely that any certificated staff development you undertake will result from consideration of AS4 and will be linked to the standards. However, it is recognized that any post-compulsory institution needs a range of different skills to ensure student achievement and therefore different standards have been designed to address the needs of specialists.

## Specialist standards and specifications

The standards aimed at raising the quality of provision across the post-compulsory sector have been introduced not only for classroom-based activities but also for the management of performance. Learning and Skills Councils (LSCs) are requiring colleges and other learning providers to demonstrate that they are meeting their responsibilities for the professional development of all their staff, including volunteers such as governors. These standards will be increasingly used as evidence in institutions' action plans to indicate their support of continuing professional development.

Teachers of literacy, language and numeracy (LLN) have their own set of specifications. These are either met through a specialised initial teacher training route or can be achieved through 'stand-alone' professional development for existing teachers who wish to move into the delivery of LLN. E-learning specifications have also being developed to recognize the competence of, and support, the post-compulsory professional who uses information and communication technology to manage, deliver and support learning.

The national occupational standards for managers working in further education colleges are also useful for staff development (LLUK 2005). Although based on generic models of management, there are discrete standards for first-line, middle and senior managers, with individuals able to progress to new standards once they are promoted to more senior positions. Many colleges are using them for appraisal and to identify professional development needs.

## Centres for excellence in teacher training

A recently established staff development resource can by found in Centres for Excellence in Teaching Training (CETTs). These CETTS have been established across England to raise standards in teaching and learning and to help recruit the best teachers into the lifelong learning sector. These partnership organizations will provide not only initial teacher training for those who are entering the profession but also continuing professional development for those already teaching or training and who wish to enhance their professional practice. The CETTs will be invaluable in supporting staff training needs and should be taken advantage of when constructing your personal development programme.

## Subject learning coaches

Subject learning coaches are another source of support that can be utilized. The Subject Learner Coaching Programme is part of the National Teaching and Learning initiative that aims to transform learning within the post-compulsory sector. The scheme was developed out of the Government's *Success for All* (DfES 2002) strategy to champion improvement in teaching and training, with the first coaches recruited in Construction, Entry to Employment, Business Studies and Science in 2003.[3] Since then other curriculum areas have been included, but even if you do not have a subject learning coach in your own particular specialism within your organization, a trained coach can still be of benefit as a mentor.

Subject learning coaches are practitioners who have been identified by organizations from within specialist curriculum areas to undertake training in order to support teaching and learning development and are pivotal in raising standards within that organization. These members of staff can be used as critical friends to improve teaching skills and can help develop a programme of professional development pertinent to your own needs. The training that the subject learning coaches undertake gives them the skills to help you focus on your practice and respond to your professional needs. They have been taught to develop skills in peer coaching and therefore, although they may not be familiar with your subject area, will be able to help you focus your reflection, experiment with new approaches and gain fresh perspectives on your practice.

Subject learning coaches will also be able to introduce you to the materials developed to disseminate best practice in teaching and learning. Again, although these materials are subject specific, the strategies used within them are transferable and will be helpful in improving your practice.

## Professional Development Portfolios

The concept of a Professional Development Portfolio (PDP) as a way of developing and evidencing continuing professional development is not a new one. It supports the notion of lifelong learning and is used by a number of professions as a method of ensuring practitioners update their skills, knowledge and understanding and is often used as a requirement for re-registration for a licence to practise. This model has now been embraced by the post-compulsory sector and teaching licences will only be renewed on the completion of an annual tariff of CPD.

There is no one way of compiling a PDP; it is simply a document that recognizes and assists professional development. However, it should include evidence of achievements and experience, for example, qualifications, courses attended, posts held and their responsibilities, skills, membership of professional bodies and any other relevant experience and, possibly more important, future plans and objectives. These should consist of the identification of learning needs and priorities, reflection on your teaching and learning that analyses strengths and areas for further development and any planning for future qualifications.

If you are beginning to prepare a PDP it may be useful to consider the CPD process developed by the Institute for Learning on its website (www.ifl.ac.uk). The Institute for Learning has played a significant part in the promotion of CPD and its value and is keen to utilize it in order to ensure that high standards are maintained within the profession. Therefore, in order to support practitioners with their plans, it has included a step-by-step guide to the planning and recording of CPD that can be used as a basis for your PDP.

> **Task 2.5: Planning for CPD**
>
> Using the 'CPD Process' on the Institute for Learning's website (www.ifl.ac.uk), undertake 'Step 1: Initial Reflection', 'Step 2: Where am I now' and 'Step 3: Compiling the Professional Development Plan' to inform the development of your Professional Development Portfolio.

## Investors in People

The Investors in People (IiP) initiative does not have a specific post-compulsory focus. It is a generic award that seeks to develop 'effective strategies to improve the performance of the organisation through its people' (IiP 2006). However, many post-compulsory organizations have adopted the IiP as a way of managing continuing professional development for their staff. It is a functional and mechanistic model built on the three key principles of 'plan, do, review' (IiP 2006). Each principle has a range of 'indicators' of good practice that have to be evidenced by the organization in order to be awarded the Investors in People standard and colleges often develop and implement a strategy of continuing professional development for staff in line with these indicators.

The above initiatives show the Government's commitment to continuing professional development and its agenda of improving students' rates of participation, retention, achievement and progress. The question for you, then, is to determine how you wish to develop as a practitioner. Continuing professional development means you must take responsibility for your own learning, planning activities to meet your developmental needs and reflecting on your experiences. This should not be an ad hoc affair, registering on courses that seem a good idea at the time. There must be careful consideration of your requirements. In order to identify what they might be, you must make a detailed audit of your current professional responsibilities to determine your current understanding and skills in your professional practice. The audit should include the teaching methodologies and curriculum models you use and take account of the judgement of others on your performance. Your audit should then be evaluated critically, identifying areas lacking in expertise so that an action plan for improvement can be devised. The plan should build on strengths as well as address weaknesses and include outcomes that are measurable, with realistic time frames.

The following section suggests some strategies that may be of use to you in planning your programme of continuing professional development.

## 2.5  Strategies for CPD

| KEY ISSUES |
| --- |
| Self-evaluation and reflective practice are useful strategies for identifying areas for continuing professional development. |
| Observation offers a more objective evaluation technique than self evaluation. |
| Appraisal procedures are a effective way to identify continuing professional development needs. |
| Collaboration with colleagues provides less formal support for continuing professional development. |
| The process of research can develop the skills necessary and self-awareness that underpin successful evaluation. |

## Self-evaluation and reflective practice

Self-evaluation and reflective practice are crucial components of all initial teaching training and can be invaluable in the development of professional practice. An evaluative or self-reflective cycle can ensure that you are undertaking a meaningful programme of CPD tailored to your individual needs as an on-going process.

The concept of 'reflective practitioner' was first introduced by Schön in 1982 as a way of introducing a new model of professional knowledge (Schön 1982). The theory has been developed into many different models that encourage reflective thinking, but the underlying principles are the same, that is, to challenge assumptions, to develop practical and theoretical knowledge and improve practice. Hillier (2005) summarizes the process neatly:

We should look at real practical situations which are problematic, complex and open to a variety of interpretations from differing points of view. This provides opportunities to develop capacities which are fundamental to competent professional practice. Thus our acquisition of knowledge proceeds interactively with reflecting about practical situations.

(p.17)

Which model you choose to undertake this process is one of personal choice. Brookfield (1986) refers to 'four critically reflective lenses', that of our own point of view, that of our colleagues, that of our students and the theoretical literature that is available. He maintains that by looking at your practice through these different lenses you will be able to identify any incongruence within your assumptions that needs further investigation. You might prefer to use Smyth's reflective cycle (1989), whereby the practitioner begins by identifying a significant event, reflects on the significance, enters into a dialogue with colleagues regarding the practice and relevant theories and finally develops new practice based upon the analysis.

Whichever model you choose you will need to begin this process to help you decide on an area of your practice that you wish to focus upon further. Self-evaluation may be of use here as it has an important place in determining your strengths and weaknesses and can be used to identify a relevant focus.

Perhaps the major tool, which will be of use to you in your professional development, is that of self-evaluation. This has an important place in determining your strengths and weaknesses and can be used with any focus you wish to give it. It could have a wide focus where you consider several or all aspects of the learning session involved, or a more narrow focus, such as the evaluation focusing on assessment shown in Example 2.1. Other objects of a narrow-focus evaluation might be:

- planning and preparation;
- teaching and learning strategies;
- communication skills and techniques;
- group management;
- managing a variety of student behavioural characteristics;
- learning resources;
- management of the learning environment;
- learning needs.

**Task 2.6: Choosing a focus for self-evaluation**

2.6(a)   Select a lesson you have recently taught. Jot down the main points for evaluation using a narrow-focus topic chosen from the list above.

2.6(b)   Do certain lessons rather than others suggest themselves for a narrowly focused evaluation?

However widely or narrowly focused your evaluation, it should attempt to measure how far your aims and objectives have been met. Of course, you may have realized as the lesson progressed that particular aims and objectives were paramount and you wished to concentrate on related activities, or that unplanned learning, a frequent and often very pleasing outcome of a learning session, had taken place. However, overall, the process of evaluation is an estimation of how far the aims and objectives have been met in terms of student learning. The level of your success will indicate areas for further possible development.

### Task 2.7: Self-evaluation

Look at the lesson plan and self-evaluation in Example 2.1. How successful is the teacher in her or his evaluation at considering the lesson's effectiveness in realizing the aims and objectives specified?

## Example 2.1

LESSON PLAN

| | | |
|---|---|---|
| *Venue*: | Christ the King Sixth Form College | *Course*: AS Law |
| *Date*: | 9 October 2006 | *Time*: 11.00–1.30 |
| *Subject*: | Introduction to Criminal Law | |

*Aims*:
- To revise and check students have an understanding of the main differences between criminal and civil law
- To introduce students to the basics of criminal law as applied by the courts, the concepts of voluntary acts and omissions to act creating liability

*Learning outcomes*:
- Students will understand how to identify a crime or a tort from a given source
- Students will understand the concept of 'Actus Reus' including liability for voluntary acts and omissions to act and will be able to distinguish a voluntary act from an automatous act

| Time | Teacher activity | Student activity | Assessment of outcomes |
|---|---|---|---|
| 11.00–11.05 | Registration and set out aims of lesson | | |
| 11.05–11.25 | Check homework – News stories collected for torts and crimes | Students will feed back crimes and torts from this week's newspapers and will be prepared to discuss any interesting points | Individual feedback of informal discussion |

*(Continued overleaf)*

**Example 2.1** *continued*

| Time | Teacher activity | Student activity | Assessment of outcomes |
|---|---|---|---|
| 11.25–12.10 | Give didactic lecture on liability including case notes and PowerPoint presentation and handouts | Students will take notes on handout and will answer and ask questions to clarify understanding | Students will be asked questions and will have to take notes in spaces provided in handouts. They will ask questions to clarify understanding |
| 12.10–12.30 | Set individual written assignment on omissions | Individual written assignment on omissions | |
| 12.30–1.00 | Split the class into half and give a case with supporting documentation | Half class to prepare the prosecution and prove the defendant committed the Actus Reus and the other half the defence | |
| 1.00–1.30 | Conduct 'mock' trial | Groups to present prosecution and defence | |

LESSON EVALUATION

The issues that arose were not classroom management issues or timing issues but seemed to relate to what the students learned and what I know that they have learned. One issue was that I was unsure how directly parts of the lesson related to the issued scheme of work and course objectives. It is true to say that all lessons should be based on achieving a certain outcome. However, by inserting an exercise that did not relate directly to the learning outcomes but helped the students' motivation or enjoyment when the subject was becoming dry, had I misused time that was allotted for different objectives? How can I assess its effect on student learning?

The other issue that arose seemed to be the lack of summative individual assessment. Where the role play was being used, there seemed to be some students that 'dominated' or received more opportunity for assessment and some students that tried to disappear and adopted a less 'front row' position. Where informal question and answer was being used, could I be sure that every student was being asked a question that gave an effective measure of their understanding?

You may have thought this teacher to have been only partially successful in judging how far his or her aims and objectives were achieved in the session taught. This is, to some extent, because we are often far more certain about student learning problems and difficulties than about whether we know what they have learned. But part of the difficulty of making evaluative judgements about students' experiences in our classrooms is how subjective these are and how problematic it can be both to teach and to observe a group at the same time. The first of two possibly more objective strategies is considered in Figure 2.4.

**Figure 2.4** Strategy 1: visual recording

The following entry was made in a student teacher's Individual Development Planner for 16 October 2006:

'While I did not want to watch the recording of my micro teaching session as I thought it would confirm how bad I really was, it was stressed that it is an important part of our development so I decided that I would have to. It was nowhere as bad as I thought and I was surprised at how different it was from my original perception of the session. The beginning was hesitant and I will try to start more confidently (by practising starting a lesson at home), but I thought I improved during it. It's interesting that I thought I was really rushing the last few minutes as I was running out of time, but it doesn't sound like that on the DVD at all. I wish I had spent more time on student activities as they did seem to be quite engaged with the activity I used and with the topic itself. The time did not really lend itself to long discussions though and I will make more use of group activities when I teach next month.'

---

**Task 2.8: Comparing strategies**

Compare the analysis in Figure 2.4 with the student's self-evaluation in Example 2.1. Which specific points in the lesson might have been more thoroughly evaluated had the session been filmed?

---

The second strategy is the student questionnaire. On the face of it, it seems odd to distribute a questionnaire to students you see on a regular basis, but a questionnaire is a more objective evaluation of your performance than others, and has the following main advantages:

- students are more likely to be open and honest than when directly questioned;
- the questions can elicit more specific responses, enabling you to focus on a particular aspect of your performance;
- individual anonymous completion reduces the possibility of conformity of response.

The major drawback is that it is not as easy as it appears to construct even the simplest questionnaire, one difficulty being composing questions of the appropriate type and wording to produce clear, useful information that will be of assistance in identifying areas for professional development.

Judith Bell, in her excellent *Doing Your Research Project* (2005), refers to Youngman's (1986) question types. The following will be of particular use in self-evaluation:

- *Verbal or open*: e.g., 'What did you feel about the discussion session?' The answer expected is a word, phrase or comment, and this can make these responses difficult to analyse. However, they can also provide some interesting responses for reflection.

- *Scale*: Various kinds of scale or continuum give students the opportunity to choose the appropriate point on the scale as in the example below.

| | Strongly agree | Agree | Neither agree nor disagree | Disagree | Strongly disagree |
|---|---|---|---|---|---|
| 1  Academic support was effective | | | | | |
| 2  Tutors marked and returned work promptly | | | | | |
| 3  Accommodation was suitable | | | | | |
| 4  Teaching was of high quality | | | | | |

Bell (2005) also draws attention to the potential dangers inherent in question wording, and these are shown in Figure 2.5.

**Figure 2.5** Dangers inherent in question wording

| | |
|---|---|
| Ambiguity, imprecision, assumption | Could your question mean different things to different students? (e.g., 'Would you describe yourself as able, average or not very good?') Could it be unclear about the kind of answer required, or already contain an answer within it? |
| Memory | Does the question rely too heavily on students' memories, which may be unreliable? (e.g., 'What level of basic skills did you achieve at school?') |
| Knowledge | Does the question presuppose the possession of information the students don't have? (e.g., 'Who sets the fee levels in your local education authority?') |
| Double questions | Are there two questions present in one? (e.g., 'Did you feel the role play and interview were worthwhile?') |
| Leading questions | Does the question lead you to a particular response? (e.g., 'Don't you think communication is the most important part of your job?') |
| Hypothetical questions | 'If you could change this lesson, how would you do it?' A pointless question if it is clear to the students they won't have that power. |

*Source*: Bell 2005: 60–4.

**Task 2.9: Devising a questionnaire**

2.9(a)    Devise a short questionnaire focusing on a lesson or series of lessons.

2.9(b)    Exchange this with a partner's and comment on question type and wording. Discuss common problems with the group.

2.9(c)    Administer the questionnaire to the relevant students.

2.9(d)    Analyse the results, question by question.

2.9(e)    Once you've analysed the results, summarize them for the rest of your group. Consider how useful the information is to you. Does any of it confirm or conflict with that gained through other evaluation methods? How might you change practice as a result of this exercise?

## Observation

Teaching observation provides excellent opportunities for continuing professional development, and yet it can still be seen as a threatening experience. Traditionally teachers have enjoyed a degree of professional autonomy and there is still a strong proprietorial feeling among many about teaching students in their own classroom. So, however experienced and professionally confident teachers are, being observed by others, whether they be colleagues, line managers or supervising tutors, is often a stressful experience. Nevertheless, such observation of and by others can be the basis of some of the most useful professional reflection you can undertake in order to improve performance. As with evaluation strategies, like the videotaping and questionnaire considered above, feedback from observation offers a more objective viewpoint on your work. The difference here is that the feedback is 'live', given immediately in an interactive context. However, there are complications that need to be discussed.

The presence of a stranger in a classroom is bound to affect the behaviour of the teacher and the students. Many teachers argue that this makes the observed session unnatural and artificial, therefore reducing the value of the feedback given. In fact there are many factors that will affect how the both teachers and students behave when a visitor is present: how used they are to visitors; whether the students know the visitor or not; whether the visitor is from inside or outside the institution; how the teacher presents the visitor. More importantly, however, is the role the observer takes in the session. Supervising tutors, for example, may insist on a non-participatory role to increase their objectivity, or a participatory one to diminish the effect of the scrutinizing assessor at the back of the classroom everyone is trying to pretend does not exist! Inspectors, on the other hand, may question students and walk around the class looking at student work. The important thing is for both the observer and observed teacher to be clear about their respective roles and the relationship between them. This will be predetermined to some extent; a line manager or supervising tutor will, however they may wish to play it down, have a supervisory evaluative dimension to their role that a peer will not. A mentor will have yet another role within the observation process.

The development of mentoring as a process in teacher education has grown

**Figure 2.6** Three models of mentoring

| | |
|---|---|
| *The apprenticeship model* | This notion is of a teacher working alongside an experienced professional, observing but also collaborating. |
| *The competence model* | Here, the mentor takes on the role of 'systematic trainer' or coach, with a predetermined list of competences to tick off. |
| *The reflective model* | The mentor helps the teacher to develop a deeper understanding of student learning by joining them as co-enquirer. |

*Source*: Maynard and Furlong 1993: 78–83.

largely as a result of the increase in school-based training in the last five or six years, as well as becoming widespread in industry and commerce. It is a practice that is now developing in post-compulsory education.

Maynard and Furlong (1993) make a distinction between three models of mentoring that might usefully be applied to the relationship between observers and the observed. The three models are shown in Figure 2.6.

---

**Task 2.10**

2.10(a)   List those who have already and may in future be observing you teach: colleague, line manager, course tutor, mentor. Try to describe how you think they see their role as an observer.

2.10(b)   If possible, present this view to them and ask them if this is, in fact, the way they do see their role. Were there discrepancies? If so, how do you account for these? How can they be minimized?

---

In order to ensure an effective relationship, it is essential that the observer and the observed be clear about the focus of the observation (in the same way as you are aware of your evaluation focus – see Task 2.6). This is particularly true if you wish to reflect on a specific area of your teaching for development. Below are some examples of communication skills and techniques that an observer of a teaching session might choose to focus on:

- giving instructions, checking understanding;
- supporting pair work – keeping a balance between enabling and spoon-feeding;
- managing attending to individuals while monitoring the group;
- effective explanation of complex points;
- appropriate use of visual aids.

---

**Task 2.11**

2.11(a)   Describe to your partner a lesson you have recently given or soon will give, detailing both student and teacher activities.

2.11(b)   Your partner should then select a focus that he or she would have chosen for an observation of that lesson, spelling out the features they would have concentrated on. They should share these with you. How far did you or would you emphasize these features in your own self-evaluation?

In considering observation, Wragg (1999) distinguishes between quantitative and qualitative methods. The former represent an attempt to quantify aspects of lessons such as verbal interaction, the use of teaching aids and classroom management as a basis for evaluation. As Wragg points out, there are many ways in which such methods can be useful and he gives examples such as an observer wanting to know how many students get to use computer equipment or the length of answers students give to questions. But such systematic analysis, as we have seen, is more suited to the competence model of mentoring. And, although whether a qualitative or quantitative approach is taken will depend on the focus of a lesson observation, it is likely that a qualitative approach with its focus on the nature of the learners' experiences will be more helpful in identifying areas for reflection and continuing professional development.

We noted above that, although observation provides a more objective approach to evaluation than perhaps the teacher's own review, this is complicated by the observer's interpretation of events in the classroom. This interpretation is central to qualitative methods of observation and will be influenced by a number of factors about the observers themselves:

- their background, experience and educational ideology;
- their awareness of and attitude to the lesson's subject/topic;
- their understanding of student responses, interactions and behaviour;
- their knowledge of and attitude to the teacher;
- their perception of their role and purpose as an observer;
- the way(s) in which they have recorded their observations.

**Task 2.12**

2.12(a)   Table 2.1 shows a series of classroom events. On a scale of 1 to 5, where 5 means 'good practice' and 1 means 'bad practice', rate each event.

2.12(b)   Would you give each the same rating if the subject of the session, where given, were different?

It is possible that there was disagreement over the ratings between the members of your group. It is likely that you needed to know a great deal more about the context of the lesson before making a judgement. Even then, however, it is possible that group members actually sitting through the lesson itself might have reached different conclusions about what was happening and its value. Nevertheless, it is only by observation that real judgements can be made about the process of teaching and learning,

**Table 2.1** Evaluating classroom events

| Classroom event | 1 2 3 4 5 |
|---|---|
| 1 Students talk frequently in a session when they're working in small groups. | |
| 2 Students are free to move around the room. | |
| 3 The teacher gives a lecture lasting 40 minutes of the hour-long session, leaving 20 minutes for question and answer. | |
| 4 Most basic skills students' work is in small groups around tables. | |
| 5 The whiteboard is the main visual aid in a lecture. | |
| 6 All teaching is one-to-one or pair instruction in a sub-aqua class. | |
| 7 Students extensively assess one another's work in a business studies class. | |
| 8 The session is based exclusively on active learning – in the above case games and role-play on a management course. | |
| 9 Students are involved mainly in recording information in a biology class. | |
| 10 The second-year degree session is a seminar where one student reads a paper and the lecturer and students discuss it. | |

therefore it is unsurprising that observation of performance has become a major part of the inspection process.

The Learning and Skills Act (2000) gave the Office for Standards in Education (Ofsted) and the Adult Learning Inspectorate (ALI) the remit to inspect all post-compulsory education and training. However, from April 2007 the inspection work of ALI was integrated into Ofsted's expanding responsibilities and Ofsted is now the inspectorate for all children and learners in England.[4]

The purpose of the inspectorate is to evaluate the effectiveness and efficiency of an institution in meeting the needs of its students and in order to do this 'inspectors will concentrate on observing lessons' (Ofsted 2001c). Inspectors will also expect to see staff development plans and details of staff development activities over the preceding two years. Therefore it is in an institution's interests to ensure not only that their staff are used to observation but also that they engage in appropriate staff development. This is often achieved by making observation the mainstay of the institution's quality assurance processes, using it as a basis for possible staff development, and it is equally likely that observation of performance is part of the appraisal system.

## Appraisal

There are as many appraisal systems as there are post-compulsory institutions, each tailored to meet the institution's own individual needs. However, every appraisal scheme should include quality assurance mechanisms not only to ensure improvement in student achievement but also to assist practitioners in their professional development and career planning.

Whatever particular methods an institution uses to appraise its staff, there are central themes that underpin all appraisal systems. First, it is a non-threatening process that operates on a regular cycle, sometimes annually, sometimes bi-annually.

Second, after an observation of performance, time is set aside to give the individual being appraised an opportunity to review their job description, to record good practice and to identify training (or other) needs. Finally, a confidential document is produced that records the matters discussed. This is used to initiate the staff development and any other agreed courses of action. Properly conducted, the appraisal process is the ideal vehicle for self-reflection and continuing professional development.

## Peer observation

Another useful strategy for professional development is through the operation of a peer observation system. The chance to view different teaching styles can focus your attention on classroom activities and lead to improvements negotiated with those who are operating in the same environment as yourself. It is a non-threatening way of providing dynamic, ever-developing practices.

There are many peer observation schemes that can be used for continuing professional development purposes. One such system is where a number of teachers from the same discipline can be paired, or even better, organized into groups of four or five, so that they can observe each other and discuss the outcomes in respect to improving their performance. This forms part of a continuous year-round cycle, with meetings held for the 'observation cell' to discuss their observations and produce an action plan, particularly useful for planning personal learning and development. An added bonus is that documentation, unlike that used for appraisal and inspection purposes, can be a great deal less formal and line managers could become part of a 'cell', so that they are observed in turn and the element of hierarchy/power removed (Brown et al. 1993).

However, peer observation is only one aspect of beneficial collaboration with colleagues. You may be following a course of study on your own or in a small group through distributed learning, but it is more common for teacher training to take place in groups comprising a wide cross-section of practitioners and students. Evaluations from such groups often cite the group that they belong to as being an important (if not the most important) learning resource they have had access to during the programme. Therefore if you are a member of a group, either as a student or as a member of a team within an institution, you need to ensure you make best use of the group for your professional development. There are a number of ways (apart from peer observation) that groups and their professional contexts can be used for developmental purposes, for example:

- developing and planning jointly run courses;
- developing new resources, particularly course materials;
- conducting trials with one another's course materials;
- trying out teaching and learning strategies seen on peer observation sessions;
- team teaching with one another's groups.

Your response to these possibilities may be to throw up your hands in despair at the narrow specialism you teach. Clearly, there are important ways in which teachers sharing a subject can collaborate, but it surprising how much you can learn from areas which at first seemed so different from your own. Indeed, so many of us are isolated in post-compulsory education that if you are undertaking a course of professional training, such experience of diverse contexts is imperative.

---

**Task 2.13: Working with others**

2.13(a)   Each group member should give a brief account to the rest of the group of their professional context, as described earlier in Task 2.3.

2.13(b)   Now select three or four individual contexts you feel it might be useful to explore and, with each colleague, specify at least one way you might collaborate.

2.13(c)   Feed this back to the rest of the group (this often sparks even more ideas and possibilities).

---

Collaboration with colleagues can also be useful if you decide to engage in the research process to enable you to critically and systematically reflect upon your practice.

## Research

The process of research can develop the skills of analysis and self-awareness that underpin successful evaluation and enable you to plan for improvement in your professional practice. There is an important relationship between teaching and research that is recognized by teacher trainers and therefore during your course you will be asked to undertake research for a number of assignments and present them in various oral and written forms. Seminar papers, course design, and essays all require research skills, but they also need to be presented in a coherent and articulate way. Students new to formal study, or returning to it after a considerable break, may find the discursive assignment or essay the most difficult to deal with and therefore it is necessary to concentrate on this form of presentation here.

A common error made by students new to writing up their research is the tendency to include everything they have researched and, in the case of assignment writing, everything they know about a topic, rather than answer the question they have been asked.

---

**Task 2.14: Answering the question**

2.14(a)   Below is a series of assignment questions about the same assessment topic. Choose one of these titles and attempt, in one or two sentences, to outline what an appropriate answer might be.

2.14(b)   Share your outlines with the group. Were there variations between answers?
    1   Outline three assessment techniques you use and explain your reasons for using them.
    2   Describe three assessment techniques you use and evaluate their effectiveness.

---

> 3   Compare and contrast three assessment techniques you use with respect to the kinds of student learning they measure.
> 4   Choose three assessment techniques you use and consider how positive student reaction is to them.
> 5   Analyse three assessment techniques you use and discuss the extent to which they measure what you say they do.

The key to Task 2.14 is to focus first on the verbs ('analyse', 'discuss', 'compare' and 'contrast'), then on the nouns that form their objects. Question 1 asks for an outline of your techniques but then wants you to explain your reasons for using them. This part of the question invites quite a wide response: you may feel the techniques will measure the kind of learning you want; or that they are easy to use; or they may be prescribed by the syllabus. Question 2 is arguably more focused, requiring you to concentrate on the techniques' effectiveness, their validity, or the extent to which they measure what they say they do, as does Question 5, which also wants you to analyse the techniques rather than just describe them, that is, you must break them down into their component parts or elements. Question 3 wants you to concentrate on comparing and contrasting, in this case, different kinds of student learning, whereas Question 4 is more interested in student response or attitude.

Once you feel clear about what the assignment title is looking for, it is time to begin the planning and research process. A useful first stage is to pool your ideas (brainstorm) and record this on a spider diagram. Figure 2.7 shows a sample spider diagram for Question 2 with one strategy, peer assessment, broken down into sub-topics. Organizing your ideas into a spider diagram helps you explore more than one way of restructuring your assignment at the next stage, the assignment plan.

**Task 2.15: Planning**

2.15(a)   Below is a series of approaches to answering Question 2. Which would be most effective?
1   In the first section, describe each assessment technique then, in the second, evaluate the effectiveness of each.
2   Describe the first technique, then evaluate it, describe the second, then evaluate it, and so on.
3   Take each element of effective assessment (e.g., objectivity/subjectivity, reinforcement of learning, ease of operation, validity, reliability) and consider particular techniques as they are relevant.

2.15(b)   Compare your views with those of other members of the group. Would group members be more comfortable with one approach rather than another? Did you think of any other approaches in addition to the three described?

You are now ready for some targeted research. There may be something to be said for a wide, scattergun approach to research at the brainstorming stage but you will soon see that the sheer volume of material available on most major post-compulsory issues makes this time consuming and of limited value. The chief resources for your targeted research are shown in Figure 2.8.

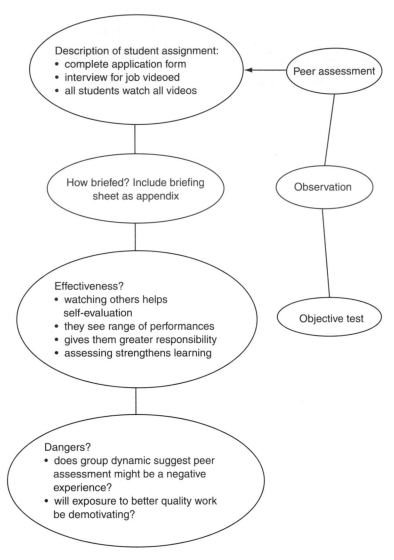

**Figure 2.7** Spider diagram in response to Question 2

**Figure 2.8** Resources for targeted research

---

Textbooks

Newspapers (particularly the *Times Educational Supplement*, the *Times Higher Educational Supplement* and other educational supplement and feature sections)

The Internet (see specifically Section 5.6 on newsgroups in Chapter 5)

TV programmers

The experience of teaching colleagues

The experience of students

The experience of group members

Educational journals, particularly:
   *Adults Learning*
   *Assessment in Education: Principles, policy and practice*
   *British Journal of Education and Work*
   *Comparative Education*
   *Curriculum Studies: A journal of educational discussion and debate*
   *Educa: The digest for vocational education and training*
   *FE Now*
   *General Education*
   *Journal of Further and Higher Education*
   *Studies in Higher Education*
   *Teaching in Higher Education*

---

**Task 2.16: Access to resources**

2.16(a)  As individuals, then as a group, which of the resources shown in Figure 2.8 do you have access to?

2.16(b)  Consider how you may go about getting access to those resources not currently available to you as a group.

---

Once you have completed your research, you must organize the material into written form as a draft. It is essential that the first attempt at the production of a paper, whether an assignment or a piece of research, is always seen as a working document. If it is an assignment, depending on the number and extent of assignments, many tutors are happy to look at drafts to help you improve and refine your paper. If not, an experienced colleague may prove helpful in playing the role of a 'critical friend'. However, if no outside help is available, you need to take responsibility for re-drafting yourself. Elements of the draft to consider are:

- Are you demonstrating an understanding of the issues you are dealing with? Have you dealt comprehensively with the subject and covered the breadth of topics required?

- Have you researched the topics in sufficient depth?

- Does your draft have balance; have you concentrated overmuch on one topic to the exclusion of others equally important?
- Have you illustrated your points with examples? In making a case or developing an argument, it is not enough simply to *state* points – you should provide *support* for them. This could be done with research evidence or arguments from literature, the use of authorities or the experience of relevant parties.
- Have you used your research reading appropriately? It is a mistake to quote chunks of books and hope they will speak for you. References should be relevant to what you want to say.
- Have you used written conventions appropriately? These may vary, but tutors normally want to see assignments written in continuous prose. A common error is to write in note form or in some other abbreviated style using bullet points, letters or numerals. Sub-headings can be used for longer pieces of work.

There are several systems of referencing, but perhaps the most straightforward (and the one used in this book) is the Harvard system. This is based on author and date of publication. In the text, you should give both, e.g.:

> . . . Bell (2005) argues that . . .

or:

> '. . . we all need to be reminded about the importance of systematic recording . . . We all think we shall remember, but after several weeks of reading, memory becomes faulty.' (Bell 2005: 62)

Note the inclusion of the page number where an author has been directly quoted.

In the bibliography, all books and articles consulted, read and referred to should be listed in alphabetical order, with the author's name and initials, followed by the date of publication, the title and finally the place of publication and the publisher. Thus for this chapter, a sample of the bibliography would be set out as follows:

Bell, J. (2005) *Doing Your Research Project*, 4th edn. Maidenhead: Open University Press.

Brown, S., Jones, G. and Rawnsley, S. (eds) (1993) *Observing Teaching*. Birmingham: Staff and Educational Development Association.

DfES (2004) *Equipping our Teachers for the Future: Reforming Initial Teaching Training for the Learning and Skills Sector*. London: HMSO.

Hillier, Y. (2005) *Reflective Teaching in Further and Adult Education*, 2nd edn. London: Continuum.

LLUK (2006) *New Overarching Professional Standards for Teachers, Tutors and Trainers in the Lifelong Learning Sector*. London: LLUK.

Millerson, G. (1964) *The Qualifying Associations: A Study in Professionalism*. London: Routledge.

Ofsted (2001) *Handbook for Inspecting Colleges*. London: Ofsted Publications.

Peters, J. M. (1994) Instructors as researchers and theorists: faculty development in a community college, in R. Benn and R. Fieldhouse (eds) *Training and Professional Development in Adult and Community Education*. Exeter: CRCE.

Wragg, E. C. (1999) *An Introduction to Classroom Observation*, 2nd edn. London: Routledge.

Judith Butcher's *Copy-Editing* (1992, 3rd edn, Cambridge University Press) gives a detailed guide to using the Harvard system.

## Related new professional standards for teachers and trainers in the lifelong learning sector

### Domain A: professional values and practice

| PROFESSIONAL KNOWLEDGE AND UNDERSTANDING | PROFESSIONAL PRACTICE |
|---|---|
| *Teachers in the lifelong learning sector know and understand:* | *Teachers in the lifelong learning sector:* |
| AK 3.1 Issues of equality, diversity and inclusion. | AP 3.1 Apply principles to evaluate and develop own practice in promoting equality and inclusive learning and engaging with diversity. |
| AK 4.2 The impact of own practice on individuals and their learning. | AP 4.2 Reflect on and demonstrate commitment to improvement of own personal and teaching skills through regular evaluation and use of feedback. |
| AK 4.3 Ways to reflect, evaluate and use research to develop own practice, and to share good practice with others. | AP 4.3 Share good practice with others and engage in continuing professional development through reflection, evaluation and the appropriate use of research. |
| AK 5.1 Ways to communicate and collaborate with colleagues and/or others to enhance learners' experience. | AP 5.1 Communicate and collaborate with colleagues and/or others, within and outside the organisation, to enhance learners' experience. |
| AK 6.1 Relevant statutory requirements and codes of practice. | AP 6.1 Conform to statutory requirements and apply codes of practice. |
| AK 6.2 Ways to apply relevant statutory requirements and the underpinning principles. | AP 6.2 Demonstrate good practice through maintaining a learning environment which conforms to statutory requirements and promotes equality, including appropriate consideration of the needs of children, young people and vulnerable adults. |

| | |
|---|---|
| AK 7.2   Own role in the quality cycle. | AP 7.2   Evaluate own contribution to the organization's quality cycle. |
| AK 7.3   Ways to implement improvements based on feedback received. | AP 7.3   Use feedback to develop own practice within the organization's systems. |

## Domain B: learning and teaching

| PROFESSIONAL KNOWLEDGE AND UNDERSTANDING | PROFESSIONAL PRACTICE |
|---|---|
| Teachers in the lifelong learning sector know and understand: | Teachers in the lifelong learning sector: |
| BK 2.6   Ways to evaluate own practice in terms of efficiency and effectiveness. | BP 2.6   Evaluate the efficiency and effectiveness of own teaching, including consideration of learner feedback and learning theories. |
| BK 2.7   Ways in which mentoring and/or coaching can support the development of professional skills and knowledge. | BP 2.7   Use mentoring and/or coaching to support own and others' professional development, as appropriate. |

## Domain D: planning for learning

| PROFESSIONAL KNOWLEDGE AND UNDERSTANDING | PROFESSIONAL PRACTICE |
|---|---|
| Teachers in the lifelong learning sector know and understand: | Teachers in the lifelong learning sector: |
| DK 3.1   Ways to evaluate own role and performance in planning learning. | DP 3.1   Evaluate the success of planned learning activities. |
| DK 3.2   Ways to evaluate own role and performance as a member of a team in planning learning. | DP 3.2   Evaluate the effectiveness of own contributions to planning as a member of a team. |

## Notes

1   A full-time member of staff will be expected to undertake 30 hours every year.
2   This continuing professional development can take many forms, e.g. external or in-service courses, relevant research, accredited courses. However, it must be designed to enhance the professional practice of the individual.

3   Subjects were chosen in response to a number of factors, for example, weak inspections findings, large numbers of learners and importance to the nation's economic needs.
4   The inspectorate is now called the Office for Standards in Education, Children's Services and Skills, although it is still known as 'Ofsted'.

# 3

# Student learning in post-compulsory education

## 3.1 What is Chapter 3 about?

Over the last decade the mantra of 'education, education, education' seems to have been replaced by one of 'learning, learning, learning'. Teaching itself has become more concerned with the promotion of effective learning than on the transmission of knowledge in one form or another, in the sense that the *process* appears to have become more important than *content*. Moreover, the traditional distinction between education and training has been obscured by this new focus on learning. Does it mean that 'skills' and 'knowledge' are no longer viable concepts in a new era of 'learning'? Does 'learning' mean inclusiveness and a sweeping away of the old education/training divide? Policy documents, in particular, reflect a shift in emphasis towards *how* we approach learning and in many cases the word 'training' has been replaced by 'learning'. We no longer have students, but learners, and learning is purportedly for everyone.

So how does what appears to be an obsession with 'learning' relate to our students/learners and what goes on in our classrooms? How does this changing understanding of what education, training, skills, knowledge and learning are, influence practice? How does a central focus on learning rather than teaching impact on the work of the tutor in PCE? Chapter 1 provided the context for understanding the changes in the post-compulsory sector and traced historical developments. This chapter seeks to develop your knowledge and understanding of selected theoretical perspectives in relation to current developments.

The chapter will explore key features of different learning theories in relation to classroom practice. Section 3.2 will examine the factors affecting students' ability to learn. What are the differences and similarities between a class of 17-year-old hairdressers, an AE French class and a group of postgraduate student teachers? What affects a student's ability to learn? We will look critically at some of the factors that have particular contemporary significance. Section 3.3 will introduce some of the theories of learning as a background to our understanding of how our students learn. How have behaviourist, cognitive and humanist ideas about learning in particular affected approaches to teaching and learning? Section 3.4 will consider what constitutes effective learning and how barriers to learning can be overcome. Are we concerned with knowledge and understanding or with skills development? We will look at how we can ensure that our students learn effectively through an understanding of their learning styles and needs. How effective study skills and learner autonomy can be developed provides the focus for Section 3.5. What is the value and role of independent learning both within the classroom and as directed self-study? How is independent learning best managed and organized? How has classroom learning become more orientated to the individual and their *personal* learning needs? These are the questions we will reflect upon and try to answer.

## 3.2 Factors affecting student learning

---

**KEY ISSUES**

What makes one group of learners distinct from another?

What individual differences can we identify in learners?

How can knowledge of factors which affect learning inform our approach to teaching?

---

**Task 3.1**

3.1(a)   Choose one of your groups of learners and write a short profile of it giving details of what you know about individuals.

3.1(b)   Look at what you have written and identify some general headings for the information you have included; for example ability, motivation, social background.

3.1(c)   Now think about a contrasting group, preferably one that you teach, or alternatively one that you have been a student in recently – perhaps a tutor training group or adult education class. Write a similar profile using the headings you identified for your first group. What are the differences? What are the similarities? Note these down to return to later. You may like to discuss your observations with a colleague.

3.1(d)   If you have been working in PCE for several years, consider what changes have taken place in terms of the range of students, the style of teaching and learning and the content of the curriculum. Do you notice a trend towards a 'personalized' approach based on individual needs? How have you adapted to new developments?

Strong claims are made for the distinctiveness of particular groups of learners. Indeed, a whole body of theory has been developed around the adult learner as distinct from younger learners. But what makes one group of learners distinct from another? Is it a question of age, motivation, ability, the chosen course of study? Every learning group is obviously different because it is made up of different individuals. Given the diverse nature of PCE you no doubt encounter a very wide variety of abilities, personalities, backgrounds and so on, among your students. These differences not only affect your approach to teaching, which will be considered in Chapter 4, but also have a marked effect on how students learn.

**Task 3.2**

3.2(a)   Here is a list of factors which affect a student's ability to learn. It is not exhaustive and you may want to add others. In your experience, are any of these factors more important than others? Place them in order of importance:
   • ability
   • motivation
   • personality
   • attitude
   • age
   • learning style
   • home life
   • previous learning experience
   • life experience

3.2(b)   Why do you consider some factors more important than others? Do some of them overlap?

3.2(c)   Now look at each factor in turn and write down an example of how learning is enhanced and how it is inhibited in each case. For example, an older student may bring to a class a great deal of previous experience and knowledge on which they can build; on the other hand, they may be anxious about having had a long period away from education and because of their age have less confidence in their ability to learn.

The order of importance and examples that one chooses will depend to some extent on who the learners are and what they are learning, but there are commonalities as well as distinctive features. Continuity of educational experience is an important influence on the way people approach learning. The 16–19-year-old in FE and the traditional HE cohort has a continuous experience of education from at least the age of 5. Schooling in one form or another has been a dominant feature of their lives. The routines and expectations of educational establishments are familiar to them. This is not generally the case for the adult learner who may not have been involved in a formal educational experience for some time and whose knowledge and expectations of education may only be based on their own school experience. Equally, the adult re-entering the education system at whatever level has many more outside responsibilities and pressures than the younger FE or HE student. That is not to play down the increased financial burdens that younger students now face in respect of tuition fees and the pressure to earn a living while studying, but these, and other pressures, are much more acute for the adult 'returner'. We shall consider these issues in more detail in Section 3.4 in the context of barriers to learning.

Social and political contexts are important influences on the way teaching and learning are approached and the relative importance given to one theoretical perspective over another. For example, the issues of ability, motivation and ageing might be considered to have particular significance at the present time given the nature of the current preoccupation with education and the new political emphasis on LLL. Let us look at these three factors in more detail with a contemporary focus.

## Ability

Ability, and more specifically, intelligence, is perhaps the most contentious and politicized aspect of learning. Even a commonly accepted definition has been elusive. Nor have approaches to measuring intelligence and establishing the intelligence quotient (IQ) of individuals been consensual. Is intelligence fixed? What are the relative influences of heredity and social circumstances on an individual's intelligence? Does IQ exist at all? Can intelligence be measured? These questions remain unresolved.

Attempts at the description and definition of intelligence have often focused on the differences between individuals. Those perceived differences have then often been used for political ends. Take for example the eugenics movement in the early part of the twentieth century whose aim it was to 'improve' the human race. Drawing on Darwin's theories of evolution as they could be applied to society (social Darwinism) and theories of heredity and genetic influences current at that time, eugenicists essentially claimed a scientific basis for white Anglo-Saxon superiority. These theories gave a justification to the sort of 'master race' ideas of Nazi Germany, and had already led to numerous pieces of legislation in the United States between 1911 and 1930. Laws were passed in some states allowing for the sterilization of 'misfits', the 'mentally retarded' and the 'insane' and to restrict marriages between certain racial groups.

Eugenics has since been discredited. And yet its spectre seems to stalk present research into genetics and IQ. Nowadays, there is general unease about aspects of genetic research from an ethical point of view. For example, the search for genes which might influence variations in intelligence is viewed with scepticism not for the scientific data researchers present, but for the implications of their findings and the uses they might be put to. What if it were true, as some scientists claim, that genetic factors account for 50 per cent of IQ variations across the population? What might be the effect of such a claim on the way teachers view their students? Other recent research claims that genetic make-up as much as the socialization process dictates differences between boys and girls in terms of how they acquire social skills, suggesting that gender differences are largely genetically rather than culturally determined (Skuse 1997). What are the implications of such claims? At the present time there seems to be a certain coyness about research into genes and IQ, perhaps due to the fear of a backlash as well as a disillusionment with social explanations. In a more confident age this was not the case.

---

**Task 3.3**

What examples can you draw on (either from observation of students, your own children or others around you) that appear to be inherited traits? Can you identify any social influence – that is, aspects of upbringing, peer influences or the wider influences in society – that might give an alternative explanation for any of these traits?

The 'nature–nurture' discussion has been a subject of research and debate among scientists and educationalists throughout the twentieth century. Intelligence testing is an attempt to identify the innate ability of the individual. Intelligence tests were first developed at the turn of the century in France by Binet and Simon. Under contract to the French government, their task was to devise a test to identify children who should benefit from special schooling. This test was adapted in the United States and in 1916 became widely known as the Stanford–Binet test (see Child 1993: 210–12). It was used widely, in modified forms, to measure normal, subnormal and superior intelligence throughout the century. In Britain, the work of Cyril Burt is perhaps the best known in the field. Burt's theories formed the whole basis of accepted wisdom on the nature of intelligence for generations of schoolchildren from the 1950s onward. He established that intelligence was partly innate and partly developed as a result of the social environment. His theories were adopted and resulted in the 11+ examination and IQ testing in schools. In later years Burt was criticized for his deterministic approach, and it has been suggested that he falsified some of his data (Hearnshaw 1979).

Since the 1960s, social and cultural factors have been considered more important determinants of intelligence than heredity. While individual differences in ability are acknowledged, educators have regarded social inequalities as influencing more profoundly an individual's capacity for learning. The abandonment (in most parts of the country) of the 11+ examination in the early 1970s was the ideological expression of an attempt at engineering a more egalitarian society through the education system. The value of IQ tests as they were conceived of in the 1950s and 1960s was called into question on the basis that they were gender and culturally biased, aimed at middle-class children who generally performed better, and were not an accurate measure of ability for most people.

The 'nature–nurture' debate usually centres on the relative importance of heredity over social factors, but it is also worth taking a step back and asking the question: does IQ actually exist? From as long ago as the beginning of the nineteenth century it has been argued in some quarters that the nature of intelligence cannot be coded, certainly not genetically coded, and that intelligence by its nature has no limitations and is not parcelled-out in specific amounts. Nor is it a merely abstract potential; rather, it has a real and determinant content. It is well known that concentrated teaching can improve IQ scores and that generation by generation IQ scores are improving. What does this tell us? It might also be argued that IQ has served the role of justifying social inequalities in that we live in a meritocracy where income is distributed according to merit and merit is defined as intelligence plus effort. Could it be that the elevation of intelligence as a defining factor of success or failure in society is a way of endorsing social divisions? As teachers and trainers concerned with helping our students to realize their potential, we might consider that humans are shaped by both nature and nurture, but that what is important is our ability to transcend both, by our capacity to overcome the constraints imposed both by our genetic and our cultural heritage (Malik 2001).

The work of Harvard psychologist Howard Gardner and his theory of *multiple intelligences* (1983, 1993) has become very popular with educationalists in recent years. This is partly because his view of intelligence reflects a current ethos of promoting self-esteem and individual achievement. Gardner sees the traditional understanding of intelligence as limiting. He suggests that traditional understandings do not recognize the range of talents and abilities that many people have who do not excel in what he describes as 'logical-mathematical intelligence'. Gardner identifies and describes six other forms of intelligence as follows: linguistic intelligence, spatial intelligence, bodily kinaesthetic intelligence, musical intelligence, interpersonal intelligence and intrapersonal intelligence. For Gardner, these distinctive forms of intelligence are genetically based and influenced by culture, but can be enhanced through practice and learning. Very recently, educationalists, particularly those working with disaffected and marginalized young people, have become interested in the idea of emotional intelligence which has been explored by, among others, Daniel Goleman (1995). Emotional intelligence appears to be similar to Gardner's interpersonal and intrapersonal intelligences in that it is concerned with such things as self-awareness and empathy, the ability to manage emotions and relationships and to motivate oneself. Emotional intelligence theory taps into the current ethos of victimhood in society (Füredi 1997, 2004) and it is easy to see why it is being used in relation to the socially and educationally excluded. Theories of multiple intelligences are attractive in that they confirm that we 'can all be good at something'. On the other hand, they might also provide what appears to be a scientifically based excuse for setting low expectations of ourselves and others rather than striving to overcome difficulties in particular areas. Such presentations of 'intelligence' bear little resemblance to other understandings described above, except in the sense that they also seem to accept the overriding importance of genetic influences. They present the contentious issue of intelligence in a non-contentious way, which might lead us to sidestep or ignore many of the, as yet, unanswered questions about the nature of ability, individual differences and their relationship to educational opportunity and equality.

---

**Task 3.4**

3.4(a)    Individual differences in ability clearly have an impact on our approach to teaching. In what ways do you take the differing abilities of your learners into account in order to ensure that each individual achieves their potential?

3.4(b)    If possible, compare your ideas with those of a partner and draw up a list together of how you differentiate your approach to teaching according to students' varying abilities.

3.4(c)    Read in more detail about multiple intelligences and emotional intelligence theories and consider whether they do indeed promote a culture of low expectations and victimhood as suggested above.

---

## Motivation

Motivation is a key factor in learning and is linked very closely to attitude. Motivation has been described as 'a person's aroused desire for participation in a learning process' (Curzon 1990: 195). How to arouse and maintain that desire is of concern both to the student and the tutor. Our students arrive in our classes with all sorts of motives for attending. Those motives may be positive and lead a student to be well motivated towards learning, or they may be somewhat negative, leading a student to be poorly motivated towards learning.

At the present time the majority of young people continue their education beyond the age of 16. HE has expanded to accommodate a much more diverse student population including a larger proportion of mature students. Unemployed people of all ages are required to attend education and training courses. An increasing number of adults attend adult education centres more for practical reasons than for the pleasure of learning for its own sake. These changes in our student population bring with them changes in student motives and motivation.

---

**Task 3.5**

3.5(a)    Choose one of your teaching groups and find out (if you don't already know) what were their individual motives for attending your course.

3.5(b)    Now consider how their initial motives for joining the course relate to their attitudes to learning during the course.

3.5(c)    Can you identify any changes in attitudes as the course has progressed? How do you account for these changes?

---

Motivation is often seen as needs-related. Perhaps the most well-known theory of motivation is Maslow's hierarchy of needs (Maslow 1970: 56–61). Maslow, whose work is closely related to humanistic psychology saw 'self-actualization' as what drives people to learn; that is, the need to make full use of one's talents, become creative and achieve one's potential is what motivates us. Self-actualization is an ultimate human goal and need, but before that need can be fulfilled a set of other needs must be met. These needs are generally presented as a pyramid, shown in Figure 3.1. At the bottom level are physiological needs that must be satisfied first, such as hunger and thirst. Once these are satisfied the next level is the need for physical and psychological well-being which if met leads on to the need for love and a sense of belonging which involves having warm, friendly relationships. Next come self-esteem needs: to achieve, be successful, have the respect of others. Finally, at the top of the hierarchy is self-actualization, the desire to fulfil one's potential. This, according to Maslow, may only be achieved by some people fleetingly throughout their lives, but the top of the pyramid is left open because human potential is not finite. The important thing to recognize about Maslow's hierarchy is that moving to a higher level is dependent on the level below. It follows therefore that a self-actualized person can only become so if all the other needs are met.

Can you identify these characteristics among the students you teach? Is it true, as Maslow seems to imply, that only well-off people in caring relationships and success-ful in their lives can achieve their full creative potential and self-fulfilment? And if so, what are the implications of this theory in relation to your students?

Maslow has been criticized for basing his theories on middle-class America in the

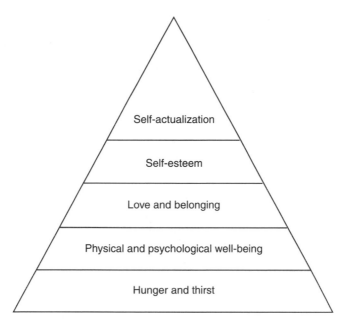

**Figure 3.1** Maslow's hierarchy of needs
*Source*: Maslow 1970.

1960s. Lessons from history as well as our own experience as teachers and learners tell us that it is not necessarily the case that motivation to learn is dependent on the fulfilment of interrelated needs in the hierarchical way that Maslow describes. Equally, the extent to which the tutor can meet certain of those needs may be limited. But what aspects of Maslow's theory are relevant to learners in PCE?

**Task 3.6**

3.6(a)    Take each stage of Maslow's hierarchy of needs and consider what the practical implications are for your teaching. For example, love and belonging might be interpreted in the classroom as creating a positive, supportive atmosphere.

3.6(b)    How will each of these practical considerations enhance student motivation?

Other theorists such as Robert Gagné have identified motivation as the first phase of the learning process. The role of the teacher, according to Gagné, is 'to identify the motives of students and channel them into activities that accomplish educational goals' (1977: 206). It is essential to student motivation that the teacher identifies and communicates goals and objectives to students and generates expectations in them. What effect do low expectations on the part of the tutor and the student have on student motivation? Is it more a problem today when students may have limited career prospects and may have chosen to continue in education and training because there was no alternative in a dwindling labour market?

**Task 3.7**

3.7(a)   Note down what strategies you use to promote and maintain the motivation of your students.

3.7(b)   Compare your strategies with a partner's. What are the similarities and differences? How do you account for these?

*Intrinsic* and *extrinsic* are other descriptions that have been applied to motivation. Intrinsic motivation is said to come from an inner drive and this is related to the human need for self-esteem and self-confidence and a desire to satisfy curiosity. Some activities are a reward in themselves and undertaken purely for the pleasure they give. Extrinsic motivation on the other hand is externally produced. Some external incentive with some sort of promise of reward, threat of punishment or need for competition or cooperation with others characterizes this type of motivation. For extrinsic motivation to be sustained, students must have attainable goals to work towards, be given immediate feedback on their performance and be rewarded for success. It is fashionable nowadays to focus more on developing an atmosphere of cooperation among students and eliminating any sort of competitive spirit in the classroom as this is seen as being harmful to students, particularly the low achievers. However, competitiveness is linked with achievement and doing one's best. Is it possible that the effect of discouraging competition is to damage motivation and ultimately the fulfilment of individual aspiration and potential?

Cyril Houle (1961) provides a similar description of motivation in what he calls the 'orientation of learning' of students, and identifies three types of learner. First, the *goal-oriented* learner who engages in a course for specific reasons with clear objectives such as obtaining a qualification, completing a task or project or solving an immediate problem. Once the objective has been achieved this type of learner generally ceases to attend her or his course of study. Second, the *activity-oriented* learner who joins a class because they enjoy the social engagement that learning offers as well as the course content. This type of learner feels as much benefit from being a part of a group as from acquiring new skills or knowledge and returns year after year moving from one course to another. If you work in an AE setting, this type of learner may be familiar to you. The third type of orientation Houle calls *learning-oriented*. This type of learner enjoys learning for its own sake and attends a course purely out of interest in the subject. Such a learner may continue to study alone long after the course has finished to extend their knowledge further.

**Task 3.8**

3.8(a)   Can you think of examples of how your learners are motivated intrinsically and extrinsically? How do these examples relate to Houle's 'orientations of learning'?

> 3.8(b)    Discuss in a small group the relative merits of cooperation and competition in enhancing motivation. Are they mutually exclusive? What might be the effects on learning of entirely eradicating the one or the other in the classroom?

## Ageing

The achievement of individual potential as a lifelong goal seems a laudable aspiration. No longer is it the case that age, in theory at any rate, is seen as a barrier to access to education. It is now clearly understood that the opportunity to continue learning throughout life is part of what it means to be a mature, healthy adult, although we might view with some suspicion current interpretations of what that means. The present-day understanding of adult learning is partly based on psychological lifespan development theories which date from the late 1960s. Up to that time it was assumed that once people had achieved biological maturity their ability to learn became 'stable' – that is, reached a plateau – and then began to deteriorate. This is called the *decrement model* of adult development. Research undertaken subsequently by a number of academics has concluded that this is not the case. The *personal growth* model which now has general currency presents ageing in a less negative light, stressing positive aspects of human development. Several similar descriptive inventories of 'phases' or 'stages' of the human life cycle are available (Tennant and Pogson 1995 and Tennant 2002). For example, Chickering and Havighurst (1981) in the United States drew on the empirical work of others (and earlier work by Havighurst) to construct an 'inventory of life': developmental tasks of the adult years. They identified six phases in the adult life cycle related to chronological ages, as follows. Late adolescence and youth (16–23) is characterized by an emphasis on achieving emotional independence, choosing and preparing for a career, preparing for marriage and family life and developing an ethical system. Early adulthood (23–35) focuses on deciding on a partner, starting a family, managing a home, starting in an occupation and assuming a civic occupation. Mid-life transition (35–45) is a period of adapting to a changing time perspective, revising career plans and redefining family relationships. Middle adulthood (45–57) is concerned with maintaining a career or developing a new one, restabilizing family relationships, making mature civic contributions and adjusting to biological change. Late adult transition (57–65) is a period of preparation for retirement and in late adulthood (65) the individual is adjusting to retirement, adjusting to declining health and strength, becoming affiliated with late-adult age groups, establishing satisfactory living arrangements, adjusting to the death of a spouse and maintaining integrity.

You may consider that Chickering and Havighurst's model is somewhat prescriptive and bears little resemblance to the lives of many people in present-day society. Indeed, one of the criticisms of their work and that of others in a similar vein is that their descriptions tended to be based on middle-class white American males at a particular time in history.

**Task 3.9**

3.9(a)   Discuss in a small group what would be the objections to the above description of adult development. How might such a model be useful to you?

3.9(b)   What sort of 'inventory of life' might apply to your students?

However, while criticisms are levelled at aspects of lifespan development theories, there is nevertheless a general professional acceptance that adulthood is a period of change and development and that in principle an adult's capacity to learn throughout life is not significantly diminished. However, it may not be generally acknowledged among the general public that this is the case. How often do our adult students use their age as an excuse for some difficulty they have with their learning?

**Task 3.10**

3.10(a)   List all the difficulties with learning something that your students (or you!) have attributed to their age.

3.10(b)   Which ones have a physical cause and which ones might be caused by other factors (e.g., social)?

3.10(c)   Discuss in a group ways of helping your students overcome these difficulties.

The demographic reality of an ageing population has contributed to some extent to changes in attitudes to age and ageing. After all, in 2001 16 per cent of the population in Britain was over the age of 64 and by 2041 this figure will reach 25 per cent. In a general sense the old cliché, 'You can't teach an old dog new tricks,' is no longer credible, although at an individual level, as we have seen, many people lack confidence in their ability to learn as they get older.

It is not surprising that ageing is a preoccupation as we begin the twenty-first century, since an increasingly ageing population is assumed to be a burden on society. Whether or not this is the case is disputed since there is little evidence to support the assertion. However, it is clearly in the interests of society to keep as much of the population as possible active and healthy for as long as possible in order to reduce the effects of that perceived burden.

An alternative to the lifespan development theories is to see adult development as a dialectical process; that is, the change and development of the individual is both a product of the change and development of society and an agent of change and development in that society. This approach to understanding adulthood rejects psychological explanations of adult development. Rather, it is argued, the development of the individual is governed by the objective circumstances of their lives. If opportunities to learn, achieve and develop potential are restricted then the potential to learn will eventually become restricted. 'Use it or lose it' is the old adage. The extent to which society can enable everyone to achieve their potential is a perennial discussion and raises the issue of whether education should be for the benefit of the individual or the greater benefit of society. In the context of our discussion of ageing and learning it is clear that the extent to which people have the opportunity to be physically and mentally active and to fulfil individual potential is important at all ages and is no less of a priority for the elderly.

In practical terms, however, we know that some older learners do experience certain physical difficulties such as hearing, sight and mobility. The important thing to remember is that these difficulties do not necessarily signal an impaired ability to learn. As you identified in Task 3.10, they merely require fairly straightforward changes of approach to learning both on the part of the tutor and the learner.

### Task 3.11

Discuss with a partner some of the difficulties you have come across with older students. What strategies have you used or could you use to overcome them?

## 3.3 Learning theories

### KEY ISSUES

What are the main theoretical perspectives that inform our approach to learning?

How does an understanding of theories of learning affect our approach to classroom practice?

It is not the intention here to provide an in-depth study of learning theories, but to present an overview of the main theoretical perspectives and to raise some critical issues related to them. Since the whole chapter is devoted to learning, aspects of theory are presented throughout and relate to the schools of thought discussed in this section. Theories of learning are based on psychological understanding and seek to describe what happens when learning takes place. Learning theory in essence is not about the conditions required for effective learning: it is for the practitioner to extract and interpret elements from theories and apply what is perceived as relevant to his or her own teaching. No one theory can supply a blueprint for how we learn, but each offers insights which are essential to us as teachers if we are to ensure that our students learn effectively.

All too often textbooks on educational psychology and learning theory, while explaining clearly the principles of learning, are less effective in the practical advice they give. As Tight (1996: 24) suggests, they offer a ' "cook book" approach to practical advice'. This is because they do not relate to the content of the learning that is to be undertaken, but to the process of learning. The application of learning theory should therefore proceed on this basis; some insights into how people learn seem more appropriately applied to certain areas of subject matter than others, as we shall examine.

The broad strands of learning theory are: *behaviourism, Gestalt theories, cognitive theories* and *andragogy*. Behaviourist, Gestalt and cognitive theories of learning have tended to centre round how learning occurs in children and date from the latter part of the nineteenth century. Andragogy and related theories, concerned with how adults learn, are more recent and derive from the humanist school of psychology.

According to behaviourist theories, which formed the basis for all learning theories, all behaviour is learned, thus eliminating any biological influences. Put crudely, behaviourists contended that all learning involves 'an observable change in behaviour' and only what can be measured can be regarded as learning. Behaviourist psychologists did not seek to discover anything about thought processes, but about how learning occurred. Experiments involving salivating dogs (classical conditioning, after Pavlov), cats and monkeys (the law of effect, after Thorndike), rats and pigeons (operant conditioning, after Skinner) are well known and are the basis of S–R (stimulus–response) theory. The earliest behaviourist was Watson who established the principle of trial and error learning which other behaviourists developed. For a full account of individuals' work in this field see Child (1993: 92–9). The American psychologist B.F. Skinner has been perhaps the most influential figure in the field. Skinner developed some of the main principles by which behaviourist theory is known (1938). His 'Skinner box' involved putting hungry rats into a box and 'training' them to pull a series of levers to release food pellets. At first, pulling the lever was accidental, but after it happened several times the rat began to associate pulling the lever with food and then did so intentionally, thus displaying learned behaviour. Such behaviour he called operant conditioning and what differentiates it from classical conditioning is that the individual is required to act on the environment (the rat operated the lever to obtain the food). The need for reinforcement, rewards and punishment and feedback are all attributable to Skinner's work. Skinner's experiments with teaching pigeons to walk in a figure of eight led to his identifying these elements as key features of learning: correct responses are reinforced by rewards, incorrect responses are ignored (or possibly punished, a negative reinforcement). Skinner subsequently made a major contribution to the development of programmed learning, the early forerunner of computer-assisted learning and mastery learning. Skinner's operant conditioning also forms the basis of behaviour modification, the technique used to bring about a change in behaviour, often used in special needs education.

In a behaviourist approach, learning should progress step-by-step and build on previously learned material. In the early stages the learner should be regularly rewarded when correct responses are given. This feedback stimulates motivation to continue. Learning is reinforced by rewards and knowledge of success. Skinner's work and the behaviourist method in general are appealing in that they identify components of learning which we can readily understand. Anyone who has trained a dog to sit on command or potty-trained a small child will recognize the features of the behaviourist method. But does all learning occur in this way? Essential to a behavioural view of learning is that any learning can be measured. Can all learning be observed? What about more abstract knowledge such as understanding Plato or appreciating classical music? Is there is a danger, therefore, that anything that cannot be measured in behavioural terms gets ignored?

**Task 3.12**

3.12(a)    Think of two examples from your own teaching where you could or do use a behaviourist approach. Describe how the learning takes place step-by-step.

3.12(b)    Discuss your examples with a partner and try to apply the behaviourist terminology to stages in the learning.

3.12(c)    Draw up a list with your partner of the types of learning activity that might best be approached through behaviourist methods.

The examples you chose in Task 3.12 may well have been drawn from a vocational or competence-based course. For example, NVQs, which are discussed in various contexts elsewhere in this book, offer the current exemplar of behaviourist theories of learning. Indeed, many professional qualifications, including the PGCE and the Certificate of Education, are competence-based courses. If you write a lesson plan or course programme with objectives which state precisely what students will be able to do (for example, 'name the parts of the internal combustion engine'), you are writing behavioural objectives intending to measure a learning outcome. The competence movement has become perhaps the most important influence in the post-compulsory curriculum today.

The contribution of Gestalt psychology to learning is particularly important with regard to perception and the role it plays in learning. Wertheimer, Kohler and Koffler founded the Gestalt school of psychology in the 1920s. Unlike behaviourists who attempted to analyse behaviour, however complex, into stimulus–response units, Gestalt theory looks at how we see patterns as a whole. In fact, Gestalt means 'pattern' or 'form' in German. The visual 'trick' silhouette pictures which have two interpretations are well-known examples used to illustrate visual perception. The Gestaltists concluded from experiments such as these that the way we look at things and the ways in which we perceive things depend on our prior experience. They emphasized closure, which is our ability to process component parts of information and create a whole, and described this as insight. Insight learning applies the laws of perception to learning. It refers to that sudden flash of inspiration that we have when we suddenly see the solution to a problem. To experience what is meant by insight learning, try doing a jigsaw puzzle without the picture to guide you. You will proceed by trial and error, but at some stage, hopefully, you will have that sudden insight as to where to place a crucial piece as you realize what the picture is supposed to be. Insight, according to Gestaltists, is a response to a whole situation, not separate responses to a series of stimuli, as behaviourists would suggest. 'The whole is greater than the sum of its parts' is a description often applied to Gestalt theory, suggesting that something is missing in the behaviourist approach. From a Gestalt perspective, learning is a complex process of interrelationships which occur as a result of engaging with a new problem in the light of previous experiences.

**Task 3.13**

3.13(a)   What other examples of insight learning can you think of?

3.13(b)   How does insight learning feature in your students' learning? Think of some examples.

Gestalt theories add another dimension to behaviourism in terms of an understanding of learning processes. Insight learning and theories of perception are often described within the cognitive theoretical framework in study texts because they have in common an emphasis on more abstract psychological concepts such as 'understanding', 'reasoning', 'thinking' and 'human consciousness' as opposed to a simplistic attempt to reduce the rich variety of human learning to 'observable behaviour'. Piaget is the most well-known of the cognitive theorists writing and researching over a period of almost 40 years from the late 1920s to the early 1960s (see Child 1993: 157–70). Although his work was focused on the development of children, he established nevertheless that learning is developmental. This has important implications for adult learning since it suggests that adulthood is a stable period in terms of intellectual development. Through experimentation, observation and research Piaget identified stages of intellectual development in children which are sequential and established that the changing nature of learning and the capacity to think throughout childhood is qualitative rather than quantitative. These developmental stages are known as: sensory motor (0–2 years); pre-operational (2–6 years); concrete operational (7–11 years); and formal operational (12 years +) (see Tennant 1988: 66–81 for a full account and critique in relation to adult learning). In short, each stage marks the development from practical thought to the abstract thought equated with mature adulthood. Is this an end point? Some theorists argue that it is not. Is the process necessarily age-related or more to do with the range and depth of learning experiences that we undergo at any age? Piaget has been criticized both for a lack of rigour in his methodology and for over-interpretation of his data. Nevertheless his analysis has been the bedrock of learning theory for a vast number of schoolteachers for the past 40 years or more (see Boden 1994).

A key feature of cognitive theory is that knowledge is constructed through interaction with the environment. It is a cognitive process which involves acquiring new information which enables the learner to develop and transform their existing knowledge and then check out and apply the new state of knowledge to new situations; and so the process goes on. New patterns of meaning and understanding are formed to enable further learning to take place. The process is dynamic. The work of Jerome S. Bruner in the 1960s to 1980s, following on from and influenced by Piaget, has made a significant contribution to cognitive theory. For Bruner, it is essential that the learner has a fundamental understanding of the underlying principles of a subject. Discovery learning, according to Bruner, is the most effective and authentic method of achieving a real understanding of the principles of a subject and then applying those principles. Discovery learning involves confronting the learner with a problem and allowing them to explore the problem and try out solutions on the basis of inquiry and previous learning under the guidance of a teacher. The newly acquired knowledge is then used to formulate a general principle which can then be applied to other situations. For example, when learning the concept of 'conservation' a young child might be given variously shaped containers, a measuring jug and a bowl of water with which to 'play'. The child is encouraged by the teacher to try pouring water from one container to another. Some of the containers, although differently shaped, contain the same amount. Gradually through experimentation, and prompting and questioning by the teacher, the child arrives at an understanding that the quantity of water remains constant and is able to articulate her or his understanding. Over a period of time, he or she would be given further opportunities to demonstrate her or his knowledge and apply the principle in other situations. This body of work on learning has led to the development of what is known broadly as *constructivism*. The central idea is that human learning is constructed, that learners build new knowledge upon previous learning and therefore learning involves constructing one's own knowledge from one's own experiences. Individuals engage in their own knowledge construction by integrating new information into their 'schemes' and negotiate meaning through a shared understanding. The teacher acts as a facilitator who encourages students to discover principles for themselves and to construct knowledge by working to solve realistic problems.

## Task 3.14

3.14(a)   Discovery learning has been a popular approach with very young learners for the past 30 years or more. Discuss in a small group examples of how it might be an appropriate approach with learners in PCE.

3.14(b)   Think of some examples from your own experience where you have encouraged discovery learning. Compare these examples with those from Task 3.15 below.

3.14(c)   What would be the role of the teacher in a discovery learning situation?

Cognitive theorists relate their theories to subject content, as do behaviourists. The approach of humanist psychologists is more concerned with the process of learning and therefore contrasts sharply with behaviourism and cognitivism. Theories of learning related to humanistic psychology were arrived at as a reaction against behaviourism and provide the intellectual basis for much adult learning theory. According to humanist insights, learning is a total personality process; life is a learning experience; true education is individual and about personal growth. Malcolm Knowles presents andragogy, 'the science and art of helping adults to learn' (Knowles 1984: 52) as a theory of adult learning. It was Knowles who developed and popularized the andragogical model, the notions of the adult as a self-directed learner and the 'learning contract'. Knowles based his model on his experiences in teaching in American universities which has been pointed to as an essential weakness of his theories. While the 'assumptions of andragogy' have been challenged and much criticized, nevertheless the notion of the self-directed learner underpins much of adult education practice and remains the keystone of adult learning theory. Many tutors working in FE colleges in particular are familiar with learning contracts which have been introduced in recent years. Knowles identified five elements of the learning process: the concept of the learner; the role of the learner's experience; readiness to learn; orientation to learning; and motivation. He contrasted a characterization of pedagogical assumptions with what he identified as andragogical. Table 3.1 sets out Knowles' 'assumptions'.

**Task 3.15**

Discuss in a group of four or five the extent to which you would support or reject the assumptions in Table 3.1. Use examples from your own experience of children and adults learning to inform your discussion.

**Table 3.1** The assumptions of andragogy

|  | Pedagogical | Andragogical |
| --- | --- | --- |
| Concept of the learner | Dependent personality | Increasingly self-directed |
| Role of learner's experience | To be built on, more than used as a resource | A rich resource for learning by self and others |
| Reading to learn | Uniform by age, level and curriculum | Develops from life tasks and problems |
| Orientation to learning | Subject-centred | Task- or problem-centred |
| Motivation | By external rewards and punishment | By internal incentives and curiosity |

Source: Knowles 1984: 116.

Humanist psychologists, in particular Carl Rogers, provided a framework of understanding upon which Knowles built, rejecting previous theories of learning as being appropriate only to children. Rogers, a therapist, applied his observations of adults in therapy to learning and conceptualized student-centred learning as a parallel to his client-centred therapy. 'Teaching, in my estimation, is a vastly over-rated function' (Rogers 1983: 119). Rogers considered that the 'facilitation of learning' with a focus on the interpersonal relationship between the learner and the facilitator based on trust, 'empathic understanding' and genuineness on the part of the facilitator is the key to effective learning. 'Changingness, a reliance on *process* rather than upon static knowledge, is the only thing that makes any sense as a goal for education in the modern world' (1983: 120, original emphasis). According to Rogers, much significant learning is acquired by doing, and therefore experiential learning is the only true learning, and the antithesis of any sort of memory learning. Like Knowles, Rogers emphasizes the 'self', self-development and self-direction. Unlike Knowles, for whom 'self-direction' involves the learner controlling the content of a course according to their needs while the tutor controls the processes, Rogers leaves the process in the hands of the learner and content appears to have little importance. Rogers, in common with Knowles, has been criticized for offering a partial theory, but both have nevertheless been very influential in the development of contemporary thinking on adult education.

Indeed, many of the ideas relating to andragogy and humanistic psychology have passed into a commonsense understanding of how learning is best 'facilitated' with learners in all sectors of PCE and are actively promoted by many mainstream educationalists. However, certain problems arise from the wholesale adoption of such an approach to teaching and learning. Tennant (1988: 23) provides a useful, if partial in itself, summary of his reservations concerning andragogy:

> . . . I have argued that the rationale and empirical support for the humanistic concepts of self-development and self-direction [have] gaps and weaknesses which need to be acknowledged. There is a need to distinguish the rhetoric of adult education from its rationale and empirical base. The prevailing rhetoric asserts that in everyday life adults are basically self-directed and that this self-direction is rooted in our constitutional make-up, it also asserts that self-development is an inexorable process towards higher levels of existence, and finally it asserts that adult learning is fundamentally (and necessarily) different from child learning. These assertions should not be accepted as articles of faith.

**Task 3.16**

3.16(a)   Reflect on your classroom practice and consider the ways in which theories of learning based on humanistic psychology have influenced your teaching.

3.16(b)   Consider the issues raised in the paragraph above and discuss with a partner your ideas for dealing with them.

It is also useful to think about the consequences of elevating process over content, by replacing the *what* with the *how* in teaching and learning. Is self direction the starting point or the goal of education? Does the practice of experiential learning reduce all learning to the functional? Is the transmission of knowledge and the pursuit of excellence redundant? What does it mean to be a 'facilitator of learning'?

## 3.4 Effective learning

**KEY ISSUES**

How do we identify learning needs and learning styles?

What are barriers to learning and how can they be overcome?

How do we help students to learn effectively?

Each group of learners is different from the next; each student is an individual with his or her own goals and expectations. These may or may not coincide with those of the tutor or the externally prescribed goals of a syllabus. A sound starting point for any course is to share those goals and where possible negotiate a consensus on what can be achieved by the group and by individuals in that group. It is often the case that some goals are predetermined by the nature of the course: preparation for achieving a qualification, for example. From the tutor's perspective, it is very useful to know what your students' learning needs are, their motives for joining the course and so on in order to support their learning more effectively. What do students need to know about you and what you are going to teach them?

---

**Task 3.17**

3.17(a)   List the information you need to know about your students and their learning needs, aspirations and expectations at the beginning of your course. Discuss your list with a partner and draw up a short questionnaire that you could use with your students.

3.17(b)   Now think about the start of your course from a student's perspective. What information could you provide them with?

3.17(c)   Why is this information exchange important? How can you use the information you obtain?

---

Of course, not all students have a clear idea what their goals, expectations or aspirations are. Is it always possible or even legitimate within the confines of a prescribed programme of study in a group situation to expect to have all of one's individual, sometimes idiosyncratic needs met? However, by discussing these issues early on, it is possible to set a mutually supportive, cooperative tone to the course conducive to effective learning.

Do all learners approach their learning in the same way? Do individuals have a 'preferred style' of learning? Within the framework of experiential learning, several theorists have developed models of learning styles. Perhaps the most well-known of these and the most frequently used with students is Kolb's (1984) 'learning style inventory'. Based on his model of experiential learning, David Kolb identified four categories of learning which occur in a cycle of concrete experience (CE), followed by observation and reflection on that experience (RO), then by the formulation of some sort of theory or hypothesis which involves abstract conceptualization (AC), and then, finally, by the testing-out of the hypothesis or theory in active experimentation (AE). According to Kolb the truly effective learner has abilities in all these four areas but most people have varying abilities in one area or another. The purpose of the inventory is to measure the relative strengths individuals have in each area by completing a questionnaire and then plotting the results on a quadrant. This enables the learner to identify her or his orientation to learning and discover how, given his or her natural inclinations, learning can best be approached. How useful is the method in identifying areas of 'weakness' and how might the information be used? There is an example recently of an individual who displayed the 'wrong' orientation to learning according to Kolb's inventory, and was refused entry onto a professional training course as a result.

**Task 3.18**

3.18(a)    Consider what practical strategies might be employed to enhance student learning as a result of using Kolb's learning style inventory.

3.18(b)    To what extent could or should such an exercise be used to assess learning needs? What other factors might be taken into account?

It is undoubtedly the case that people learn in different ways partly because they are different individuals and partly as a result of the subject matter on hand. It is important that the tutor has a clear understanding of what is to be learned in order to teach it effectively. If we are all individuals, all with our own learning styles, does that mean that we all need an individual learning programme? If that is the case, then what is the value of learning as a social activity? Would people gain more from learning alone in their own way?

Clearly, teaching methodology and course content need to be considered in relation to the learning styles of students. Discussion of appropriate methodology and classroom management issues can be found in Chapter 4. The task here has been to consider the role that learning styles have in relation to effective learning. If students are aware of their strengths and weaknesses in their approach to learning and are given consistent guidance by the tutor as to how they can build on their strengths and improve on their weaknesses, then they are more likely to have been successful in their studies. Robin Barrow (1984: 107) suggests that 'People come to learning in different ways, partly as a result of content, partly as a result of being different people preferring to or finding it easier to acquire understanding in different ways' and points to the importance of the relationship between how people learn and a clear understanding by the teacher of what is to be learned. Let us now turn to how effective learning can best be promoted.

We have already looked at various theoretical perspectives on learning, and the point has been made that learning is related to content. Any number of claims can be made about how learning is best achieved, but what is learned is the test of how effective the learning has been. Let us consider a typical classroom scenario on a post-compulsory PGCE course. The topic for the session is 'equal opportunities in PCE'. The sequence of the lesson is as follows:

1    Tutor 'brainstorms' ideas with students about what equal opportunities issues they have come across, either from their own experience or the experience of others.

2    Tutor gives a short talk about legislation and its impact/success/failure and invites the questions/comments/views of students.

3    In groups of four, students discuss various short case studies of practical equal opportunities issues and are asked to offer possible solutions to the problems.

4    Small groups feed back their ideas to the whole group.

5    Tutor leads group in a discussion of the underlying causes of inequality and draws together key points from the session.

**Task 3.19**

3.19(a)   What are the strengths and weaknesses of the lesson? Look at each stage, preferably with a partner, and discuss how you would ensure that students learned effectively.

3.19(b)   What is missing? For example, no mention is made of the tutor introducing the topic or stating any aims or expectations. Does this matter?

3.19(c)   Now draw up a five-point 'recipe for successful learning' from a student's perspective based on your discussions about the above lesson sequence.

This sort of lesson format is probably familiar to you. It begins with the students' own experiences and broadens out by introducing new knowledge and challenging students to think about practical and finally abstract principles. This is one way of approaching learning. How else might the topic have been addressed? It could be argued that a good, informative, challenging lecture would have been as effective. What do you think? Your own lessons provide useful 'real-life' case studies for reflection along these lines and will enable you to consider how effectively your students learn. Chapter 6, on assessment, will also introduce another dimension to the subject of effective learning.

**Task 3.20**

3.20(a)   Consider in turn the following short 'pen sketches' of typical students. What barriers to learning might they encounter?

Julie is a 17-year-old who left secondary school a year ago with no qualifications. She has been unsuccessful in finding a suitable job although she has done some casual work in a fast-food restaurant. Julie is about to begin, somewhat reluctantly, a GNVQ intermediate course in hospitality and catering at her local FE college.

Steve is at the beginning of a three-year BA course in media studies and sports science at a 'new' university. He is 18 and has just left school with two A levels at grades C and D. Steve tried to get a job in leisure management, but has realized that he needs a degree if he is going to build a good career. His parents are unable to support him financially.

Mary is a 30-year-old mother of two, recently divorced. Her children are both of school age and she has now decided to do an access course at her local FE college with a view to going on to HE. Mary left school at 16 with 4 O levels and did office work before her children were born.

Frank has recently retired at the age of 57. He left school at 14 and had been a shopkeeper all his life, working long hours. He now wants to keep his mind alert by joining a beginner's Spanish course at his local AE centre because he hopes to buy a holiday home in Spain.

3.20(b)   Try to place the barriers you have identified into the categories of educational, institutional and societal. Do some of them overlap?

Some educational barriers might equally be considered to be institutional problems. For example, a tourism tutor might be ill-equipped to help a student deal with a severe spelling problem. We might expect a learning support workshop to be available to give expert guidance and tuition. However, it is the responsibility of that tourism tutor to ensure that the student is aware of the problem, to mark the student's work carefully and ensure that she or he gets whatever support is available. Many mature students lack confidence in their ability to learn, have low expectations of themselves or have memories of bad educational experiences. These, and other barriers to learning may have an educational aspect but are intrinsically linked with institutional and particularly societal barriers.

Institutional barriers are sometimes harder to overcome. Any tutor who has fought to have a lift or even ramps installed to enable wheelchair access to parts of the building will know that while everyone agrees that the facilities are essential, the money is often slow in coming. The Association of University Teachers (AUT), in a summary of a piece of research into barriers to learning, identified the following institutional barriers: poor quality of information; the high cost of many courses; the distance to travel; a confusing array of options; the time students have to give up to attend courses. This, they concluded, leads to a 'vicious spiral of unequal opportunities' (AUT 1997). The less people's potential is fulfilled, they observed, the less able and motivated they are to develop themselves.

The huge expansion in FE and HE in recent years has eroded some of the barriers to access that existed in the past. We have already mentioned the greater diversity of the post-16 student population. How have institutions fared in meeting the needs of such a wide range of students? Have new barriers to learning been created within institutions as a result?

This leads us into a discussion of the societal barriers to learning that people encounter, since education is a key part of social policy and is certainly the service which attracts the most attention and concern in the early years of the twenty-first century. As we have already noted at the beginning of this chapter, the present government has expressed a firm commitment to LLL and a widening of access to education for all sections of society. Numerous studies have confirmed that participation in PCE is predominantly composed of socioeconomic groups A, B and C1. Certain groups of people continue to be under-represented: unskilled/semi-skilled manual workers; unemployed people; women with dependent children; older adults (aged 50+); and ethnic minority groups. For people in these groups, there is a wide range of reasons why they do not continue their education beyond school, some of which have already been mentioned. But the overarching barrier may be that education is something that other people do and is perceived as not something they need. Since the late 1990s a plethora of reports and policy initiatives have focused on these 'excluded' groups and vast sums of money have been channelled into courses and other provision. Widening participation has become the cornerstone of higher education policy and has therefore increased the pressure on schools and colleges to prepare a much wider range of young people for university study. Already, over 80 per cent of young people stay on in some form of education after 16, but it is uncertain whether the real barriers to learning have been overcome by many of them. Financial incentives in FE may encourage participation, but they do not necessarily foster commitment on the part of young people. Furthermore, the introduction of higher education tuition fees and the abolition of student grants seem something of a contradiction to a widening participation agenda.

---

**Task 3.21**

3.21(a)   Consider what changes have taken place in either the FE, AE or HE sectors.

3.21(b)   What new barriers to learning have emerged and how has participation been widened and improved as a result of these changes?

3.21(c)   How do societal barriers to learning link with educational and institutional barriers?

---

The aim of the legislation was to encourage participation by people from poorer backgrounds while offsetting the burgeoning cost of HE by making the more well-off pay for their education. However, it is now clear that it has done little to democratize the HE system and may well have restricted participation by people on average and below-average incomes still further. There is little evidence that young people from less well-off backgrounds are willing to burden themselves with debt in order to continue their education, despite the range of initiatives to open access. What does seem to be happening is that more young people from middle-class backgrounds are entering HE with lower A level grades (Hayes and Wynyard 2002a).

This section has cast the net very widely over practical issues concerned with learning and has aimed to promote discussion about how we can ensure that our students achieve to the best of their ability and have high expectations of themselves. The next section will explore the concept of learner autonomy.

## 3.5 Learner autonomy

---

**KEY ISSUES**

What distinguishes autonomous learner from learning autonomy?

Is learner autonomy concerned with the process of learning or is it an educational goal?

How do students develop good study skills?

What do we mean by 'personalized learning'?

---

If we brainstorm the variety of terms used to describe learning which is not teacher-centred, the list seems endless with little apparent distinction in the way labels are used. Tight (1996: 89) makes a distinction between what he calls 'learning concepts' which 'focus mainly on the perspective of the organisation providing education or training' and 'those which are more concerned with the perspective of the individual learner'. In the first category he places distance, flexible and open learning (which will be discussed in Chapter 5) as distinct from experiential, independent and self-directed learning where the shift from institutional responsibility to the individual leaves the learner in charge of and supposedly in control of their own learning.

The notion of the self-directed learner comes, as we have already seen, from the andragogical model of learning. While a variety of criticisms have been ranged at andragogy, nevertheless many aspects have been incorporated into our understanding and practice in PCE, not least the self-directed, autonomous learner. Moore (1983: 163) suggests that:

> Autonomous learners – and this means most adults, most of the time – sometimes formally, often unconsciously, set objectives and define criteria for their achievement. Autonomous learners know, or find, where and how and from what human and other resources they may gather the information they require, collect ideas, practise skills and achieve their goals. They then judge the appropriateness of their new skills, information and ideas, eventually deciding whether their goals have been achieved or can be abandoned.

To what extent and to which groups of learners in PCE might this description fit? Perhaps not the average FE student, but what about groups in AE, or HE undergraduates? How many of the characteristics described by Moore do your learners display? Are our students 'naturally' self-directing, or is self-direction or learner autonomy something which the tutor can encourage through a particular style of teaching and which learners develop over a period of time? More importantly, should autonomy be more than knowing how to study and direct your learning? Can independent, critical thought be achieved autonomously? What are the implications for the role of the tutor?

It is increasingly the case that learners in all sectors of PCE need to develop their ability to study independently, to increase their 'learner autonomy'. Whatever the educational justifications that are made for 'learner autonomy', the reality is that cuts in course hours and the shift away from examination to project and assignment work mean that students do spend much more time working alone or in groups without constant tutor guidance and supervision.

In FE, GNVQ is a good example of this. Moreover, independent study is now an integral part of all vocational courses and therefore the demands on both students and tutors are different from the tutor/student relationship associated with traditional craft courses. The 'autonomous learner' may seem to be an idealized description of many young people in FE and developing that autonomy is indeed a challenge for all concerned. This curriculum change is coupled with an explosion in the FE student population due to the collapse of the youth labour market in the mid-1990s and substantial budget cuts.

The shift in the AE curriculum towards more accredited courses puts more pressure on learners and tutors to achieve qualifications. In order to keep fees within affordable limits, course hours are often inadequate to cover all the syllabus in class time. It is therefore essential that students engage in a significant amount of independent study. In HE the shift is slightly different. Independent research and study has always been a defining feature of academic study and quite rightly so. In some respects the undergraduate epitomizes the autonomous learner described above. However, the recent massive expansion in HE has created several new problems. To begin with, the new expanded HE student population is much more diverse. There is now a greater proportion of mature people, part-time students, a slightly higher social and ethnic mix and, perhaps more importantly, a wider range of ability entering HE. Alongside this, the rise in student numbers has not been accompanied by a parallel increase in funding. Not surprisingly this has led to cuts in course hours and thus a much greater emphasis on independent study.

The possible reasons for these curriculum changes throughout PCE are discussed elsewhere (see Chapters 1 and 7 in particular). However, it is useful to consider how you would interpret 'learner autonomy' in your work and what emphasis you would place on it. Across the board in PCE, information and communication technology has made its presence felt. The use of ICT in just about any education or training course is considered desirable if not obligatory and it has become synonymous with autonomous learning. The use of IT is discussed in depth in Chapter 5 but it is mentioned here since one of the claims made for it is that it promotes learner autonomy. Data-mining – searching for and retrieving information (Woudhuysen 1999) – is the most popular feature of the Internet and often seems to be equated with learning, which clearly it is not. Certainly the availability of information through ICT is infinitely wider than what is on offer in the average library, but depth of knowledge is questionable. To what extent can knowledge be 'packaged' in the way that we tend to see in web-based learning programmes? Can real learner autonomy be achieved by the sorts of interpretations described above? The concept of 'autonomy' has taken on a new meaning in that it describes how learning takes place. What if, however, we define 'learner autonomy' as the achievement of intellectual freedom and critical thought through the mastery of a subject? Is this still an appropriate goal to aspire to? Can it be achieved through the process of 'autonomous learning', independent study, workshops, resource-based and 'e-learning'? What of the social aspect of learning?

**Task 3.22**

Note down some of the arguments for and against autonomous learning.

In Section 3.4 we considered learner needs and the learning styles of our students. What often emerges from such analyses is that many students do require help and support in the way they approach learning. Learning how to learn is something that both students and tutors often ignore. We also considered effective learning in the classroom in Section 3.4. What we shall explore in Task 3.23 are the skills that students need to enable them to learn and how they can be developed by the tutor. As teachers we routinely offer ad hoc guidance on how to approach a piece of work, or perhaps we have a 'study skills' handout that we give to each student with advice on time management and approaches to reading and so on. Some courses begin with a study skills module covering much the same ground. The essential point about study skills or learning to learn is that it must be done in context; it must be applied to the subject to be studied.

**Task 3.23**

3.23(a)   Choose one of your typical teaching sessions and write down the sequence of activities in the lesson. Organize the information in three columns. In the first column write down what you do throughout the lesson; in the second column record the parallel student activity. When you have done that, look at each student activity and identify what learning strategies your students need at each stage. For example:
- Teacher activity strategy: introductory talk.
- Student activity: listen, take notes.
- Learning: assimilate information, extract key points and write them down.

3.23(b)   Now examine the learning strategies you have identified. Are all your students able to apply these strategies effectively? Which ones could you give help with during the lesson? Which ones require a longer-term plan to develop? How can you facilitate and support this?

Whatever subject you are teaching, students need to develop effective study skills. It is essential that learning strategies are acquired and practised in the classroom if students are going to be able to learn effectively on their own. *Learning to learn,* that is, supporting students as they develop appropriate attitudes, strategies and approaches to learning, has become an important focus of professional development for teachers in both the compulsory and post-compulsory sectors. On some courses, the way that students approach their learning is given as much time and attention as what they are learning. Personalized learning has recently become a notable concern for policy-makers and academics (see, for example, Johnson 2004; Leadbeater 2004a, b; and Pollard and James 2004) and is beginning to impact on the work of teachers in PCET. Indeed, personalized learning has been hailed as the new 'big idea' in government education policy. It is, however, somewhat conceptually obscure, although linked to other policy initiatives such as *Every Child Matters* and *Assessment for Learning*. The thrust of personalized learning is seen as a solution to the protracted problems of underachievement, particularly among disadvantaged children and young people. The 'personalization' of learning can be seen partly as developing out of theories of multiple intelligences, emotional literacy and learning styles and based on the perception that education must meet individual needs. As such, it reflects a focus on developing learning behaviours, and on the construction of 'personal understandings' redolent of constructivist theories of learning. Pollard and James (2004), who provide a useful examination of personalized learning, note that '[it] is not a matter of tailoring the curriculum, teaching and assessment to "fit" the individual, but it is a question of developing social practices that enable people to become all that they are capable of being'. The key document to consult is *2020 Vision: Teaching and Learning in 2020*. It is here that personalization is set out as that which will liberate children and young people from the perceived failures of education. However, critics suggest that far from being a radical step forward in promoting educational achievement, personalized learning reflects a retreat from the idea that education has the capacity to transform people's lives. The focus on developing learning behaviours is being substituted for knowledge and learning to learn is seen to be more important than what is learned. The extent to which personalized learning promotes learner autonomy in the way it has been discussed above, is uncertain. Nevertheless, it is an approach to classroom practice that is likely to change the PCE classroom radically, as well as teacher/student relationships and, fundamentally, how student learning is understood.

The diversity of learners in the post-compulsory sector of education is as wide as the types of courses and programmes on which they enrol. Faced with such diversity, and the pressures on tutors to respond to every individual's learning needs, it is not surprising that we sometimes lose sight of the similarities between learners and their common goals. This chapter has introduced a variety of aspects of learning and has sought to relate theoretical perspectives to contemporary issues and professional practice.

## Related new professional standards for teachers and trainers in the lifelong learning sector

### Domain A: professional values and practice

| PROFESSIONAL KNOWLEDGE AND UNDERSTANDING | PROFESSIONAL PRACTICE |
|---|---|
| Teachers in the lifelong learning sector know and understand: | Teachers in the lifelong learning sector: |
| AK 1.1 What motivates learners to learn and the importance of learners' experience and aspirations. | AP 1.1 Encourage the development and progression of all learners through recognizing, valuing and responding to individual motivation, experience and aspirations. |
| AK 4.1 Principles, frameworks and theories which underpin good practice in learning and teaching. | AP 4.1 Use relevant theories of learning to support the development of practice in learning and teaching. |

### Domain B: learning and teaching

| PROFESSIONAL KNOWLEDGE AND UNDERSTANDING | PROFESSIONAL PRACTICE |
|---|---|
| Teachers in the lifelong learning sector know and understand: | Teachers in the lifelong learning sector: |
| BK 1.3 Ways of creating a motivating learning environment. | BP 1.3 Create a motivating environment which encourages learners to reflect on, evaluate and make decisions about their learning. |

BK 2.2   Ways to engage, motivate and encourage active participation of learners and learner independence.

BP 2.2   Use a range of effective and appropriate teaching and learning techniques to engage and motivate learners and encourage independence.

BK 2.3   The relevance of learning approaches, preferences and skills to learner progress.

BP 2.3   Implement learning activities which develop the skills and approaches of all learners and promote learner autonomy.

BK 2.5   Ways of using learners' own experiences as a foundation for learning.

BP 2.5   Encourage learners to use their own life experiences as a foundation for their development.

BK 2.6   Ways to evaluate own practice in terms of efficiency and effectiveness.

BP 2.6   Evaluate the efficiency and effectiveness of own teaching, including consideration of learner feedback and learning theories.

BK 2.7   Ways in which mentoring and/or coaching can support the development of professional skills and knowledge.

BP 2.7   Use mentoring and/or coaching.

## Domain C: specialist learning and teaching

*PROFESSIONAL KNOWLEDGE AND UNDERSTANDING*

*PROFESSIONAL PRACTICE*

*Teachers in the lifelong learning sector know and understand:*

*Teachers in the lifelong learning sector:*

CK 3.1   Teaching and learning theories and strategies relevant to own specialist area.

CP 3.1   Apply appropriate strategies and theories of teaching and learning to own specialist area.

CK 3.2   Ways to identify individual learning needs and potential barriers to learning in own specialist area.

CP 3.2   Work with learners to address particular individual learning needs and overcome identified barriers to learning.

# 4

# Teaching and the management of learning

## 4.1 What is Chapter 4 about?

This chapter deals with the relationship between teaching and learning as two inseparable processes and examines the prerequisites for success in teaching for learning. The phrase *teaching for learning* has become increasingly dominant in recent years as a result of a growing awareness that teaching and learning must be considered as complementary activities. So, in any planning and curriculum development activities, the aims of the teacher must be to ensure that the learner is placed at the core of the structure, content and delivery of the teaching lesson.

The teacher has two major responsibilities of equal importance which will determine the success of a learning experience for individuals and groups. One responsibility is the planning of well-structured, stimulating and effective taught lessons, with coherent, appropriate aims and learning outcomes and clear assessment strategies. The other is the management of the learning environment, so that learners can achieve their potential in a safe, efficient and mature environment which is fair and inclusive to all, while recognizing the differences which characterize each individual within a group of adult learners. Thus, planning and managing the learning environment are parallel activities. It is possible to plan a good teaching lesson, with appropriate goals, interesting material, varied teaching and learning experiences and excellent resources. If, however, a teacher is unable to manage the learners, then the planning is wasted, since barriers to learning will arise and these will diminish learning potential. Adults do not learn effectively in an environment in which they feel psychologically or physically uncomfortable. There are many distractions to the learning process, and while not all of these can be eradicated all of the time, the exercise of sound management skills in the learning environment is essential to learner success, not to mention teacher satisfaction.

Similarly, if no real planning has taken place, there is little likelihood that learners' needs will be met. To the casual observer and even the learners themselves the learning experience may seem unproblematic, even worthwhile, but without due consideration having been given to the range of factors which make up the planning process such learning experiences are likely to suffer from real limitations.

Finally, given the plethora of factors which form part of the teacher's role in the lifelong learning sector, it is important not to lose sight of our own individual ethos and worth as teachers. Much emphasis is placed currently on the diversity of learners and their different learning styles. Teachers too are diverse and have different teaching styles and this is worth stating clearly. We should remind ourselves that, as teachers, we have 'theories and belief systems that influence our perceptions, plans and actions' (Calderhead 1987: 107). These are moulded by our own learning experiences, our political beliefs, our personalities and our ideological views on education. While we can be inspired by other teachers and want to model ourselves on them we need to be true to ourselves in the articulation of our beliefs and our response to the shifting paradigms of change in the sector. We cannot, and should not, eliminate our *selves* in the planning and delivery of our teaching and learning experiences.

The remainder of the chapter is devoted to the two parallel themes of planning and the effective management of the learning environment. In Section 4.2 planning is examined under the key issues identified below and Section 4.3 explores the various factors which account for a well-managed learning lesson.

## 4.2 The planning process

**KEY ISSUES**

How can we plan for the delivery of effective and well-structured lessons, with coherent aims, learning outcomes and a clear assessment strategy?

How can we plan for the *range* of learners we may encounter within a teaching group?

How can we ensure that we plan for individual achievement, so that learners achieve their goals, assume responsibility for their own learning and are encouraged to become lifelong learners?

In what ways can we plan for 'wider' learning, i.e., that which goes beyond our subject specialism?

## Planning teaching lessons and schemes of work

The first stage in planning a teaching lesson is to assemble all the information which is relevant to the needs of the learners. This includes practical information such as the length of the lesson, the environment, and the ages and abilities of the learning group. It also includes the following: the subject or topic to be taught; an understanding of how formal or informal the teaching context is; the balance between teaching knowledge and demonstrating skills and a view of the best strategies for achievement in these areas. Other influences include health and safety considerations, the availability of resources and the actual time which is at our disposal to plan lessons. When gathering this information it is normally essential to liaise with colleagues, especially if we are new to an organization or to teaching itself.

This information can then be translated into a lesson plan, which acts as a *planning tool* prior to the lesson and a *guide* to the teacher during that lesson. The lesson plan can be produced in different formats. Provided a plan covers essential detail the format chosen will be determined by personal preference, but a useful test in determining a good lesson plan is to ask whether it is clear and coherent to anyone who might need to teach from it and not just ourselves!

So what detail should a lesson plan contain? The minimum requirements are that it should outline the following: the aims and objectives; the activities undertaken by the teacher and those by the student and how these link to the objectives; the structure and timing of each activity within the lesson; use of resources and the assessment strategy. Later in this section we will be considering the inclusion on the plan of the non-specialist elements of learning which may form part of the learning process. Lesson plans can follow several formats and it is personal choice which should really dictate the style of plan we write, although many institutions now require their staff to follow an established template in the interests of quality assurance and consistency. Some prefer a 'linear' template, which contains sections for each of the planning elements, such as 'resources' and 'assessment', as well as a step-by-step description of what will be happening during the lesson. Others might prefer a 'read-across' format, which shows what is happening at each stage of the lesson. Petty presents a lesson plan format that organizes planning into columns listing timings, content, teacher activity, student activity and resources. (Petty 2004: 425). Reece and Walker also discuss lesson plan formats in terms of possible layouts and offer examples (Reece and Walker 2003: 253–7).

The starting point for the plan is the establishment of aims and objectives. Settling these not only gives confidence to our teaching but often eases the rest of the planning process. A series of questions which you pose for yourself before you begin writing the plan can be useful in determining the aims which you as a teacher have for your learners and translating these into the learning outcomes – in other words stating clearly what the learners will be able to do by the end of the lesson as a result of what they have learned. The formulation of coherent aims and learning outcomes requires practice, even although on the surface it may seem straightforward. As a novice it is probably worth collaborating with more experienced practitioners when first establishing these learning *goals*. There are, however, basic guidelines which can be used for formulating aims and outcomes.

Aims are statements of *general* intent. Usually aims will be written as long–term statements of intent to cover an entire programme, as well as aims that are specific to each lesson within that programme. The aims spell out for the teacher what she wishes to achieve in the lesson, giving the teaching a structure and direction and helping to break learning down into manageable units. From the aims the objectives are derived, and these are statements of *specific* intent, which give a clear indication of what a student will be able to do as a result of the learning. These are also known as *learning outcomes*. There should always be a 'match' between aims and objectives/ learning outcomes, showing how the objectives are achievable *through* the aims. Example 4.1 gives two examples.

## Example 4.1

**A**

*Aim:*         To instruct the learner to produce a simple diagram which explains how a
car engine functions.

*Objective:*  By the end of the lesson the learner will be able to draw a simple diagram
explaining the function of a car engine.

**B**

*Aim:*         To demonstrate the safe and hygienic application of a bandage to a cut.

*Objective:*  The learner will be able to apply a bandage safely and hygienically.

---

**Task 4.1**

Choose a topic which you teach and formulate aims and objectives for a lesson. Try to
specify conditions and standards for your objectives.

---

Furthermore, objectives need to be as specific as possible. Sometimes we will
want to specify the *level* or *standard* at which a learner is expected to achieve. So, in
example B above, standards meeting health and safety requirements were specified.
At other times we may wish to outline the *conditions* under which a task might be
completed. In example A, we may have specified that the task was to be completed
without copying any practice diagrams.

Now that we have a sense of the goals for the lesson we can consider how best to
help learners achieve them. For this purpose we need to consider the many teaching
and learning strategies at our disposal and make a choice about which are most suited
to our purposes. These choices can be determined by a further set of questions which
we need to pose in relation to the ages and abilities of our learners, the resources at our
disposal and, to some degree, our own confidence in and preferences for using a
particular strategy. While being aware of personal reactions to particular strategies,
the needs of the learners are key to our choices and this is where our evaluations of
what works well with groups in terms of activities are crucial to successful outcomes.
There is no doubt that some methods lend themselves more readily to certain types of
learning than others. The issue of appropriateness is not usually difficult to determine
if we know our learners well and think carefully about the subject matter. Experience
will also assist with the selection of methods. Variety is a key factor in sustaining
learner interest, and so normally a varied diet of methods will ensure motivation. We
also need to be open to new methods and be prepared to experiment. As Petty says: 'If
you don't have the occasional disaster when you are learning to teach, you are not
experimenting enough' (Petty 2004: 125).

Minton (1991) provides a useful approach to the use of methods by organizing
them into those which are teacher 'controlled' and those which the learner has the
more control over (see Figure 4.1). The usefulness of this matrix is in helping us to
think through the *balance* of methods in a lesson.

**Figure 4.1** Minton's matrix of control

| Teacher control | | Lecture |
| --- | --- | --- |
| | | Demonstration |
| | | Discussion (structured) |
| | Less control | Discussion (unstructured) |
| | | Seminar |
| | | Tutorial |
| | Shared control | Practical |
| | | Simulation and games |
| | | Role-play |
| | | Resource-based learning |
| | | Films/TV programmes |
| | | Visits |
| | Student control | Distance learning/flexistudy |
| | | Discovery projects/research |
| **Least control** | | Real-life experience |

*Source*: Minton 1991: 112.

The development of a clear assessment strategy is an integral part of the planning process and should be thought about at the same time as the objectives or learning outcomes are being formulated, since it is these outcomes that we are assessing. Very often considerable effort is put into deciding what we want our learners to be able to do in their classes, but far less thought is given to how we can know that they have achieved. Put simply, if we want to know whether learning has taken place we need to be able to check this through assessment techniques. Each learning outcome should be assessed in some form in order to ascertain that learning has taken place. In this way we will also know whether there are gaps in understanding, in which case we will need to revisit particular parts of the learning experience, possibly adopting different strategies. More guidance on establishing assessment criteria to meet learning outcomes is given in Chapters 6 and 8.

As teachers in the lifelong learning sector we are no longer simply delivering our subject specialism, and we have to adjust our mindsets to take account of this fact, as for many of us our own experiences as learners have been those of learning one particular subject and only that subject. Along with our subject specialism, we are expected to embed a range of generic skills into our teaching. These are often referred to as *key* and *transferable* skills and their exact nature is determined by the level and age of learners we are teaching. The skills are derived from government initiatives, supposedly designed to improve employability and raise levels of literacy and numeracy. The skills initiative is the subject of lively debate and the 'embedding' of skills a constant challenge, particularly in vocational programmes, where there is often resistance among learners to any component of the teaching which is not perceived to be strictly relevant to the subject area. The challenge takes two main forms. One is *how* to embed skills – a task which has proved demanding for even experienced practitioners – and the other how to make the skills relevant to the needs of learners. So, during our planning stage, we need to be sure that we are clear about which skills we are embedding and how we can embed them. These are processes on which we will undoubtedly need to collaborate with colleagues.

It is usual for trainee teachers to practise their planning skills initially by writing individual lesson plans. With confidence the transference of these skills into long-term planning should become straightforward. Again, experienced colleagues should be able to offer model schemes of work and often teachers in a new post will find that schemes of work are already in existence. Not always however! A *scheme of work* is a long-term planning document, which will present a view of what is to be learned over a period of several weeks or even months. It is made up therefore of a number of individual plans which link together, and when perusing a scheme of work it is this sense of linkage which is a key feature of a good scheme. When looking through the plans it should be possible to see how learning from one lesson is reviewed briefly in the subsequent plan and leads logically into that plan. It is through this process that the scheme of work becomes a coherent and cohesive planning tool and not just a series of lesson plans.

One very important factor to be borne in mind in longer-term planning is the need to review learning on a regular basis. This helps to consolidate this process over a period of time and ensures that learners are given opportunities to revise material which they may have experienced difficulty with on first exposure. Learning is, after all, a cumulative process.

Once the planning stage has been completed it is important to communicate the learning outcomes to learners, so that they understand fully the goals which have been established for them. This will normally happen at the beginning of a programme, but it is an on-going process, in the sense that learners need to be given short- as well as long-term goals, and the goals need to be monitored on an on-going basis. We will look in greater detail at the communication of learning goals later in the chapter, but this process is integral to planning as well as managing learning, since we may have to adjust planning if learning goals are not being reached.

**Task 4.2**

Look at the different lesson plan templates which are available and plan a lesson you might deliver using two *different* formats. Try to get a sense of which of the two you have a preference for.

## Planning for a range of learners

Our second key issue in this section is that of planning for a *range* of learners. Government-led policies in the past decade governing access, inclusion and widening participation, have meant that learning opportunities have been opened up to a larger spectrum of the adult population. This has meant not only a larger number of partici-pants in formal and less formal adult settings across the UK, but also an increased mix of adults within individual learning groups.

Few learning groups nowadays are homogeneous in terms of their identity, although some uniformity can more commonly be found among groups of 14–19-year-olds in further education settings who are studying for vocational or academic qualifications. Even within these groups, however, more mature adults, often returning to study after a period away from school or college, will mix with younger learners. Within one class setting, therefore, it is usual to find learners with very different attitudes to and experiences of learning and teaching.

The presence of a range of learners within one group can affect planning considerably. In varying degrees, and depending on the teaching context, learners will vary in obvious and less obvious ways. The more obvious differences will be in terms of age and an often-related issue of prior learning experience. Gender, personality and social class are other factors which produce differences in attitudes and behaviour among learners.

When we meet a new group the issue of motivation can be hard to determine. Are the members attending the group for social and personal advancement, intellectual satisfaction and career development? Is their attendance mandatory or voluntary? Again these reasons are often clearer, or apparently clearer, with younger adults on college-based vocational programmes, but are less obvious where the choice to attend a programme has been voluntary. As a course progresses, motivations for attending a course will become more obvious, and biographical details about each member of the group will begin to emerge. Working with a group is rather like character development in a novel. In the beginning we make guesses as well as assumptions about who the characters are and how they will develop, but, as with a novel, some of these assumptions are naïve, partial or simply wrong.

As time progresses, learners' likes and dislikes in relation to particular styles of learning and teaching strategies will of course become apparent, and such information can be helpful to the tutor in the planning process, although we have to be wary of planning our teaching wholly to satisfy the strategies our students state a preference for, since these may not be the most effective for delivering the learning. Additionally, sometimes, useful learning can be gained by a person through moving outside their comfort zone. It is not only teachers who have from time to time to be prepared to move outside their comfort zones.

Planning for a range of learners with different experiences and expectations of learning reinforces the need to have a repertoire of ways to deliver learning. We have already discussed the need for such a varied diet in terms of sustaining interest during a lesson. Meeting the learning preferences of different personalities in a group is another good reason for varying our modes of delivery.

Another very important factor in planning for a range of learners is to plan for *inclusiveness*. As Wallace says, we should 'create learning activities which are accessible to all the students and which do not make any student feel excluded, directly or by implication' (Wallace 2005: 47). In order to promote a climate of inclusiveness and guard against exclusion it is of course essential that we gather as much information about individual students as possible before we begin teaching them, so that we are aware of factors which will affect their ability to perform certain tasks or engage in particular forms of learning. A key to planning activities which are accessible for all is to think about disability, both seen and unseen. Nowadays, learners are usually asked to declare forms of disability on enrolment so that appropriate adjustments can be made to facilitate the learning process prior to commencement of the course, although not all learners venture such information in the case of unseen disabilities, and sometimes, of course, learners are unaware of any disability. The information we have from learners gives us the opportunity to preview the learning experience prior to the commencement of a programme. One example would include organizing the classroom in such a manner that a wheelchair user could participate in group activities with the same ease as other learners; another would be preparing PowerPoint presentations and handouts in a larger font for a partially sighted learner. The use of certain coloured paper in handouts may be helpful to somebody who is dyslexic. Encouraging individual learners to be open with us about their needs is crucial if we are to plan for them, and so trust must be built early on in a course if we are to know about the factors we need to take into account when planning learning. We need to promote the idea of a joint responsibility, where the learner feels able to disclose the information we need to plan efficiently for them, and where we make sure that we use this information to make the arrangements necessary to facilitate learning for that person. Finally, on this point, it is essential as teachers that we have some knowledge of the various pieces of legislation, such as the Special Educational Needs and Disability Act 2001 (SENDA), which impact on learner entitlement. In this way we can harness the support of other professionals in assisting all learners to access the curriculum equally.

**Task 4.3**

Take a group you are currently teaching or observing. What individual needs and abilities do you need to take into consideration when planning a lesson for these learners? How will these affect the planning process – both on paper and practically?

The ultimate goal of our planning, whether we are working with small or large groups or with individuals, should be to enable each learner to achieve their potential during the learning experience. We are, in effect, planning for *achievement* and the achievement of the individual is a much valued aspect of our learning culture today. If we are to plan for everybody in a group to reach their potential we may have to *differentiate* learning. Differentiation is the response to a recognition that not all learners learn in the same way, more especially at the same pace, and the consequent organization of learning activities according to certain needs and abilities. By differentiating learning we can allow a person to learn successfully as part of a group while achieving different outcomes from a fellow student. To some degree, we will all recognize differentiation from our own learning experiences, in the sense that we have probably all been in learning situations where we have been aware that we have been progressing more quickly or slowly than others in a group. In such a case there is often a sense of pressure, of having to 'keep up', and this in itself can create a barrier to a learning task, as well as feelings of stress, negativity and demotivation. For adults who have already experienced such barriers in previous learning experiences, a sense of despondency can descend and adversely affect their attitude to the learning.

Differentiation can be planned in a number of ways. It is possible to set tasks at varying levels for small groups within a whole-group setting, so that individuals can be grouped according to ability. Indeed this kind of differentiated learning is very useful for teaching mixed-ability groups. Alternatively, a teacher might set each group the same basic task but prescribe different outcomes.

How do we show differentiation in our planning then? It may be that we spell out on the lesson plan our differentiated learning objectives, as this is evidence that differentiation has featured in our planning. Equally, we may have written differentiated goals into the rationale of our scheme of work. Most important of all, of course, is the need to communicate the differentiated learning goals to learners, so that they are aware of what is expected of them. This is crucial to planning for *success*, which is the third issue we need to focus on in this survey of planning learning.

## Planning for individual achievement

So far in the chapter we have focused largely on planning for group learning. In the previous section we turned our attention to individual achievement through differentiation of activity and assessment; this is only one example of how we can help adult learners to achieve goals. Part of the responsibility of a teacher in the lifelong learning sector is to identify and support individual learning needs – a skill which is integral to their professional role, and one which is constantly being developed as new challenges from learners present themselves. The concept of learning as a personalized affair is a dominant force in current educational thinking.

In planning terms this involves first diagnosing need, a skill for which knowledge and understanding of potential barriers to learning is essential. Sometimes we are able to readily identify such barriers and address them in our planning. At other times we may need to enlist the support and guidance of more experienced practitioners in assisting our understanding of how best to plan for a particular learner's needs and this is where the use of referral systems has a part to play. As a teacher, for example, we may have generic knowledge of a learner's difficulties, but may require assistance from a specialist in knowing how best to plan to meet his or her needs in a classroom setting. This demonstrates our dependence on a wider network of professionals, assuming one is available, for our planning. There is clearly a link here between planning for inclusiveness and planning for individual need.

Nowadays, planning for individual success and achievement is a purposeful and well-refined activity. There is currently a requirement for all learners in a formal lifelong learning situation to have an individual learning plan. This is a tool which is negotiated between learner and teacher and which is designed to support and maximize achievement through the establishment of learning targets. While the targets are individual, they should be achievable within the framework of the learner's everyday classroom experiences, so that they link very clearly to the learning objectives which form part of the scheme of work.

The individual learning plan will normally follow a format which has been prescribed by the learning establishment, and newly appointed staff will need to acquaint themselves with the format in use. There are, however, features which are common to all individual learning plans. These include: clearly communicated short- and long-term learning goals; a record of all forms of assessment which relate to these goals and document their achievement, and evidence of regular review and updating of the plan. This is a basic analysis of a learning plan. The Learning and Skills Network has produced a useful 'ILP checklist' which outlines good practice in the creation and use of such plans (see www.lsneducation.org.uk/skillsforlife).

It goes without saying that helping learners to plan for individual achievement involves us as teachers in ensuring that we create time for the review of our learners' plans within our scheme of work. This entails building regular review and tutorial time into our teaching schedules, in order to avoid an ad hoc approach, which will surely result in a failure to find time to see each learner properly.

Ultimately, of course, success will only occur if the learner, supported by the teacher, has a commitment to the goals which have been established. After all, these goals have been *negotiated* between teacher and learner, rather than imposed by the former. Within a post-compulsory setting there is a clear duty to encourage and support learners of whatever age. When working with those who have recently left school, however, there is an increased responsibility towards preparing them for further study and/or the world of work. Part of this is planning to promote independent learning through involving learners in regular self-evaluation and review of targets, so that they too have a hand in modifying learning plans where necessary. We are, in effect, planning for 'wider' learning – for *lifelong* learning. Earlier, we discussed the fact that a learning programme often reaches beyond the subject or programme to encompass key skills. The function of the key skills initiative is to improve the employability of young people through enhancing their literacy, numeracy and IT skills. A further aim is to create lifelong learners through promoting learner independence. Such independence can only be acquired through teaching those skills which enable learners to learn effectively on their own as well as in a formal classroom setting. In addition to key skills, therefore, learners need study skills. These include effective reading and writing skills, research techniques, time management and organizational skills. There is not often much time to plan formal study skills components into our everyday teaching, but we can plan to include teaching, learning and assessment strategies which allow learners to practise and hone these skills. Furthermore, we can and should make time to induct learners into the 'learning support' units which exist nowadays in post-compulsory settings to help with the acquisition of these skills.

**Task 4.4**

Select *two* of your learners and construct for each of them an individual learning plan which takes account of the factors discussed above. Don't forget to negotiate the plan with them!

In this first section we have reflected on the centrality of sound planning in the creation of effective learning. We have seen that a teacher needs to be equipped with not only the knowledge and skills to plan varied and purposeful lessons, but also an understanding of the needs of individual learners. We have established that planning is an activity requiring practice and one which must be thought of in both the long and the short term. Finally, we are contributing not only to a learner's immediate goals but also to developing them as lifelong, independent learners. Our legacy therefore is one of importance.

## 4.3 Managing the learning environment

| KEY ISSUES |
| --- |
| How do we create a good learning environment which is safe, efficient and stimulating? |
| How do we recognize and deal with the attitudes and behaviours of a variety of adult learners? |
| How do we manage learning *outside* a classroom setting? |
| In what ways can we help learners to manage their own learning? |

### Managing the physical environment

As has already been noted in the introduction, we can have planned effectively for learning to take place, but without sound management skills our planning will go to waste. We now consider the knowledge and skills that are necessary to ensure that the learning environments which we manage are indeed conducive to learning. At this point it is important to emphasize also the role of the teacher as the only person who should be managing the environment of the classroom. This is not to introduce a flavour of authoritarianism into the discussion, rather to highlight the responsibility we as teachers have to take charge of the classroom environment. It is often assumed that adult learners will be easy to manage in comparison with children. The reality is that the management skills required are just as demanding, but that they are of a different order.

A good illustration of this and a starting point is the classroom itself: practical aspects of the physical environment. An examination of a teaching room should alert us to general issues, such as whether furniture is laid out to allow sufficient room for the traffic that will be in the room and if wires are arranged in such a way that learners are unlikely to trip over them. In the event of an emergency, it is important that all members of a group can exit a room swiftly and that they are aware of the meeting point. Fire, accident and emergency procedures are essential information for all students and should be clarified when you first meet a new group. This is part of your professional responsibility and in the litigious climate in which we operate it is worth remembering this. In addition to these general safety points we need to be aware of potential health hazards in relation to particular students and use the information we have about our learners to avoid problems.

A growing proportion of students nowadays are sensitive, for example, to substances we find in seemingly harmless tools, such as felt pens, dyes and plastics. To these we can add pollutants such as fumes from chemicals, particularly where ventilation is not good. Solvents are another issue, the effects of which have been widely publicized. A suggested approach to managing safety in the particular environment in which you teach is to consider carefully the substances, equipment, tools and/or furniture which form part of the essential working conditions for delivering your subject and to create an inventory of any part of this paraphernalia which you consider could be risky for an individual. In this way you can 'tailor' your safety checks and thus avoid wasting time checking details which are not relevant to the delivery of your subject.

There are, however, a few generic aspects of the learning environment to which all teachers should pay attention and these are heating, lighting and ventilation. Ventilation is a much-ignored feature of good classroom practice and yet is often a simple technique for keeping learners alert. Without adequate ventilation students become sluggish and their performance is impaired. Even in winter, windows need to be opened for a few minutes several times a day, particularly between classes in a room which is going to be filled with people for much of the day. If not, the environment will become stuffy and increasingly unpleasant as the day wears on. Attention should also be paid to lighting. The widespread use of PowerPoint means sometimes that classrooms are dark places and while this may be good for illuminating the slides themselves it is not good for note-taking. It is good to try to strike a balance. Last, there are few teachers who have not experienced problems with heating. Often the issue of heating is outside our control, but we need to take any sensible measures to ensure that reasonable temperatures are maintained at different times of the year, by reporting extremes of heating. There are a few simple and practical tips to remember as well. Sitting for a long time in a cold classroom makes people unhappy, so find some pretext for getting them moving from time to time. In periods of hot and cold weather you will need to think of strategies for re-energizing learners if you want to get the best out of them and this is part of managing an efficient environment. An efficient environment is one in which the opportunities for learning are maximized not only by good planning but also by attending to the welfare of the learners. Your classroom might be very safe in terms of some of the issues already discussed here, but if your learners are tired, cold or lethargic then learning will be minimized. Classroom management is the axis on which planning turns.

## Learning contracts

Continuing the theme of keeping learners energized, we need now to consider how to make the learning environment a place where boundaries are established and channels of communication are clear. Managing these features of the learning process allows learners to feel positive about their commitment to learning and ensures that our planning for inclusion, equal opportunities and fairness to all learners is effective. Creating this type of environment does not just happen of its own accord, however, and needs to be managed; an effective tool for this purpose can often be a learning contract.

A learning contract is a set of what might be loosely termed *rules*, governing the way in which learners behave with respect to each other and the teacher. The contract should be negotiated by the learners themselves, with varying amounts of assistance from the teacher, usually depending on the age of the group of learners. Early on in a course it is worth taking time to establish such a contract with the learners and to make a copy available to all members of the group. The contract may specify a number of ground rules for the way in which individuals within the group interact with each other and with the teacher and often specifies 'rules' concerning their commitment to the learning process. From time to time, and depending on how long the group is to be together for, it may be necessary to revisit the contract and use it as a reminder about boundaries. This can normally be an effective way of reaffirming the principles to which the group signed up – principles of which they have owner- ship. Moreover, of course, use of the contract is not confined to whole-group man- agement, but can be used during personal tutorial time with individual learners who have crossed particular boundaries. It may also be the case that there will be a need to add to the original list of rules, in order to take account of changing dynamics within the classroom. Learners should feel free to raise issues of concern to them through evaluation processes and need to know that these will be considered carefully by the teacher and not disappear without trace. This is a way of strengthening the learning environment and making learners feel valued.

---

**Task 4.5**

Think about the type of 'rules' which you might wish to negotiate with a learning group, including one of which you yourself might be a member.

---

## Managing group behaviour

An essential aspect of managing adult learners is to recognize and deal with the variety of behavioural characteristics that they display when learning in groups, and this is the second issue for consideration in this section on managing learning. It is important for us as teachers to understand both how groups function and the roles that individual members of a group play as contributory factors in this process.

Each learning group develops a unique culture, which is one of the reasons why teaching can be such a fascinating profession. So it is possible to have two parallel teaching groups, in other words two groups working on identical programmes, that behave very differently and require different management skills.

How is a group culture created? It is produced by the interaction and inter- dependence between its members and the beliefs, feelings, attitudes, personalities and life experiences which they bring to the group. Drawing on the ideas of Freire and Rogers, Jarvis (1995) informs us that learning is an 'emancipatory experience which may involve a change in self-organization and perception' and that 'much socially useful learning is learning the process of learning and retaining an openness to experi- ence, so that the process of change may be incorporated into the self' (1995: 99). If we accept this view, it follows that the group is not a static entity, and that it will be constantly reshaping itself according to the way in which its individual members respond to their learning environment. It should not surprise us, therefore, if we find the behaviour of a particular group mercurial and unpredictable and therefore, on occasions, difficult to manage, for their behaviour is the product of a complex network of interactions which are in part to do with the learning process, as described above, but also in part to do with individual life experiences, of which we often have only partial knowledge. The latter are played out within the group and affect the learning process. What is perhaps important here for us as teachers is to recognize our *limitations* in managing lessons and realize that we cannot always change behaviour, despite our best efforts. This will make us more realistic with ourselves when dealing with groups. Rogers (1996: 148) makes the useful observation that the group has a life of its own which is outside of the tutor's control.

In addition to thinking about group culture, we need also to recognize 'stages' in the life of a learning group. Tuckman (Napier and Gershenfeld 1989) talks of the following stages in group development: forming, informing, storming, norming and performing. In the first stage of forming, a collection of individuals come together with a common goal and express their willingness to interact and signal a common bond. Following this is the *informing* stage, during which individual members set and explore goals, aligning individual goals with the agreed goal. During this stage, members interact because they see that others are looking towards the same or similar goals. They express their mutual dependence and begin to explore other bonds they may share, such as common interests, concerns or acquaintances. Next, the group begins to structure itself and its members begin to adopt roles, roles which – after a period of experimentation, jostling and even conflict (the storming stage) – stabilize into the formation of agreed role identities and the acceptance of common roles for all members of the group. Finally, the individuals become a working group: dynamic and not static, with interlocking roles, specializations and division of functions. At this stage the group has become in effect a team, ready to commit to the achievement of commonly agreed goals.

Bearing in mind what has already been said about our limitations in managing the functioning a group, and if we accept Tuckman's ideas, we need to reflect carefully on the manner in which we handle the stages of the group. First of all, it can be a useful exercise to actually share with the group the idea that, as a group, they will experience highs and lows, although this is debatably a more risky strategy with younger learners. In this way the group shares an understanding of the notion that they are a dynamic entity and will need to accept the positive with the less positive in terms of their experience of being part of that group. Second, it seems clear that the trickiest stage to handle will be the *storming* phase, for it is a safe passage through this that will allow the group to function well in the long term. During this phase there can be a number of sources of conflict: personality clashes, manifestations of dislike for others in the group, including the teacher, concerns about achievement of the goals and/or the amount of work needed in pursuit of this. Managing the storming phase requires a blend of strategies to minimize personality issues, offer reassurance about the goals and to sometimes engage the learners in open and frank discussions, allowing them to air grievances and then setting an agenda for 'recovery'. The skills required for this will develop with experience and trial and error and teachers must be realistic in their expectations of themselves in this regard.

**Task 4.6**

Discuss with others in your group to what extent you recognize the ideas of Tuckman in groups you have taught or been part of.

## Managing individual behaviour

Turning our attention away from the notion of the group per se, we need to think about the very obvious issue of individual behaviours which can limit the effectiveness of a group and which require our attention. Some individuals within a group setting, and this is not confined just to learning situations, are inclined to play out particular roles. The roles that they play are determined by a plethora of factors, including: roles they have played in previous groups, perceptions of how they wish to be seen by others, a natural predisposition towards certain behaviours, and emotional and intellectual needs. In a learning situation some behaviours are shaped by the nature of a school experience, such as memories of inadequacy and the subsequent strategies an individual employed to counteract such feelings. Conversely, if the school experience and parental pressure focused on high achievement, then it is possible that such standards will still be fixed as the norm and that any failure to reach these in a new learning situation will have a detrimental effect on the learner's motivation and behaviour within the group. Roles can be adopted for a range of reasons, some of which may be conscious, others less so. Some individuals may wish to court popularity and others may wish to be the group leaders. Other roles which are recognizable are: the 'smoother', the aggressor, the distractor, the joker, the rescuer – and the person who tries to monopolize all of these!

It is difficult to eradicate role playing in learning groups and some roles are of course healthy for the well-being of a group anyway. To a certain degree adults will tolerate otherness, particularly during the *forming* stages of the group. At the same time they will be interested, albeit covertly at times, in how we as teachers deal with these emerging patterns of behaviour. It is only when the behaviour which follows from the role becomes problematic that we need to act. For example, it is sometimes useful to have a 'joker' in the group. If, however, there is an attempt to sabotage the group dynamics through the overuse of unwanted wisecracks, then the behaviour needs to be dealt with, for such behaviour has now reached the point of being difficult.

And it is up to us, as managers of our groups, to decide on that point of intervention, a point normally reached when particular behavioural patterns are beginning to threaten the effectiveness of the group in terms of cooperative learning. We will normally be aware of this phenomenon through the body language of those in the group who are upset or distracted by such behaviour. Having watched us for a while to see how we have reacted, they will often suddenly tell us either verbally or through their body language that they have had enough. Sometimes a group reaches a point where they feel that the rules of respect have been flouted; normally we as teachers will have intervened before this stage has been reached.

A number of factors will need to be considered in our decisions about handling *unwanted* behaviour – as we might term it. One may be the age of the student in question, as clearly our strategies with a 16-year-old just out of school enrolled in full-time learning in a further education college will require different tactics from those used with a 40-year-old trainee teacher on a postgraduate programme. Both learners may manifest similar behaviour, but the type and level of intervention on our part will differ. Whatever the situation, however, it is crucial that we are not tempted into playing games in the classroom with such learners, i.e., entering into psychological warfare! Neither is sarcasm an effective tool on a long-term basis, tempting though it may be to draw on it in the short term. To use sarcasm, far from promoting appropriate behaviour as is our duty as professionals, is to ourselves engage in unwanted behaviour.

One-to-one interventionist strategies can often be the most effective, whereby we address the issue personally with the learner in question. This has the advantage of allowing us to probe possible root causes of the behaviour and enables us to offer the learner an opportunity to reflect on the effect they are having on their own learning and that of others. Again, this is where the learning contract can have its uses. We should not forget the use of referral systems either, needing to recognize where our ability to deal effectively with difficult and challenging behaviour is limited.

In addition to talking through behavioural issues with individuals there are general classroom management techniques that we can learn about and practise and which will be advantageous to us throughout our teaching careers. Sadly, these are sometimes ignored on teacher training programmes. These involve the use of our own body language to transmit messages to those who are undermining the well-being of both the group they are in and possibly our own authority as manager of that group. We can often minimize unwanted behaviour through simple gestures, such as where we stand in the classroom and the use of eye contact. A full discussion of such techniques can be found in John Robertson's *Effective Classroom Control* (1989). His *Teaching Young Adults* (2001) is also useful in its treatment of the role of the teachers in effective learning.

Finally in this section on the management of behaviours which are detrimental to the group's well-being, we need to address the issue of *discriminatory* behaviour. This type of behaviour must be dealt with quickly and effectively. We need also, of course, to include ourselves in this challenge, ensuring that we are non-discriminatory in our treatment of others. Discriminatory behaviour and attitudes emanating from any individual(s) towards another or others should be challenged directly and discussed openly, if this is appropriate, before it escalates out of control. A zero-toleration attitude on the part of the teacher towards such behaviour is vital.

It is in this way that we can actively promote equal opportunities and deal with prejudice. For younger adults this is an important part of their social as well as intellectual development. If we have created the safe environment discussed earlier in this chapter and established a learning contract, then it should not be too difficult to facilitate open discussions on key issues such as gender and race.

To summarize the first two sections of this second section of the chapter, our role as teachers in the lifelong learning sector is to manage the learning environment in such a way that learners can work effectively in an atmosphere of safety, mutual respect and tolerance, in which communication channels among themselves and between themselves and the teacher are open. In this way a purposeful learning environment has been established.

---

**Task 4.7**

Specify two learners you have encountered whose behaviour has been problematic. With a partner or in a group, consider the following:
- What were the causes of the behaviour?
- How did you deal with them?
- How successful were your strategies?

---

## Managing non-classroom-based learning

Our third key issue in this section is that of our responsibility in managing learning which takes place outside the classroom. An increasing amount of usually formal learning fits into this category, with *blended* learning (a mix of classroom-based and e-learning) becoming increasingly popular and possible with the widespread use of technology.

In addition to blended learning, we may work on distance learning programmes, where for certain programmes face-to-face contact is minimal or non-existent. This type of learning offers a number of advantages to adults whose lives are busy and for whom regular attendance at classes is difficult. For teachers it requires a review of the respective responsibilities of learners and themselves in managing the learning process. Clearly, the successful management of this type of learning is no less challenging than regular face-to-face contact with students, but are the skills different? The answer lies in a detailed consideration of how the essence of the learning situation is in itself different. This type of self-directed learning relies heavily on the presence of two conditions. One is that the learner is motivated to engage in learning on their own, without constant group support, and the other is that they possess the study skills necessary to be able to work efficiently on their own. Even although the teacher can be on hand for email and telephone communication, for some learners this is more difficult to handle in actuality than face-to-face contact. If either of these two conditions is not present, then managing this type of learning becomes problematic for the teacher. This may account for the formal and anecdotal evidence that suggests that dropout rates on such programmes can be high. So what can be done to ensure that learners who elect to work in this mode are supported, yet made aware of their own obligations in the process? We are back to the learning contract. Such a contract might establish important patterns of communication between ourselves and the learner, so that the latter feels secure in terms of a regularity of contact and the teacher confident that boundaries have been set around those patterns. The idea of flexible learning patterns is attractive to many learners for reasons already outlined, but boundaries can often be transgressed and then neediness can take over. We need to preserve our sanity as teachers in being firm about our own boundaries. We also need to be highly organized in managing this type of learning, ensuring that we give the learners that we do not meet on a regular basis the same support as we give to those we see daily or weekly. We need, for example, to be careful with deadlines for distance learners, ensuring that we adhere to both those we set for learners and our own marking deadlines.

In addition to good lines of communication we need to get learners to realize that they can acquire the all-important study skills that will facilitate their success outside the classroom as well. If the learner is part of an educational establishment then often they will have access to study support mechanisms, either on a 'drop-in' basis or by appointment. There is also a good selection of literature on this subject, such as Stella Cottrell's *The Study Skills Handbook* (1999). This is a user-friendly text which offers invaluable assistance to learners on a range of skills, including time management, research skills and learning styles.

## Independent learning

Encouraging learners to develop autonomy is a theme which has run throughout this chapter. Ultimately, it is the best gift we can offer our learners, for it is a truly transferable skill which will serve a lifetime of learning. Many of the skills discussed so far in the chapter favour the development of active and reflective learners, from taking responsibility in negotiating a learning contract to agreeing to ground rules which commit an individual to patterns of study. There are a number of absolute 'basic' skills which learners need to acquire in order to begin the road to autonomy and which we should be able to teach them through working with them in the classroom. First, learners should be able to plan and prioritize, in other words manage their time efficiently. These and other organizational skills, such as meeting learning targets, can be covered in an individual learning plan. Other skills, relating to reading, writing and critical thinking can be developed as part of classroom and assessment activity, with the teacher helping to increase confidence, through praise and identifying with students through feedback areas for development. As already mentioned, there are usually a number of support mechanisms within an educational establishment to which we can refer learners for further advice on study skills and we have a role to play in referring learners to the appropriate unit for them. Our role, while our learners are with us, is to *help* them manage learning, particularly if they are not used to this. This has been the subject of this chapter. Their goal is to become gradually less dependent on us and to manage learning for themselves. This is the essence of independent learning.

## Related new professional standards for teachers and trainers in the lifelong learning sector

### Domain A: professional values and practice

| PROFESSIONAL KNOWLEDGE AND UNDERSTANDING | PROFESSIONAL PRACTICE |
|---|---|
| *Teachers in the lifelong learning sector know and understand:* | *Teachers in the lifelong learning sector:* |
| AK 2.1 Ways in which learning has the potential to change lives. | AP 2.1 Use opportunities to highlight the potential for learning to positively transform lives and contribute to effective citizenship. |
| AK 3.1 Issues of equality, diversity and inclusion. | AP 3.1 Apply principles to evaluate and develop own practice in promoting equality and inclusive learning and engaging with diversity. |
| AK 6.2 Ways to apply relevant statutory requirements and the underpinning principles. | AP 6.2 Demonstrate good practice through maintaining a learning environment that conforms to statutory requirements and promotes equality, including appropriate consideration of the needs of children, young people and vulnerable adults. |

### Domain B: learning and teaching

| PROFESSIONAL KNOWLEDGE AND UNDERSTANDING | PROFESSIONAL PRACTICE |
|---|---|
| *Teachers in the lifelong learning sector know and understand:* | *Teachers in the lifelong learning sector:* |
| BK 1.1 Ways to maintain a learning environment in which learners feel safe and supported. | BP 1.1 Establish a purposeful learning environment where learners feel safe, secure, confident and valued. |
| BK 1.2 Ways to develop and manage behaviours which promote respect for and between others and create an equitable and inclusive learning environment. | BP 1.2 Establish and maintain procedures with learners which promote and maintain appropriate behaviour, communication and respect for others, while challenging discriminatory behaviour and attitudes. |

BK 1.3   Ways of creating a motivating learning environment.

BP 1.3   Create a motivating environment which encourages learners to reflect on, evaluate and make decisions about their learning.

BK 2.2   Ways to engage, motivate and encourage active participation of learners and learner independence.

BP 2.2   Use a range of effective and appropriate teaching and learning techniques to engage and motivate learners and encourage independence.

BK 2.4   Flexible delivery of learning, including open and distance learning and on-line learning.

BP 2.4   Apply flexible and varied delivery methods as appropriate to teaching and learning practice.

BK 3.1   Effective and appropriate use of different forms of communication informed by relevant theories and principles.

BP 3.1   Communicate effectively and appropriately using different forms of language and media, including written, oral and non-verbal communication, and new and emerging technologies to enhance learning.

BK 3.3   Ways to structure and present information and ideas clearly and effectively to learners.

BP 3.3   Structure and present information clearly and effectively.

BK 3.4   Barriers and aids to effective communication.

BP 3.4   Evaluate and improve own communication skills to maximize effective communication and overcome identifiable barriers to communication.

## Domain D: planning for learning

| PROFESSIONAL KNOWLEDGE AND UNDERSTANDING | PROFESSIONAL PRACTICE |
|---|---|
| *Teachers in the lifelong learning sector know and understand:* | *Teachers in the lifelong learning sector:* |
| DK 1.1   How to plan appropriate, effective, coherent and inclusive learning programmes that promote equality and engage with diversity. | DP 1.1   Plan coherent and inclusive learning programmes that meet learners' needs and curriculum requirements, promote equality and engage with diversity effectively. |
| DK 1.2   How to plan a teaching session. | DP 1.2   Plan teaching sessions which meet the aims and needs of individual learners and groups, using a variety of resources including new and emerging technologies. |
| DK 1.3   Strategies for flexibility in planning and delivery. | DP 1.3   Prepare flexible session plans to adjust to the individual needs of learners. |

# 5
# Resources for teaching and learning

## 5.1 What is Chapter 5 about?

This chapter examines how resources can be effectively deployed by teachers and trainers in PCE to aid the learning of students. It is not primarily concerned with the technicalities of the production of teaching and learning resources, although it does contain some straightforward advice in this area, which can be used as 'revision' material, as a stimulus for new ideas or, in the case of the new teacher or trainer, as a list of starting points for further reading.

These are exciting times in the field of teaching and learning resources, with the introduction of new technologies in particular playing an increasingly important part. However, it is acknowledged that for many tutors and trainers in the sector these developments have to be viewed against the backdrop of a 'more for less' ideology where diminishing or, at best, the same financial resources are deployed for increasing numbers of students and trainees. It is for this reason that this chapter does not neglect the 'traditional' teaching and learning aids which constitute the majority of the resources currently available for our use while at the same time devoting a considerable part to those new technologies which seem to promise so much for the future.

Section 5.2 considers the nature of teaching and learning resources and how these may be linked to both ideologies of the curriculum and the management of learning. The production and development of learning resources can be one of the most creative and satisfying aspects of our professional lives. However, it must be accepted that in many cases there is no formal or organized attempt to assess the effectiveness or even the appropriateness of these resources. Section 5.3 examines the implications of published reports on the use of learning resources in the post-compulsory sector. Section 5.4 looks at four models for the organization of learning resources in a typical establishment. Audio-visual learning resources, including, penboards, handouts, overhead projectors (OHPs) and overhead transparencies (OHTs), data projectors, videos, DVDs and more specialized types of resource are described and assessed in Section 5.5. Section 5.6 covers a broad range of what can be loosely termed IT learning resources, including software (e.g., computer-based learning) and the Internet, and this is followed by a consideration of various aids and techniques for the production of learning resources in Section 5.7. Open and flexible learning (OFL) and resource-based learning (RBL) are somewhat interconnected developments and these are described in Section 5.8 which also speculates on what learning spaces of the future may look like for our students.

## 5.2  What is a learning resource?

> A human being should not be wasted in doing what forty sheets of paper or two phonographs can do. Just because personal teaching is precious and can do what books and apparatus cannot, it should be saved for its peculiar work. The best teacher uses books and appliances as well as his [*sic*] own insight, sympathy and magnetism.
>
> (Thorndike 1912)

Teaching and learning resources should be used to promote and enhance student learning. This seems an obvious statement, but resources can be used as 'decoration', with no clear purpose in mind apart from some vague belief that they ought to be used. Careful consideration is required as to how the resources should be used, especially with the more 'sexy' technologies as used in media and music production for example, where there is a temptation to 'replace' the tutor with the resources, reducing their role to that of technician or supervisor. To ensure maximum benefit from aids and resources, some analysis is required, so their use can be directed towards maximizing student learning. For example, in many models of curriculum design (see Chapter 7), the consideration of appropriate teaching and learning resources arises as a consequence of the desired learning outcomes, the teaching and learning styles and the subject matter. Often specific learning resources are linked, albeit sometimes only indirectly, with specific learning outcomes. The question then becomes one of just how effective the particular learning resources are in helping students achieve those particular learning outcomes.

It is important therefore to think critically about what various stakeholders in education and training, and authors, mean by the term 'teaching and learning resources'. But first, your own thoughts.

---

**Task 5.1**

What is a 'learning resource'? Give one example each of a learning resource that you use which addresses all three learning domains.

How does this resource promote and enhance student learning?

---

Definitions of what constitutes a 'learning resource' often arise as a consequence of the curriculum design adopted (and more specifically its underlying ideology – see Chapter 7) and implicit theories concerning the acquisition of learning (see Chapter

3). This is equally true of the form of selection of those resources. There are historical examples which illustrate this: consider Skinner's behaviourist theories of learning (see Chapter 3, page 72) and the development of 'linear programmed learning' packages. Equally difficult to pin down is the meaning of terms such as 'teaching resources' and 'learning resource centre'. In fact the phrase 'learning resource centre' has been applied in the past, particularly in the AE and FE sectors, to provision ranging from a reprographics room containing a couple of photocopiers to a fully fledged multimedia centre/library.

We may, however, at the outset attempt a broad distinction between a 'teaching resource' and a 'learning resource'. Put at its simplest, a 'teaching resource' is material, hardware, software or services designed and intended for use by a teacher or trainer to enable, enhance or extend their teaching, whereas a 'learning resource' is designed so that a student or trainee may use it directly to complement their understanding or even as an alternative to a 'traditional' taught approach. In these terms a chalkboard is a teaching resource and a 'gapped handout' (written material with gaps where students can add their own responses, such as an answer to a question or a missing word) is a learning resource. In practice, of course, the distinctions are not clear-cut: the same teaching resource used in a different manner or context becomes a learning resource.

**Task 5.2**

Categorize the following resources as teaching resources, learning resources or both:
- data projector
- OHT
- textbook
- a pond
- Wikipedia

You no doubt gave the response 'both' to most if not all of the listed resources. It is for this reason that for the remainder of this chapter we will only draw the distinction between 'teaching resource' and 'learning resource' where it appears important to do so: otherwise we use the terms interchangeably.

Learning resources can support learning in the cognitive domain, to explain the overt curriculum content. Aids and resources can also be used within the affective domain; indeed anything that keeps students in the mood for learning (or even just in the training room) is promoting learning. For learning in the psychomotor domain, real or model equipment provides the opportunity to demonstrate and practise activities.

Aids and resources may also help learning to continue after the initial contact, in the student's own time, or in subsequent structured learning sessions. It is an advantage if the aid can promote learning over a period of time; this will increase the input-to-learning ratio (the 'cost-effectiveness').

To reiterate, as Thorndike (1912) suggests in the extract at the beginning of this section, learning resources work best when they complement or extend the work of a lecturer, teacher or trainer rather than supplant it. Even when used as part of an OFL scheme, learning resources are most effectively deployed in collaboration with a tutor (see Section 5.8). This seems reasonably obvious now, but has not always been so in the past: for example, in the 1960s a widespread belief (or at least an oft-repeated assertion) was that 'teaching machines', 'programmed instruction' or 'computer-assisted instruction' would not simply form an alternative to traditional or 'conventional' teaching and learning methods but would actually replace them. Even the most cursory of glances into many of today's training or lecture rooms would suggest otherwise.

Aids and resources may be used in the cognitive domain as 'advance organizers' (advocated by Ausubel as cited by Curzon 1990) to set the scene for the introduction of a new topic, and to encourage students to make connections with their existing knowledge. For example, consider a teacher of biology using tomato seeds over a number of years as a learning resource in the topic of seeds and germination. Each student is given a seed. Handling the seeds might remind them of occasions outside their formal educational experience, and should trigger any knowledge they have about seeds and germination. As seeds and their cultivation are fairly familiar, they provide a good starting point for discussing how scientific investigations are designed and carried out. The everyday nature of seeds will allow students to concentrate on the principle behind investigation design, rather than simply on the details of one particular method. It is interesting to note that no new cognitive information has been transferred; rather, students have been encouraged to use their existing knowledge, and this obviously has links with the affective domain. Resources therefore play an important role in the construction of knowledge, especially with the linking of new knowledge to prior knowledge, learning and experience.

There are, however, many more subtle messages communicated by aids and resources. For example, an aid acts as a third party in a teaching and learning situation. The student and teacher momentarily have the same role as they look at or interact with the resource. This could be seen as the teacher inviting the students to share the status of the teacher during those moments: a discreet communication of the teacher's high expectations of their students. Sharing is also occurring as aids and resources are used, and this could also have connotations of the teacher giving something of value to students, possibly with caring parental overtones.

There may also be the perception among more mature students that the teacher has taken time to produce or even prepare resources, which should encourage students to persevere, as it indicates the teacher's belief in the students' abilities, and provides a role model of dedication to learning.

## 5.3 The effective use of learning resources

The current climate illustrated in policy and strategies (DfES 2006a; Golden et al. 2006) emphasizes the use of information technology as a means of improving teaching and learning. CPD requirements to evidence continuation of QTLS status will include that of the 'development of skills in subject teaching, including the effective

application of e-learning techniques' (DfES 2006a: 52). ICT will also be a requirement of the minimum core in addition to that of literacy and numeracy for new
trainees from 2007. ICT is seen as key to the development of personalized learning
programmes: 'a range of practices to personalise learning, including the effective use
of e-learning and new technology, aim to make the system as a whole more capable of
responding to individual needs and aspirations' (DfES 2006a: 48). Others, such as
Cuban (2001), question the amount spent on these resources in relation to their
effectiveness as a tool for improving learning and, indeed, teaching.

The allocation of ICT resources within PCE has improved dramatically over the
past decade. The number of computers in English FE colleges more than doubled
to 380,000 in 2006, of which 95 per cent allow for Internet access. Eighty-two
per cent of colleges used a VLE as their main learning platform as compared to 53 per
cent in 2003 (BECTA 2006).

However, the effective use of ICT to enhance teaching and student learning
remains patchy. Where this occurs, it is usually the attitude of the tutor towards the
use of new and emerging technologies that is the key factor. While 78 per cent of
tutors feel competent or advanced in the use of ICT (BECTA 2006), ICT's main use
remains that of preparing, planning and researching for sessions.

It remains clear that in order to engage tutors at a higher level in terms of
*enhancing* teaching and learning, access to support and development continues to be
fundamental in the drive for e-enabled educational organizations.

> Teachers . . . need training and support to adapt successfully to flexible learning,
> managing independent learning, involving people in the community and making
> full use of advanced educational technology.
>
> (National Commission on Education 1993: 104–5)

> Many institutions have a ratio of work stations to students of 1:10 or better. This
> measure, while useful, does not adequately convey whether information technol-
> ogy is being employed effectively to improve students' learning. Colleges now
> need to develop better ways of using information technology within courses.
>
> (FEFC 1996: 24)

The conclusion of many independent and government reports would appear to
be that, while there is some evidence of underprovision of learning resources, there is
also an indication that existing resources are underutilized in PCE. This may be for
a number of reasons:

- the inappropriateness of the resources (e.g., to the learning outcomes of a particular course);
- inherent structural difficulties within the organization;
- ignorance of the availability of learning resources;
- the anxiety or inexperience of some staff in the use of the learning resource
  (particularly true, perhaps, of those that utilize IT).

**Task 5.3**

5.3(a)   How satisfied are you with your own understanding and use of teaching and learning resources?

5.3(b)   If you feel that you could make better use of learning resources in your own teaching, how much of this is attributable to one or more of the reasons listed above?

5.3(c)   Construct an inventory of your own use of learning resources (e.g., handouts, software, etc.) in the last week of teaching. Now place them in rough order of frequency (rather than total time in using each). Compare your list with a colleague's in the same broad area of work. How well do they compare?

5.3(d)   Within your organization identify where you would be able to get support/training to enhance your use of learning and teaching resources.

## 5.4 The organization of learning resources

**Task 5.4**

Does your organization have a strategy or policy for the use of learning resources (including IT)? If so, what is it? More specifically, can you name the person or unit/section, etc. responsible for: assistance with the photocopier (e.g., paper, what to do if it gets jammed); assistance with IT resources?

It has been suggested (e.g., Davies 1975) that there are four main models for the organization of learning resources within an institution and these are outlined below.

### All resources centralized

In this model most of the teaching and learning resources tend to be under the direct control of a central institutional body, sometimes accountable to a committee or 'user groups'. Typically, requests for audio-visual equipment loan, the purchase of new software or even a simple increase in the photocopying allowance are made to this controlling body. 'Technicians' tend to be deployed and controlled by the centre.

### Only commonly used resources centralized

In this model the 'centre' retains control of those teaching and learning resources that tend to be used by most staff or students and often those which are particularly expensive to purchase, because of considerations for the security of the equipment. However, departments or units are permitted to control some learning resources which may well be specifically related to their own function or curriculum area. For example, a typical police training centre in England would place responsibility for its OHPs, reprographic services, books and periodicals on general policing matters with central agencies but its firearms simulator would be under the control of the appropriate training branch.

## All resources localized but staff retain control

All resources are placed where teachers and trainers have the easiest access to them, often on a departmental, section or unit basis. Budgets are devolved as closely as possible to the level of use. However, particular staff may have an important role as gatekeepers to these resources controlling their use by teaching staff and students. 'Technicians' may also be employed by the departments to help develop and maintain the resources.

## All resources localized allowing near-complete access

'Localized' here is meant in the sense of the greatest possible devolution of access to learning resources. In practice it may mean that these learning resources are placed in a central position (such as the college open learning centre) but students in particular have unrestricted use of them. It may be that a distinction between teaching resources and learning resources is introduced, with the former being controlled by the audio-visual department. It is doubtful whether this model in its purest form is operated by more than a very small number of organizations.

---

**Task 5.5**

Can you locate your own institution within the list of organizational models above? List the advantages and disadvantages of each approach.

---

## 5.5 Audio-visual learning resources

Many books about teaching and learning published even just a couple of decades ago would have assumed that a 'teaching and learning' resource meant an audio-visual aid. New ways of teaching and new technologies have combined to dramatically broaden the term. However, penboards, OHPs and the like are still widely used in PCET and it remains important therefore that sufficient attention is given to their effective use as teaching and learning aids.

## Penboards

It is acknowledged that penboards (often called 'whiteboards') are not the most exciting of teaching and learning resources. However, we offer no apology for beginning a section on audio-visual learning resources with the humble yet ubiquitous penboard. If a defence is required, however, we would point to the fact that penboards are everywhere, they are sometimes all that you will have, and perhaps most importantly, they do not 'break down'.

A more positive defence would rest upon the essential democracy of the penboard. It is usually blank before you start and student contributions can be added as the session progresses and easily changed with the slightly less ubiquitous board wiper. The penboard can also be used collaboratively with the students, providing the opportunity for students 'to do' as well as 'be told'. This is a somewhat more difficult task to perform with the OHP. However, we are not seriously suggesting that the penboard should be used to convey large amounts of information that students simply copy (although even recently the authors have witnessed it used for just this purpose). However, penboards can be useful as supplementary aids to capture impromptu student contributions, to summarize unexpected conclusions, to highlight key information and terms and to serve as a written cue which can aid memory retention and recall.

---

**Task 5.6**

Leave the board uncleaned at the end of a teaching session when you have used a penboard as your only teaching aid and you know that it is unlikely to be used by anybody soon after. Thirty minutes later look again at the board. How much of it now makes sense and is a clear representation of the ideas or material covered? It is a sobering thought that this is perhaps the only record some of your students may have of several hours' work!

---

**Use of penboards**

- While writing or drawing on the board it is best if the teacher is angled in such a way that they can still see the class. This not only helps to retain the attention of students but also allows the teacher to access visual cues to understanding. You don't need to be a contortionist to do this but you do often need to remind yourself not to stand with your back squarely to the class in the early stages of writing on the board.
- Can the work on the board be clearly read from all parts of the teaching room?
- Clean the board regularly during the session when the information is no longer needed (check with the students first). Visual information often has a more powerful pull on the attention than that given verbally and even the most attentive and well-meaning of learners can find themselves reading the contents of the board rather than listening.
- A penboard used as a form of class notebook can often be a highly ambiguous teaching aid (particularly when used as an 'impromptu' aid); think back to the results of Task 5.6. For example, arrows are often used by teachers and trainers when describing or explaining a concept on the board. It is reasonably clear what the arrow signifies when it is actually used, but this clarity may be lost when next encountered by students in their notes.

> In this example is it meant that A leads to B, or that A and B are connected in some fashion, or that A becomes B or . . .?
> - Check your pens before you use them to ensure they are drywipe pens. One of the 'rites of passage' that most new teachers or trainers in PCE undergo is to use a permanent marker pen on a whiteboard with all-too-visible results!

## iWB

Although common in secondary schools, interactive whiteboards (iWB) are not as readily available in the PCE sector, although their use is becoming more widespread This is an 'electronic' whiteboard with the ability to capture the written material for later use, either as a networked or written resource. There is some evidence that, as with the use of other audio-visual resources such as the data projector, these are often underutilized, a means of displaying or presenting information (a teaching resource), rather than an interactive learning resource (Golden et al. 2006). The iWB when blended with traditional methods of teaching can enrich the learning experience and bring the subject matter directly into the teaching room through on-line collaboration via on-line conferencing or webcams for example. Webcams and a cross-border webserver have been used successfully in the Dakini project (a project embracing all secondary school geography teachers across Kent and the north of France) to bring the subject to life in a classroom setting. All GIS data satellite images, OS information can be downloaded and is bilingual, allowing the teachers to share good practice and exchange information while enriching the learning experience for the students. The use of additional software, such as Active Vote, allows students to participate in interactive learning quizzes. The benefit of this type of software is that it allows individuals and groups to access their results immediately. Research suggests that the use of e-learning technologies in terms of presentational tools has 'a strong impact on *engagement* factors' (Finlayson et al. 2006: 10).

## Handouts

Handouts (predominantly written materials which have been pre-prepared and are given to students) are a useful and popular learning resource commonly used throughout PCE. In fact they are so common that students often react as if they have been 'cheated' in some way if they do not walk away at the end of a session with a pile of handouts! At its simplest, a handout can be a straightforward record of the teaching that has taken place (e.g., a set of lecture notes). However, anecdotal evidence at least would indicate that handouts used solely in this manner (although they can be a useful record) rarely lead to sustained learning. Instead it would appear likely that successful handouts have the extra capability to *engage* students with the material.

---

**Use of handouts**

---

- 'Gapped' handouts are a popular way of involving students in the active learning of subject material. Essentially, gaps are left in the text of the handout which may represent single words, whole phrases, mathematical formulae or parts of a diagram. Students then complete the handout using their own understanding, other materials (including videos), attention to the lecture and so on. However, it is difficult to make gapped handouts non-trivial and unambiguous.
- So-called 'skeleton' handouts are sometimes used, particularly in HE. As the name suggests, a skeleton handout gives the bare bones of the session with plenty of gaps where students are encouraged to make their own notes, comments and so on. However, this requires that students have a relatively advanced set of study skills.
- A useful combination is the gapped or skeleton handout combined with a similar style of OHT (see below). This can increase the sense of ownership in students if completed at the same time as the teacher or trainer and particularly if the additions made are in the students' own words.
- It is worth thinking carefully about the design and look of your handouts. For example, a handout which is designed to be physically cut up by students can help to undermine the apparent 'inaccessibility' of some subject areas. Coloured paper can be used to emphasize the importance of a particular handout, for example if an important summary is produced.

Tutors often produce handouts that reflect their own learning preferences, for example, information presented in linear format as a series of points, and which reflect their own personal ideologies. These often perpetuate stereotypes. Instead of merely presenting information, design handouts that ask questions or serve as cues to promote learning rather than rely on a student's ability to simply recall information. Images or prompts in call outs or bubbles, for example, are easily digested, visually attractive and are more easily remembered than chunks of information; graphs can be displayed using questions as opposed to a series of statistics. This type of handout engages the learner and can be used to promote active thinking environments.

**Task 5.7**

Conduct an audit of the handouts you produced for your last taught course or topic.
- Is there a pattern in terms of how the information is presented?
- Do they promote active thinking and enhance learning?
- Do they reproduce stereotypical attitudes in terms of race, gender or disability?

Produce one new handout using different presentational techniques.

## OHPs and data projectors

The OHP remains the teaching aid most likely to be found in any or all teaching rooms. These are increasingly being supplanted in use by the data projector (a projector linked to a personal computer or computer network, often either portable or permanently fixed to a classroom ceiling). The availability of the data projector is now much more widespread than it was even three years ago. Ninety-eight per cent of colleges have display screen technologies (data projectors or iWB); 'however, there is still some way to go until a tutor can expect to find these in any teaching room' (BECTA 2006: 23). A conventional surface is often used to project onto. OHTs are no longer used in this arrangement; instead, what are the equivalent of acetates are produced using presentational software such as Microsoft's PowerPoint.

---

**Use of OHPs**

- Health and safety issues are important with OHPs, and particularly so with the trailing electrical cable.
- A fundamental skill is knowing how to position and focus the OHP. Be aware of the 'keystoning' effect if the screen is angled and know how to remedy it:

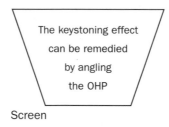

The keystoning effect
can be remedied
by angling
the OHP

Screen

- If you have a choice, position the OHP and screen so that the image can be seen clearly from all parts of the room (but bear in mind that students are often sitting down while you may be standing). A corner is often good for this.
- Bear in mind that most older-style OHPs have a square 'platen' area (where the OHTs are placed) whereas most OHTs that are likely to be produced are A4 (rectangular) in shape.
- If you are an OHP novice then practise in an empty room before you go live!

---

The advantages of a data projector system when connected to an Internet-enabled computer are:

- Whatever you can display on a PC monitor you can display on a conventional screen to a class. This gives the potential for dynamic graphics, greater and easier use of colour and 'live' demonstration of interactive software and the Internet (transforming a teaching resource into a learning resource). This capability is obviously very useful when trying to teach how to use a particular piece of software, or when bringing to life subject matter – the use of film footage from World War 2 for example or simulated environments such as a hospital.

- The need to use a printer and photocopier to produce OHTs is reduced (although copies may be produced for students).
- A large number of presentations can be stored on disk or the organization's network. This allows presentations to be easily shared with other members of the teaching team or posted onto VLEs for student use.
- As a teaching resource they promote focus and provide a means of presenting information in the planned sequence (can reduce the likelihood of going 'off task').
- Presentations can be shared more easily between staff and learners through posting onto a shared VLE or emailed as an attachment.

The main disadvantages would appear to be:

- A reasonable understanding of the principles of IT is assumed of the user.
- It is currently difficult to 'write' student contributions or amendments on the presentation (although a text box can be used for this purpose).
- Even though a special projector is used the image on the screen still requires the light level to be reduced.

Slides or acetates are easy to produce and use. It is clear to most that these are not simply a reproduction in another form of the handout. However, it is important to appreciate that, in common with any other teaching or learning resource we may choose to employ, the way we structure and use slides or acetates influences both the way our students feel about their learning and how effectively they learn.

---

**Use of presentational slides and OHTs**

- The size of font that you use is important. For an 'average' sized room with a maximum of 25 students the font size should be about 20pt for bold Times New Roman or:

# about this big

whereas for a large lecture room with up to 100 students it should be at least 30pt bold, or:

# about this size

Alternatively, an OHT can be constructed in a normal-sized font and then enlarged on the photocopier (illustration modified from Gibbs and Habeshaw 1989).
- Information on acetates or slides is easier to assimilate if the acetate/slide has only a relatively small amount on it. The general rule is that more white space is needed than you think.
- Remember that the edges of the acetate may not be projected onto the screen: this means that your margins probably need to be larger than normal so that text is in the middle of the OHT.

- Both permanent and water-soluble marker pens can be used to produce hand-written OHTs. In fact a combination of the two is often a successful approach: water-soluble pens being used to add to a 'skeleton' OHT as a session progresses (e.g., by adding, at the same time as students, parts or labels to a diagram).
- A common way of producing an OHT is by first printing to a sheet of paper and then using this to photocopy onto an acetate. Laser printers are also able to print directly to an acetate.
- Use images to engage students and, if connection to a computer is available, use sound and other multimedia technologies to enhance learning.
- The design and subsequent use of the OHT as a learning aid is very important. One particular technique of retaining student engagement with the material is to adopt the 'progressive disclosure' approach (a sort of a dance of the seven veils with paper and acetate). An aid (usually a piece of paper) is used to obscure a part or parts of the acetate but is then subsequently moved to reveal the 'answer' or the next part of the argument. However, the overuse of this approach can build up a form of tension within the group as learners mentally try to guess what is next or what it is that is hidden. The technique also tends to reinforce the notion of teacher as giver and omnipotent, but with adult students in particular we may be trying instead to encourage greater learner autonomy. Therefore, it might be more appropriate to think about a design that allows information to be added rather than revealed (e.g., by adding to the OHP using a water-soluble pen).
- Slides can be animated for text to appear as the lesson progresses – do not overuse animation in presentations as learners often focus on where the text will appear from and how, rather than on the subject content.
- Overlays are another popular way of adding to an OHT. In this case additional, pre-prepared, acetates are laid over the original to build up a concept. This technique is easier to produce in presentational software slides.
- Memory sticks are an excellent way of storing information, leave a much lighter carbon footprint and are superbly portable.

## Videos and DVDs

### Task 5.8

Watch a pedagogical short video or DVD (or part of a video, say five to ten minutes) and make a note of just how much needs to be visual, how much benefits from being visual and how much could just as easily be conveyed using the spoken or written word.

Just as with other teaching and learning resources, students can react in very different ways to the use of a video or DVD. This may be for a variety of reasons: for example, the age of the student could be a factor (the video and the DVD are now unremarkable parts of every youngster's life). It is likely that different students may have different combinations of preferred learning styles. However, most direct classroom observation and research seems to suggest that the more active the learning that takes place using a video or DVD the better.

| Use of visual recording |
| --- |
| • The use of the video can be made more active/interactive by showing manageable lengths of video (after about ten minutes most people's attention begins to wander) and/or using a gapped handout or other mechanism to elicit responses to the video.<br>• Use up-to-date videos. Showing a video with kaftan-clad presenters may hold a certain nostalgic charm for some but is unlikely to impress most younger students.<br>• Particular care and preparation is required if students use videos without the involvement of a tutor as part of an open-learning resource centre.<br>• DVDs provide greater flexiblity: for example, in selecting a particular sequence to view, in the choice of language (for non-English speakers) and (in some cases) a choice of viewing angle. |

## Specialized audio-visual learning resources

We began this chapter with a discussion of how the selection of teaching and learning resources is often a factor of the learning objectives of a programme. It follows that particular types of programme may require specialized audio-visual resources for their effective delivery. Examples include the use of models in the teaching of anatomy, 'breadboards' in electronic circuit design and the employment of simulators in judgemental firearms training in many police forces.

### Task 5.9

Does your main area of teaching require any specialist learning resources? Are those used because:
- They are simplified versions of the real thing?
- They are simulations of processes?
- They give the ability to touch and/or experiment?

## 5.6 IT learning resources

Recent years have witnessed a dramatic increase in the impact of IT both in the production of teaching and learning resources and on the nature of those resources themselves. This is no doubt partly because of the potential IT possesses for improving the quality and effectiveness of learning resources as well as the obvious virtues of automation, capacity, interactivity and 'provisionality' (the relative ease of changing a learning resource). However, there must surely also be a case for IT being seen as a means of delivering learning to yet greater numbers of students, in a more flexible and cost-efficient manner. Preliminary research (e.g., the 'TILT' (Teaching with Independent Learning Technologies) project) indicates that IT can be a valuable learning resource in particular subject areas rather than all aspects of the curriculum. Among others, TILT identified the following subjects as benefiting greatly from IT:

dentistry, engineering, maths, statistics, zoology, languages, music and history. The message with IT appears similar to any *other* learning resource: appropriateness is measured by how effectively it helps our students achieve their learning objectives. A blended approach to the use of e-learning allows for the benefits of each to be utilized.

## Multimedia software

A large number of software packages have been developed both by teachers and trainers themselves but more so by commercial companies which aim to exploit the potential of the PC as a learning resource. Often the software is designed so that it can be used by students working independently of a teacher. This type of software has been given a variety of names, including computer-based learning (CBL) and computer-aided learning (CAL).

---

**Use of CBL/CAL**

- There are a number of advantages of CBL/CAL when compared with other more traditional learning resources:
  1  A software package can be designed to have endless patience!
  2  The resource can be made available at any hour and most can be used (almost by definition) without the assistance of a teacher.
  3  The 'neutrality' (non-human nature) of the PC allows students the risk-free ability to make mistakes, to experiment and also, on occasions, to be subversive.
  4  Students are able to access these resources at home as well as within the organization at a time that suits them.

  There are, of course, disadvantages:
  1  A number of students (by popular reputation particularly mature ones) are fearful of using a PC. This fear may have to be overcome by other means before any meaningful learning can take place.
  2  After a sustained period of using CAL many students begin to experience a feeling of isolation and quite naturally miss the human interaction available in a classroom. The establishment of on-line learning discussion groups can help to alleviate this and the promotion of on-line learning communities should be encouraged. In order to promote on-line discussion groups ensure clear guidelines are provided (and monitored via the tutor). Larger groups can be split into specialist interest groups or subject specialism areas (Wenger 1998; Salmon 2002).

- If you are designing your own CBL/CAL for students, don't try to compete with the commercial software available: you are likely to come off worse. Instead, a more useful skill to develop is to be able to customize professional packages for the use of individual students or groups of students. In some cases this is already acknowledged and encouraged by the software developers themselves. For example, Mathcad allows the writing of workbooks on particular topics within mathematics. Examples of workbooks can also be downloaded from the Internet.

- A useful software programme is 'Hot Potatoes'. This allows the tutor to design multiple choice quizzes, short answer quizzes, matching games, crosswords and much more. You can design them so they give immediate feedback to the learner. Tutorials and examples are available and you can also record student results. Although not freeware, you can install this free of charge if you are working for a non-profit educational organization. You will need to comply with the conditions.

---

- CBL/CAL software should make good use of the strengths of PCs. For example, the ability to carry out tedious statistical calculations quickly and correctly, to construct graphs and alter them instantly as data is changed.
- In many ways the characteristics of good CBL are the same as those for other forms of OFL.

Most new computers come with an array of software including that of multimedia. If you have not used these before, have a go! Once you have got used to them you will find them an invaluable tool in the production of interactive and engaging teaching and learning resources. 'New' ICT-based resources such as digital cameras and recorders are now commonplace and relatively cheap to purchase. Digital cameras can be used by students and tutors to record evidence of learning and promote motivation. Recording teaching sessions is invaluable in terms of self-assessment.

### Use of multimedia software

- Be critical of multimedia software which claims to be 'educational' (or even 'edutainment' or 'infotainment'!). The best allows and encourages student interaction which goes beyond the exercise of simple choices. Where possible use a copy of promising multimedia software under evaluation conditions before recommending that your organization purchases it. Alternatively, post a message to a usenet newsgroup or appropriate mailing list to see if anybody else has tried it. The *Times Educational* and *Higher Educational* supplements also review multimedia software on a regular basis.
- Multimedia software should be just that – multimedia (not simply a few token video clips). It follows that it is of greatest value as a learning resource in those subject areas and skills that benefit most from animation, sound and so on. Few teachers of a certain generation can fail to be impressed when the birdsong of the chaffinch can be played instantly when 'looked up' in a multimedia encyclopaedia.

## The Internet and the web

The Internet should not be confused the World Wide Web. The former is the collection of interconnected networks and the latter comprises the documents and other resources accessible via hyperlinks and URLs. This collection of resources and information is arguably one of the key changes to the way in which tutors and students research and find information. It is quick, (relatively) cheap and accessible at any time. A word of caution, however: users should be critical when using information from the web as anyone can publish. It does not have to go through any quality assurance or editorial systems. The sheer volume of information can be confusing and unmanageable, so refine search terms and criteria to target your searches. Many of you will be familiar with realizing that you have spent two hours surfing with nothing concrete to show for it.

- Google is the most widely used search engine. In 2007 using the search term 'learning and teaching resources' elicited 1,090,000 responses. You can, however, refine your search; in this instance, the search engine found all pages with 'teaching', 'learning' and 'resources' ('and' is automatically ignored). The use of quotation marks refines your search to pages containing the exact phrase. This reduced the number of hits to 35,300. In both cases, a search of pages from the UK only was used.

- Although there appears to be an abundance of material 'out there' on the Internet you will soon discover that much of it is repeated from site to site, some of it you have to pay for and some of it you can't trust. This is not to say that there isn't much of value and interest, but such information has to be searched for (and added to favourites). Government and academic sites often provide the best repositories for 'quality' information (e.g., Ofsted reports are available from the UK government site).

## Netiquette

Make sure students are aware of the rules of netiquette prior to the planned activity. Many colleges have systems in place to restrict access to certain sites. Students should be informed of any rules and regulations concerning the use of the Internet, including that of antisocial behaviour such as flaming (the posting of messages deliberately intended to cause hostility on discussion boards) or pie fights (normally short in duration and extremely heated and found on blogs and bulletin boards). It is especially important to explain netiquette conventions for VLEs and discussion group forums.

The Internet arguably has changed the way in which we communicate and seek information. Significant changes in recent years have included personal use of a much greater range of applications beyond the basics of word processing or email. The development of wi-fi technologies means we have finally cut those apron strings to the home or office and digital video now accounts for 60 per cent of Internet traffic. Portable technologies allow us to be in touch wherever we are, although we are still limited through battery life, in terms of whenever we like. The marked difference here is the use of new technology as an interactive social platform – social networking sites, blogs, wikis-users have become the publishers. Web 1.0 could be summed up as passive, while Web 2.0 is active. Perhaps one of the simplest comparisons to illustrate this point is the difference between Encarta, a static source of information, and Wikipedia, where you are able to engage in collective editing (O'Reilly 2005).

**Task 5.10**

Constant connectivity is now the norm for many users. What are the benefits, or drawbacks, in social terms?

User e-sophistication, in other words one's ability to utilize technology, especially emerging technologies, remains spiky and uneven. Most users feel confident with the basics such as word processing and email, but are unaware of the wider implications and benefits of emerging technologies. Discussions with colleagues suggest that this is not because staff are resistant to technology and change, but rather, they feel unsupported and, more importantly, uninformed. 'A lack of confidence or competence with ICT was cited by 38 per cent [of college staff] as reasons for low use' (BECTA 2006: 7). For example, if you do not know what a blog is, how will you be aware of its uses and, further, who could show you how to use this? An important aspect of teacher training in any sector is that of the placement and the role of the mentor. Evidence suggests that a 'key factor in determining the contribution of the mentor appears to be the level of confidence in his/her ability to use ICT, both personally and in the classroom, which in turn has an effect on both the nature and range of the support given to the trainee teacher' (Muttona et al. 2006: 1). In the light of the new standards and guidance for the training of tutors in the PCET sector (DfES 2004b) where there is a clear emphasis on the centrality of the mentoring role, this has implications in terms of the training and up-skilling of mentors. While tutors will need to evidence CPD, it is not clear yet how this will be defined. It is hoped that managers of educational organizations will take a positive approach to the CPD requirements and arrange programmes of personal learning specific to individual tutors' needs. It is clear that in order to remain updated, colleges and other educational organizations will need to provide supportive training packages to staff for these new and emerging technologies as well as maintain the current 'robust ICT infrastructure' (BECTA 2006: 5).

---

**Task 5.11**

Read the following list of terms and then specify one advantage of each as a learning or teaching resource:

- VLE
- blog
- podcast
- wickis
- iPod
- iWB
- wi-fi
- Skype
- MMS/SMS
- e-portfolio

---

The following section focuses on those aspects that are of most relevance to the development of teaching and learning resources.

## Email

For many of us, email is considered the most accessible and efficient means of communicating. Email predates the Internet and was used by multiple users of the same mainframe to exchange information from the mid-1960s. Internet email followed. Its use as a household communication system has grown exponentially over the last decade. Within colleges, email is now used extensively between staff and to a lesser extent between tutors and learners. Eighty-two per cent of colleges use a VLE.

**Table 5.1** Use of email

|  | Email between learner and tutor | Tutor moderated on-line discussion | Unmoderated learner on-line discussion | Learners make use of personal websites and blogs |
|---|---|---|---|---|
| Not used | 1% | 17% | 53% | 36% |
| Some or few programmes | 74% | 81% | 45% | 66% |
| All or most programmes | 25% | 2% | 2% | 2% |

*Source*: BECTA 2006: 19.

---

**Use of email**

- Posting an email is like posting a letter but with one important difference: it is almost instantly delivered. This has major advantages but one big disadvantage: it encourages a lack of reflection before sending. This is particularly true if you feel strongly about something. With a conventional letter there is usually time to reconsider the wisdom of something you have written. Email is currently in a strange middle ground between a letter and a telephone conversation, and protocols have only recently been established.
- Email is an excellent way of keeping in contact with students who may be embarking on an OFL programme (see Section 5.8). Course materials can be sent via attachments, and if your email software has a 'read acknowledgement' capability then use it. That way you can be reasonably certain that students have received your message or the materials.
- Use email to stay in touch with your students on a regular basis. This is particularly important if your students spend a considerable amount of time on placement. VLEs allow you to select individuals or groups, or you can create distribution lists in your address book; this means one email does all. Emails are an excellent way of supporting your students.
- It is possible to use email as a means of running workshops or seminars on-line to eliminate the need for all participants to be physically present at the same time. There may also be a number of other less obvious advantages to this arrangement:

  Classrooms are limited by a defined place and fixed periods. Yet email allows everyone to come and go when they can and encourages longer and more effective discussions. People reshape their ideas in the light of their ongoing understandings and reflections. They can also go back to previous conversations and resume them.

  (Pincas 1997)

## Mailing lists

By electronically joining a mailing list on the Internet you will automatically receive (by email) all the messages sent to the members of the mailing list. You are of course able to send messages yourself. Mailing lists are used to conduct discussions on particular subjects, to disseminate information (e.g., the various HEFCE mailing lists), to share early drafts of academic papers and so on. At least some of the educational mailing lists are moderated, in other words, a person is responsible for checking that a contribution sent to the rest of the mailing list is relevant. Others (probably most of those on the Internet) though are unmoderated and so anything can be sent to all. You will need to subscribe to these.

---

**Task 5.12**

How often do you use email to communicate with your students? Create a distribution list for one of your groups and stay in touch with them for four weeks using email to:

- answer questions;

- pose questions and promote discussion;

- provide support and advice;

- prepare your students in advance of your sessions with tasks and information.

Remember that although this can be time consuming in the beginning in the design and creation of supporting material, the long-term benefits are far-reaching.

---

**Use of mailing lists**

- It is difficult to estimate the number of mailing lists on the Internet but it must run to many thousands. It is reasonably certain therefore that there is a mailing list (or possibly several) in existence that deals with your particular subject specialisms. For example, if you are involved in police studies there is the mailing list 'crimnet'.
- www.wired.gov.net is an email alert service from the Home Office giving you the option to register your preference for announcements by agency, department or key word searches.
- If you are developing learning materials for students there are several mailing lists of interest, including several devoted to open learning.
- At the same time as joining a mailing list you are also given instructions about how to unsubscribe. Don't lose them!

---

## Usenet newsgroups

Whereas mailing lists consist of a defined group of contributors and are essentially private in nature, usenet newsgroups (or simply newsgroups) are open to anyone to browse and (in the case of unmoderated groups which constitute the majority) contribute to. Each newsgroup covers a particular subject area, topic or interest group.

## Blogs

These have replaced many of the usenet and mailing systems and typify Web 2.0 technology. They can be simply defined as an e-diary or journal – the break from traditional diaries here is that they appear in reverse chronological order and are social in nature rather than private. Many students prefer to use blogging as their means of communication or instant messaging. Email is considered by many to be a long-winded old-fashioned formal means of communicating as opposed to virtual social interaction. Blogs have the advantage of creating informal learning environments to promote discussion and critical thinking in subject-specific areas.

## Podcasting

Simply put, podcasts are typically audio files which can be downloaded onto PCs, mobile phones, MP3 players and iPods. They are not static like other material posted on VLEs. Feed and podcast aggregating software (e.g., iTunes) are required in order that individuals can subscribe to this service. This alerts the user to the availability of new episodes. The advantage of this type of service is that students can listen at a time and place of their convenience – on the journey to college using their iPod or at home when revising at their PC. Students are used to receiving information in this way. The audio medium suits the learning preferences of some students and can have other advantages such as the development of English speaking skills of students whose first language is not English. Keep podcasts small – students are used to listening in terms of the length of a song. Lecturers in HE have used this to replace traditional lectures suggesting that it frees up time for smaller group activities and promotes widening participation (Stothart 2006). It should be remembered that these are not just recordings of lectures, they are specifically created, and use emerging teaching strategies that incorporate new technologies. The auditory medium is often associated with passive learning; care should be taken to include the use of questioning to promote active thinking environments (for blogs on this topic see www.mobile-learning.blog-city.com).

## On-line discussion groups

These are essentially on-line forums that are *user generated*. Unlike podcasts where subscribers are notified of new episodes, members need to log in and check for postings. The advantage of creating on-line discussion groups in educational establishments is that it allows the organization authority in terms of membership and the ability to moderate content. The absence of anonymity is an effective subliminal control measure. On-line discussion groups can be used effectively to support peer learning, collaboration and student-generated research.

## VLEs

These are software systems that facilitate course management, administration and information. 'In 2006, 82 per cent of colleges used a VLE, compared to 59 per cent in 2003. However, not only did use of these VLEs increase across colleges, they were also most widely cited as a college's main platform' (BECTA 2006: 6). VLEs such as BlackBoard can be utilized in a variety of ways and have many useful features all within one site including email (individual, group or select users), e-portfolios, discussion boards and announcements. The real advantage of VLEs is their simplicity – you do not have to be a web editing specialist. Word, PowerPoint, audio and visual files can be directly input.

**Task 5.13**

- Identify the VLE in your own organization.
- Research its use and functions.
- Use one tool that you have not previously used and incorporate this into your teaching offer.

## E-journals and books

E-journals can be accessed at any time and are cost-effective and kinder to the environment. Encourage students to access these to enhance knowledge and understanding before and after taught sessions. Some journals are readily available on-line. Many larger organizations provide students with a wide range of on-line databases from which to choose (for example, the basic skills magazine from www.basic-skills.co.uk). EBSCO is a useful database for researching educational issues.

## Audio-visual technologies

These include a range of technologies such as digital cameras and recording facilities, video-streaming and -conferencing. The use of these technologies as a learning resource in addition to a teaching resource can enrich learning.

## E-portfolios

These are a collection of digitalized evidence to record learner achievement. Limited use merely provides a digital copy of a paper-based portfolio. However, with imagination, these can represent evidence of the learning journey at a variety of levels, as evidence of CPD, for example, or to provide prospective employers with interactive information. The e-portfolio can store a variety of files – video evidence of completion of tasks or effective communication skills, for example. It can be useful should employers request such visual evidence of skills prior to interview. Again, the advantages are clear in terms of access at a student's convenience and for personalized learning.

## Shared resources

An emerging use of Web 2.0 technologies is the creation of your own personalized homepage. A free example of this is Pageflake (http://www.pageflakes.com/). Why not create your own homepage for yourself and your students. These homepages can be personalized to include all your favourite websites, links straight to email and your favourite sites on one page. Each section or tab is called a 'flake' and you can add as many flakes as you like. Stay updated with your specialist subject area and interests with podcasts and blogs straight to each flake. Instead of logging into your email, then onto your search engine, then entering your search and finally going to the relavant site, everything here is on one page. This does not sound that useful until you use it! Consider the news, add the feed and this will be delivered to your page every day; you do not need to go and find it. Think of the uses of creating a homepage to share with your students providing everything they need for their course in one place. You need to organize and set up the homepage and then invite your students to share. You will need to make a decision about moderation or editing capability. If you choose to retain all control, students will be able to view these resources but not add or delete them. However, if you allow the students editing capability, imagine how rich in information your page could be. A useful flake is the 'sticky note' which amounts to a virtual Post-it note. Use these to remind students of deadlines, tutorials, tasks or appropriate radio programmes.

**Task 5.14**

Choose!
  Either:

1    Create a course study guide to Internet resources for your particular specialism. This should be selective and include only those links that are still 'live' (you will need to check them – don't trust another person's links!) and contain quality information (e.g., not just another set of links). The course study guide might contain lists of:

 • websites;

 • mailing lists and how to subscribe;

 • any regular Internet conferencing (e.g., IRC (Internet Relay Chat) channels);

 • CBL/CAL learning packages, either for downloading or for accessing on-line (e.g., PowerPoint demonstrations);

 • discussion groups;

 • links to e-journals and e-books and a 'how to' guide for accessing on-line databases such as EBSCO.

    or

> 2   Create a personalized homepage for yourself and your students. Try Pageflake first as this is free and simple to use once you have practised. Then add audio, music or video files (e.g., www.jisc.ac.uk/whatwedo/programmes/elearning_pedagogy/elp_learneroutcomes/elp_learnervoices.aspx). This contains video interviews of how students in FE and HE used technology to enhance their learning. Include feeds from:
>
> - DfES;
> - BBC;
> - your own specialist subject area.

## A note on security and misuse of the Internet

Security is a big issue with the Internet in two main respects: the misuse of private networks for malicious or illegal purposes and the transmission of viruses. To counteract the spread of a computer virus a regularly updated proprietary virus scanner is probably the best protection.

A number of educational organizations have expressed concern over the availability of pornography (some almost certainly illegal in the UK) through the Internet. Certainly, it is easy to inadvertently stray onto pornographic sites and a number of software programs have been marketed to try to deal with this problem, with varying amounts of success. A more serious problem is the occasional student who will purposely misuse the Internet connection, either to seek out offensive material or for other possibly unlawful activity. Students may also waste their time in other ways: for example, by visiting chatrooms available through the Internet. It is easy to overstate this phenomenon, for it can be considered a manifestation of an age old problem in a new technological guise. Our own view is that those approaches to the problem which emphasize the degree of punishment for misuse, rather than the likelihood of detection, are largely ineffective. Rather, if students know that their activities are either continuously logged (including the web addresses 'visited') or are randomly viewed (such as placing a monitor with the librarian) they are less likely to misuse the system. All students who access the Internet through their college will need to be made aware of the acceptable user policy of their institution. There have been a number of cases of the networks of educational providers being used, without their knowledge, to share offensive materials such as paedophile material. If you have any suspicions about the misuse of your networks you should inform the appropriate person. A growing concern in the educational community is the misuse of the Internet for 'academic' reasons. There is evidence of an increasing problem with a minority of students using the Internet as an aid to plagiarism. This takes the form of either copying unattributed sections of text into an assignment or even the purchase of essays. If you suspect this may be occurring then you need to consult with colleagues on the best approach to detecting and countering the problem.

## 5.7 The production of learning resources

### Word processing

Word processing documents are, and have been for some time now, universal and many educational institutions require that their students word process all assessed work. One section in one chapter of a book is hardly sufficient to cover the rudiments of word processing. However, there are many excellent learning packages available and short courses offered by local colleges (such as ECDL – the European Computer Driving Licence). Alternatively, like many teachers in PCE, you could simply sit down at a PC and experiment. Most word processing packages have a tutorial capability (the effectiveness of which as a self-study learning process you will no doubt assess!) and the use of templates can provide a useful short cut to a good-looking document.

---

**Use of word processing**

- Presentational style is obviously related to personal preference. A page of word processed text can contain much more than a handwritten page and this is not always a good thing in learning resources. Hence you may need to leave more gaps and white space, and spread the text out.
- Don't subject your students to a dizzying array of typefaces and font sizes, and avoid the overuse of capitals.
- Avoid the standard clipart that comes with many word processing packages. For an unknown reason this all seems to have been designed for a child of the 1950s and has become clichéd through overuse.
- Paginate your handouts. This makes it easier for you to refer to a certain page and for your students to check that no pages have gone missing during collation.
- Do use images, graphs, timelines, etc.
- Make it *active*: include tasks and questions.

---

The advantage of electronic documents is that they can be posted on a VLE or emailed to students prior to your teaching session. You can edit and update with ease and hyperlinks can be added to direct students to relevant links including multimedia links. This is especially useful for extension tasks and differentiated learning.

**Task 5.15**

Create an interactive electronic learning resource for your students. This should include:
- links to other relevant websites;
- links to appropriate documents;
- links to a relevant e-journal or book;
- links to a multimedia file (animated).

## Photocopiers and photocopying

Read the following quotation. While this refers to the use of photocopiers, it is easy to see how new technologies very quickly become yesterdays technologies. 'The introduction of the photocopier demonstrated the degree to which teaching can be revolutionised by the use of new technology' (National Commission on Education 1993: 95).

Photocopiers occur in a bewildering variety of types and sophistication and, like the average word processing package, it is doubtful that we use anything like the full potential of facilities available. There are a number of alternatives to the photocopier which can be cheaper to use, particularly if more than about 20 copies are likely to be made.

---

**Use of photocopiers**

1   Make sure that you are able to do at least the following on a photocopier to which you have access:
   - copy a single page of A4 size;
   - copy multiple pages of a single page of A4 paper;
   - enlarge and reduce (and the relationship between A4 and A3);
   - change the tone (lighter/darker);
   - produce double-sided copies;
   - collate;
   - staple;
   - copy onto OHTs.
2   Be aware of the limitations that copyright legislation imposes. Most educational institutions or centres hold a licence administered by the Copyright Licensing Authority (CLA) and it is worth finding out what this allows you to copy.

---

## 5.8 Open and flexible learning

---

KEY ISSUES

OFL has many advantages but the importance of teacher–student and student–student interaction in the classroom should not be lost sight of.

The library is of vital importance in OFL but as a resource centre not a storage facility.

Students need particular skills if they are to take advantage of OFL.

---

Open and flexible learning (OFL) is not new. It has been around in some form for quite a time, although without many of the features we believe are important to its success today. Most people have heard of correspondence courses and the Open University even if they have not had direct experience of them. It is these initiatives that were the forerunners to today's systems of OFL. Increasingly, OFL is being linked to the development of CBL and the use of electronic communication such as email and video-conferencing. However, OFL as an approach to assisting learning is a concept that would exist regardless of the technology used to deliver it.

We are focusing on OFL in this part of the chapter for two reasons:

1   OFL appears to be an increasingly important dimension in the work of many post-compulsory establishments (helped no doubt by a clear funding stream in the LSC). Many colleges for example are now investing in open learning centres. No doubt they see this partly as a sound economic development but they may also sense a growing popularity for this type of approach among individual students and businesses approaching colleges for training.
2   OFL is very dependent on good quality resources. The choice and design of these resources play a vital part in helping students achieve their learning objectives. Part of this section will be devoted to the preparation of 'conventional' open learning materials. We have looked elsewhere at some aspects of IT-based approaches.

You will encounter a variety of terms in the literature of learning resources including distance learning and 'flexistudy', which quite often mean the same thing or at least share many attributes. However, 'open learning' is a term generally used to describe courses flexibly designed to meet individual requirements. It follows that open learning systems try to remove barriers that prevent attendance on more traditional courses and therefore usually include arrangements for people to learn at the time, place and pace that suits their circumstances. Restrictions placed on students are under constant review in open learning systems. Another key characteristic of open learning is its student focus. There is often an emphasis on learner choice, on negotiation of outcomes, on student self-assessment and on learner evaluation of the modules. Materials are designed to suit the learner. Finally, most open learning systems require specially prepared or adapted materials with which students can interact. There should be a variety of resources available for use in different ways. OFL is not, however, 'old-fashioned' distance learning, and appropriate tutorial support and the use of support groups are important elements in any OFL arrangements. In this sense the mode of tutorial support (e.g., 'face-to-face' or email) is largely unimportant: it is the quality and effectiveness of this support which really counts. It is not difficult to see why OFL is growing rapidly: busy adults prefer flexible arrangements which fit round their lives; they like to work at their own pace (without being embarrassed); they like access to tutorial support, but are less keen on teachers 'leaning over their shoulders' all the time. OFL can give learners ownership of the process through the ability to negotiate how learning is achieved. It can allow students to gain confidence by working through a course in manageable chunks achieving success at each step. OFL can make it easy to revisit the 'difficult bits' whenever necessary. Businesses have also been quick to see the benefits of this approach to training. It causes less disruption of work schedules, training resources are better used and, after initial 'tooling-up costs', it can be a relatively cheap option for developing some skills, freeing resources to be spent in other areas. OFL can target specific training needs as employees can tackle only those modules that are needed; they don't have to sit through an entire taught course. Many large enterprises like Ford and British Airways use OFL extensively. They are attracted by the best schemes which use a range of very sophisticated technologies to put over information in a way that speeds understanding and helps retention.

For colleges and training centres the advantages are various. The institution may attract more students and therefore much-needed cash, and OFL has been used to reduce programme costs in some college courses. Some lecturers are attracted to it because it is learner-centred, and enables them to adopt a number of different support roles.

---

**Task 5.16**

It has been suggested that elements of one of the courses you teach could be redesigned as open learning modules. Students would be expected to use self-study packages, work at their own pace, and use a range of resources. Tutorial support would be available, but not necessarily from you. Choose one of the courses you teach and consider the following:

5.16(a)   Which elements might it be possible to deliver through open learning modules? Why have you chosen these elements as the most appropriate for open learning?

5.16(b)   What would be the major advantages and disadvantages of using open learning for parts of the course you have chosen?

5.16(c)   In order for open learning to be successfully integrated into your course, what organizational elements would need to change in your establishment (e.g., timetabling)? What training would you and your colleagues need to enhance your skills and to enable you to support open learning most effectively?

---

The best OFL schemes use high quality, carefully designed resources such as interactive video and CD-ROMs, access to on-line databases, audio tapes, articles and study guides. Such resources are expensive because they take time to prepare. There are numerous problems facing anyone trying to design open learning materials, as well as problems facing those trying to use them. The materials tend to be 'one-way'. You do not get the instant feedback of the classroom where, if a topic is difficult or your approach ineffective, learners will soon let you know one way or another. Therefore, great care has to be taken when choosing or preparing resources for open learners and when writing the instructions or guides that tell the learners how to use the resource.

For example, when preparing open learning materials for your students or when using commercially produced resources, you need to know your students' characteristics as independent learners. What is their reading level, for example? If you write in too abstract, technical or complex a manner they might be easily lost – but if you simplify your language too much they may feel patronized. Factors such as motivation, peer group support and study skills are also important to consider in this respect.

In the classroom you can provide many different forms of support for your students: arousing interest through enthusiastic delivery, and linking ideas to students' interests; clarifying objectives and their relevance to the students; presenting difficult concepts or skills in a number of different ways; providing opportunities for practice and giving immediate feedback. Can open learning materials be a satisfactory, if not perfect, substitute?

Open learning materials cannot be written like an ordinary textbook. Textbooks focus on content and not support or guidance. Textbooks are usually organized according to the logic of the subject rather than the logic of learning. They take the perspective of the subject specialist rather than that of the learner. They require the physical presence and support of a teacher. Open learning materials are more complex in structure and function.

**Task 5.17**

Do this activity with a colleague if you can. You might choose a resource that you both use.

5.17(a)   Select a written learning resource currently in use on one of your courses. It may be an instruction booklet, an introduction to a topic, a written briefing for a task or assignment, a list of legal definitions, etc.

5.17(b)   Examine your chosen material for readability, clarity, layout and tone.

5.17(c)   Comment briefly on how you would improve the chosen resource to enhance communication with the learner.

Staff who are integrating open learning into their courses often want to use existing materials and packages such as standard textbooks, videos, CD-ROMs and computer programs. They do not want to design and produce all their own resources. The solution is to write a study guide to supplement the existing materials, to compensate for any weaknesses those materials might have and to guide the learner through the resources.

A study guide might include any or all the following features (adapted from Powell 1991: 45–8):

- your overviews and/or summaries of the topic;

- concept maps or other diagrams showing how the main topics and ideas are related;

- learning objectives;

- an annotated bibliography;

- guidance as to which chapters/sections to study and which to ignore;

- specially written (or audiotaped) alternative explanations, to be studied instead of sections in the material that you think are inaccurate, biased, out of date or confusing;

- local examples or case studies which you have prepared because they will be more appealing than those (if any) in the existing material;

- your paragraph-by-paragraph commentary on the argument expressed in the text;
- questions and activities based on the material, section by section;
- model or specimen answers to activities, and/or checklists whereby learners can evaluate their own responses to questions or activities that seem likely to produce unpredictable responses;
- suggestions for practical work or experimental activity (e.g., guidelines or worksheets);
- a glossary of technical terms;
- a self-assessed test related to the objectives;
- questions to discuss with fellow learners;
- instructions for an assignment to be sent to a tutor for comment and/or marking.

## The role of the library resource centre in supporting learning

Inspection reports and research into the use of libraries have drawn attention to a valuable, and very expensive, learning resource frequently underused and under-valued. In the past the library has often been seen as a 'warehouse' for books and of marginal relevance to many of the practical subjects taught in PCE. This has recently been changing. The growth of OFL, more assignment-driven courses, assessment criteria that include research skills and processing information, and an increase in the number of part-time adult learners who want to do independent work have brought radical changes to the 'old college library', turning it, in many cases, into a learning resource centre.

In such centres, the range of resources available is obviously important but the atmosphere, the provision of spaces for different types of work, and the skills support available are equally important. The JISC Report (2006) emphasizes the need for particular attention in the design of new learning spaces. Awareness of the learning environment and its effect on learning and motivation has long been recognized. It is clear that the lines between learning and social environments are becoming blurred. The role of the library, for example, has changed dramatically over the last decade. These are now considered to be key elements of the community where access to resources should be available to all. These spaces have become much more people-centred, interactive hubs, rather, than hideouts and places of isolation. The emergence of the Internet café illustrates the benefits of open access spaces where individual activity co-exists in mutually supportive and collaborative surroundings. The opportunities for peer support to enhance less structured or informal learning atmo-spheres are optimized. A fundamental difference to the design of learning spaces is the change in attitude to that of 'enabling, rather than controlling, access to learning' (JISC 2006: 8). Learning spaces that are designed to encourage and foster the co-existence of informal and formal learning, are a feature of modern design, as is mobile technology and greater use of audio-visual resources such as webcams and video-conferencing/streaming.

While dominant teaching styles have moved from a pedagogical to an andragogi-cal approach, this has not been reflected in the layout of teaching rooms which remain very much tutor-focused as opposed to collaborative and active learning environments. Twenty-first century teaching suites such as the Robinson Rooms at the LSE incorporate and make use of the full range of emerging new technologies. The dominant emerging use of technology is the use of audio-visual resources – not only used to connect people over a wide geographical area but also to record tutor demonstrations that can be placed on VLEs for later viewing and revision. A feature of this type of technology use is its impact on personalized learning and development. Students can be assessed in their work or learning space. These sessions can be stored for later analysis by the student, peers or tutor at a time, place and *pace* that is beneficial to them. In Lewisham College's 'interactive catering theatre', classes can be filmed by digital cameras controlled by the learners themselves, so that they can view in detail on flat screen monitors on their desks the techniques and skills being demonstrated' (JISC 2006: 23). Continuous filming of teaching sessions, controlled by the learners, has enormous benefits – the students control which aspects of their learning they need to improve. Analysed recorded sessions can later be edited to produce individually tailored interactive learning resources, or to produce interactive quizzes (e.g., using Hot Potatoes) based on identification of common group errors, or audio commentary used to explain and correct errors as well as examples of good skills.

**Task 5.18**

5.18(a)   What role(s) does the library resource centre play in your institution?

5.18(b)   How important is your library resource centre in the development of your students' skills and abilities? Would your students' learning suffer if you didn't have a learning resource centre? How?

5.18(c)   What changes would you like to see to the learning resource centre in your institution to make it a better support to learning? Think broadly: for example, range of resources, layout, staffing, access, etc.

5.18(d)   Identify the technologies that would be required to modernize open access learning areas in your organization.

5.18(e)   Identify good practice in relation to new and emerging technologies.

5.18(f)   Design a creative learning environment: what could your teaching room look like, how would this promote learning?

5.18(g)   What are the implications for enabling as opposed to controlling learning spaces?

## Development of student skills in using learning resources

It is a cliché to say that students now have access to more information and a wider range of resources than ever before. The question is, can they make effective use of these resources? This question has become more pressing in recent years because of the changing patterns in PCE. Many courses, for example those approved by Edexcel, require students to tackle complex assignments needing a lot of research. Open learning is very resource-based and poses enormous problems for students without information handling skills. Many adult learners have not studied for years and find the battery of resources facing them very daunting. Many professions (such as policing and nursing) now require critical reflection as part of their training. The responsibility is much more on students to carry out their own independent study and research. Without adequate skills, students learn ineffectively and increase their chances of failure. To help students become effective and successful learners and achieve their potential, teachers need to consider the following:

1   What study skills do students need to possess in order to get through the courses they follow and to cope with the work they are set? For example, do they need to be able to take notes, to extract information from written and visual sources? To synthesize information from different sources? Can they formulate good questions? Can they analyse data and generate hypotheses? (These skills apply to the use of IT as well as to printed resources.) Student-centred learning and independent learning can place enormous pressures on students, highlighting any problems that they have studying and dealing with information.

2   Who should develop these skills? Many lecturers believe that students should have developed key skills by the time they get to college or training school. They feel that there is no time to spend on general study skills in an overcrowded course. Help and support are usually available to those students who conspicuously lack certain skills, for example literacy (as a form of 'crisis management'), but what about those students who struggle through assignments, learning very inefficiently but passing? Should they go to special skills workshops or should skills work be provided as an integral part of their subject courses?

3   How can these skills be developed? Research has shown that there are some clear principles underpinning the development of these key skills:

   •   Relevance is crucial. Skills are developed using realistic and purposeful tasks, not little 'made-up' exercises. Skills need to be 'built into' coursework, but not buried in it. Skill development doesn't take place where skills are invisible to the students using them, which leads on to the next point.

   •   Students need to use their skills, to reflect on what they have done and then to try out improved strategies. Students react badly to being told the 'right way' to take notes, write essays, etc. They need support as they examine their existing study skills and strategies and work out how to make them more effective.

   •   Effective use of study skills needs to be valued in assessment and direct feedback on the use of such skills should be given to students.

   •   A variety of teaching approaches is needed to suit different styles of learning.

When considering resources to promote effective learning, the question of students' abilities to use the resources must surely be a central issue.

   The notions of OFL, 'distance learning' and RBL can easily become confused and even treated as aspects of the 'same thing'. However, RBL is a term most properly restricted to, in the words of Gibbs and Parsons (1994), 'the use of mainly printed materials, written, collated or signposted by tutors, as a substitute for some aspects of teaching and library use . . . The focus is on full-time students, learning "on campus" but more independently through the use of print-based learning resources'. It does not follow however that these resources need necessarily be accessed by students in the conventional manner: they can just as easily be provided to students by the use of remote and mobile technology.

## Related new professional standards for teachers and trainers in the lifelong learning sector

### Domain A: professional values and practice

| PROFESSIONAL KNOWLEDGE AND UNDERSTANDING | PROFESSIONAL PRACTICE |
|---|---|
| Teachers in the lifelong learning sector know and understand: | Teachers in the lifelong learning sector: |
| AK 3.1  Issues of equality, diversity and inclusion. | AP 3.1  Apply principles to evaluate and develop own practice in promoting quality and in inclusive learning and engaging with diversity. |
| AK 4.3  Ways to reflect, evaluate and use research to develop own practice, and to share good practice with others. | AP 4.3  Share good practice with others and engage in continuing professional development through reflection, evaluation and the appropriate use of research. |
| AK 5.1  Ways to communicate and collaborate with colleagues and/or others to enhance learners' experience. | AP 5.1  Communicate and collaborate with colleagues and/or others, within and outside the organization, to enhance learners' experience. |
| AK 7.1  Organizational systems and processes for recording learner information. | AP 7.1  Keep accurate records which contribute to organizational procedures. |

### Domain B: learning and teaching

| PROFESSIONAL KNOWLEDGE AND UNDERSTANDING | PROFESSIONAL PRACTICE |
|---|---|
| Teachers in the lifelong learning sector know and understand: | Teachers in the lifelong learning sector: |
| BK 1.3  Ways of creating a motivating learning environment. | BP 1.3  Create a motivating environment which encourages learners to reflect on, evaluate and make decisions about their learning. |

| | |
|---|---|
| BK 2.2 Ways to engage, motivate and encourage active participation of learners and learner independence. | BP 2.2 Use a range of effective and appropriate teaching and learning techniques to engage and motivate learners and encourage independence. |
| BK 2.4 Flexible delivery of learning, including open and distance learning and on-line learning. | BP 2.4 Apply flexible and varied delivery methods as appropriate to teaching and learning practice. |
| BK 3.1 Effective and appropriate use of different forms of communication informed by relevant theories and principles. | BP 3.1 Communicate effectively and appropriately using different forms of language and media, including written, oral and non-verbal communication, and new and emerging technologies to enhance learning. |
| BK 3.5 Systems for communication within own organization. | BP 3.5 Identify and use appropriate organizational systems for communicating with learners and colleagues. |
| BK 5.1 The impact of resources on effective learning. | BP 5.1 Select and develop a range of effective resources, including appropriate use of new and emerging technologies. |
| BK 5.2 Ways to ensure that resources used are inclusive, promote equality and support diversity. | BP 5.2 Select, develop and evaluate resources to ensure they are inclusive, promote equality and engage with diversity. |

## Domain C: specialist learning and teaching

| PROFESSIONAL KNOWLEDGE AND UNDERSTANDING | PROFESSIONAL PRACTICE |
|---|---|
| *Teachers in the lifelong learning sector know and understand:* | *Teachers in the lifelong learning sector:* |
| CK 3.5 Ways to support learners in the use of new and emerging technologies in own specialist area. | CP 3.5 Make appropriate use of, and promote the benefits of new and emerging technologies. |
| CK 4.2 Potential transferable skills and employment opportunities relating to own specialist area. | CP 4.2 Work with learners to identify the transferable skills they are developing and how these might relate to employment opportunities. |

## Domain D: planning for learning

| PROFESSIONAL KNOWLEDGE AND UNDERSTANDING | PROFESSIONAL PRACTICE |
|---|---|
| *Teachers in the lifelong learning sector know and understand:* | *Teachers in the lifelong learning sector:* |
| DK 1.2   How to plan teaching sessions which meet the aims and needs of individual learners and groups, using a variety of resources, including new and emerging technologies. | DP 1.2   Plan teaching sessions which meet the aims and needs of individual learners and groups using a variety of resources including new and emerging technologies |
| DK 1.3   Strategies for flexibility in planning and delivery. | DP 1.3   Prepare flexible session plans to adjust to the individual needs of learners. |

## Domain E: assessment for learning

| PROFESSIONAL KNOWLEDGE AND UNDERSTANDING | PROFESSIONAL PRACTICE |
|---|---|
| *Teachers in the lifelong learning sector know and understand:* | *Teachers in the lifelong learning sector:* |
| EK 1.2   Ways to devise, select, use and appraise assessment tools, including, where appropriate, those which exploit new and emerging technologies. | EP 1.2   Devise, select, use and appraise assessment tools, including, where appropriate, those which exploit new and emerging technologies. |

# 6

# Assessment

## 6.1 What is Chapter 6 about?

The formal and informal assessment of students is becoming a large part of the work of teachers throughout PCE. Although external awarding bodies may offer guidance and training with respect to assessment, and assessor awards aim to equip tutors with the ability to assess students taking a wider range of qualifications (see Section 6.5), it is the responsibility of tutors in their classrooms to assess and monitor student progress. This chapter aims to provide a basis for developing tutors' expertise in creating and using the range of assessment strategies necessary to do this.

Section 6.2 looks at our experience of being assessed, both inside and outside an educational context, emphasizing the significance of key events both to ourselves and to our students. Our negative experiences could have resulted from errors in the construction and use of the assessment concerned and there will be a consideration of the concepts of validity and reliability and the role they play in the structure and use of assessment. Crucial too are the type of referencing used and its relation to the aims and objectives of learning, and this is considered in Section 6.3. Section 6.4 will examine a range of assessment techniques and their suitability for particular learning strategies, while Section 6.5 looks particularly at the elements of evidence-based assessment. Section 6.6 considers how experience of assessment itself can form the basis of positive student learning. Finally, if assessment is to be of any enduring value in the learning process, it must be appropriately recorded and reported and Section 6.7 considers how most effectively the reviewing of student progress can be achieved.

## 6.2 Assessment: ourselves and our students

| KEY ISSUES |
| --- |
| How might assessment affect teachers and learners? |
| Why do we assess? |
| How might we improve the quality of assessment? |

Just as many of us, consciously or unconsciously, tend to use those teaching strategies we experienced as learners, so our own experience of being assessed plays a key role in the development of our repertoire as a teacher.

---

**Task 6.1: Our own experience**

6.1(a)  Consider the experiences you've had of being assessed, either in an educational setting, such as the 11+, GCSE, A level or vocational exam, or outside, such as scout or guide badges, life-saving awards or job interviews. Choose one example of assessment which had a positive effect and one which had a negative effect.

6.1(b)  Share these with the group. Are there particular features common to the group regarding what was positive or negative in their experiences?

---

At the risk of stating the obvious, assessment which had a positive effect on you was more likely to be that which you were successful at. But, quite apart from the high quality of your performance, this could have been because you were aware of what was required or that the assessment itself was a fair test of your learning. Conversely, negative experiences could have been the result of misunderstanding the nature of the assessment or not having any feedback on your performance. Figure 6.1 presents a list of remarks made by a range of students in post-compulsory settings about the assessment of their work.

---

**Task 6.2: Assessing your students**

6.2(a)  Repeat Task 6.1 only this time choose three examples of assessment you have recently completed with your students. How do you think they felt about these experiences?

6.2(b)  Share your views with the rest of the group.

---

Under the pressure of day-to-day teaching and training it's easy to forget the power and significance of assessment for ourselves when setting assessment tasks for our students. We can also be tempted to include assessment automatically in our programme of work without considering its appropriateness or the way in which it will affect individual or group learning.

**Figure 6.1** Reactions to assessment

---

'When we have a test, I forget everything straight afterwards.'

'Our teacher takes so long to mark our work, we've forgotten what it was about by the time we get it back.'

'I'd like more constructive criticism from our art tutor. She just says "Great" all the time. When I challenge her, she claims she doesn't want to be too prescriptive.'

'I was delighted to get 85 per cent for my last essay . . . until I discovered everyone in the group got between 85 and 95 per cent.'

'Our lecturer only points out what you get wrong at the bottom of a piece of work . . . never how you could have got it right.'

'My mate's dad does all his assignments. My mate just word-processes them. It doesn't seem to matter.'

'Our "Introduction to Italian" tutor refuses to assess us. He says if we did badly we'd lose interest. But all of us want to know how we're doing.'

'Everybody in our group passes everything. We're getting a bit worried.'

'We have to write our own assessment of ourselves on our report forms. I never say I'm good at anything because it sounds like I'm showing off.'

'I understand all the work but I'm no good at getting it down on paper.'

'Our teacher sets our exam paper. But, of all the topics she revised, only one came up.'

'We do a lot of presentations, which I reckon is unfair as some people are more extrovert than others.'

'We took the exam at the end of the course, so, by the time the teacher discovered I hadn't understood a lot, it was too late.'

'My work experience supervisor resented having me foisted on him, so when my college tutor visited me and asked him how I was doing he dropped me in it.'

'I got confused by all the possible answers in the multiple choice test so I just started guessing.'

---

**Task 6.3: Why assess?**

Choose one of the assessment examples from Task 6.2.

- Why did you assess at this particular moment? To check learning, because of awarding body requirements, the structure of the course (end of a module or unit), institutional demands?
- Why did you choose this form of assessment? Is it easy to use, prescribed by the awarding body?
- What feedback was there to students? How was it done? How will it help them to learn?
- What action will be taken as a result of assessment? Will you cover the same content in a different way? Will individual students get particular attention?

One reason for our positive and negative experiences could be that the assessment itself didn't measure what it was intended to, or was invalid. So, a written exam is an invalid test of the ability to speak a language. A conversation with a native speaker would be more valid. More valid still, arguably, would be the ability to perform a range of oral tasks in a variety of contexts. Experienced drivers often claim the driving test to be an invalid means of assessing the ability to drive, suggesting the test is only a valid means of assessing the ability to pass the test itself. The introduction of a written test to supplement the practical driving test was criticized by some as an invalid method of assessing knowledge and awareness that is only demonstrable in real driving conditions. Those unfortunate enough to take a driving test on several occasions should, all things being equal, have the same chance of passing it each time, since the examiners base their judgements on a series of objectively demonstrated practical skills. The test, then, is reliable. It could be made more reliable if the same skills were required to be demonstrated on more than one occasion to several examiners, thus, for example, making examinees' nerves and any individual examiner's subjectivity less influential.

## Task 6.4: Rating assessment methods

Table 6.1 shows a series of learning tasks and the method selected to assess each one. Decide, with a colleague, using a scale of 0–5, where 0 is low and 5 is high, how you would rate the methods in each case for both validity and reliability.

**Table 6.1** Rating methods of assessment

| Learning | Assessment method | Validity | Reliability |
|---|---|---|---|
| The causes of World War 1 | Essay | | |
| Empathizing with the emotional problems of 16-year-olds | Multiple choice test | | |
| Memorizing chemical elements | Short answer questions | | |
| Metaphor patterns in *Antony and Cleopatra* | Open book exam (text taken into exam and used for reference) | | |
| Dribbling in football | Skills test | | |
| Typical high street shopping habits | Assignment/research task | | |
| Knowledge of road signs | Written test | | |
| Improving accent in a foreign language | Peer assessment | | |
| Using 'Table' in Microsoft Word | Self-assessment | | |
| Punctuation | Oral exam | | |
| General receptionist duties | Discussion | | |
| Dealing with customer complaints | Role-play | | |
| Domestic mobility for the physically disabled | Case study of physically disabled client | | |

Satterly (1990) points out that validity and invalidity aren't absolute qualities of assessment: '. . . one cannot meaningfully talk of an assessment or test being valid or invalid, but only of its *interpretation* as valid or invalid *for some specified purpose*' (p. 224, original emphasis).

---

**Task 6.5**

Where validity or reliability was low in the examples above, how could you increase it, or what other method would be a more valid or reliable one?

---

A valid assessment method is one which tests whether the aims and objectives of a learning experience have been achieved. Discussion with a student would have a fairly low validity rating where general receptionist duties were concerned. Much more valid would be observation by a tutor in a real or simulated situation with a structured checklist or questionnaire relating to the skills and abilities specified in aims and objectives such as handling phone calls and dealing with clients. Although an essay would have high validity in testing a student's grasp of the causes of World War 1, allowing discursive analysis of complicated processes, it could be relatively unreliable. A detailed marking scheme would increase reliability by ensuring that the same abilities and qualities were being credited for all students by all assessors.

## 6.3 Referencing

---

**KEY ISSUES**

The type of referencing we select will depend on the nature of our aims and objectives.

Criterion referencing is arguably the most effective at giving a picture of learning achievement.

---

To find out how effectively learning has taken place, we need to compare a performance, a demonstration of skill, knowledge or ability with something else as a way of characterizing it. This choice of a relation or correspondence is a choice of referencing type. Our selection of referencing type should follow from the aims and objectives we have set for student learning.

Should we wish to compare an individual student's achievement with that of the group she or he is a member of – whether that be a class, year group or national cohort – we would select *norm referencing*. The assumption here is that the performances of any group follow a normal curve of distribution – put simply, small per centages achieving high and low scores, with the majority achieving average marks. Raw scores are therefore adjusted to fit this normal curve and a picture given of any individual's performance in comparison with the group as a whole. This approach has drawn criticism from those claiming standards have fallen in public examinations. Norm referencing, they argue, bears no relation to absolute standards of achievement:

should standards actually fall, grade distribution would mask this by remaining the same. Its defenders claim that it is fairer to assume a conformity of ability in successive year cohorts than exact conformity of question or overall exam paper level of difficulty. Those hostile to 11+ testing have argued that norm referencing allows authorities to select at random according to the resources they choose to allocate to selective education. A further argument against norm referencing challenges any claim it may make to tell us anything of value about an individual's learning achievement.

An approach that does do this, it is argued, is *criterion referencing*. Here the correspondence is between the performance and an objective standard or criterion. The difference between this and norm referencing can be seen in the following example: X may be regarded by all in her group as having by far the best singing voice, but measured against criteria relating to, say, enunciation, pitch, tone, interpretation and expressiveness, she may fare differently.

---

**Task 6.6**

6.6(a)    Reflect on your own experience of both norm and criterion referenced assessment.

6.6(b)    Compare your experiences with those of the rest of the group. How did they help or hinder your learning and overall educational achievement?

---

Criterion referencing may be combined with *grade referencing*, where criteria and levels of achievement relating to them are connected with points on a scale, literal or numerical. But they need not be and, as we shall see in Section 6.6, much recording of achievement in PCE is descriptive of that achievement with little or no use of grades or marks.

Other types of referencing widely used in the sector include *comparisons with a scale of dependence* moving to independence, and *ipsative referencing*, where the comparison is with own previous performances. Both of these are prominent features of assessment in special needs education.

---

**Task 6.7**

6.7(a)    Choose two assessment tasks you have recently set. What type of referencing did you use in each case? Why did you choose them?

6.7(b)    Share this with the rest of the group. Were particular referencing types prominent in certain subject areas or on specific courses?

---

The selection of referencing type is, as we mentioned earlier, connected with your aims and objectives. If, for example, a central aim was about skill development, then ipsative referencing should be part of your overall assessment. And, as we shall now see, it is your aims and objectives which should also determine the assessment techniques and strategies you use.

## 6.4 Assessment techniques

| KEY ISSUES |
| --- |
| Assessment techniques are used in specific contexts. |
| These contexts may limit our freedom to use particular strategies. |
| Where possible, assessment strategies should be related to the aims and objectives of learning. |

Before looking at particular assessment techniques or strategies, it is worth considering the contexts in which we intend to deploy them. Rowntree (1987) identifies a range of assessment features or modes. Assessment is variously formal or informal: at one extreme a degree finals paper, at the other, very generalized judgements made by a teacher as he or she observes an individual or group. It is formative or summative, its prime purpose being either to support student learning or, on the other hand, to gather information about it. It is continuous or terminal, taking place throughout a course of study or on its completion. It may focus on coursework or examinations, concern itself with process (the learning activities of students) or with product (something generated by that process, such as a drawing, an essay or a display, for example). The assessment may be internal, carried out by those within an institution, or external (an examining body). Rowntree applies to assessment Hudson's (1966) distinction between convergent thinking, where students excel at a rational task with a single answer, and divergent thinking, which thrives on open-ended tasks allowing creative freedom and imagination. And finally, he describes assessment as tending to be idiographic or nomothetic, that is, either concerned with characterizing or describing an individual's uniqueness or more interested in comparing individuals with others in an attempt to arrive at a more general understanding of achievement.

### Task 6.8

Consider the assessment you undertake as part of your teaching. Which of Rowntree's features can be accurately applied to it?

We will have more or less choice as to how we assess according to the context we work in. Our institution may, for example, prefer a particular examination board, require us to assess internally and continuously and report achievement terminally. But, where we do have choice, both the features of assessment and the particular strategies we use should be determined by the nature and purpose of learning, as expressed in our aims and objectives.

**Task 6.9**

Table 6.2 presents a set of aims with related objectives as well as a series of assessment strategies. Match the aims and objectives to the most suitable strategies.

**Table 6.2** Choosing suitable assessment strategies

| Aims | Objectives | Strategies |
| --- | --- | --- |
| A  To exercise overall command of emergency services throughout a major incident | Maintain clear and accurate communications through changing circumstances | 1  Objective/multiple choice test |
| B  To reflect on clinical practice | Evaluate positive and negative aspects of interactions with patients | 2  Self-assessment |
| C  To handle TV interviews effectively | Demonstrate an ability to use appropriate body language on camera | 3  Demonstration of skills/ routine (e.g. resuscitation) |
| D  To be aware of a range of sources of information | Search the library catalogue by author, subject or title | 4  Examination consisting of long essays |
| E  To develop and retain knowledge of costs of building materials | Know the costs of a variety of types of bricks | 5  Role-play |
| F  To understand the meaning of vocabulary | Define key words in a given passage | 6  Interview |
| G  To bring about an awareness of health and safety matters | Indicate where fire exits are | 7  Group discussion |
| H  To deal with major technical malfunctions | Describe action which would cancel or override malfunctions | 8  Simulation exercise |
| I  To converse fluently in Spanish | Conduct a one-to-one conversation about everyday topics | 9  Display |
| J  To identify major literary themes | Trace and describe ideas of kingship in Shakespeare's history plays | 10  Short answer test |
| K  To be able to support clients in expressing their emotions | Draw out clients' feelings about a traumatic incident | 11  Seminar presentation |
| L  To monitor own progress | Aware of level of own achievement | 12  Problem-solving exercise |
| M  To develop an argument and defend own views | Present an analysis of the causes of inflation and respond to questions from colleagues | 13  Information-gathering exercise |

| | | |
|---|---|---|
| **N** To understand the structure of the British constitution | Describe broadly the functions of executive, legislature and judiciary | 14 Peer assessment |
| **O** To be able to give positive feedback | Appraise colleagues' work without giving rise to animosity | 15 Audio/videotaping |
| **P** To develop the capacity to work as a member of a team | Contribute ideas to a team project | 16 Comprehension test |
| **Q** To develop a sense of design | Able to use colour, shape and image to present a concept visually | 17 Log/diary |

A suggested matching for Table 6.2 is as follows:

| | | | | | | | |
|---|---|---|---|---|---|---|---|
| **A** | 8 | **G** | 3 | **M** | 11 | | |
| **B** | 17 | **H** | 12 | **N** | 10 | | |
| **C** | 15 | **I** | 6 | **O** | 14 | | |
| **D** | 13 | **J** | 4 | **P** | 7 | | |
| **E** | 1 | **K** | 5 | **Q** | 9 | | |
| **F** | 16 | **L** | 2 | | | | |

**Task 6.10**

Now undertake a similar exercise with your own work. Consider the aims and objectives either of a scheme of work, a series of sessions or of a single lesson. Look at the strategies you use to assess learning. How far do your strategies match your aims and objectives? Are there more suitable techniques you might use?

We have seen above that there can be at least two reasons for our use of some assessment strategies rather than others: a syllabus or our institution may require us to follow a particular pattern of assessment; or certain strategies may be more or less appropriate for the learning we wish our students to experience – that is, they fit our aims and objectives. But there are other reasons why teachers use particular assessment techniques and not others.

**Task 6.11**

Choose three assessment strategies you use frequently and three you never use. Apart from the two reasons specified above, are there further reasons for your using or not using those you have chosen?

When we conducted Task 6.11 with Certificate of Education students, the following reasons came up most frequently. Time constraints often preclude the use of more elaborate assessment – teachers are often wary of allowing the assessment tail to wag the learning dog. Teachers themselves admit to lacking confidence in their skills to devise and use particular strategies, particularly more complex ones such as role-play. Others doubt whether students themselves have the skills to deal with the demands of specific strategies, such as peer assessment. Many teachers feel they lack the resources to use certain techniques, for example, access to a video camera, a library or a PC. Teachers can be deterred by the comparative difficulty of some strategies – a log or diary is often cited – where they feel complex, often subjective judgements are required of them and there is the associated problem of reporting such achievement to third parties.

One of the reasons above mentions student skills. We saw in Chapter 3 how particular learning strategies suit some individuals rather more than others. Similarly, individuals find that particular assessment strategies allow them to perform to their maximum potential, and differentiation in assessment, even when the same learning, the same knowledge or skills acquisition is being tested, offers them the flexibility to be able to do just this. Differentiation may mean selecting different assessment methods for different groups, or alternative tasks and questions within a given assessment exercise. Certificate of Education students have given the following examples of how they have used differentiation in their assessment:

- men and women were placed in single-sex groups for a simulation exercise on a management course after it was discovered that men in mixed-sex groups dominated the organization of the task, relegating the women to secondary roles;

- on a floristry course, some students with limited literary ability were examined for part of their assessment by oral interview;

- in a comprehension exercise, assessment material was provided using examples relating to students' ethnic or cultural background;

- numeracy test papers were set in a student's first language.

---

**Task 6.12**

6.12(a)   Differentiation often raises the issue of equal opportunities. Discuss the examples above in your group. Do they give the students concerned a more equal opportunity to have their knowledge and skills properly assessed or an unfair advantage over others?

6.12(b)   Do you use differentiation in your assessment? Do you now feel there are situations where you could and should use it?

---

## 6.5  Evidence-based assessment

The use of evidence-based assessment, and particularly that relating to learning outcomes such as competences, has grown from changes in both work-related and vocational education and training as well as new programmes established by initiatives such as Curriculum 2000. A range of education initiatives in the 1980s, such as the

Certificate of Pre-vocational Education (CPVE) and the TVEI, attempted to broaden the academic, subject-centred secondary and FE curricula to provide opportunities for learning and achievement for the many curricula excluded. Out of these initiatives grew the GNVQ, but agreement on the nature and relationship of the general and vocational elements of post-14 education is far from being reached (for a detailed treatment of 'vocationalism', see Chapter 1). However, such a broadening of the curriculum required assessment that was more flexible and equipped to measure a much wider range of demonstrated ability than previously. At the same time, new approaches to the assessment of work-based training were pioneered in the succession of initiatives launched to combat the spiralling youth unemployment of the early 1980s. As these developed, they became the template for a much broader range of work-based assessment strategies as the structural changes in the economy, such as the expansion of the service sector and the contraction of manufacturing, meant that a workforce was required which was more flexible and adaptable, equipped with generic, transferable skills rather than specific skills limited to a narrow occupational role. There was also disenchantment with the capacity of existing vocational qualifications to guarantee the ability to perform occupational tasks satisfactorily at work and to offer opportunities for development and progression. The review of the National Council for Vocational Qualifications (NCVQ) led to a framework of NVQs with occupational standards set by 'industry-led bodies'.

There are four major issues at the centre of the debate about competence-based assessment. The first concerns charges that it is unable to distinguish between levels of performance. Competences cannot be graded: you are either competent at something or you are not. You can't be 'very', 'fairly' or 'just about' competent. Critics argue that motivation is therefore affected; there is simply no incentive for students to strive to do better, when a less thorough performance could be sufficient evidence to gain a 'competence'. Defenders of this approach to assessment point out that it is its avoidance of grading which is its strength; that individual achievement is related to performance criteria and underpinning knowledge rather than being compared to the achievement of other students or some absolute, unattainable standard.

The second issue concerns the extent to which competences focus on the performance or behavioural aspects of learning, rather than, say, cognitive aspects which are not so easily demonstrable publicly. While some may be happy with this focus for more obviously skill-based learning, it is argued that its application is inappropriate to professional contexts which require greater knowledge and understanding, such as nurse education, social work training, teacher education or police training. Many Post-compulsory Certificate in Education courses are now assessed using a competence-based approach. The five competences shown in Figure 6.2 are examples from one such course.

**Task 6.13: Sufficient evidence?**

In pairs, specify the evidence you think would be sufficient for the demonstration of each of the five competences shown in Figure 6.2. As a group, to what extent was the public demonstration alone considered sufficient evidence?

**Figure 6.2** Examples of competences used to assess a Post-compulsory Certificate of Education course

---

*Core competence*: demonstrate within a teaching programme practical presentation skills, flexible modes of delivery, awareness of social and cultural issues and skill in classroom management.

*Specific competences*:

- can use a variety of teaching approaches, methods and strategies appropriate to learners' needs;
- can manage a variety of learning environments to the optimum advantage of learners;
- can demonstrate a range of communication skills and techniques which meet learners' needs (including non-verbal);
- can demonstrate and create positive attitudes towards equal opportunities in a variety of learning situations;
- can demonstrate an awareness of stereotyping, labelling and rule-making and their significance in learning situations.

---

Even though these five competences are concerned with classroom practice and therefore appear to be performance oriented, it is likely that each needed supplementary evidence. We can observe (1) teaching approaches, methods and strategies but how do we judge if they are appropriate to learners' needs? Equally, we can observe a teacher establish and operate a rule (5), but how are we to know if they are themselves aware of the rule's significance in learning situations? The relationship between knowledge and performance has been considered in some detail (see Wolf and Black 1990), with some arguing that knowledge evidence waters down competence-based assessment, since assessing performance should equally be an assessment of any knowledge underpinning it. On the other hand, three major inquiries into post-16 qualifications have highlighted the importance of supplementing performance evidence with that from a range of other assessment strategies, particularly externally set and marked tests (Beaumont 1995; Capey 1995; Dearing 1996).

The third issue concerns the reliability of competence-based assessment. Although, on the surface, performance criteria can be spelled out in detail, assessors' interpretation of such criteria can vary. Systems of internal and external verification do, of course, help to minimize such variation but, as Wolf (1993: 17) points out:

> the [assessment] process is complex, incremental, and, above all, *judgemental*. The performance observed – directly, or in the form of artefacts – is *intrinsically* variable: one person's playing of a piano piece, one person's essay, is by definition not exactly the same as another's, and cannot be fitted mechanistically to either a written list of criteria or an exemplar.

**Task 6.14: Acceptable evidence**

If possible, this exercise should be carried out in curriculum groups, or in groups of closely allied subjects (e.g., hairdressing and health and beauty). Select a task which a student would be asked to perform as a part of their assessment. If you have a common framework such as an NVQ, agree a level at which such a task would be assessed. Now, individually, try to describe – *in your own language*, not that of a set of performance criteria, and in as much detail as possible – what you would accept as performance evidence for the successful completion of this task. Compare your accounts.

Finally, some argue that a competence-based system makes learning assessment-led. That is, for students at least, one eye is always on the competences that have yet to be awarded and the entire course of study then becomes skewed towards ticking off such competences. This can lead to extreme behaviour illustrated by the following (true) incident which occurred on a Certificate of Education course. A college student had been knocked down by a vehicle on campus and (fortunately only slightly) injured. A Certificate of Education student, a member of college staff, had, being a first-aider, attended and dealt with the incident. Arriving late for the Certificate of Education session, he explained the reason for his lateness. The tutor made a concerned inquiry about the injured student. 'He'll be OK,' was the reply. 'But what a stroke of luck! I've been waiting for something like this to come along for months to give me the evidence for that health and safety competence!'

## Evidence-based assessment in action

Example 6.1 presents assessment material relating to NVQ Beauty Therapy. Example 6.2 presents material relating to the Applied GCE in Health and Social Care (AQA 2005) and Example 6.3 presents material relating to key skills Working With Others. Familiarize yourself with this and then complete Task 6.15.

**Task 6.15**

Look through the evidence of direct observation. Describe the different aspects of the trainee's performance the assessor focuses on.

Example 6.2 is guidance on the assessment of portfolios for the Applied GCE AS and A levels in Health and Social Care. The key skills material shown in Example 6.3 is from Level 2, Working With Others. The candidate's outline plan and confirmation sheet, plan, log and witness testimony and candidate review are included.

**Task 6.16**

What are the main similarities and differences between assessment in NVQ, Applied AS and A level GCE and key skills?

Example 6.1

**Sheppey College Beauty Therapy Department**
**Temporary Record of Practical Assessment**

Assessor ..Katrina. McIntyre.............. Candidate name...Maya. Gurna.............. Unit ..BT7..............

| Date of assessment | Range | Start Time | Finish Time | Comments | Feedback given |
|---|---|---|---|---|---|
| 2.11.06 | Female. exfoliater. mask + mitts french. | 10.48. | 11.51 | Remove client jewellery. Good presentation. Checked visually and manually. Sanitised hands correctly. Removed varnish correctly. Good filing technique. Cleansed products correctly. Good communication. Explained cuticle work. good use of cuticle knife. Good use of exfoliator mask. Bardi. Good application of mask. Checked client comfort with mitts. correct timing. Home care conds roll ready. Tidy work area. Correct removal of mask + mitts. Good massage. good buffing technique. lovely french paint. | Excellent afterna. all covered. C ✓ |
| | | | | | |
| 2.11.06. | Female. Paraffin wax. ext. mani. | 2.30 | 3.00. 3.25. | Thorough consultation. Removed jewellery. Good communication. Checked client comfort. discussed filing shape. good use of the cuticle knife. tested generously. Checked client comfort. lovely application of paraffin wax. tidy work area. good removal of paraffin wax. lovely massage technique. | Futher treatment have care advisi. Excellent aftercare C ✓ |
| 9.11.06 | male. whole hand mani. | 1.12. | 1.50. | Removed jewellery. Good communication. Sanitised hands correctly. Sanitised correctly. discussed nail shape. Sanitised emery board. good use of cuticle knife. checked client comfort. lovely massage. thorough technique. good buffing technique. natural squeaky nails. | Home care CU. |

Sheppey College Beauty Therapy Department
Temporary Record of Practical Assessment

Assessor ...Katrine McIntyre............... Candidate name ...Maria Gwin............... Unit ...BT8...............

| Date of assessment | Range | Start Time | Finish Time | Comments | Feedback given |
|---|---|---|---|---|---|
| 16.11.06 | Basic manicure Dept. BT5 | | | lovely painting. | |
| 16.11.06 | General pedicure Dept. massage | 12.00. | 1.50 | Sanitised toes. Checked feet for contra-indications. minimal filing needed. decanted products correctly. good use of cuticle knife. chest. prepared correctly. Sanitised rasp. Correct removal of hard skin. Wrapped feet not working on. lovely massage technique. good buffing. Finished good speed and rhythm. Supported toes correctly. Checked client comfort. | thorough aftercare. all covered. ✓ |
| | | | | | |
| 16.11.06 | Remove existing polish, shape, buff, oral treatment, massage, polish | 2.20. | 3.23. | Sanitised. Checked for contra-indications. Discussed nail shape. Good communication. moved trolley to correct position. Client checked comfort. good use of whole knife. good removal with rasp. good application of mask. Corner things. lovely massage. good buffing. | homecare Contra-action advice. Return when. 4 wk. ✓ |
| | | | | | Checked client comfort at all times around small toe. good painting. |

## Example 6.2  AQA Advanced Subsidiary and A-Level Teachers' Guide – Health and Social Care

| 5 | | *Portfolio Assessment* |
|---|---|---|
| 5.1 | Good portfolio work | To produce good portfolio work, students should be encouraged to provide clear, accurate evidence, which demonstrates their understanding. |
| | | The work should be focussed on the requirements of the unit and should not include appendices and/or additional material. |
| | | The form of evidence, i.e. questionnaire/report, should be as indicated in the 'How you will be assessed' section of the unit. |
| | | The content of the evidence should also be restricted to that detailed in the unit. In this way students should be able to produce concise portfolios. |
| | | There should be a clear structure to the work, with a logical approach and avoidance of repetition. |
| 5.2 | Quality of written communication | The quality of written communication is important, especially relating to the Research and Analysis and Evaluation sections of the assessment criteria and, as such, students should be encouraged to: |
| | | • use a style appropriate to the topic<br>• use specialist terminology, where appropriate<br>• use written communication adequately to convey meaning<br>• use written communication to facilitate the use of reasons/ explanations and/or analysis. |
| 5.3 | References | Students should also be encouraged to include references, where appropriate, in the body of the evidence. Detail should be sufficient to refer back to the source of the information and to acknowledge that source, e.g. page of text/web page, author, publisher, date etc. The inclusion of large sections of unreferenced (plagiarised) material should be strongly discouraged; it is not a sensible use of time/effort and will not gain any marks. |
| 5.4 | Group work | While students may work in groups to facilitate learning, all evidence submitted must be authentic and individual. Where help/advice is given by the teacher, this should be taken into account when assessing the work. Teachers should acknowledge that the 'What do I do next?' query from the weaker student constitutes a greater degree of assistance compared with the 'I'm thinking of doing this' approach, where the more able student seeks reassurance for individual ideas. |
| 5.5 | Referring back | Students should be discouraged from repeatedly submitting their work to teachers for assessment/advice and having it referred back with comments. Teachers should receive the work, refer back once, if necessary, with appropriate advice, then receive the completed work as a final submission. |

| 5.6 | Confidentiality | Students should maintain confidentiality of clients and other individuals throughout their portfolios. Witness statements should not be included in any of the portfolio units. Forms of evidence other than written should also be discouraged, as they produce many problems both for teacher assessment and subsequent moderation, not least of which is the provenance, validity and reliability of the evidence. |
| 5.7 | Assignments | Teachers should not find it necessary to provide assessment assignments for any portfolio unit, but may choose to do so as part of the learning/teaching of the subject content. A danger of using assignments is that the focus of the unit requirement/ details may be lost when rewriting/contextualising the work, and teachers are advised, therefore, to work from the specification itself. |
| 5.8 | Time allocation | Each unit should be allocated 60 hours of guided learning and as a general rule should be split into 30 hours for learning and teaching and 30 hours for producing assessment evidence. The nature of each individual unit will help determine whether or not all the 'What you need to know, understand and be able to demonstrate' should be completed prior to beginning the assessment evidence, e.g. in Unit 3, having covered the Concepts of Health and Ill Health and the Factors Affecting Health and Well-Being sections, it may be appropriate to construct the questionnaire at that point. The Immunisation against Disease section could then be covered and the report produced, before completing the work on the Value of Screening and its report. |
| 5.9 | Assessing the portfolios | Using the mark bands |

The portfolio assessment criteria use levels of response. Four bands of marks are available for each of the four assessment objectives. Completed portfolios should be marked holistically, i.e. the entire body of evidence should be taken into account when making decisions on the marks to be awarded for the individual assessment objectives.

The marking criteria should be applied top-down, i.e. for each assessment objective, work should be compared with the criteria in the top band of marks. If no suitable match in that band can be found, then the same work should be compared with the next band of marks down and so on until an appropriate mark band is found.

Assessors should then select a mark within the band identified from the range provided.

For example, AS unit HC02 AO3, if the second from the top mark band is selected, a mark between 9 and 12 can be used. The mark selected within this band will depend on the degree to which the evidence exemplifies the mark band's descriptors.

The total mark for a unit is calculated by adding up the individual marks awarded for each assessment objective.

*(continued overleaf)*

**Example 6.2** (*continued*)

| 5 | Portfolio Assessment |
|---|---|

For example, AS unit HC02:

| Objective | AO1 | AO2 | AO3 | AO4 | Total |
|---|---|---|---|---|---|
| Mark band | 3 | 2 | 2 | 2 | |
| Mark | 11 | 9 | 6 | 5 | **31** |

This candidate achieved a mark of 31 out of a possible 80. The level of performance was just above average for AO1, but lower for AO2, AO3 and AO4.

If an Assessment Objective consists of more than one strand and not all strands within a particular mark band have been met in full, then clearly a mark at the lower end of that mark range is more appropriate than awarding full marks.

When assessing the work, teachers are advised to read through the work in order to consider a rank order within the student group based on Knowledge, Understanding and Skills (Assessment Objective 1) and the Application of Knowledge, Understanding and Skills (Assessment Objective 2).

It is advisable to do this with a maximum of 3–5 portfolios at a time, deliberately selecting those at the top, middle and lower levels of achievement. The whole group should then be ranked against these two sets of criteria.

The rank order may then be adjusted when assessing the criteria for Research and Analysis and Evaluation (taking into account assistance the teacher has provided and the quality of written communication).

Once the final rank order is established, students' work may be 'moved' on to the grids using benchmark exemplar portfolios for guidance and marks awarded appropriately. In this way, students may arrive at the same/similar mark, but in a variety of ways.

Example 6.3

# WORKING WITH OTHERS LEVEL 2 – CANDIDATE PLAN, LOG AND WITNESS TESTIMONY (OTHER EXAMPLE)

Candidate _ Gina Hale _____     Supervisor _ ALISON ABRAHAM _

| List all the things that I have to do to get the job done | Person/people I will be working with on this task | When do we plan to start and finish? | Venue, resources, who to ask for support/advice | Health and Safety points | Supervisor's comments (on how the candidate met their responsibilities, worked safely, worked with others and checked progress) |
|---|---|---|---|---|---|
| Took notes during study of content, checked/wrote up bullet point on flip chart paper for presentation and prepared OHTs | Risk Assessment team members / consulted team on layout of flip chart | Monday 19.3.07 / Monday 26.3.07 | College Crèche, tutor Alison Abraham / use of Powerpoint, Photocopier | Research on child behaviour and College safety policy in conjunction with risk Assessment | Gina worked well with others in inform in in time making sure. She was Creative to her planning and structure of presentation. |
| was responsible for section of presentation | Planned structure of presentation with team members | Monday 26.3.07 | team members | use of equipment check for trailing wires | |

Assessor's feedback _____

SUPERVISOR _A. Abraham_   ASSESSOR _____   CANDIDATE _Gina Hale_
DATE _23.4.2007_   DATE _____   DATE _23.4.07_

# WORKING WITH OTHERS LEVEL 2 – CANDIDATE REVIEW

Candidate _____    Supervisor *Alison Abrahams*

| | |
|---|---|
| What went well in working with others on this job | i thought our presentation was very clear and each part of it followed on from the section before. |
| What did you do to help achieve things together? | We planned the presentation carefully, each person being responsible for a different aspect of the risk assessment. |
| What difficulties were there in working with others on this job? | We didn't sit down and plan the project thoroughly before we carried it out and so some of us were carrying out the same tasks which was a waste of effort. |
| What feedback did you get from the other people involved on how effectively you worked with others? | The group members appreciated my suggestion that we each presented a different section and that I put the powerpoint together. |
| What ways of improving your work with others did you agree with the other people involved? | We all agreed that more thorough planning before taking action would have improved the project |

**Supervisor's comments**
On how the candidate responded to
The feedback provided, if not included
above)

Gina demonstrated real leadership skills and proved to be very effective at enabling the group to solve problems

**Supervisor's signature**

A. Abrahams        Date  23.4.2007.

SUPERVISOR _____    CANDIDATE  Gina Hale

DATE _____    DATE  23.4.07

**Task 6.17**

From the limited information available to you, how far does each piece of assessment answer criticisms of competence-based assessment that it:

- fails to distinguish levels of performance;
- focuses on performance/behaviour;
- can be unreliable;
- can be assessment-led?

It is likely that the professional skills required by teachers new to competence-based assessment are in two areas: first in devising and using strategies which produce the appropriate evidence to indicate competence and second in judging whether such evidence is acceptable.

**Task 6.18: Devising assessment**

In the same curriculum groups as Task 6.14, specify between two and five performance criteria.

Now devise the strategies you would use which together could generate sufficient evidence to indicate competence with relation to all your criteria.

Some of the questions which frequently arise with regard to devising competence-based assessment and judging the acceptability of evidence are as follows:

- Are witness statements acceptable alone as third-party evidence or do they always need further verification?
- Should self-assessment be corroborated by supplementary evidence?
- How many times and in how many contexts should a skill be performed to establish a competence, bearing in mind that range statements and evidence indicators offered as guidance often specify content alone?
- How far is jointly authored/produced work acceptable as evidence?
- For how many competences can any one piece of evidence be acceptable?
- To what extent is a demonstration of competence dependent on the assessor's skill rather than the candidate's ability (in, say, a carefully managed review of progress)?

**Task 6.19**

How important were any of the above issues when you undertook Task 6.18? Were there any further issues which arose for your group?

## 6.6  Assessment for learning

In their work with teachers, Paul Black, Dylan Wiliam and their colleagues (Black and Wiliam 1998; Black, et al. 2002) found that:

> An assessment activity can help learning if it provides information to be used as feedback, by teachers, and by their pupils, in assessing themselves and each other, to modify the teaching and learning activities in which they are engaged. Such assessment becomes 'formative assessment' when the evidence is actually used to adapt the teaching work to meet learning needs.

Their findings detail best practice of assessment for learning under four headings: questioning, feedback through marking, peer- and self-assessment and the formative use of summative tests.

### Questioning

'Research has shown', say Black et al., 'that many [teachers] leave less than one second after asking a question before, if no answer is forthcoming, asking another question, or answer their own question' (Rowe 1974, in Black et al. 2002: 5).

---

**Task 6.20**

In pairs, review one another's questioning practice. Consider the following points:
- Are you too hasty in asking a second question or answering the first yourself if no answer is forthcoming?
- For what purposes do you use questioning – to test learning and knowledge, to deepen understanding, to stimulate thinking and ideas, to establish a logical chain of thinking?
- Do you use mainly closed or open questions, those factual in nature, inviting one-word responses, with one right answer, or those wider in nature, capable of being answered in a variety of ways?
- Do you consider a number of student responses?
- Do you target and distribute questions or concentrate on students whom you know will give a (positive) response?

---

### Feedback through marking

Black and colleagues (2002: 9) summarize the main ideas for improving written feedback to students as follows:

- Written tasks, alongside oral questioning, should encourage pupils to develop and show understanding of the key features of what they have learnt
- Comments should identify what has been done well and what still needs improvement, and should give guidance on how to make that improvement

- Opportunities for pupils to follow up comments should be planned as part of the overall learning process

---

**Task 6.21**

The following written comments were made by different tutors as feedback on a GNVQ leisure and tourism assignment. In pairs, consider which you think comprise effective feedback and which less effective?

'The assignment asks you to analyse/explain points but you have simply presented information.'

'You could have considered the following aspects of the company's operation – customer profiles, advertising, market research. Please write a paragraph on each and resubmit.'

'You need to work at your spelling, the grammatical structure of your sentences and your punctuation.'

'Although you have included sufficient information from your sources, your presentation of it is unclear and confused.'

'Read through the assignment and write down the following, indicating how they should be used and what they mean:
- Their, there, they're;
- Its, it's;
- Here, hear.'

'The following words were used in your assignment. Check in a dictionary whether you spelt them correctly: promosional, commercial, destination, inconsistent, somone, amenitys, consessionary.'

'You might want to try grouping your information in categories such as train routes, then fare structure, employees, marketing approaches.'

'Your account needs to be far more detailed than it is.'

'Pick out the following key points you present in the assignment and write down what the reasons for them are: the London–Manchester and London–Birmingham routes are the most popular; the company needs to reconsider its public image; there has been an overall loss from rail to bus and air services.'

'A good piece of work B+'

---

**Task 6.22**

In pairs, swap four or five pieces of work you have recently marked. Assess your partner's feedback in each case. How effective was it? In cases where it might be improved, what could be amended or added?

## Peer and self-assessment

Black et al. make a strong case for this and feel classroom practice could be improved through:

- [making transparent] the criteria for evaluating learning achievements – to pupils to enable them to have a clear overview both of the aims of their work and of what it means to complete it successfully
- Pupils should be taught the habits and skills of collaboration in peer assessment
- Pupils should be encouraged to keep in mind the aims of their work and to assess their own progress to meet these aims as they proceed.

(2002: 12)

### Task 6.23

Task 6.22 was an example of peer assessment carried out by you and your partner. Reconsider your assessment of each other's feedback with the following points in mind:
- What were the criteria used for judging effective feedback?
- What advantages were there in peer assessment over assessment of your feedback by your tutor?

## Formative use of summative tests

Black et al. consider that a creative and active approach to summative test revision can help students learn more effectively. Techniques here include students being 'asked to "traffic light" a list of key words or topics', flagging as green, amber or red, according to whether they have 'good, partial or little understanding'. Peer marking of tests is also recommended as is students generating and then answering their own questions.

### Task 6.24

The following revision techniques have been used by teachers and students. Which of these have you used with your students and which do you know they use themselves? In pairs, share your experience and the effectiveness or otherwise of the techniques you have used. Which have led to the most effective student learning and why?
- students testing each other;
- mind maps/spider diagrams;
- colour coding/highlighting points;
- timed answers to past paper questions;
- summarizing key points;

- explaining work to someone who knows little about it, e.g., parent/friend;
- audio-taping key points;
- students setting own questions;
- use of revision guides/notes;
- putting notes onto postcards;
- others . . .?

## 6.7 Reviewing, recording and reporting achievement

The development of new courses involving a wider range of teaching and learning strategies is requiring teachers to be involved in much more complex assessment procedures. Typically, assessors are often now required, among other things, to:

- negotiate an assessment plan;
- discuss this plan;
- allow the candidate to express views/participate;
- document the process of evidence collection;
- give feedback which is specific, constructive and supportive;
- use questions which are open, clear and justifiable, not leading, probing or searching.

There is recognition here that assessment is more than an isolated judgement of a specific performance; that it should be integrated into a system of reviewing, recording and reporting achievement which teacher and student are at the centre of.

### Task 6.25

6.25(a)   Working in pairs, choose a recent piece of assessable coursework each of you has completed. With one of you as the student and the other as the tutor, assess the work and record your interaction involving all the skills listed above. Then swap roles and repeat the exercise.

6.25(b)   Which stage of the process proved the most difficult?

Many teachers find giving feedback the most problematic area of reviewing learning. This could be for a number of reasons: the tutor has the difficult task of bringing together a range of evidence of performance which she or he may not have assessed themself; balancing feedback which is constructive and supportive but at the same time an accurate reflection of achievement is far from straightforward; negotiation assumes equality between participants when, in truth, the trainer rather than the candidate is finally empowered to make a decision about the acceptability of evidence. Francis and Young (1979), and others, have specified features which tend to characterize the giving of effective feedback. Good feedback is:

- clear and direct, whereby the reasons for assessment decisions are fully explained in language which is direct and unambiguous rather than vague or beating about the bush;

- constructive, because it is important to offer advice for further action which is in the student's capacity to take;

- descriptive of what the tutor has seen/observed/thinks rather than overevaluative or judgmental;

- helpful and supportive on the tutor's part (this attitude must be fully communicated to the student);

- well timed, being given as soon as is practicable after evidence has been demonstrated and at a time when the student is receptive to feedback;

- fully understood by the student, with the tutor making every effort to ensure this, leaving no unresolved questions, misunderstandings or confusions;

- specific, being related to particular incidents or learning events.

**Task 6.26**

How far could the features above be applied to your pair work in Task 6.25?

The recording and reporting of achievement is usually based on records or profiles which vary in structure and style. Often, an awarding body will prescribe its own format but there may be institutional, departmental or curriculum area profile reports which are related to this or are freestanding. Most are variations of the four profile formats considered below.

## The graded scale

These can take a variety of forms but their common feature is their placing of performances somewhere on a given scale. In Table 6.3 the assessor ticks a box on the continuum between one pole and another. In Table 6.4 the assessor inserts a number signifying a level of achievement for each assessment, where 1 equals good, 2 equals adequate and 3 equals poor.

**Table 6.3** Polar graded scale for communication skills

| Writes precisely, clearly with few errors | | | | | | Expression is vague, difficult to understand with frequent errors |
|---|---|---|---|---|---|---|
| Written accounts are comprehensive and coherent, etc. | | | | | | Written accounts are brief and bitty, etc. |

**Table 6.4** Numerical graded scale for communication skills

|  | 1st assessment | 2nd assessment | 3rd assessment | 4th assessment | 5th assessment |
|---|---|---|---|---|---|
| Precision and clarity in writing |  |  |  |  |  |
| Comprehensiveness of written accounts |  |  |  |  |  |
| Etc. |  |  |  |  |  |

The strengths of the graded scale are:

- it is visually straightforward and easy to read;
- it can indicate progress when used formatively;
- it refers to specific skills/abilities.

Weaknesses include:

- the difficulty of representing precisely two ends of a real continuum by the descriptors at each pole;
- the absence of any criteria which might help the learner understand the basis of grading;
- a tendency to use ipsative referencing in the absence of assessment criteria.

## Grid profiles

Grid profiles share a visual simplicity with graded scales but attempt to relate performance to assessment criteria, as shown in Table 6.5.

**Table 6.5** Grid profile for communication skills

| Written communications | Can express and reply to simple information | Can express and reply to simple information in a variety of contexts | Can express and reply to complex information | ✔ Can express and reply to complex information in a variety of contexts |
|---|---|---|---|---|
| Oral communications |  |  |  |  |

The advantages of grid profiles are:

- they are quick to complete;
- they specify what a student can do;
- they can be used formatively to plot development.

Disadvantages are:

- the descriptors may not do justice to learner achievement (a student who is outstanding at handling inquiries in reception might nevertheless have a tick only in the first box);
- grids are not tailored to individual students.

## Open portrayals

This is essentially a blank sheet of paper on which an assessor is free to write what he or she chooses to. In practice, some are more open than others. The NVQ comments in Example 6.1 on page 156, although representing an open portrayal are closely related to a particular piece of work. A summative report at the end of a college year or course may offer a much wider portrayal.

The strengths of open portrayals are:

- they are highly dedicated to individual students;
- they are informative;
- they are comprehensive.

Weaknesses include:

- tutors have a habit of wanting to fill blank space if it exists;
- they can be unstructured;
- they can be time consuming both to write and to read.

## Criterion-referenced competence statements

This is an approach now widely adopted in PCE. The strengths of an approach using such statements are:

- they are positive, framed in 'can do' terms;
- they lend themselves to negotiation and the reviewing of learning;
- they are related to learning/performance evidence.

Weaknesses include:

- relating evidence to competences can be complex and time consuming;
- there is no opportunity for levels of achievement to be acknowledged;
- learning outside the scope of particular competences is not credited.

Many teachers working in PCE express two major anxieties about assessing their students: first, they are concerned about the increasing prominence of assessment and the time devoted to it often at the expense, they feel, of student learning; second, they worry that much assessment they are required to carry out does not do justice to the richness of the learning experience they know their students have undergone. We hope this chapter has helped them to reflect on these matters and deal with them more effectively in practice.

## Individual learning plans

The use of individual learning plans has become widespread across the sector in recognition that the more involved learners are in monitoring their own progress, the more effective it is going to be.

### Task 6.27

Consider the ILP in Example 6.4 below and the record of tutorial meeting in Example 6.5. How do you think those who devised these expected them to be used? What features of learning and development does the ILP presuppose?

**Example 6.4** Sample ILP

## STUDENT INDIVIDUAL LEARNING PLAN

Your Individual Learning Plan is a running record of action agreed between you and your personal tutor. Ownership of the plan is yours, but it will be of most use to you if you discuss and agree it with your course or personal tutor.

Use of an individual learning plan is designed to help you:
- Plan the way forward rather than leaving things to chance
- Recognise your range of options
- Show others that you have a plan so that they can help you achieve it
- Record the advice and guidance you have received
- Make the right career decisions
- Set targets to reach your goals

This plan summarises your current position and identifies the goals you are aiming at; you will use it at your individual tutorial meetings when you will review your progress, agree actions and amend or confirm your goals.

| NAME: | COURSE | YEAR |
|---|---|---|
| *Georgina Hale* | *Diploma in Childcare Level 3* | *2006-7* |

| TUTOR: |
|---|
| *Alison Abrahams* |

| FUNDING/WELFARE ADVICE IN PLACE? | STUDENT UNION CARD/LIBRARY ACCESS IN PLACE? |
|---|---|
| (YES)          NO | (YES)          NO |

**SECTION 1: WHERE AM I NOW?**

EXISTING QUALIFICATIONS
List the qualifications you have gained so far

GCSE: English C    Health and Social Care CC
      Maths C      Sociology B
      Science C    ICT        C
                   First Aid certificate

PREVIOUS EXPERIENCE

A - list your previous and current experience of work (including voluntary work)

Summer work in children's holiday club
working at stables for friend's mum
Work experience in a primary school

B – list any training that you have undertaken (excluding those leading to a qualification)

First Aid

C – list your outside interests and activities

Horses
Going to the cinema

D – What was the result of your initial assessment at college?

Literacy level 2, Maths Level 2

E – Have you got an up to date National Record of Achievement?

yes

**Section 2: WHERE AM I GOING?**

QUALIFICATION AIMS
A – programme of study (list all subjects/modules to be gained including key skills)
1. Working with babies & young children
2. The developing child
3. Health & Community care
4. Play & Early Learning
5. Working with Others Level 2
6. Improving Own Learning & Performance Level 2

B – list any work experience you hope to gain while at college

Experience of working in a nursery

C – List anything that might affect your ability to achieve (eg job domestic issues)

Saturday job in department store

**Section 3: WHERE DO I WANT TO BE IN 5 YEARS TIME**

I do not know yet whether I want to go straight into employment working with children or go on to university to study a child and health related course or become a primary school teacher.

**Section 4: WHAT DO I HAVE TO DO?**

ACTION AGREED – between yourself and your tutor. These will indicate how you will achieve the targets you have set

ACTION TO BE COMPLETED BY STUDENT
1. full attendance and arrive for all sessions on time
2. bring all necessary equipment to classes
3. hand in work on time
4. show respect to others at all times
5. participate in sessions and complete necessary homework, reading etc
6. contact the college if unable to attend

ACTION TO BE COMPLETED BY TUTOR
1. arrange regular tutorials
2. monitor the learning and progress and give useful suggestions on how student can improve
3. set targets for the student to support them to achieve their qualifications with the best possible grade

**If you do not complete these actions you will find you have been placed on Academic Performance Review (please see your college diary). Meeting the actions agreed here are essential to making progress on your course**

| SIGNATURE OF STUDENT: Gina Hale | DATE: 22nd September 2006 |
| --- | --- |
| SIGNATURE OF TUTOR: A. Abrahams | DATE: 22.9.2006 |

## Example 6.5

### RECORD OF TUTORIAL MEETING

Student Name _GINA HALE_    Date of Meeting _Friday 30th March 2007_

| WORK OUTSTANDING | EVIDENCE OF WORK COMPLETED OR GRADED |
|---|---|
| None | Gina has completed work at a high standard throughout the year. |

ATTITUDE TO LEARNING
_Good_

ATTENDANCE _3 day's absence_    PUNCTUALITY _Excellent_

WELFARE FINANCIAL SUPPORT IN PLACE?    STUDENT UNION/LIBRARY ACCESS IN PLACE?
_N/A_    _Yes._

---

PROGRESS SINCE THE LAST MEETING – How have you performed against the previous actions set?

Gina has missed some assignment deadlines and needs to work harder at planning and organising her assignments.

---

NEW LEARNING TARGETS SET (these should include targets for grades)

1. Improve planning + organising of assignment work

2. Finalise arrangements for last work experience placement

3. Revise for Play + Early Learning test next term.

POINTS RAISED BY THE STUDENT

Gina feels she needs more detailed
advice and guidance about routes
into child care work and applying
to university.

ACTION AGREED AGAINST TARGETS – between yourself and your tutor. These should
indicate how you will achieve the targets you have set.

Action to be completed by the student

1. Improve planning + organisation of time
2. Complete own research on childrelated courses an university
3. Ensure contact made with placement organisation

Action to be completed by the tutor

1. Refer to college advice + guidance
2. Discuss planning skills
3. Monitor through tutorials + reviews.

DATE OF THE NEXT MEETING

Fri 20.4.2007

Student
Signature _____

Tutor
Signature _____ Alison Abrahams

## Related new professional standards for teachers and trainers in the lifelong learning sector

### Domain E: assessment for learning

| PROFESSIONAL KNOWLEDGE AND UNDERSTANDING | PROFESSIONAL PRACTICE |
| --- | --- |
| *Teachers in the lifelong learning sector know and understand:* | *Teachers in the lifelong learning sector:* |
| EK 1.1 Theories and principles of assessment and the application of different forms of assessment, including initial, formative and summative assessment in teaching and learning. | EP 1.1 Use appropriate forms of assessment and evaluate their effectiveness in producing information useful to the teacher and the learner. |
| EK 1.2 Ways to devise, select, use and appraise assessment tools, including, where appropriate, those which exploit new and emerging technologies. | EP 1.2 Devise, select, use and appraise assessment tools, including where appropriate, those which exploit new and emerging technologies. |
| EK 1.3 Ways to develop, establish and promote peer- and self-assessment. | EP 1.3 Develop, establish and promote peer- and self-assessment as a tool for learning and progression. |
| EK 2.1 Issues of equality and diversity in assessment. | EP 2.1 Apply appropriate methods of assessment fairly and effectively. |
| EK 2.2 Concepts of validity, reliability and sufficiency in assessment. | EP 2.2 Apply appropriate assessment methods to produce valid, reliable and sufficient evidence. |
| EK 2.3 The principles of assessment design in relation to own specialist area. | EP 2.3 Design appropriate assessment activities for own specialist area. |
| EK 2.4 How to work as part of a team to establish equitable assessment processes. | EP 2.4 Collaborate with others, as appropriate, to promote equity and consistency in assessment processes. |
| EK 3.1 Ways to establish learner involvement in and personal responsibility for assessment of their learning. | EP 3.1 Ensure that learners understand, are involved and share in responsibility for assessment of their learning. |
| EK 3.2 Ways to ensure access to assessment within a learning programme. | EP 3.2 Ensure that access to assessment is appropriate to learner need. |
| EK 4.1 The role of feedback and questioning in assessment for learning. | EP 4.1 Use assessment information to promote learning through questioning and constructive feedback, and involve learners in feedback activities. |

EK 4.2  The role of feedback in effective evaluation and improvement of own assessment skills.

EP 4.2  Use feedback to evaluate and improve own skills in assessment.

EK 5.1  The role of assessment and associated organizational procedures in relation to the quality cycle.

EP 5.1  Contribute to the organization's quality cycle by producing accurate and standardized assessment information, and keeping appropriate records of assessment decisions and learners' progress.

EK 5.2  The assessment requirements of individual learning programmes and procedures for conducting and recording internal and/or external assessments.

EP 5.2  Conduct and record assessments which adhere to the particular requirements of individual learning programmes and, where appropriate, external bodies.

EK 5.3  The necessary/appropriate assessment information to communicate to others who have a legitimate interest in learner achievement.

EP 5.3  Communicate relevant assessment information to those with a legitimate interest in learner achievement, as necessary/appropriate.

# 7

# Exploring the curriculum

## 7.1 What is Chapter 7 about?

Why do our courses look the way they do? How have they developed over time to become the courses they are today? Can we understand our courses better in order to help improve the quality of our students' learning?

For many of us, working as busy teachers and trainers in a variety of organizations, scheduled to work with the maximum number of students in the minimum amount of time, the 'curriculum' is all too often simply whatever course we happen to be teaching at the time! This chapter provides an opportunity to pause and consider just what our courses are really about. Remember, unless we really know the answer to this question, that is, understand what it is we are meant to be doing and why, how can we be sure that what we are doing is the best for our students?

In order to understand how the chapter is organized, compare a course to a building. Consider what needs to be done before starting to build a new building or prior to adding an extension to an existing building. Sections 7.2, 7.3, 7.4 and 7.5 will pose some fundamental questions about the nature and organization of our courses in order to expose their foundations, rather as structural surveys and groundworks expose the fundamental state of the ground and dictate the foundations required to build a new structure or an extension.

Section 7.6 is the tea break, giving you some time to stop and consider your position in the light of all this new information before moving on to Chapter 8 which will help you to design, build and evaluate your new or revised course.

## 7.2 What is the curriculum?

---

**KEY ISSUES**

What is the curriculum and who dictates it?

Why is it continually changing?

Should it be continually changing?

---

As professionals working in the post-compulsory sector, we teach and train through many different courses covering a huge variety of subject matter and areas of skill development. However, one thing we have in common is that we all have some kind of curriculum through which we aim to help our students to learn.

**Task 7.1: What is this notion of curriculum all about?**

Drawing on your own experience and subject expertise, take a moment to think and then jot down a sentence explaining your own definition of 'curriculum'. Figure 7.1 shows some writers', teachers' and trainers' responses to this question.

**Task 7.2: Comparing definitions**

7.2(a)   Which, if any, of the definitions presented in Figure 7.1 fits most closely with your own ideas?

7.2(b)   What are the key differences and similarities when compared to your definition?

**Figure 7.1** Some definitions of 'curriculum'

1   The curriculum is what happens to students because of what teachers/ trainers do.

2   The curriculum is a formal course of study as at a college, university or training institution.

3   The curriculum is a teacher's or trainer's intention or educational plan.

4   The curriculum is a group of subjects and/ or skills which make up a programme of study.

5   The curriculum is a formal, timetabled programme of lessons.

6   The curriculum is everything that happens to students at a college, university or training organization.

7   The curriculum is an attempt to communicate the essential principles and features of an educational proposal.

8   The curriculum describes the results of instruction.

9   The curriculum lays down what's to be covered and to some extent the teaching and learning methods to be used.

10   The curriculum is the organization's plan to guide learning towards pre specified learning outcomes.

11   The curriculum is a structured series of intended learning outcomes.

12   The curriculum consists of every learning experience planned and provided by the organization to help pupils attain learning outcomes.

13   The curriculum is the public form of attempting to put an educational idea into practice.

14   The curriculum is a menu presented to students for consumption.

Figure 7.1 presents a diverse set of definitions, but here is one view of the key similarities and differences. See how it compares with your responses to Task 7.2.

Definitions 1 and 3 emphasize teacher and trainer planning while 10 mentions planning across an organization. Definitions 2, 5 and 12 also have an institutional emphasis but 4 is the only one which explicitly mentions subjects and skills although these must be implicit in many of the others. Definitions 6 and 12 provide an interesting contrast in that 12 only mentions the planned curriculum whereas 6 includes the totality of a student's experience at an institution, the planned and the unplanned, recalling the notion of a hidden curriculum (Jackson 1968). Definitions 8, 10, 11 and 12 are similar in that all make particular mention of learning outcomes. Definition 9 alone seems to hint at ideas of curriculum content and process and 14 is unique in presenting learners as explicitly passive consumers of the curriculum. Finally, both 7 and 13 mention the notion of the curriculum as conveying a particular vision of learning while 13 emphasizes the public nature of a curriculum once it is in place.

From this, it's possible to identify what seem to be some key issues to consider in any definition of curriculum and these are shown in Figure 7.2.

**Figure 7.2** Some key issues in defining 'curriculum'

---

- Evidence of planning (on a variety of scales) for student learning;
- statements of what's to be learned;
- indications of how it's to be learned;
- pointers as to the outcomes of this learning;
- statements on the role of learners in all this;
- explanations about the vision behind the curriculum;
- some dissemination or publication showing the public nature of the formal curriculum.

---

This section has begun to expose and consider our own ideas about curriculum. What does some of the literature on curriculum tell us? Goodson (1994) makes the interesting point that, while curriculum development and implementation have been written about by many people, the more fundamental issues of curriculum definition, who constructs it, why and for whom have been more neglected. However, one writer who did address these questions was Stenhouse (1975), who starts by quoting the *Shorter Oxford English Dictionary* which defines curriculum as 'a course: especially a regular course of study as at a school or university'. Thus, curriculum may be viewed as the planned intentions of Government and of teachers/trainers in their organizations. These plans often take the form of a public, written prescription detailing intended learning outcomes and Stenhouse goes on to mention that in many countries the curriculum is a state-controlled, legal requirement. For many of us, this resembles the national curriculum, GCSE, BTEC, AS and A2 level specifications, NVQ specifications for vocational qualifications and the police and nurse training programmes, all of which can be viewed as public, published documents. Indeed, Higham et al. (1996) portray the 16–19 curriculum for schools and colleges as simply comprising the courses or qualifications (academic, vocational and core/key skills) for which students are studying.

A second view of curriculum outlined by Stenhouse (1975) asks us to concentrate not just on the planned curriculum but on the reality of teaching and learning for teachers and students. Stenhouse challenges us to view the curriculum as what really happens in our classrooms and training areas. He also points out that the key reason teachers and trainers need to study the curriculum is to examine this balance between intentions and realities and use this information to improve their work and enhance students' learning.

Taylor and Richards (1985), on the other hand, have little patience with any of the broader definitions of curriculum which try to include all the planned experiences, not just the formal things to be learned. They see these as the context within which the curriculum operates and which can affect the curriculum:

> '. . . the course of study to be followed in becoming educated' is in fact the oldest known meaning of the word [curriculum]. In contemporary writings, however, the phrase is frequently translated into 'the subjects to be studied' or 'the educational experiences to be provided' and not infrequently into 'the actual subject matter to be covered'.
>
> (Taylor and Richards 1985: 3)

Taylor and Richards argue that each of these definitions has its uses depending primarily on the context to which it is applied. Thus, an Early Years curriculum might be better viewed as educational experiences such as the sand tray; a school curriculum might consist largely of subjects, whereas in PCET the curriculum is more closely associated with courses of study. The key issue, they say, is to choose whichever definition seems most appropriate and use this consistently and accurately.

So, bearing in mind Goodson's (1994) cautionary note, both Stenhouse (1975) and Taylor and Richards (1985) present notions of curriculum as public plans (often written) about what is to be learned, increasingly described as 'learning outcomes', and this is reflected by Higham et al.'s (1996) more recent contribution. However, Stenhouse adds a further idea, that of curriculum as the reality of learning for teacher and student. Whatever definition we choose to use, Taylor and Richards emphasize the need to be consistent and accurate in our use of the term 'curriculum'.

### Task 7.3: Do you agree?

Set your original definition of curriculum against those above. Where do you stand now? Why do you believe this?

Having arrived at a working notion of curriculum, ask yourself a question. How much curriculum change has taken place in the last few years? The answer, of course, is that a tremendous amount has altered.

### Task 7.4: Curriculum change in your work

In your own specialist area, note down the key changes you know about that have taken place in recent years. Include both the large-scale changes, often imposed by others, and the smaller-scale changes you, your colleagues or your organization have introduced.

Figure 7.3 presents a few examples of large-scale curriculum change. See if any of these figure in your list. These are curriculum developments on a national scale, but interestingly it is relatively easy to produce such a list without too much searching of the archives. The amount and rate of change in the last 15 years of the twentieth century was remarkable. Of course, curriculum development has always taken place on a smaller scale. No doubt you will have been able to recall instances of specific course developments in your own work and organization. All this begs two key questions. Jot down your responses to Task 7.5 before reading on.

**Figure 7.3** Examples of large-scale curriculum change

- Schools have had numerous versions of the national curriculum to contend with since 1988.
- The changes to the academic post-16 curriculum associated with Curriculum 2000 (since much discussed, e.g., Hodgson and Spours 2003; Priestley 2003) involving the introduction of AS and A2 specifications, virtually the first full review of A level since it was introduced in the early 1950s.
- The changes associated with a general vocational strand to the curriculum with GNVQs being introduced in 1992, their on-going development including the Curriculum 2000 innovation of AVCE, the subsequent ending of GNVQ, the introduction of Applied GCSE and A level, the re-appearance of BTEC and other national qualifications and the 14–19 diplomas to be introduced from 2008.
- Occupation-specific vocational qualifications are in the process of being transformed by the steady introduction of NVQs, first devised in 1988 and revised throughout the late 1990s.
- National police training was completely revised in the mid-1980s, further change took place in the late 1990s and is on-going with the 2005 introduction of the Initial Police Learning & Development Programme (IPLDP).
- Nurse training was radically altered in the late 1980s with Project 2000 and developments in both this and associated areas of medical training have continued ever since, not least since the publication of *Making a Difference* (DoH 1999).

**Task 7.5: What do you think?**

7.5(a)    Just why does the curriculum change?

7.5(b)    Should it be continually developing?

At this point, many teachers and trainers might well be tempted to mutter something about the Government (or whichever agency is in overall charge of their area of work) never seeming to provide enough time or resources to do a proper job; never allowing enough time for any change to settle down before introducing yet more alterations; and, perhaps, never really seeming to know what they really do want! In particular instances, this may well be true. Indeed, some writers such as Ahier and Ross (1995) talk about curriculum being the result of a creative tension. Think of the haggling you can see taking place in many market-places abroad when you're on holiday. Seller and prospective buyer engage in a process of bargaining (arguing, debating, sometimes almost coming to blows!) until, if it works out, a compromise is reached. Each is out to get what they want. This is another form of creative tension and many curricula are the final outcome of argument, debate and conflict over different ideas about what should be taught and learned, how this should take place and the best means of assessing learning. Thus, all present curricula could be represented as simply the best compromise (hopefully) or the least bad compromise (more realistically) that can be achieved until new knowledge and ideas, together with evaluation data, make a revision necessary.

More cynically, the bargaining might be distorted by one of the hagglers threatening to use physical force whereupon the other calls her or his friends over to help! Thus, in this view, the curricula many of us have to deal with at present might simply be a dominant power group's position which will be replaced as soon as the balance of power shifts, with less importance being attached to the quality of education and training involved than to the political kudos attached to having produced change. The works of Ball (1987) and Goodson and Hargreaves (1996) largely on schools, and of Hyland (1994) on NVQs, all provide some fascinating insights into the politics of curriculum change but perhaps it might all be summarized by someone writing much earlier.

Taba (1962) was moved to use the term 'tinkering' when she portrayed curriculum as being the result of constant and on-going modification. Think of 'tinkering' and imagine when you have been endlessly trying to get something, often some domestic gadget or part of a car, working properly. That's the image to hold in your mind and this helps us to avoid becoming too cynical.

---

**Task 7.6: Which parts of the curriculum are you tinkering with?**

7.6(a)   Do you always teach the same thing in exactly the same way every time you teach it?

7.6(b)   Should we teach students of science, of nursing, of motor vehicle maintenance, to exactly the same curriculum, in the same ways as we did and with the same assessment methods as we had twenty, ten of even five years ago?

---

We, the writers of this book, believe that the curriculum must develop continually. All of us will sometimes hanker for a supposed golden age of education and training lost somewhere in the mists of time but it is deceptively easy to lose sight of the fact that, in every field, knowledge has progressed and the demands made on those educated and trained in that field have changed and intensified. All of this means that the curriculum must change.

However, remember your answers to Task 7.6 about your own everyday teaching and training. Most of us continually develop our teaching and training as we learn more about them over the years. The important thing is to ensure that the curriculum is changed – not to glorify an individual's or group's political position, but simply to improve the quality of student learning. To summarize, therefore, this section has begun a structural survey of the notion of curriculum by asking you to consider your notion of curriculum and to set it against those of other teachers and trainers and against ideas from the literature. It has examined some reasons for curriculum change and concluded that the key criterion of initiating such change should be the improved quality of student learning. The next section will ask you to consider the nature of your own curriculum in more detail.

## 7.3  What are the key features of our courses?

| KEY ISSUES |
| --- |
| What are the key features of our courses? |
| How does your course look in relation to others? |
| What are the key models from the literature on curriculum? |
| What can curriculum models tell us about our courses? |

This section will help us to identify, analyse and review the key characteristics of our courses in terms of purposes, what our students learn and how they learn. To help us to do this critically and rigorously, four curriculum models will be used. This section continues the structural survey of curriculum begun in Section 7.2 and prepares us for a detailed analysis later. Figure 7.4 presents some teachers' and trainers' statements about how they view the key characteristics of learning in their courses. Notice how each of these statements conveys a sense of purpose and meaning about student learning. Thus, for instance, can you see how Sarah's aims and outcomes (purposes) include students learning the biology content well enough to achieve GCSE? However, Sarah also says that her students need to begin thinking as scientists, implying that her view of GCSE biology content is to teach students not simply a set of facts, but also a process of thinking, so that they can gain a better GCSE grade and use scientific thinking in their everyday lives.

**Task 7.7: What are the key features of other people's courses?**

Choose three of the statements in Figure 7.4 and identify what the teacher/trainer says or implies about:
- the aims and outcomes (purposes) of the course;
- the content of what is being learned;
- the process of that learning.

**Figure 7.4** Teachers/trainers talking about their courses

'Our aromatherapy course is about getting students to learn skills, acquire knowledge and to work with clients in a very special way.'
*(Suzanne and Nicole)*

'My art foundation course tries to help students to assume responsibility for developing and testing their own artistic knowledge, skills and understanding and to take control of their own careers as artists.'
*(Mathew)*

'My degree courses in different science specialisms all aim to produce practical, all-round scientists who are technically very knowledgeable, but who can also operate very effectively in practical situations and who can communicate and work closely with others.'
*(Sam)*

'My IT NVQ course gets students to learn how to use a piece of software as required in their workplaces.'
*(Angie)*

'My first aid course demands students learn basic procedures by heart but that they develop their common sense when dealing with emergency situations.'
*(John)*

'My bricklaying NVQ course means students need to learn the basic techniques but also need to be able to see how these will lead to a construction . . . see the potential their skills provide.'
*(Andy)*

'In their initial training on dangerous driving, my police trainees must know their law to the letter but they must also learn how to read a situation and to deal with the public in positive ways.'
*(Bob)*

'My GCSE biologists must know the biology syllabus content really well but they must also learn about thinking like scientists.'
*(Sarah)*

---

**Task 7.8: Key features of your course**

Pause before reading on and try to summarize student learning in one of your own courses, or a part of it, in a sentence or so. Make sure you say something about the:

- purposes, often expressed as aims and outcomes;
- content;
- process of learning.

Keep your statement handy so that you can refer to it when attempting Task 7.9.

So far in this section we have concentrated on exposing the key features of other teachers' and trainers' courses and comparing them with our own. Let's test our thinking more fully by examining some of the literature on curriculum models. All these ideas can then be used to examine our own courses in more detail.

Interestingly, systematic approaches to developing the curriculum are relatively new, having first appeared in the USA in the 1940s before spreading to the UK in the 1960s. Four curriculum models appear consistently in the curriculum literature and these are summarized below.

### The product or objectives model: a focus on *behavioural targets* for learning

This model has a behaviourist learning basis (see Chapter 3) and is interested in the product of a curriculum: just what does it equip a learner to do?

It is closely associated with Ralph Tyler (1971), was one of the earliest curriculum models and has become one of the most influential. Indeed, Tanner and Tanner (1980) argue that it is the dominant model of twentieth-century thought about curriculum design. Tyler organizes his model around four fundamental questions which, he claims, must be answered when developing any curriculum (Figure 7.5).

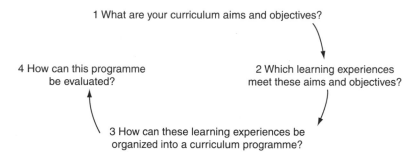

**Figure 7.5** Tyler's model (1971)

Tyler argues that each of these questions requires careful thinking including an element of needs analysis (of both students and others such as employers). Thus, aims and outcomes (the purposes of the curriculum) need to rest on the overall purposes (philosophy) of the relevant college, university or training organization, on the view of learning held by the curriculum developers and teachers/trainers, and on the subject matter itself. Once determined, these aims and outcomes must specify as clearly and unambiguously as possible what is to be learned. In turn, this will aid the selection and organization of the learning and assessment experiences and the evaluation procedures. All this, of course, links closely into the issues raised in Chapters 3, 5 and 9 of this book.

It is worth noting at this stage that Tyler concentrates on the how of curriculum-making not the what of the curriculum itself (Walker and Soltis 1997). Thus, it is possible to use his four questions to develop courses which will rest on very different notions of learning, teaching and assessment.

However, in practice, this model is widely associated with behaviourist approaches to learning and the curriculum (see Chapter 3). Behavioural objectives are devised which pre-specify measurable learning outcomes. Learning and assessment experiences are then selected and organized to meet these outcomes and evaluation takes place to establish how well the course has enabled the specified behaviours to be learned. Students play a largely passive role in all this.

Nevertheless, the Tyler model remains probably the most influential of all and its clarity and simplicity mean that it is an accessible mechanism for curriculum design and development.

## The content model: a focus on the *what* of learning

This is an approach to curriculum rooted in an instructivist view of learning (Reigeluth 1999) which is interested in the transmission of existing knowledge to new learners.

This curriculum model was developed in the 1950s and 1960s and rests on the work of, among others, Paul Hirst (1974). The emphasis is on the intellectual development of learners. Hirst believes that there are seven or eight forms of knowledge which represent the ways in which people experience and learn about the world. These are mathematics, physical science, knowledge of persons, literature and fine arts, morals, religion and philosophy. The curriculum is, therefore, designed to enable learners to develop their understanding of these areas which usually assume the form of curriculum subjects. Such a curriculum uses outcomes but of a broader kind than the purely behavioural type mentioned earlier. The prime aim of the curriculum is the transmission of wisdom – that is, knowledge already developed – often in the form of disciplines or subjects. It is this knowledge that becomes the chief factor influencing any curriculum decisions.

## The process model: a focus on the *how* of learning

This is an approach to curriculum which is interested in the processes and procedures of learning so that the learner is able to use and develop the content, not simply receive it passively. In this it can be seen to have links to what we now see as the individual constructivist (Bruner 1990), social constructivist (Daniels 1996) and situated cognitivist (Lave and Wenger 1991) views of learning.

The model was explicitly developed by Lawrence Stenhouse (1975) as a response to the product or outcomes model described earlier. The emphasis is on defining content in cognitive terms as concepts and broad-based skills and this, in turn, defines the ways (processes and procedures) through which students need to learn. There is a reliance on teachers being relatively autonomous and possessing a high degree of professional ability since they must have a thorough understanding and judgement of *the* concepts, principles and criteria inherent in their own subjects (Taylor and Richards 1985).

Thus, teachers need to define the content of their course, define what constitutes a teaching procedure acceptable in subject terms and make clear the criteria by which students' work is to be judged (Stenhouse 1975). In this way, Stenhouse sees teachers as being able to plan rationally without using (behavioural) outcomes.

## The situational model: a focus on the *cultural context* of learning

Dennis Lawton (1983) and Malcolm Skilbeck (1976) are linked to this approach which emphasizes the context in which the curriculum exists. This approach to curriculum seems now to echo some of the situated cognitivist (Lave and Wenger 1991) view of learning mentioned above.

In short, Lawton sees education as being about the transmission of the key elements of a society's culture to the new generation. His work sees culture as existing in eight subsystems such as economic, technological and aesthetic. The curriculum should then be organized in terms of the knowledge and experiences most appropriate for each subsystem. Skilbeck sees the culture of the college, university or training organization as a key factor in determining the eventual shape of the curriculum. He advocates what he terms 'situational analysis' – a review of the internal and external issues affecting the organization – as a precursor to using one of the other models. Thus, the situation in which the curriculum will operate becomes a key determinant of its eventual shape.

---

**Task 7.9: What are these curriculum models all about?**

Summarize the key aspects of each model (product/objectives, content, process and situational) in your own words. What are their key similarities and differences? Remember to refer back to the statement you made in response to Task 7.8.

---

At this point it is important to note that all these models are directive in that each lays down a prescription for carrying out the processes of curriculum design and development which allows different views on aims and objectives, content, learning, teaching and assessment to be combined so as to produce a curriculum. As such, theoretical models are useful in helping us to review an existing course or to design a new course since they also carry these proposed solutions to the problems of curriculum design and development.

Let's see if these models can help us in practice by enabling us to identify the key features of our courses. Remember, most of us teach on courses that others have designed even though we usually have some degree of freedom to interpret, sequence and manage the learning experiences of our students. This means that many of our courses are, in practice, a combination of different curriculum models.

For example, take the GCSE biology course mentioned in Figure 7.4. Sarah went on to describe her course as being 80 per cent content, product and situational and only 20 per cent process. That is, the curriculum seems most focused on getting students following a one year retake course in an FE college department with a particular way of doing things (situational) to learn biology and to remember it for the examination (content) with the course itself being simply a passport to employment or higher level courses (product), a view echoed by Sarah's students. The small proportion of process is Sarah trying hard within a tightly defined course and timescale to develop more scientific thinking and behaviour in her students.

In contrast, Andy described his NVQ bricklaying course as being 80 per cent product and 20 per cent content and process. He and his students see the NVQ as mainly a measure of their craft skills and as a means of obtaining and keeping employment. The content and process aspects simply refer to the basic knowledge required by NVQ and the ways in which Andy helps his students to learn.

Finally, Suzanne and Nicole described their aromatherapy course as being one-third product, one-third content and one-third process and situational. This reflects the students' need for qualification in order to practise in many places (product), their need to know what they are doing (content) and the ways in which they must learn to work with clients in an often quite intimate fashion (process), something both Suzanne and Nicole felt to be particularly important in their profession (situational).

**Task 7.10: Your course and the four models**

Consider a course you teach in relation to the four curriculum models. Make a rough judgement about which of the models features in your course and in what proportions. What are the reasons for your answer?

There is a key lesson in all of this regarding how to treat theoretical models: use them not as a 'quick fix' but as tools to analyse the aims and outcomes (purpose), the selection and organization of learning and assessment activities and evaluation procedures.

Most teachers and trainers in PCE find that their courses are a particular combination of product, content, process and situation. Each course will have its own points of emphasis. Take a teacher training programme for instance. It has a clear product emphasis, the outcome being that of a trained teacher/trainer with a national qualification and meeting the national standards (LLUK 2006), a content dimension (the knowledge and understanding required of a fully trained professional) and process and situational aspects (the ways in which you learn and gain the qualification and the context in which the qualification is provided). While each of the four models seems to claim that it presents the correct way to develop a curriculum, in reality we need to balance a wide range of factors in order to arrive at a workable curriculum that can operate in practical situations. The value of curriculum models is that they can help us to be more thoughtful and professional in this process.

One further point is worth making. Although four models have been outlined and examined in this section, many of us have found that, in practice, we end up using the set of four questions posed by Tyler (1971: 201). This is certainly not because we are all behavioural outcomes enthusiasts but because the questions provide a straightforward framework for developing our courses. Indeed, many of our own students have pointed out that, in essence, the other models eventually arrive at a similar set of questions. The key thing is to ensure that, before you begin the curriculum development process, you have a clear idea about how you view learning and your subject matter. Then, Tyler's questions can help you build a practical curriculum.

To summarize, this section has continued the structural survey of curriculum by asking you to identify the aims and outcomes (purposes), content, process and context of your courses in relation to similar statements from other teachers and trainers. It has presented and examined four curriculum models and identified their key characteristics. You have set your own courses against the four models in order to clarify the precise nature of your courses. Finally, the section has provided advice on the use of theoretical models and has concluded that, in practice, all our courses contain elements of all the models, and it is the proportions that expose the differences. Bearing this in mind, Tyler's questions might be a useful framework provided we have already thought about our positions on learning and subject matter.

Having identified the key characteristics of our courses, the next section will ask why our courses possess these characteristics and investigate the assumptions, values and purposes that underpin them.

## 7.4  What ideologies (values, assumptions and purposes) underpin our courses?

| KEY ISSUES |
| --- |
| Why are courses organized so differently? |
| Why are there so many different curriculum models? |
| Should there be this variety in both theory and practice? |

The previous section used practical and theoretical methods to help us to begin a review of our courses but it also showed the variety in curriculum theory (four different models) and practice – just look at the different responses of those teachers and trainers talking about their courses in Figure 7.4. This section asks why this variety exists, if it is necessary and, if so, why it is so important.

The 1980s saw the start of a concerted effort by Government to reduce curriculum variety (see Chapter 1), and in particular since 1988 the compulsory education sector has seen the continuing evolution of the national curriculum in an attempt to establish national benchmarks and to raise standards. Meanwhile PCET has seen, among other changes, the on-going development of NVQs to bring national standards to vocational training, the introduction of GNVQ (a supposed mix of academic education and vocational training) followed by the introduction of key skills, further revisions to GNVQ and, with Curriculum 2000, a wholesale revision of the A level and the ending of GNVQ with the introduction of Applied GCSE and AVCE, later called Applied A level.

These processes have continued apace. In 2002 the Green Paper *14–19: Extending Opportunities, Raising Standards* (DfES 2002) envisaged, among other things, changes to the national curriculum at Key Stage 4 (GCSE) and the introduction of a matriculation diploma. The Tomlinson Report (2004) revisited the whole area of 14–19 and the Government response (the White Paper *14–19 Education and Skills*, DfES 2005) has led to the current development of 14–19 diplomas and associated changes including those to functional skills and apprenticeships.

HE is also involved in wholesale curriculum change with the development of the Quality Assurance Agency Benchmarks and the HE National Qualifications Framework, as are a number of professions.

In addition, recent years have seen the complete reorganization of both the nurse and police training curricula to produce nurses and police officers with the knowledge, skills and abilities required for their rapidly changing roles in society. Meanwhile, don't forget the introduction and on-going development of national standards for the education and training of teachers and others working in schools by the Training and Development Agency for Schools (TDA), by LLUK for those working in the post-compulsory sector and the establishment of the Higher Education Academy for university lecturers.

However, even if the formal curriculum, the printed syllabus or specification is standardized, does that mean the curriculum in practice – as taught by lecturers, teachers and trainers, and experienced by learners – is standardized?

---

**Task 7.11: Same course, same learning experience?**

7.11(a)   When you were at school, did all the teachers of the same subject, say maths, teach in the same way? Explain your answer.

7.11(b)   In your own area of teaching/training, does every lecturer/teacher/trainer work in an identical way? Explain your answer.

7.11(c)   Do you think that the following groups of learners have identical learning experiences? Explain your answers.
   • All the first-year economics degree students in a university.
   • All NVQ Level 3 beauty therapy trainees in college or a workplace.
   • All police probationary constables in a training centre.

---

So, assuming that your answers point towards some variation, however much the formal curriculum is standardized, the question remains as to why this variation exists. And we still haven't answered the question about variation existing between the theoretical models and between curricula. For instance, why is NVQ different from the national curriculum which is different from A level? And why has GNVQ undergone successive changes since being introduced in 1992?

In short, the answer is that every curriculum represents a set of fundamental beliefs, assumptions and values, collectively termed 'ideologies', about the nature of education and training. As Barnes (1982: 60) says:

No curriculum planning is neutral: every curriculum is imbued with values. These values embody a view of the kind of people we wish our pupils to become . . . and of the kind of society that such people could live in . . . As Eisner (1985) once wrote when discussing the idea of neutral curriculum planning, under the rug of technique, there lies an image of man.

We can cluster these beliefs about education and training into groups and call these 'educational ideologies' – that is, systems of meaning about education. In order to review and develop our own courses as teachers/trainers, we need to be able to identify these ideologies and hold our own considered position about them. This is important because these ideologies include assumptions about learning, teaching, the nature of subject knowledge and how education and training are linked to the wider economic, political, moral and social circumstances of the time. All this sets the context for making decisions about what to teach, how students should learn and how such learning should be assessed.

So, just what are these ideologies and how do they relate to education and training? Scrimshaw (1983) identifies five major educational ideologies which together represent over 2000 years of thinking about the nature and meaning of education and training. They are now briefly described.

### Classical humanism: maintaining a stable society by transmitting society's cultural heritage to students

Over 2000 years ago in ancient Greece, Plato, in the *Meno*, developed a view of education as being a way of producing a just and harmonious society made up of rational and reflective individuals. His notions of just and harmonious were tied to a hierarchical society with the role of education being to train people to take up their proper roles. Thus, people at different levels in the hierarchy would require different curricula with only the rulers needing a full education in philosophy and the mathematical sciences because they were the only people who would need to develop wisdom.

Interestingly, around 1000 years later, Augustine of Hippo devised a very similar proposal. He wanted a general education consisting of seven liberal arts to be provided to most pupils while a select few were to be given studies in philosophy and theology, ready to command a society dominated by the Christian Church.

### Liberal humanism: the use of the intellectual disciplines in developing individuals and, thus, a fairer and more equal society

In the eighteenth century as, post-Renaissance, the thinkers of the Enlightenment period attempted to envisage a society beyond that controlled by hereditary monarchs, Rousseau (see Boyd 1956) advocated a view of society which assumed people to be naturally good but too often corrupted by their social environments.

For Rousseau, education was about providing structure, order and discipline to help learners develop into morally mature individuals. The curriculum would be developmental, take great account of individual differences and begin with everyday situations before moving on to a systematic study of the essential disciplines of literature, history, science, mathematics, etc. (Taylor and Richards 1985). All this would, argued Rousseau, produce free thinking, responsible individuals able to play their full part in a free and democratic society.

## Progressivism: meeting individuals' needs and aspirations so as to support their personal growth and strengthen a democratic society

In the early twentieth century in the USA, Dewey (1915) developed an approach which saw both the above ideologies as problematic. He saw classical humanism as too teacher-centred, too concerned with existing knowledge and with fitting people into an existing society. Liberal humanism, on the other hand, he considered too student-centred, ignoring the importance of the social contexts of learning and development. So, he developed a middle way between these two.

This involved Dewey's own vision of democracy as the best way for people in a society to live together and for individuals to grow and develop. He wanted schools that replicated democracy in an 'embryonic social community' in which students were encouraged to cooperate and work together and learn from each other as well as from their teachers (Walker and Soltis 1997). Education was to extend people's powers and possibilities as human beings. The curriculum would be based around active problem-solving in a variety of social contexts and be constructed of topics which interested and challenged students (learning from experience) with the aim that people would learn how to think for themselves, make decisions, cooperate and participate as makers of a democratic society.

## Instrumentalism: a curriculum delivering a specific product such as the development of a skilled workforce

This ideology has become an increasingly important element in UK Government policy since the Great Debate was initiated in 1976 and given that the education policies of all major political parties in England, Scotland and Wales share this emphasis, shows every sign of remaining at the heart of Government policy.

Instrumentalism, as it operates in the UK in the early years of the twenty-first century, sees the development of a highly educated workforce as essential in meeting growing international competition and values high levels of numeracy and literacy, subject areas covering aspects of science and technology and anything else seen as relevant to achieving this goal. Publications including the Foster Report (DfES 2005d), the 2006 White Paper *Further Education: Raising Skills, Improving Life Chances* and the Leitch Report (DfES 2006a) all provide evidence of this.

The instrumental curriculum sees knowledge in factual terms and is clearly lecturer/teacher/trainer led. Thus, through instrumentalist education and training, students are preparing themselves for their roles in the global workplace and in society as a whole.

## Reconstructionism: education to change society

In stark contrast to the other ideologies, reconstructionism sees education as the means of moving society in a particular direction; in effect, as a tool of the state. In many developing countries, some degree of reconstructionism is, perhaps, necessary, as they seek to raise the living standards of their populations through a largely product-oriented curriculum.

However, totalitarian Governments have always used education as a means of getting people to serve the interests of those in power and there are numerous past examples including Nazi Germany, the Soviet Union and, at the time of writing, China, where the purpose of education is described in Taylor and Richards (1985: 21) as being 'to serve the ends of proletarian politics, not the pursuit of individual goals and aspirations'. Interestingly, by 2007, China is many years into a policy of using education as part of its attempt to move towards a more open, market-based economy while maintaining the political and social status quo. Clearly, China is now an increasing force in the global economy but time will tell if this use of education to support an economic, social and political balancing act will be successful.

---

**Task 7.12: What are these five ideologies all about?**

Summarize the key aspects of each educational ideology by commenting on the following:
- What is the historical origin of the ideology?
- How does it view the role of education and training?
- What kind of curriculum is advocated?
- What is the value given to individual learners?

---

Most courses in PCET are influenced fairly clearly in their make-up by an ideology even if this is applied inconsistently, mixed with another and applied without universal agreement.

---

**Task 7.13: Spot the ideology**

Look at a course you teach and see if you can link it to a particular ideology. Explain your responses. Or, looking at the following courses, which ideology(ies) would you associate with any three of them? Explain your responses.
- NVQ;
- nurse education;
- A level;
- adult education courses in sugarcraft;
- MBA;
- police training;
- applied GCSE and A levels; 14–19 specialist diplomas;
- university degrees in English and in travel and tourism;
- skills for life and functional skills courses.

---

Having arrived at your responses to Tasks 7.12 and 7.13, consider one further issue. Are these fundamental assumptions, values and beliefs which underpin every course made explicit to teachers/trainers and learners? Is it simply assumed either that these are matters too obvious to be missed or that everyone else agrees and, therefore, no mention is necessary? What does your course documentation say about any of this? It is the unspoken and, all too often, the non-debated nature of ideologies in education that can cause difficulties for everyone.

In conclusion, this section has tackled the question as to why courses seem to vary so much both in theory and in practice. In essence, it is because course developers and those commissioning courses have their own assumptions, beliefs and values about the nature and purpose of education and training and these ideologies affect course design. In an age when courses seem likely to become more, rather than less, standardized, variation will still occur because teachers/trainers have their own ideologies and this will affect the ways they teach and train their students.

In terms of helping us with our own work, two issues need mentioning. First, as we review and develop our own courses, we must be explicit about our ideologies so that our colleagues, and other teachers/trainers and students, will understand our intentions. Second, when we come to use other people's courses, we need to be able to identify the ideological underpinnings in order to arrive at how we will operate the course in practice.

## 7.5 The 14–19 reforms

| KEY ISSUES |
| --- |
| What are the major features of the 14–19 reforms? |
| What light does our discussion of curriculum models and ideologies shed on these reforms? |

Given the early stage of these reforms at the time of writing, this section will first outline the nature of what is being undertaken and the associated rationale.

The story of 14–19 curriculum reform in recent years has already been referred to in this and other chapters, not least in the references to the Curriculum 2000 changes to A levels and in the many and various attempts to develop general vocational programmes, not least the now discontinued GNVQ. However, the most important recent changes can be traced to the publication by Government of two Green Papers, *14–19: Extending Opportunities, Raising Standards* in 2002 and *14–19 Opportunity and Excellence* in 2003. These set out a broad vision for the future of 14–19 provision which included greater flexibility at Key Stage 4, students to progress at a pace consistent with abilities and interests, a range of opportunities to include apprenticeships, increased collaboration across schools, colleges and work-based providers, higher quality teaching and learning, improved employer involvement and financial support for students (DfES 2002a, 2003b).

In the longer term, the Government wanted a much stronger vocational offer with a firm underpinning of general education, assessment within programmes which was fit for purpose and the development of a unified framework of qualifications suitable for young people across all abilities (DfES 2002a, 2003b). As a key element in driving this agenda forward, the Government appointed Mike Tomlinson, ex-Chief HMI, to head a working group for long-term 14–19 reform, to advise on these reforms.

In 2004, the working group published its final report, what has come to be known as the Tomlinson Report. In introducing the report to the Minister, Tomlinson left no doubt about the conclusions from their work. He wrote:

> It is our view that the status quo is not an option. Nor do we believe further piecemeal changes are desirable. Too many young people leave education lacking basic and personal skills; our vocational provision is too fragmented; the burden of external assessment on learners, teachers and lecturers is too great; and our system is not providing the stretch and challenge needed, particularly for high attainers. The results are a low staying-on rate post-16; employers having to spend large sums of money to teach the 'basics'; HE struggling to differentiate between top performers; and young people's motivation and engagement with education reducing as they move through the system.
>
> (Working Group on 14–19 Reform 2004: 1)

Tomlinson's proposed system set out a vision of a broader range of learning experiences and qualifications all of which would be recorded on a 'personal transcript' held on-line for each 14–19-year-old. In summary, the report recommended the following:

- Secondary school students would take fewer exams. GCSEs and A-levels, along with their vocational equivalents, would become part of a four-stage, graded diploma.

- From the age of 14 onward, every student would study core skills, 'functional' maths, English and IT, and would only receive a diploma if mastery of these skills had been proved.

- Core skills and advanced qualifications would be externally examined. GCSEs and vocational courses at 16 would be assessed internally by teachers, trained and accredited as examiners.

- Vocational training would be offered to all students that want it, often in FE colleges.

- More students would have the option of taking bonus questions to earn an A+ or an A++ at A-level, and some could even take university courses while still at school.

- Every student's achievement, including work experience, community involvement, sport and arts, would be recorded in detail in an online 'transcript'. Universities and employers would use this to select students and employees.

- Schools would be held to account and measured on the proportion of students achieving a pass, merit or distinction diploma, and the numbers demonstrating the required literacy, numeracy and IT skills.

(*Financial Times*, 19 October 2004)

Intriguingly, there was a broad consensus about these recommendations with many educationalists and employers agreeing on the broad direction. Indeed, expectations for radical change were generally raised by the work of Tomlinson and the working group.

Equally intriguingly, the response from Government was to reject many of Tomlinson's recommendations and to water down many of those that remained. The Government response was contained in the 2005 White Paper *14–19 Education and Skills* which, in summary, outlined the following:

> New vocational diplomas will be introduced in schools and colleges from 2008 under plans to raise the 'scandalously' low proportion of English teenagers staying on in education past the age of 16. The work-related qualification is the central proposal in a White Paper, which ministers said would transform secondary education, published in response to the 18-month Tomlinson inquiry. There will also be a new diploma for 16-year-olds. To get it they will have to get five Cs or better at GCSE, including at least a C in both English and maths. This measure of success will also be used in league tables next year. GCSE English and Maths will be redesigned to make it impossible to get a C without having mastered 'functional' aspects of the subjects.
>
> (*Times Educational Supplement*, 25 February 2005)

The reaction to this White Paper was marked:

> There has been widespread dismay at ministers' decision to reject Sir Mike Tomlinson's central recommendation: a diploma including both vocational and academic courses. A-levels and GCSEs, which he wanted scrapped, will continue alongside the new vocational diploma . . . there will be no basic English or Maths exams, as Tomlinson wanted . . . Union leaders, educationalists and bodies including the Independent Schools Council said the White Paper represented a missed opportunity to put vocational and academic courses on an equal footing. The Government's 2003 Green Paper, which set up the Tomlinson review, said it should move to a 'unified qualifications structure suitable for all young people'. But this has been rejected. Instead, it focused on streamlining the current 3500 vocational courses for 14 to 19-year-olds to three-level diplomas in 14 subjects by 2015.
>
> (*Times Educational Supplement*, 25 February 2005)

Notwithstanding the disappointment expressed about the limited nature of their reforms, the Government set about putting them into action and, at the time of writing, the DfES 14–19 website outlines the following as the four key priorities:

- A greater focus on the 3Rs – the functional skills needed for everyday life, demonstrated through real life application.
- Stronger vocational routes, where young people develop in part through

practical experience, with qualifications that give them a broad enough education to progress further in learning as well as into employment.

- More stretching options on both general and applied routes and activities which extend young people, backed by greater flexibility for young people to accelerate through the system, or to take longer in order to achieve higher standards.
- New ways to tackle disengagement and to ensure that those in danger of dropping out can be motivated to stay in learning.
        (http://www.dfes.gov.uk/14–19/dsp_stakeholders.cfm?page_id=1)

The major curriculum developments at the heart of the reforms involve the development of new diplomas and, in particular, the specialized diplomas, revisions to A levels, functional skills with revisions to GCSE English and Maths and a re-engagement initiative for 14–16-year-olds.

## Specialized diplomas

Of all these innovations, it is the diplomas that have generated the most interest, perhaps since they are the 'new' element that DfES describes thus: '[Diplomas have been] created to provide a real alternative to more traditional education and qualifications, and are the most important change to the country's education system since the introduction of GCSEs' (DfES 2006b: 1). They are aimed at the full range of students and will be available as shown below:

- *Level 1 diploma*: equivalent in size to 4–5 GCSEs at grades D to G;
- *Level 2 diploma*: equivalent in size to 5–6 GCSEs at grades A* to C;
- *Level 3 'progression' diploma*: equivalent in size to two A levels;
- *Level 3 diploma*: equivalent in size to three A levels.

As DfES explains:

In the future, we want every young person in a school or college to be entitled to pursue any one of the Diploma courses at an appropriate level for them, wherever they are in the country. This entitlement will be put in place in 2013, once all of the Diplomas have been tested.
        (http://www.dfes.gov.uk/14–19/index.cfm?sid=3&pid=224&lid=
                185&ctype=Text&ptype=Single)

The timescale for the introduction of the specialized diplomas is shown below:

1   **From September 2008**

- IT
- Society, health and development
- Engineering

- Creative and media
- Construction and the built environment

## 2  From September 2009

- Land-based and environmental
- Manufacturing
- Hair and beauty
- Business administration and finance
- Hospitality and catering

## 3  From September 2010

- Public services
- Sport and leisure
- Retail
- Travel and tourism

Each diploma will consist of three components:

- *Principal learning*: developing the knowledge, understanding, skills and atti-tudes relevant to a sector or sectors using realistic contexts and materials wherever possible.
- *Additional/specialist learning*: allowing learners to specialise further or to select units that will complement their programme.
- *Generic learning*: providing the learner with the essential skills including Maths, English and ICT, which will prepare them for successful employ-ment, training and further study.
(http://www.cbcdiploma.co.uk/thediploma/aboutspecialiseddiplomas/)

The diplomas are being developed by multi-agency Diploma Development Partnerships (DDPs) led by the relevant Sector Skills Councils as representatives of employers, with members representing a number of key stakeholders, including higher education and education professionals. The DDPs are meant to ensure that the content of the qualifications meets the needs of employers and higher educa-tion, including a requirement to succeed in achieving functional English, Maths and ICT.

At the time of writing, only outline content for the first five diploma lines is available. Awarding bodies (for example, AQA, Edexcel and OCR) will work with DDPs as they turn the content into qualifications. An example of what is available (in early 2007) is shown overleaf in Figure 7.6. In this case the diploma is for construc-tion and the built environment but similar information is available for all the vocational areas scheduled for a 2008 introduction.

**Figure 7.6** An example of a specialized diploma: construction and the built environment

---

The construction and the built environment diplomas are designed to introduce young people to the fabric of the world in which we live and its impact on individuals and communities. They progressively build up an understanding of the physical extent and significance of the built environment and of the activities which shape, develop and influence it.

Young people taking a Construction and the Built Environment Diploma course will study how things get built and the factors that affect this, such as the planning process and social and environmental factors. They will also start to develop skills which are widely used across the built environment industries; the practical techniques used in the design, construction, maintenance and management of the built environment.

The industries covered by the Construction and the Built Environment Diplomas range from construction craft areas, such as carpentry, brick laying and decorating, through building services, such as electrical installation and plumbing, to management of the built environment, such as facilities management and estate agency. The Diplomas will enable young people to go on to degree courses such as Construction Management and Apprenticeships across the industry areas.

They will prepare young people for a range of occupations and professions within construction, specialist building, building maintenance services, utilities services, facilities management, property and asset management and housing.

This is a summary of the content of the Construction and the Built Environment Diplomas. It gives a flavour of the kind of areas that would be studied by young people but by no means describes the full content at each Diploma level. For more information please visit: www.cbediploma.co.uk

**Mandatory Learning**

Functional skills in maths, English and IT user skills.
Personal, learning and thinking skills.
Work experience.
Project.

**Design the built environment:**
   design; planning; materials; economic, social and environmental issues.

**Create the built environment:**
   job roles; tools; materials; and processes; construction techniques; health and safety and environmental protection; project management.

**Value and use the built environment:**
   Impact of the built environment on individuals and society; housing and property; maintenance and support.

*Learners would have to apply principles, for example, by designing a complex structure, carrying out tasks safely using appropriate tools and safety gear and evaluating the contribution of the built environment to the community.*

**Optional Learning**

Learners must select topics organised into three pathways (four at level 3), either concentrating on one or two pathways or selecting from across the range:

**Construction:** including surveying, civil engineering and craft skill options.

**Building Services Engineering:** including electrical or mechanical services.

**Management of Built Assets:** including valuation, sales and letting and housing management.

**Management in the Built Environment (level 3):** financial or project management, supply chain relationships.

There are also a number of other topics such as CAD, science and materials, customer management, heritage and languages.

---

*Source*: www.cbediploma.co.uk/

## Functional skills and revised GCSE English, ICT and mathematics

In relation to functional skills and the revised GCSEs in English and Maths, QCA has produced a draft set of standards for functional skills, with initial focus on levels 1 and 2, following consultation on these over summer 2006 and are trialling, then piloting developments from 2006/07. Awarding bodies are meant to provide specifications to schools and colleges by September 2008 for revised English and ICT GCSEs, and by September 2009 for the revised GCSE maths so that schools and colleges can introduce the revised GCSEs in English and ICT which includes functional skills in September 2009 and the revised GCSE in Maths including functional skills in September 2010 (see: www.dfes.gov.uk/14–19/index.cfm?sid=3&pid=225&lid=189&ctype=Text&ptype=Single).

## Changes to A level

At A level, the situation at the time of writing is as follows. The emphasis is on providing more stretching questions so that from September 2006, QCA has been trialling different options to introduce new stretch and challenge at A level for our brightest students. These options are not meant to affect the existing A level standard and the trials are designed to be evaluated and incorporated into A levels from September 2008. Similar options will be included within specialized diplomas (which may of course include A levels), so that at advanced level, all young people, whether they have taken a specialized diploma or general qualifications, will have had the opportunity to demonstrate their capabilities.

Two other options are also being introduced: the extended project at A level and higher education modules in schools.

## The extended project

This will be a single piece of work, requiring a high degree of planning, preparation, research and autonomous working and will be available for first teaching from September 2008. The project must be distinct from A level coursework units and a common framework will apply to both the stand-alone version for A level students and the extended project within level 3 specialized diplomas. The consultation revealed support for the extended project being completed in Year 13 because the skills the extended project will test were more likely to have been developed in Year 13 as students mature.

In 2008, the DfES will consider whether more breadth needs to be introduced into A levels in 2008 and will also look at the progress made to introduce harder questions and the extended project. This review will not be looking at the future of A levels. They will remain long term as free-standing qualifications. In the future DfES is also intending to introduce the A* grade to reward achievement in the more challenging questions in A level exams (see: www.dfes.gov.uk/14–19/index.cfm?sid=3&pid=233&lid=231&ctype–Text&ptype=Single).

## Higher education modules

The 2005 Education Act allows for limited courses of higher education to be provided in schools. Colleges can already do this. The availability of HE modules is designed to help young people to study in greater breadth and/or depth and to develop independent learning skills and help prepare for entry to HE.

One final feature of the 14–19 reforms addresses the issue of disengaged 14–16-year-olds.

## 14–16 Re-engagement programme

The new 14–16 re-engagement programme is designed to:

- provide a tailored programme for each young person and intensive personal guidance and support;
- involve significant work-based learning, probably amounting to two days each week;
- involve courses that could lead towards a level 1 [specialized] Diploma;
- lead on to a range of further options, including Apprenticeships.

The programme will be aimed at young people who are lower achieving, at risk of disengagement and likely to benefit from a work-focussed programme. The content of the programme focuses on vocational development and experience, personal and social development and a catch-up on basic and Key Skills. Participants will be expected to continue with the Key Stage 4 statutory curriculum alongside the scheme.

(www.dfes.gov.uk/14–19/index.cfm?sid=28&pid=235&lid=199&ctype=
Text&ptype=Single)

Having outlined the nature of what is being undertaken and the associated rationale, this section will now consider these reforms in the light of our previous discussion concerning curriculum models and ideologies and ask whether these reforms are consistent with any fundamental beliefs concerning the purpose of a PCET curriculum.

The fundamental assumptions underpinning the 14–19 reforms seem to be as follows:

The primary problem lies with the design of the qualifications and therefore this should be the starting point (rather than, for instance, with the design and implementation of learning programmes, the availability of appropriate staff (or their performance), or the quality of facilities). The key to the improvement of qualifications is the involvement of employers in their design. (In fact, 'involvement' appears to be a weak version of the Government's intention. Employers are being asked to take the lead). Employer involvement will lead to their valuing the resulting qualification and to their using them for the purposes of recruitment. There is at present an 'alphabet soup' of over 3,500 vocational qualifications (taken by 14–19 year olds), leading to confusion amongst various user groups.

(Stanton 2005: 1)

**Task 7.14: What are the values and beliefs underpinning these 14–19 reforms?**

Go back and re-read the four key priorities listed earlier in the section (a greater focus on the 3Rs; stronger vocational routes; more stretching; new ways to tackle disengagement) and the assumptions identified by Stanton above.

Which ideology or combination of ideologies from Section 7.4 might help you to analyse the core values and beliefs underpinning these 14–19 reforms?

There are some changes being made to A levels but the curriculum innovations attracting the most interest are of course the specialized diplomas which at the time of writing are still in the very early stages of development. Nevertheless, if they genuinely are 'the most important change to the country's education system since the introduction of GCSEs' (DfES 2006b: 1) we need to examine what we do know about them in order to understand better their nature and intended purposes.

Raffe (2005) points out that, in contrast to Scotland and Wales (with the Welsh Baccalaureate) which have developed unified academic and vocational qualification systems at 14–19, England has opted for what he terms a twin-track model, but with 'linkages' between the tracks (p.1). In essence, England has kept the academic A level and is developing a parallel qualification route, the specialized diplomas (which may include some A levels of course), as the latest solution to improving the quality of pre-vocational and early vocational education and training.

Remember that each diploma will consist of three elements (principal learning, additional/specialist learning, generic learning) which are being developed by multi-agency Diploma Development Partnerships (DDPs), and which are led by the relevant Sector Skills Councils as representatives of employers.

**Task 7.15: What kind of curriculum thinking underpins the 14–19 reforms?**

Use this information and the outline of a specialist diploma in Figure 7.6 above to consider the following:

7.15(a)   Do you agree with the Government that A levels are still needed or should we have moved to develop a wholly new integrated qualifications system (an English Baccalaureate?) as the Welsh have done?

7.15(b)   Use the curriculum model or a combination of models from Section 7.3 to help you analyse the new specialized diploma as outlined in Figure 7.6 above. What kind of curriculum does the diploma seem to be?

7.15(c)   Why do you consider the Government has employers leading on diploma developments? Where do you stand on this issue? Use the models and ideologies to explain your position.

The changes to GCSE English, ICT and Maths and the use of the phrase 'functional skills' seem to signal a move forward from the Basic and Key Skills initiatives that have existed for some years. Moreover, the emphasis on incorporating these 'functional skills' into core national curriculum GCSEs (which of course are now deemed to form the benchmark for student success and organization league table positions!) at Key Stage 4 (five GCSE grade Cs or above including English and Maths) seems to indicate a much sharper and more integrated approach.

However, the task might not be a simple one. As Wake (2005) explains, although there is increasing recognition that current mathematics curricula do not adequately equip people to use and apply mathematics effectively in different spheres of their lives, there is also clear evidence that we can develop qualifications that seem to fail comprehensively: '. . . in this relatively recent development (Key Skills Application of Number) we have evidence of how a qualification can prove unattractive to both learners and teachers, and apparently lack value to employers and higher education institutions' (2005: 1). Wake goes on to assert:

> I consider it essential to take into account the likely experience of learners from the outset of the development of the crucial design features of a 'functional mathematics' curriculum, as not to do so will almost inevitably result in another unsuccessful attempt to develop a core or key skill qualification in the area of mathematics such as we have recently experienced with Application of Number.
>
> (2005: 1)

---

**Task 7.16: What about 'functional skills'?**

7.16(a)    Do you think that moving away from separate key skills towards integrating 'functional skills' into GCSE and diplomas will improve learning?

7.16(b)    Will involving schools much more closely than before in the 'functional skills' agenda by integrating them into GCSE English and maths make any difference?

---

The final element of the 4–19 reforms covers the new 14–16 re-engagement programme which is designed to support young people who are lower achieving and at risk of disengagement. This of course is a particular example of a major aim of the whole reform programme, that of improving the qualifications, knowledge and skills of the future workforce. This issue is discussed by Winch (2003) who identified a curious paradox. The school national curriculum has two aims neither of which is explicit about working life:

- To provide opportunities for all pupils to learn and achieve
- To promote pupils' spiritual, moral, social and cultural development and prepare all pupils for the opportunities, responsibilities and experiences of life.
                (www.teachernet.gov.uk/management/atoz/n/nationalcurriculum/)

Even the QCA which expands on the aims at some length still only manages one explicit reference to this:

- [young people] are well prepared for life and work
(www.qca.org.uk/secondarycurriculumreview/lenses/
curriculum-aims/index.htm)

Winch explains the paradox as follows: '[the educational aim of preparing young people for paid employment] is a key theme of the [14–19] review, but not, paradoxically, one that receives anything more than a glancing mention in the aims of the school curriculum . . .' (Winch 2003: 1). He argues that this key difference between the national curriculum and the 14–19 curriculum causes real problems for young people and asserts that there is a 'need to state clearly that it is a central and desirable aim of the school curriculum to prepare young people, not only for engagement with their cultural heritage and for civic participation, but for fulfillment through the exercise of their active powers through paid employment' (Winch 2003: 1).

He goes on to point to the differences between the educational aims for 14–19 in developing more vocational qualifications at levels 1, 2 and 3 and the needs of the economy and of economic policy. In effect, he describes the UK economy as requiring increasing numbers of highly qualified personnel but no more at levels 1, 2 and 3. This leads him to question the apparent difference between education and economic policies and to call for Government economic policy to support the growth of jobs requiring these level 1, 2 and 3 vocational qualifications. Otherwise he says:

> If young people realise that the employment opportunities they are being offered are essentially quite limited if they do not decide to go on to higher education, then there is a real likelihood that disaffection with school will not diminish at all, as the premise on which higher achievement has been sold to them is a largely false one. This point illustrates the need for 'joined up' policy, that ensures that the Treasury's concern with narrowing the UK productivity gap by increasing supply of level 3 skills is matched by policy that encourages demand [for more highly qualified people] amongst employers, so that young people are given compelling occupation-related reasons for continuing with their education.
>
> (Winch 2003: 10)

---

**Task 7.17: Curriculum aims and the 14–19 reforms**

7.17(a)   What is your perspective on the (essentially instrumentalist) re-engagement programme for 14–16-year-olds?

7.17(b)   How do you respond to Winch's critique of the mismatch between 14–19 policy and economic policy? What might be some implications of this for the 14–19 reforms?

## 7.6 Where do you stand so far?

---

**KEY ISSUES**

---

What is your working definition of curriculum?

How can the four curriculum models be of help?

Where do you stand in terms of educational ideology?

---

The purpose of this section is to provide an opportunity for us to pause a moment so as to review and record where we have got to in thinking about the theory and practice of curriculum matters. On the basis of this, we can then move forward to plan and develop a new, or revised, curriculum.

**Task 7.18: Reporting on your review of curriculum**

7.18(a)   What is your definition of curriculum?

7.18(b)   Why should the curriculum always be developing?

7.18(c)   Use the curriculum models to help analyse a course you teach on. What mixture of product, content, process and situation is it?

7.18(d)   What educational ideology do you feel most comfortable with? Why?

7.18(e)   What ideology lies behind a course you teach on? If it's different from your response to 7.18(d), does this raise any practical issues?

As practising teachers/trainers, this chapter has presented you with opportunities to consider your own work and that of other teachers/trainers. In order to help you, some of the theoretical work on curriculum has been introduced so that you can become more critical and thoughtful. However, have you noticed the different ways we can treat curriculum theory? The curriculum models are there to aid review and development and they provide ways of sorting out curriculum matters. So, in practice, our own courses often represent a particular combination of models.

Ideologies, however, are different. They represent our fundamental beliefs about the nature and purpose of a curriculum. Although some overlap of ideas is natural, we can only really embed the ideas of one ideology in any curriculum. So, having completed our structural survey of the curriculum, it's time to start planning and building. All this now means we can move on to Chapter 8 where we will begin to design and develop a new or revised curriculum, establish thorough evaluation mechanisms and be able to present and justify our new or revised course to others.

# Related new professional standards for teachers and trainers in the lifelong learning sector

## Domain A: professional values and practice

| PROFESSIONAL KNOWLEDGE AND UNDERSTANDING | PROFESSIONAL PRACTICE |
| --- | --- |
| *Teachers in the lifelong learning sector know and understand:* | *Teachers in the lifelong learning sector:* |
| AK 1.1 What motivates learners to learn and the importance of learners' experience and aspirations. | AP 1.1 Encourage the development and progression of all learners through recognizing, valuing and responding to individual motivation, experience and aspirations. |
| AK 2.1 Ways in which learning has the potential to change lives. | AP 2.1 Use opportunities to highlight the potential for learning to positively transform lives and contribute to effective citizenship. |
| AK 3.1 Issues of equality, diversity and inclusion. | AP 3.1 Apply principles to evaluate and develop own practice in promoting equality and inclusive learning and engaging with diversity. |
| AK 4.1 Principles, frameworks and theories which underpin good practice in learning and teaching. | AP 4.1 Use relevant theories of learning to support the development of practice in learning and teaching. |
| AK 4.3 Ways to reflect, evaluate and use research to develop own practice, and to share good practice with others. | AP 4.3 Share good practice with others and engage in continuing professional development through reflection, evaluation and the appropriate use of research. |
| AK 5.1 Ways to communicate and collaborate with colleagues and/or others to enhance learners' experience. | AP 5.1 Communicate and collaborate with colleagues and/or others, within and outside the organization, to enhance learners' experience. |
| AK 7.3 Ways to implement improvements based on feedback received. | AP 7.3 Use feedback to develop own practice within the organization's systems. |

## Domain B: learning and teaching

| PROFESSIONAL KNOWLEDGE AND UNDERSTANDING | PROFESSIONAL PRACTICE |
|---|---|
| *Teachers in the lifelong learning sector know and understand:* | *Teachers in the lifelong learning sector:* |
| BK 2.1 Principles of learning and ways to provide learning activities to meet curriculum requirements and the needs of all learners. | BP 2.1 Provide learning activities which meet curriculum requirements and the needs of all learners. |
| BK 2.5 Ways of using learners' own experiences as a foundation for learning. | BP 2.5 Encourage learners to use their own life experiences as a foundation for their development. |
| BK 3.5 Systems for communication within own organization. | BP 3.5 Identify and use appropriate organizational systems for communicating with learners and colleagues. |

## Domain C: specialist learning and teaching

| PROFESSIONAL KNOWLEDGE AND UNDERSTANDING | PROFESSIONAL PRACTICE |
|---|---|
| *Teachers in the lifelong learning sector know and understand:* | *Teachers in the lifelong learning sector:* |
| CK 1.1 Own specialist area including current developments. | CP 1.1 Ensure that knowledge of own specialist area is current and appropriate to the teaching context. |
| CK 1.2 Ways in which own specialism relates to the wider social, economic and environmental context. | CP 1.2 Provide opportunities for learners to understand how the specialist area relates to the wider social, economic and environmental context. |
| CK 3.1 Teaching and learning theories and strategies relevant to own specialist area. | CP 3.1 Apply appropriate strategies and theories of teaching and learning to own specialist area. |
| CK 3.2 Ways to identify individual learning needs and potential barriers to learning in own specialist area. | CP 3.2 Work with learners to address particular individual learning needs and overcome identified barriers to learning. |
| CK 4.2 Potential transferable skills and employment opportunities relating to own specialist area. | CP 4.2 Work with learners to identify the transferable skills they are developing, and how these might relate to employment opportunities. |

## Domain D: planning for learning

| *PROFESSIONAL KNOWLEDGE AND UNDERSTANDING* | *PROFESSIONAL PRACTICE* |
| --- | --- |
| *Teachers in the lifelong learning sector know and understand:* | *Teachers in the lifelong learning sector:* |
| DK 1.1  How to plan appropriate, effective, coherent and inclusive learning programmes that promote equality and engage with diversity. | DP 1.1  Plan coherent and inclusive learning programmes that meet learners' needs and curriculum requirements, promote equality and engage with diversity effectively. |
| DK 1.3  Strategies for flexibility in planning and delivery. | DP 1.3  Prepare flexible session plans to adjust to the individual needs of learners. |

## Domain E: assessment for learning

| *PROFESSIONAL KNOWLEDGE AND UNDERSTANDING* | *PROFESSIONAL PRACTICE* |
| --- | --- |
| *Teachers in the lifelong learning sector know and understand:* | *Teachers in the lifelong learning sector:* |
| EK 1.1  Theories and principles of assessment and the application of different forms of assessment, including initial, formative and summative assessment in teaching and learning. | EP 1.1  Use appropriate forms of assessment and evaluate their effectiveness in producing information useful to the teacher and the learner. |

## Domain F: access and progression

| PROFESSIONAL KNOWLEDGE AND UNDERSTANDING | PROFESSIONAL PRACTICE |
|---|---|
| *Teachers in the lifelong learning sector know and understand:* | *Teachers in the lifelong learning sector:* |
| FK 1.1  Sources of information, advice, guidance and support to which learners might be referred. | FP 1.1  Refer learners to information on potential current and future learning opportunities and appropriate specialist support services. |
| FK 3.1  Progression and career opportunities within own specialist area. | FP 3.1  Provide general and current information about potential education, training and/or career opportunities in relation to own specialist area. |

# 8

# Course design, development and evaluation

## 8.1 What is Chapter 8 about?

Given the increasing degree of central control over courses evident in recent years, we might be forgiven for assuming that, as teachers and trainers, we have little or no role to play in course design and development. This is far from true.

Even highly prescribed courses such as NVQ, A level, the new 14–19 specialist diplomas or occupation-specific training programmes such as those for police officers or nurses still leave us, working as individuals or as part of a team, relatively free to interpret, sequence, resource and emphasize the various course elements in our own way, drawing on our own professional judgement to decide what will maximize opportunities for our students to learn. In this way we are able to design and develop the curriculum. This is a vital element in our work as teachers and trainers. Indeed, in examining curriculum design and development in some detail, this chapter views it as something which contributes to the overall aim of the book – to develop teachers' and trainers' professional abilities and to nourish their critical awareness.

This chapter focuses on the ways that we, as teachers and trainers, structure and organize students' learning. It challenges readers to examine the courses they teach. Sections 8.2 and 8.3 ask how a curriculum might be designed and developed, and how its effectiveness can be evaluated and judged. Section 8.4 examines how such new developments can be presented to colleges and training organizations so that they might be put into operation.

## 8.2 Designing and developing your course

| KEY ISSUES |
| --- |
| How can we develop or revise a course? |
| What is the role of ideology and curriculum models? |
| How can we identify what's needed in the new or revised course? |

> How can we specify course purposes?
>
> How can we sequence and organize course content into learning and assessment experiences?

Sooner or later, as teachers or trainers, we all need to handle aspects of course design and development: for instance, starting a new job and planning our teaching, planning how we will put into practice a current NVQ/A level or diploma specification by turning it into a practical course, revising a course that has been running for a while, or setting up a new course from scratch are all tasks that we need to be able to carry out professionally. The question is, how?

This section will provide some practical answers based on a straightforward model derived from the theoretical and practical work described in Chapter 7. It makes no claims for being anything more than a practical framework by setting out a sequence of seven stages for curriculum developers to follow, shown in Figure 8.1.

**Figure 8.1** A model for curriculum design and development

---

Stage 1    Select a manageable course development task (it's got to be practical!)
Stage 2    Consider the ideological basis for the course, to identify the key values, beliefs and assumptions.
Stage 3    Conduct a needs analysis: if favourable, continue development work to ensure the proposed course really is worthwhile and practical.
Stage 4    Develop statements of purpose (aims and objectives) to set clear intentions and outcomes in the light of the above.
Stage 5    Specify content and sequence, then organize appropriate learning and assessment experiences to enable learners to achieve the intentions and purposes.
Stage 6    Consider how your proposed course fits into the curriculum offer of your institution.
Stage 7    Establish appropriate evaluation and feedback procedures, to review and improve the effectiveness of the course for learners.

---

This section will cover Stages 1 to 6. That is, it will take you from identifying a manageable course development task through to selecting content, designing a full scheme of work and considering the place of your course in the curriculum of your institution overall. The final stage, that of course evaluation and feedback, will be tackled in the next section. This is to provide sufficient space for the important issue of evaluation, something which, all too often, is simply tacked on at the end of a course, seemingly as a bit of an afterthought.

## Stage 1: select a manageable course development task

The starting point is defining the kind of course that is needed – something that might be easier said than done. However, in order for you to gain the maximum benefit from the remainder of this chapter, you should have a curriculum development task to work on. Examples of courses developed by teacher training students in recent years are shown in Figure 8.2. Whatever you choose to focus on, try to make sure it's relevant to your work as a teacher/trainer and that it's something manageable.

**Figure 8.2** Examples of courses developed by teacher training students

- Driving instructor training
- Brass band music for beginners
- Introductory sculpture
- Preparing for life at university
- Equal opportunities for special constables
- Outreach course for deprived youngsters
- Induction for early years workers
- NVQ IT training
- Bricklaying for DIY-ers
- Students with special needs: a course for FE teachers
- How to have a good time and stay healthy
- LGV driver training
- Introductory reflexology
- Conflict management
- Introduction to a new IT system
- Minibus driver training
- Art and group therapy
- Various A level courses
- BA/BSc modules and units
- French for shopworkers
- NVQ customer care
- Health and safety at work
- Presentation skills
- Police promotion skills
- European art summer school
- Bereavement care for nurses
- Women's health and body care
- Applied GCSE and A level business units
- C&G gardening
- Suturing for nurses
- Applied GCSE health and social care

---

**Task 8.1: What curriculum to develop?**

Select a course (or a part of it) you teach that you need to revise, or identify a syllabus, specification or subject you would like to teach (or that your organization has decided you should teach) but which needs developing into a practical course.

---

Once you have identified your curriculum development task, the next question for you to address is just what kind of course do you want it to be?

## Stage 2: consider the ideological basis for the course

**Task 8.2: What kind of course and why?**

Remember Chapter 7 and your own educational ideology that it helped you to define.

8.2(a)    What educational ideology (fundamental values, beliefs and assumptions) will you bring to the job of course design development?

8.2(b)    If you are revising an existing course, or developing a course from a pre-set syllabus or specification, what seems to be its underlying ideology?

8.2(c)    If your answers to 8.2(a) and (b) are different, can you balance the two? Explain how.

---

Your responses to Task 8.2 will act as a framework around which you can begin to develop your course. However, now that you have clarified the kind of course you want to develop, what needs must the course meet, and how are you to identify these, especially students' learning needs?

## Stage 3: conduct a needs analysis

What needs must this course meet? Perhaps this is better rephrased to read *whose* needs? Quite naturally, this will depend on a whole range of factors including you, any of your colleagues who might be involved, the organization within which you are working, those who might use the course to make judgements (such as employers, colleges, universities) and, most important of all, the learners themselves.

---

**Task 8.3: Whose needs and why?**

List those with needs to be taken account of in planning your course. Why do you have to take their needs into account?

---

So, given these needs must be met, how are you to identify and analyse them? Just what is a 'needs analysis'? In short, it involves the collection and analysis of information from all those who will be involved and affected by the proposed course so that the planning stage can take account of as wide a range of needs as is practicable.

Obviously, this requires careful handling because every course demands a different level of needs analysis. For instance, if you are revising an existing course you should already have at least some basic information about needs which might simply need reviewing and extending in places. If, on the other hand, you are developing a brand new curriculum then a much more detailed needs analysis will be required before you make any further progress. Figure 8.3 provides a set of suggested questions, the answers to which would result in a full needs analysis report. If you are revising a course, choose whichever seem most appropriate. Having identified the kind of needs analysis you intend to carry out, you have then to decide how this information will be obtained. Figure 8.4 provides some suggestions. However, don't set up complicated surveys involving large numbers of people or feel obliged to cost everything to the last penny unless you are involved in a really large-scale development. Use your organization's support staff to help (e.g., if a technical costing is required) and be realistic. It's a matter of generating sufficient information on the basis of which you, your colleagues and your organization might make a professional judgement.

---

**Task 8.4: Conducting a needs analysis**

8.4(a)   Using Figures 8.3 and 8.4, conduct a needs analysis for your proposed course.

8.4(b)   Summarize your findings in a report which will form part of your curriculum development documentation.

---

**Figure 8.3** Questions for a needs analysis

1   What are your organization's criteria for numbers, costs, accommodation, staffing and resources?
2   Is there any demand for the course?
3   How long is the demand estimated to last?
4   Are there any similar courses running in the area? If so, will there be sufficient demand for all to run?
5   What is the estimated size of the potential student population?
6   What would a profile of the prospective students show?
7   Will the course appear in league tables?
8   What costs will the course incur?
9   Will the course attract any funding?
10   For those courses attracting fee-paying students, what price will prospective students be willing to pay?
11   What does the assessment and evaluation data from previous cohorts contain?
12   How was any previous needs analysis carried out? What information does it contain?
13   Can other staff who have been involved provide you with any additional information?
14   Will your course meet the organization's criteria?

**Figure 8.4** Possible strategies for needs analysis data collection

- *Meeting the organization's criteria*: liaise with others in the organization to clarify criteria and report back with information.
- *Judging demand size and longevity*: monitor any feeder routes for prospective students, e.g., conduct surveys of schools, employers, colleges, universities.
- *Identifying the competition*: survey other providers.
- *Profiling prospective students*: once you have identified feeder routes, survey these prospective students to identify their particular needs.
- *Costing*: accurate estimated costs of staffing, accommodation, resources, food/drink, administration, examination, etc., as appropriate.
- *Funding*: checks with organizations such as LSC, HEFCE, LAs (local authorities), NHS (National Health Service) trusts, police forces, etc., as appropriate.
- *Pricing*: survey of prospective students and of competition prices.
- *Learning from previous experience*: use existing assessment and evaluation data; liaise with other staff.

Having conducted and reported on the needs analysis, and assuming we are going ahead, the next stage is to specify or review the purposes of the course, often presented as aims and objectives.

## Stage 4: develop statements of purpose (aims and objectives)

Course purposes are shaped by two key things. First, the ideology underpinning the course (already specified in Task 8.2). Second, the curriculum model, or combination of models, representing the key features of the intended course. For example, a progressive ideology and process curriculum model would lead to aims and objectives emphasizing individual learner development and growth whereas classical humanism and a product curriculum would aim for learners gaining specified kinds and quantities of knowledge in order to fulfil specified roles in society.

---

**Task 8.5: Factors affecting course purposes**

Consider what model or combination of curriculum models will best support the course you are developing. Take into account your own preferences and, if relevant, the emphasis apparent in the syllabus of specification.

---

There is another dimension to stating purposes. You may recall that Chapter 3 introduced several different approaches to learning which would have a clear effect on aims, which are broad statements of purpose, and, in particular, objectives, which are much more specific course or lesson targets and learning outcomes. For example, an expressly behavioural perspective on learning will lead to objectives very different from those generated from a purely cognitive approach. Figure 8.5, adapted from Cohen and Manion (1989: 32–41) presents some guidance on two different types of objective.

**Figure 8.5** Defining, writing and using two types of objective

---

*Key characteristics of behavioural objectives*
- specify who is to perform the desired behaviour;
- specify this behaviour clearly and unambiguously;
- specify the conditions for the behaviour to be demonstrated;
- specify the standard used to determine success or failure.

*Using behavioural objectives*
- requires great care because it defines learning in one particular way (behaviourally);
- requires teachers/trainers to be sure this is appropriate for the course and the intended learning;
- is better not done unless these conditions are met.

*Key characteristics of non-behavioural objectives*
- may be more flexible and open-ended;
- still need expressing simply and linking to learning experiences;
- allow for broader notions of learning to be used, not just behaviour.

*When to use each type of objective*
- Behavioural objectives might well be most effective when the subject matter and intended learning is skill-based and can be demonstrated easily, or where overt writing or speaking can demonstrate appropriate levels of learning, or where learners need small, behavioural stages brought into the subject matter to provide clear, attainable targets.
- Non-behavioural objectives might be best used when the intended learning is more complex or less specific, is developmental and almost impossible to view in terms of behaviour without reducing the learning to an absurd level.

---

*Source*: Cohen and Manion 1989.

Task 8.6 provides some examples of behavioural and non-behavioural objectives from Certificate of Education students' course development work.

---

**Task 8.6: Examples of course objectives**

From the list below, identify which objectives are behavioural and which are non-behavioural, and think about why.

The student will be able to:

- demonstrate how to grip the (golf) club correctly;
- demonstrate how to place a casualty into the recovery position;
- increase their understanding of the theories of loss and bereavement;
- appreciate the importance of taking responsibility for their own health;
- open a file, input data, save the data and exit from a database program;
- identify and meet necessary health and safety regulations;
- feel more confident about using the specialist equipment;
- understand the thinking behind a theoretical model in economics;
- become a more reflective and critical professional;
- drive a minibus to Driving Standards Agency standards.

---

Having identified the main issues involved in expressing the purposes of a course through aims and objectives, there are two further points to make. First, when you come to write your course aims and objectives, keep them to the minimum necessary to specify the course intentions fully. Second, don't be afraid to mix behavioural and non-behavioural objectives provided you make it clear that you are doing this deliberately.

For example, in an NVQ healthcare assistants' course, your students will certainly need to meet the performance criteria which are, as with all NVQs, behavioural objectives and learning outcomes. However, you might also want to include in your practical operation of the course some more broadly based, non-behavioural objectives to cover the less obvious but very important aspects of working with patients on a busy ward. So, if your course intends learning of different kinds to take place, the objectives must recognize this. Just be honest and show you have been thoughtful about it.

All this means that we have reached the next stage, that of identifying and sequencing appropriate teaching/training and assessment experiences for our prospective students.

## Stage 5: specify content and sequence, then organize appropriate learning and assessment experiences

For many of us, these are the tasks we immediately associate with the notion of course development. Indeed, we might well relish the work because it involves us in working out what we consider to be the programme through which students can learn our specialist subject most effectively.

However, it is not too long before a number of key questions arise. How is content chosen, or rejected? What makes for a correct sequence? How are learning and assessment experiences linked to all this? Is a detailed plan required for each session or will a scheme of work suffice? Just what level of detail is required at this stage in the development of a new or revised course? The remainder of this section will provide some practical answers to these questions.

How is content chosen? In many cases course content is already specified by a syllabus or course specification. In other cases, teachers/trainers might have a much freer choice. However, don't forget our earlier work in this chapter which indicated that, however tightly specified the course content might be, and no matter how well known and commonly covered it is, individual teachers/trainers will always provide their students with (however slightly) different experiences. We can take nothing for granted here. All of us need to consider the content we teach and the basis on which we have chosen it.

---

**Task 8.7: Thinking about content and sequence**

Choose one of the following contexts:

1   Ben, a 9-month-old baby, is with you in his bedroom playing. Please get him bathed and changed etc. ready to go to sleep.

2   Jo, a learner driver, is going along a residential road at 25 m.p.h. and needs to turn the car around and drive back the way she has come. What does she need to do?

8.7(a)   Using one of the above contexts what, in your opinion, is the best practice sequence in which the activity should be carried out?

8.7(b)   What content do learner parents or drivers need to understand in order for them to achieve the objective of a (near) perfect performance?

---

Figure 8.6 presents two sets of responses from teacher training students to the first context in Task 8.7, bathing a baby. Note the differences. Is one of the sequences better? Why? What about the content involved? Would either or both sets of responses achieve the objective?

Group A explained that their objective was to achieve the bathing of the baby and that safety, hygiene and careful handling were the prime objectives and content to be used. In contrast, Group B stated that, for them, bathtime was an important element in the baby's routine, in elementary learning about water and hygiene, but that it can be fun too and an aid in developing the child's relationship with its parent(s) and, thus, its overall development. It was also seen by one student as having been an enjoyable time for the parent too! In other words, ideologically and in terms of curriculum models, these groups had very different starting points which led, in turn, to different content and, to a lesser extent in this example, differences in sequence.

**Figure 8.6** How to bathe a baby?

| Group A response | Group B response |
|---|---|
| 1  Warm baby clothes | 1  Make sure baby is happily and safely playing in bedroom |
| 2  Warm towel | 2  Warm clothes, run water, test, put in bath toys and bubbles |
| 3  Run bath | 3  Bring in baby, start tape of bathtime songs and sing along |
| 4  Take baby to bathroom | 4  Remove soiled nappy and clean baby as needed while singing |
| 5  Test water temperature | 5  Place baby gently in bath, reassure using toys and music |
| 6  Undress baby and remove nappy | 6  Wash baby carefully, using different cloth for face, still singing and playing |
| 7  Place baby carefully in bath | 7  Carry on playing, etc., as seems best |
| 8  Wash carefully and hygienically | 8  Gently remove baby from bath and wrap in warm towel |
| 9  Remove baby from bath carefully | 9  Dry baby carefully and apply cream/powder as appropriate |
| 10  Wrap baby in towel and dry | 10  Dress baby and begin playing going to bed game |
| 11  Use cream etc. and put on fresh nappy | 11  Turn off music, take baby to bedroom and lay him in cot |
| 12  Take baby to bedroom | 12  Play going to sleep game, read, play music, etc., as appropriate |
| 13  Dress baby | 13  Bring game to an end and settle baby safely down to sleep |
| 14  Lie baby safely in cot | 14  Clean and tidy bathroom |

---

**Task 8.8: Reviewing your sequence and content**

Look back at your response to Task 8.7. How did you define the objective? Which ideology and curriculum model(s) influenced your sequence and content? Would you want to revise your response at all?

---

In order to identify the appropriate content and sequence for your proposed course, it is important to take account of two key factors. First, the syllabus or specification and its associated content, ideology and model(s). Second, your own educational ideology and what seems to you to be the most appropriate curriculum model(s), as expressed in your aims and objectives. You must strike a balance between the course as laid out and your own ideas if your content and sequence are to enable the students to achieve your aims and objectives.

Assuming you were about to teach parents to bathe their babies, what kinds of learning and assessment experiences would you use to help them learn? Again, the answer is linked to the balance struck between the course and your own ideas. Thus, to caricature Group A's position, they might be tempted to hire an expert to run a series of lectures entitled 'How to bathe a baby: the way to infant hygiene and safety', with slides, data on water temperature and accidents to babies in bathrooms. Worksheets might be used to enable learning facts and procedures by rote, there would be practice sessions with dolls and participants' performance might be assessed through observation of the practice and some written tests.

Being equally unfair to Group B, on the other hand, they might run a series of workshops entitled 'Hygiene and hugs: making bathtime an enriching experience for all – a holistic perspective'. These would involve parents, a health visitor and a child psychologist working with a facilitator who would start from everyone's own experiences. Through discussion, inputs and home visits by the professionals, some reflection (a reflective log?) and the use of students' own children (and bathrooms!) everything would be brought together. Assessment would be informal and based on participants' contributions, involvement and evidence of their reflection. Thus, your selection of learning and assessment experiences will emerge directly from all your previous work on developing the course. Assessment was handled fully in Chapter 6. It is mentioned here simply to emphasize its role in providing information to all those involved about what has and has not been learned.

One further question remains with regard to selecting content, sequence, and learning and assessment experiences. As part of the process of course development or revision, is every session to be planned in detail? At this stage, the simple answer is no, unless what is being planned is a short event of some kind, say a one-day introduction to a new IT program. In this case, the full day's programme, resources and materials would be required.

In other cases, where longer and more involved courses are under development, what's needed is an outline scheme of work for the course and, usually, one short session (about an hour) which is planned and resourced to provide an indication of quality. As an illustration, Table 8.1 provides an example of part of a scheme of work.

---

**Task 8.9: Selecting and sequencing content and deciding on learning and assessment experiences**

Begin working on an outline scheme of work for your proposed course which will show how you intend students to achieve the aims and objectives specified earlier. Select and sequence your course content and, given practical limits to time and resources, decide on the kinds of learning and assessment experiences which will be most appropriate. Present them using the exemplar scheme of work layout in Table 8.1 or use one of your own.

**Table 8.1** An example of a scheme of work from a curriculum development proposal

GNVQ Advanced Business scheme of work for Elements 1.1, 3.1, 3.3: 'Marketing and Effects of Supply and Demand on Business' (1996)

| Session | Performance criteria (PC) | IT key skill | Content | Methods | Resource | Outcome | Assessment |
|---------|---------------------------|--------------|---------|---------|----------|---------|------------|
| 1 | PC 1.1.1 PC 3.1.1 | | Introduction to marketing principles | Lecture, discussion, brainstorm | Students' ideas, teacher input, OHPs | Initial thinking and ideas | Informal through class discussion |
| 2 | PC 3.1.2 | | Case study of a marketing function (traditional) | Individuals summarize main points from case study | GNVQ advanced textbook | Recognize main points in a sales and marketing plan and where they fit in | Informal through viewing individual findings, formal via individual reports |
| 3 | PC 3.3.3 | | Launching a new product onto the market | Guest speaker (medical company sales rep) | Speaker's handout on what to include in plan | Commercial company's perspective on a real problem | Written notes by each student |
| 4 | PC 3.1.3 | | The marketing mix | Video and discussion | Video | Theoretical base | |
| 5 | PC 3.1.4 PC 3.1.3 PC 3.3.4 | | Analysing marketing activities | Visit to blood transfusion centre and presentation by manager | Video, OHP, speaker's ideas and information package | Assignment set and budget limits set giving a real task and consultancy feel to work | |

(Continued overleaf)

**Table 8.1** continued

GNVQ Advanced Business scheme of work for Elements 1.1, 3.1, 3.3: 'Marketing and Effects of Supply and Demand on Business' (1996)

| Session | Performance criteria (PC) | IT key skill | Content | Methods | Resource | Outcome | Assessment |
|---|---|---|---|---|---|---|---|
| 6 | Evidence indicators for not-for-profit organizations in 3.1 and 3.3 | PC 3.1.2 PC 3.2.1 | Pooling of ideas | Ideas from all students noted | Flip chart and ideas | Central pool of ideas for all students to access | Informal through student discussion |
| 7 | | PC 3.1.2 PC 3.1.5 PC 3.1.4 PC 3.3.3 | Initial work on plan | Individual study and research, formal review of progress with teacher | Books, computers, information packs, students' and teachers' ideas/notes, central pool of ideas | Progress on sales and marketing plan, basic groundwork and initial drafting | Informal through teacher and student discussion |
| 8 | PC 3.1 PC 1.2 PC 3.3 | PC 3.2.3 PC 3.3.7 PC 3.3.1 PC 3.3.6 | Prepare presentation | Individual preparation on aspects of plan | Flip chart, computer, book, notes | Structure for presentation arrived at | |
| 9 | | | Presentation given and assignment submitted | Individuals present aspects of work to class | Flip charts, OHPs, assignments | Sharing ideas, constructive evaluation of others' ideas | Completed assignment and student presentations |

Source: Dunnill et al. 1995: 135.

## Stage 6: consider how your proposed course fits into the curriculum offer of your institution

Few courses are taught entirely in isolation, and many students are following more than one course in their programme of learning. For example, the idea of a coherent 14–19 curriculum was at the centre of the ill fated Curriculum 2000 reforms which began in September 2000. Reviews of this process of reform (Hodgson and Spours 2001, 2003; Hodgson et al. 2001a, b; Ofsted 2001b; QCA 2001a, b) have highlighted the importance of the issues below:

- The breadth requirements of Curriculum 2000 were limited by a range of factors, including funding, sixth-form size, content and assessment requirements.

- The GCSE five A*–C threshold had a powerful effect on how students are seen as being able to study subjects post-16.

- How universities perceived the new qualifications (AS and key skills in particular) was a major determinant of their value in the eyes of both teachers and students.

- The content requirements of AS and AVCE limited the time for enrichment activities and squeezed the time allocated to each course.

- Emphasis on knowledge and understanding was perceived to be greater in enhanced courses than on the ability to analyse, synthesize and evaluate or on research and study skills.

- The pressure to cover content, in part resulting from a modular curriculum, led to teachers using more didactic, instructional approaches.

- Excessive assessment demands on students and in consequence on staff and on the work of awarding bodies.

> **Task 8.10: Your course as part of an institutional curriculum**
>
> In the light of the issues above, consider the relation of your planned course to the students' overall programme of learning.

To summarize, therefore, this section has presented you with the challenge of developing or revising your own course. On the basis of the work presented in previous sections a seven-stage model for course design and development has been used and this section has taken you through six of these stages, to a point where your course is beginning to take practical shape. The importance of the definitions, ideologies and curriculum models handled in earlier sections has been stressed as a means of ensuring continuity and coherence of learning in your new course. The next section will address the final stage of course development, that of devising effective and appropriate evaluation and feedback procedures.

## 8.3 Evaluating your course

---

**KEY ISSUES**

---

What is evaluation?

Why evaluate? For what purpose and for whom?

What are you going to evaluate?

How and when will you evaluate?

How can you ensure evaluation data feeds back into your course planning cycle?

---

Just as you thought you were safe! Having put time and effort into the processes of reviewing your existing course and then developing a new course or revising an existing one, you assumed that was that. A job well done. The course is ready to run and you're rightly proud of your work. But no! Here is one last stage to work your way through. Surely, you groan, evaluation is just about filling in a form (sometimes) at the end of a course and little or nothing being done afterwards?

So, just what is evaluation and why is it so important? Before going further, consider your responses to Task 8.11.

---

**Task 8.11: Evaluation – your starting point**

8.11(a)   How regularly does evaluation take place?

8.11(b)   How appropriate and user-friendly are your evaluation methods?

8.11(c)   Do you let people use their own words at all?

8.11(d)   Do you evaluate in ways other than end-of-course forms?

8.11(e)   Do you evaluate against practically described learning purposes?

8.11(f)   Do you discuss the results internally, externally, never?

8.11(g)   Does anyone else get to know of the results?

8.11(h)   Do you ever change anything afterwards?

---

Evaluation is all about finding out if our new course is working properly. This, of course, is what Ofsted means by 'self evaluation' which lies at the heart of its inspection methodology. In general, therefore, evaluation involves generating data through a process of inquiry and then, on the basis of this, making judgements about the strengths and weaknesses and the overall effectiveness of the course, and making decisions about how to improve it further. As Cronbach (1980: 14) says: 'the history of social reform . . . is littered with examples of large-scale and costly catastrophes as well as more modest mistakes . . . evaluation offers to certify that a programme will live up to its advertising'.

There are people who use the words 'evaluation' and 'assessment' as if they were the same thing. Be careful. Assessment refers to information and judgements about individual students' learning. Evaluation is about gaining information and judgements about course effectiveness. It is important to see if our development work has succeeded and that our new course is meeting its aims and objectives. But there are others who are interested in our work and evaluation has to meet their needs too. So just who are these others?

Earlier sections of this chapter listed several groups who will be interested. As well as the course developers these include the students, the teachers/trainers, others such as managers in our organization together with employers, colleges and universities. We might well add funders, as many funding organizations such as the TECs, organizations within the NHS or the police service, charitable trusts, research sponsors and private companies will insist on evaluation as part of their funding criteria. Finally, in a wider national and global sense, given the increasing climate of accountability, the community in general is often involved and interested in evaluation findings.

All this means that evaluation can become very complicated, an issue we will deal with later in this section. However, in general, it means that any evaluation must specify its intended audience and then ensure it covers all their interests and not simply those of the course developer(s).

---

**Task 8.12: Evaluation – what, why and for whom?**

8.12(a)   Provide a definition of evaluation and say why it is not assessment.

8.12(b)   Why is evaluation an important part of course development?

8.12(c)   For your course, who might be interested in an evaluation and why?

---

Having established the need for an evaluation, what is going to be evaluated? Partly, as was argued in Chapter 7, this will depend on the course ideology and curriculum model(s) – that is, the kind of curriculum you have developed. However, you must also be clear about the main purpose of your evaluation. Is it to help course improvement, to establish its impact and outcomes or some combination of the two? And how much time and money is available, if any? Whatever you decide, ensure you are undertaking something which is practical. Considering these questions will help you to identify what you want to evaluate.

Even when you know the course well there may still be difficulties in deciding what to evaluate, or, as is often the case, what to leave out of an evaluation. Figure 8.7 presents two approaches to this question generated by groups of Certificate of Education students. Which seems the most appropriate to you and why?

In general, Group B's approach is to be recommended simply because it maintains a tight focus on the evaluation work. Even if you have limitless time, money and other resources for evaluation, you still need to be clear about what you are evaluating.

**Figure 8.7** Deciding what to evaluate: two approaches

Group A listed the main things that seem to happen in the course, e.g.:
- Are aims and objectives being achieved?
- Is it effective for the learners?
- What are the outcomes for the learners?
- What has been the impact on staff?
- Is there the right balance of process, content and product?
- Was there any evidence of enjoyment?
- What have the costs really been?
- What have the benefits really been?
- What do employers, colleges or universities think?

Group B identified broad areas for evaluation before generating specific questions, e.g.:
- The quality of classroom/training area experience;
- The organization of the course;
- Levels of student motivation and attainment;
- The organizational context for the course.

---

**Task 8.13: Deciding what to evaluate in your course**

8.13(a)   What is/are the purpose(s) of your evaluation?
8.13(b)   What broad evaluation areas can you identify?
8.13(c)   Why have you decided on these?

---

Having established the purposes and focal points of the evaluation, what specific issues do you want information about under each of the broad headings and how will you gain this information? The close link between these two is, in reality, a reflection of your educational ideology and the theoretical basis of your course, and this will identify the practical methods of any evaluation. Figure 8.8 presents three theoretical evaluation models to show this. Remember, as with all theoretical models, including those discussed in Chapter 7, you need to use them to help you review and develop your own practice rather than allow them to dictate your approach.

As teachers/trainers, most of us need evaluation data on a range of course issues, both because we want to monitor and improve our work and because others require data for their own purposes. For example, every FE college must collect a wide range of statistical information for the FEFC about levels of recruitment, retention and attainment. This points clearly to you needing to employ a variety of evaluation methods (although very few people adopt the classical approach which is more suitable for a formal research project). This variety is certainly acceptable provided, as before, you acknowledge it openly in your course proposal to show you are aware of what you are doing.

**Figure 8.8** Three models of evaluation

1   *Scientific evaluation I: classical evaluation*
Features:
- views the course as an experiment or treatment to be administered to the students;
- solely interested in measuring course effectiveness defined by the intended outcomes;
- will have test group(s) following the course and control group(s) not following it;
- tests all the students before and after the course to judge course effectiveness and to compare the course with others;
- data and reports very statistical/quantitative.

This is rather like the late Geoff Hamilton on BBC *Gardeners' World* testing the effectiveness of his organic methods against the use of chemical fertilizers and pesticides. Indeed, classical evaluation is directly descended from these physical science traditions: 'Students, rather like plant crops, are given pretests (seedlings being weighed and measured) and then submitted to different experiences. Subsequently, after a period of time, their attainment (growth or yield) is measured to indicate the relative efficiency of the methods (fertilizers etc. used)' (Hamilton 1976. 13).

2   *Scientific evaluation II: evaluation via behavioural objectives*
Features:
- still views the course as something of an experiment;
- draws on behavioural notions of learning and curriculum design;
- specifies the intended learning outcomes as behavioural objectives;
- records the proportion of students attaining/not attaining the specified behaviours;
- data and reports very statistical/quantitative.

This approach possesses all the advantages and disadvantages of behaviourist perspectives on education and training that were discussed in Chapter 3. For example, can all learning be expressed as behaviours? If not, then this reduces learning to a simplistic shadow of its true nature. However, there is an elegant simplicity to the approach which has seen it become ever more popular in a wide variety of education and training courses.

3   *Qualitative evaluation*
Features:
- views the course as a human, social activity, not as a scientific experiment;
- interested in a host of content and process issues but especially the course intentions and organization, the experience of the course in practice and the range of outcomes including the unintended;
- also interested in the perspectives of everyone involved, not just the course designer(s);
- uses methods such as observation, interviews and questionnaires as well as assessment and other data;
- reports more language-based than statistical.

This approach draws more on the arts and social sciences so that, rather than aiming for a simple rating of achievement, there is a more complex approach to the measurement of course effectiveness. This means that the aim is to present an holistic picture of the new course in operation which is designed to illuminate the reality of the course for all those involved. Thus, it is hoped, the various strengths and weaknesses might be identified.

> **Task 8.14: In your own words**
>
> 8.14(a)   Summarize the main points about these three evaluation models.
> 8.14(b)   Why, in practice, are a variety of approaches usually adopted?

Now you are in a position to identify what issues you want to evaluate within each of the broad evaluation areas identified in Task 8.13(b) and to specify how information about each could be collected. At this stage, just work through all the issues you would like to evaluate. To help you, Figure 8.9 shows how the same student Group B from Figure 8.7 turned their broad evaluation areas into a series of possible evaluation issues and strategies.

**Figure 8.9** Suggested evaluation issues and methods

---

*1   The quality of classroom/training area experience*

Specific issues worth evaluating:

- Purpose
- Pace
- Clarity of teacher talk
- Quality of student activity
- Teaching/learning resources
- Tutor–student and student–student relationships
- Discipline
- Teacher subject knowledge, etc.
- Quality of formative and summative assessment strategies

Suggested evaluation strategies/evidence sources (in no order):

- Teacher observation:
  by peer?
  by outsider/manager?
  by self?
- Ask the students:
  verbally?
  in writing?
  in writing?
  open or closed questions?
- Teacher qualifications
- Evidence of record-keeping/tracking and final success rates

*2   The organization of the course*

Specific issues worth evaluating:

- Planning – on the basis of any earlier evaluation?
- Resources
- Tutorials and support systems
- Staffing
- Monitoring and evaluation procedures

Suggested evaluation strategies/evidence sources (in no order):

- Evidence of schemes of work and resources available
- Course handbook on tutorial and support
- Evaluation data
- Staffing details
- Evidence of record-keeping/tracking and final success rates
- Ask the students:
  verbally?
  in writing?
  open or closed questions?

*3  Levels of student motivation and attainment*

Specific issues worth evaluating:

- Attendance
- Results
- Destinations
- Are students' ideas valued?

Suggested evaluation strategies/evidence sources (in no order):

- Registers
- Retention rates
- Formal results
- Teacher observation:
  by peer?
  by outsider/manager?
- Ask the students and note student demeanour, non-verbal behaviour etc.
- Are there any indications of fun, enjoyment, humour etc. demonstrated by staff and students?
- Any earlier evaluation data?

*4  The organizational context for the course*

Specific issues worth evaluating:

- Accommodation
- Resourcing
- Staffing
- Library, etc.
- Management and communication

Suggested evaluation strategies/evidence sources (in no order):

- Visit accommodation, view resources and library
- Ask the students:
  verbally?
  in writing?
  open or closed questions?
- Staffing details
- Formal question and answer systems:
  on paper
  face-to-face

---

**Task 8.15: Identifying specific evaluation issues and methods**

Use the suggestions in Figure 8.9 to help your thinking about evaluation.

8.15(a)    Select the specific issues you would want to evaluate in your course.

8.15(b)    Select the evaluation strategies you think would give accurate data.

8.15(c)    When would you collect the data? Why is the timing important?

8.15(d)    Explain your choices. How practical do you think they are?

8.15(e)    Revise your list of issues and strategies in the light of 8.15(d) so that you have a practical as well as an effective evaluation strategy.

Task 8.15(e) raises another major consideration, that of ensuring the evaluation you plan is able to operate in practice. Thus, your original choices in Task 8.15 might well have needed revising. Remember, a small-scale evaluation, properly thought through and carried out will be far more useful than a large, impractical and poorly implemented version.

Finally, what will happen to the results of your evaluation? They will need analysing and presenting in a clear format so that the findings can be conveyed to whoever requires them and, more importantly, so that you can identify those areas of the course that need improving and build these into your next course planning session (we should not forget that, in certain circumstances, there may well be a good case for not changing things). Whatever the situation, your report must explain the reasons for whatever action or non-action you propose to take.

To summarize, this section has defined course evaluation and has differentiated this from assessment. Evaluation has been presented as a means of judging course effectiveness for a range of interested parties and for a similar range of reasons. Advice has been provided about what to evaluate by suggesting the selection of a small number of key, broad areas as a starting point. Three theoretical models of evaluation have been used to explain the link between what is to be evaluated and how it can be evaluated, followed by an opportunity to make some of these links and to develop a practical and worthwhile evaluation programme. All this is presented as a sequence in Figure 8.10.

**Figure 8.10** Suggested sequence for developing a course evaluation

---

1  Identify the purpose(s) of the evaluation.
2  Identify the broad areas to be evaluated.
3  Consider the kind(s) of evaluation best suited to your needs.
4  Identify the specific issues to be evaluated and the methods.
5  Ensure the evaluation will be able to operate in practice.
6  Collect the data, analyse, and report to all involved.
7  Explain any proposed changes with reasons.
8  Build changes into next course planning cycle and evaluate.

---

Note the final stage. Evaluation is a continuous process if it is to help you keep improving the quality of your course. Moreover, given the moves towards increased accountability in all areas of education and training, as Hopkins (1989) notes, evaluation now often leads to a public discussion and to subsequent action or judgement. There are league tables for almost every aspect of education and training. If we are to engage in evaluation for reasons other than simply our own professionalism, and it seems we must, then any evaluation we carry out must be of high quality in order to promote and develop high quality education and training.

## 8.4  Scrutinizing your course

---

**KEY ISSUES**

---

Why not allow new and revised courses to operate as soon as they're worked out?

The scrutiny process: what's it all about?

How can a new or revised course be made ready for the scrutiny process?

What does a formal course proposal document contain?

What's involved in presenting a course and in scrutinizing other people's courses?

---

You might well ask, given all the hard work you have put in already, why you can't just run the course? There are two reasons. First, in line with the notions of increased efficiency and accountability mentioned frequently in this and other chapters, education and training organizations now expect new courses to be developed and presented to set criteria and then examined rigorously and, if necessary, revised, before being allowed to operate. In most colleges and universities, this is called the scrutiny process. National qualifications such as A level, the 14–19 diplomas and NVQ are offered by awarding bodies and they have a similar process, as do the academic examining boards, for those who wish to develop new or amended versions of such courses.

Second, there is a professional development dimension. Given that we might well have spent time and energy on developing a new course and this might well have been a team effort, there is still a danger that, being so involved and committed to it, we will fail to spot all the flaws in our work. A scrutiny process helps by allowing the organization to take some responsibility for helping us avoid making mistakes. As will be seen later in the section, it also provides us, our colleagues in the organization and in other similar organizations with opportunities to learn about curriculum development by taking part in it. It is the scrutiny process which lies at the heart of this section.

What is the scrutiny process? It is a set of procedures designed to support staff in the development and revision of courses. It ensures that such courses meet the criteria set by the organization and other relevant bodies, are planned to the highest standards, are examined by experts (internal and external to the organization) and are only then allowed to operate.

In most cases, the organization will provide staff with guidelines and some support in the scrutiny process. In this instance, some guidelines are set out in Figure 8.11, while this section and the book as a whole act as support.

**Figure 8.11** The scrutiny process

*Phase 1: Course development or revision*

1.1   The course development team plan what they consider to be an appropriate course following the appropriate framework (NVQ, degree, BTEC rules, police/nurse training regulations, etc.)

1.2   The proposed course is organized into a course proposal document and distributed to the others involved in the scrutiny process.

*Phase 2: Internal scrutiny*

2.1   The course development team makes a formal presentation of their proposed course and document to an internal scrutiny panel composed of the organization's representatives and a number (three?) of staff colleagues acting as internal scrutineers.

2.2   The internal scrutineers use the course document to become familiar with the proposal, listen to the presentation, discuss it and pose searching but not unfriendly questions to the course development team on any issues of concern.

*(Continued overleaf)*

**Figure 8.11** *continued*

2.3 At the end of this meeting, the internal scrutiny panel must pass one of four judgements on the proposed course:
1 accept unreservedly in which case the proposal goes forward to Phase 4;
2 accept subject to minor changes in which case the proposal moves to Phase 3;
3 accept subject to major changes in which case the proposal moves to Phase 3;
4 reject, which means the proposal has no chance of becoming an approved course.

*Phase 3: Revisions to original proposal*
3.1 Depending on the scale of the changes imposed by the internal scrutiny panel, the course development team works to amend the course proposal in line with the panel's requirements and resubmits a revised course proposal document.
3.2 Once the organization can see that all the necessary changes have been made, the proposal proceeds to the next phase.

*Phase 4: External scrutiny*
4.1 The scrutiny panel will reconvene but this time with two or three external validators.
4.2 The external validators are specialists in the field but from other organizations. Their role is to carry out an expert and impartial critical scrutiny of the proposed course.
4.3 The course development team makes another formal presentation of their proposed course and document.
4.4 The panel listens to the presentation, discusses it and poses more questions to the course development team on any issues of concern.
4.5 At the end of this meeting, the external scrutiny panel must again pass one of four judgements:
1 accept unreservedly in which case the proposal goes forward to Phase 5;
2 accept subject to minor changes in which case the proposal moves to Phase 5 after these changes have been made;
3 accept subject to major changes in which case the proposal might well need further external scrutiny;
4 reject, which means that the proposal has lost its chance of becoming an approved course.

*Phase 5: Course approved to operate*
5.1 The organization will allow the course to be run for up to five years subject to satisfactory levels of recruitment, retention and student success and to satisfactory annual evaluation reports.

What does a course proposal document contain? Figure 8.12 shows the content normally required. In addition, such documents are always presented in as professional a manner as possible. After all, the document represents the quality of your proposed course to those on the scrutiny panels.

**Task 8.16: The scrutiny process – what's it all about?**

8.16(a) Why shouldn't we just put our new courses straight into operation?
8.16(b) What are the purposes of a scrutiny process?
8.16(c) How does it work and what is the role of the course proposal document?

**Figure 8.12** Contents of a course proposal document

1   A brief rationale for the proposed course explaining why it is such an important development. Add information about student and market needs analysis. Add reasons for sizes of: recruitment targets; minimum and maximum numbers; staff/student ratios.
2   A statement of course aims.
3   An outline of course content expressed as objectives and outcomes.
4   A description of the course organization including: an outline scheme of work; one fully detailed session plan; a typical student's experiences; a typical student's attendance pattern.
5   Details of teaching and learning strategies to be employed.
6   An outline of the assessment framework to be used.
7   An outline of the evaluation framework to be used including sample materials.
8   An indication of any resource implications arising from the new course including accommodation, equipment and staffing (expertise and training as well as number).
9   A costs table including, if possible hourly staffing costs, any other support costs, accommodation and equipment, recurrent costs, overheads, etc. These are usually available from organizations' administrators.
10  An indication of revenue from the course showing sources and levels both short and (estimated) longer term together with some comment as to how certain and long-lasting the revenue might be.

This all looks like a pretty large piece of work, and so it is. This is a full course proposal and getting a new or revised course off the ground is a serious business. So, how can you make what you have already produced in terms of your new or revised course into a formal course proposal ready to go forward to the scrutiny process? For quick reference, Table 8.2 links each task from Chapters 7 and 8 with sections in the course proposal document.

**Table 8.2** Tasks linked to creating a course proposal document

| Proposal document content | Section | Task | Course development activity |
|---|---|---|---|
| 1, 2, 3, 4, 5, 6, 7 | 7.6 | 7.15 | Sharpen thinking on curriculum, ideology, curriculum models |
| 1, 2, 3 | 8.2 | 8.1 | Identify your curriculum development or revision task |
| 1, 2, 3 | 8.2 | 8.2 | Decide on the kind of course it will be |
| 8, 9, 10 | 8.2 | 8.3 | Identify the organization's criteria for costs, numbers, etc. |
| 2 | 8.2 | 8.4 | Conduct a needs analysis |
| 1, 2, 3 | 8.2 | 8.5 | Decide on the broad purposes for the course |
| 2, 3 | 8.2 | 8.6 | Specify the course aims and objectives |
| 4, 5, 6 | 8.2 | 8.7, 8.8, 8.9 | Specify content, sequence, learning/assessment experiences |
| 7 | 8.3 | 8.11, 8.12, 8.13, 8.14, 8.15 | Establish a set of evaluation procedures |

**Task 8.17: Writing most of your course proposal document**

8.17(a)   Using Table 8.2 collect all your responses to earlier tasks together.

8.17(b)   Write them up in full and arrange them under the ten headings of a course proposal document, as outlined in Figure 8.12.

You should find that the only areas requiring further work are 8, 9 and 10 on resources, costs and revenue. Once again, don't worry. Even if you hate working with figures Task 8.18 will show you how to tackle this area.

**Task 8.18: Writing the rest of your course proposal document**

Your own organization will have ready-made lists of costs for most kinds of course and will usually help refine these for your particular course. Ask for their standard costings and for additional advice if needed.

If you are hoping to run a self-financing course, hotels, conference centres and other venues all provide cost schedules on request. Just ask for them.

Revenue is more a matter of estimation. Work out what income you expect the course to generate and consider how certain you are of your figures and for how long you expect revenue to be earned. Write this up including the basis for your estimates. Ask your organization for help if you need it – they should be used to assisting their staff with this kind of issue.

8.18(a)   Write up your work on these areas and add to your course proposal document.

8.18(b)   Check through your document to ensure that every heading is complete and that the spelling, layout and general feel of the document is as professional (not flashy) as possible.

What is involved in being a presenter and a scrutineer at one of these scrutiny panel meetings? In order to gain the maximum quantity and quality of professional benefit from this chapter, you are strongly advised to work with at least one other person to reproduce a scrutiny process for yourself. If you are a member of a group, all the better. Several of you can work together to develop a proposal, perhaps starting with one person's idea or a real course development task someone has been given. Others can act as scrutineers of that group's proposal. Then you can reverse the roles.

In essence, what is being asked of you is to work from two perspectives: that of the curriculum developer and that of the scrutiny panel member. Things can often look different from someone else's perspective and you will learn a great deal by having your own course development scrutinized by someone else and by scrutinizing someone else's course proposal yourself. It will also be invaluable preparation for working on similar tasks in your teaching and training work. Indeed, a fair proportion of Certificate of Education course proposals become real courses and go into operation very smoothly because of their careful planning and preparation. To help you to prepare for a scrutiny panel meeting, Figures 8.13 and 8.14 provide guidance on how

**Figure 8.13** Being a scrutiny panel member

The role of a scrutiny panel member is:
- to complete a comprehensive evaluation of the proposal focusing on the use of curriculum ideology and design model(s) as well as evaluating the proposal as set out in Figure 8.12;
- to help the course development team to make progress and suggest action points as needed (unless the proposal is a non-starter, in which case the organization should have stopped it earlier);
- harder than it might seem!

We must therefore be critical where necessary, award praise where appropriate and, above all, be positive. We are there to help another set of professionals with their work, not to turn it into our work!

Tasks of a scrutiny panel member:
- Before the scrutiny panel meeting to read the course proposal document thoroughly and draw up a checklist of questions and comments.
- During the scrutiny panel meeting to listen to the presentation and delete or add questions and comments to the checklist.
- Immediately following the presentation to ask questions of clarification.
- During the post-presentation discussion to ask questions, discuss and provide feedback in a critical and/or positive manner as appropriate, perhaps by always having a positive suggestion to make following any criticism. If changes are needed, the job is to help them be made, not simply point out the problem.

**Figure 8.14** Being a course presenter at a scrutiny panel

The role of a course presenter is:
- to provide as professional a proposal document as possible well in advance of the meeting;
- to provide evidence of depth of information and thinking through the presentation;
- harder than it might seem!

We must, therefore, plan and prepare for the presentation very carefully. We are there to help other professionals to gain an accurate picture of our proposals, not to 'sock it to 'em'!

Tasks of a course presenter:
- Before the scrutiny panel meeting to supply sufficient copies of a high-quality course proposal document.
- To plan and deliver a professional presentation. There will usually be at least 20 minutes for your presentation and plenty of time for discussion and for the scrutineers' questions afterwards.
- To ensure that the style of the presentation reflects the course: give a sample of how students will experience it and use any techniques you feel are appropriate. Above all make it interesting (and fun!)
- During the scrutiny panel meeting to listen as well as talk, and not be too defensive.
- Immediately following the presentation to answer questions of clarification.
- During the post-presentation discussion to answer questions, discuss and respond to feedback as appropriate, avoiding defensiveness and always having a positive approach to the meeting. If need be, ask for positive action points to follow any criticism. Remember, if changes are needed, the job of the scrutiny panel is to help to develop the course.

to be a member of a scrutiny panel and how to be a course presenter. In order for scrutiny panel members to operate as effectively as possible, a sample checklist and form is provided in Figure 8.15. This would normally be printed over two sides of an A4 sheet and completed copies would be given to the presenters as well as to the organization's representatives.

**Figure 8.15** Suggestions for a scrutiny panel evaluation form

*Presenting team:*

*Course title and details:*

*Scrutiny panel criteria:*

Use the following checklist to make brief notes here as needed.
1  Is there a brief rationale for the proposed course? Does it include:
   • a student and market needs analysis?
   • recruitment targets?
   • minimum and maximum numbers?
   • staff/student ratios?
2  Is there a statement of course aims and objectives? Are these appropriate to the needs of the client group? Do they specify the kinds of intended learning outcomes?
3  Is there an outline of course content which is linked to the intended aims/objectives/outcomes?
4  Is there a description of the course organization, an outline scheme of work and a session plan, outlines of staff/student ratios, and a typical student's experiences and attendance pattern?
5  Are there details of teaching and learning strategies/materials to be employed which seem to match the intended aims/objectives/outcomes?
6  Is the assessment framework to be used appropriate to the intended aims etc.?
7  Is the evaluation framework to be used appropriate to the intended aims etc.?
8  Is there evidence that the following have been considered?
   • resource implications;
   • costs;
   • revenue.

*General comments and any recommended revisions/additions:*

*Overall recommendation* (delete as appropriate):
   • Accept now
   • Accept with minor/major revisions as specified above
   • Reject

*Name of scrutineer:*

*Date:*

---

**Task 8.19: Preparing for a scrutiny panel**

If you are able to attend a scrutiny panel meeting, either as a presenter or as a scrutineer, use Figures 8.13, 8.14 and 8.15 to help you prepare for the event.

To summarize, this section has examined the process through which most organizations now support and approve the development and revision of new courses. The scrutiny process has been explained and a framework provided for the new course to be presented as a single document. Furthermore, explicit links have been made between this final document and the tasks spread through this chapter so that readers are able to see how their work can contribute to a full course proposal.

Finally, the section has advised all readers to take part in the scrutiny process or something similar because of the tremendous amount of professional learning that will emerge from such an experience. To this end, guidance and advice have been provided covering both the roles of course presenter and scrutineer.

## Related new professional standards for teachers and trainers in the lifelong learning sector

### Domain A: professional values and practice

| PROFESSIONAL KNOWLEDGE AND UNDERSTANDING | PROFESSIONAL PRACTICE |
| --- | --- |
| *Teachers in the lifelong learning sector know and understand:* | *Teachers in the lifelong learning sector:* |
| AK 1.1 What motivates learners to learn and the importance of learners' experience and aspirations. | AP 1.1 Encourage the development and progression of all learners through recognizing, valuing and responding to individual motivation, experience and aspirations. |
| AK 3.1 Issues of equality, diversity and inclusion | AP 3.1 Apply principles to evaluate and develop own practice in promoting equality and inclusive learning and engaging with diversity. |
| AK 4.1 Principles, frameworks and theories which underpin good practice in learning and teaching. | AP 4.1 Use relevant theories of learning to support the development of practice in learning and teaching. |
| AK 4.2 The impact of own practice on individuals and their learning. | AP 4.2 Reflect on and demonstrate commitment to improvement of own personal and teaching skills through regular evaluation and use of feedback. |
| AK 4.3 Ways to reflect, evaluate and use research to develop own practice, and to share good practice with others. | AP 4.3 Share good practice with others and engage in continuing professional development through reflection, evaluation and the appropriate use of research. |
| AK 5.1 Ways to communicate and collaborate with colleagues and/or others to enhance learners' experience. | AP 5.1 Communicate and collaborate with colleagues and/or others, within and outside the organization, to enhance learners' experience. |

AK 7.1 Organizational systems and processes for recording learner information.

AK 7.2 Own role in the quality cycle.

AK 7.3 Ways to implement improvements based on feedback received.

AP 7.1 Keep accurate records which contribute to organizational procedures.

AP 7.2 Evaluate own contribution to the organization's quality cycle.

AP 7.3 Use feedback to develop own practice within the organization's systems.

## Domain B: learning and teaching

*PROFESSIONAL KNOWLEDGE AND UNDERSTANDING*

*Teachers in the lifelong learning sector know and understand:*

BK 1.1 Ways to maintain a learning environment in which learners feel safe and supported.

BK 2.1 Principles of learning and ways to provide learning activities to meet curriculum requirements and the needs of all learners.

BK 2.4 Flexible delivery of learning, including open and distance learning and on-line learning.

BK 2.5 Ways of using learners' own experiences as a foundation for learning.

BK 2.6 Ways to evaluate own practice in terms of efficiency and effectiveness.

BK 3.1 Effective and appropriate use of different forms of communication informed by relevant theories and principles.

BK 3.5 Systems for communication within own organization.

*PROFESSIONAL PRACTICE*

*Teachers in the lifelong learning sector:*

BP 1.1 Establish a purposeful learning environment where learners feel safe, secure, confident and valued.

BP 2.1 Provide learning activities which meet curriculum requirements and the needs of all learners.

BP 2.4 Apply flexible and varied delivery methods as appropriate to teaching and learning practice.

BP 2.5 Encourage learners to use their own life experiences as a foundation for their development.

BP 2.6 Evaluate the efficiency and effectiveness of own teaching, including consideration of learner feedback and learning theories.

BP 3.1 Communicate effectively and appropriately using different forms of language and media, including written, oral and non-verbal communication, and new and emerging technologies to enhance learning.

BP 3.5 Identify and use appropriate organizational systems for communicating with learners and colleagues.

## Domain C: specialist learning and teaching

| PROFESSIONAL KNOWLEDGE AND UNDERSTANDING | PROFESSIONAL PRACTICE |
|---|---|
| *Teachers in the lifelong learning sector know and understand:* | *Teachers in the lifelong learning sector:* |
| CK 1.1 Own specialist area including current developments. | CP 1.1 Ensure that knowledge of own specialist area is current and appropriate to the teaching context. |
| CK 1.2 Ways in which own specialism relates to the wider social, economic and environmental context. | CP 1.2 Provide opportunities for learners to understand how the specialist area relates to the wider social, economic and environmental context. |
| CK 3.2 Ways to identify individual learning needs and potential barriers to learning in own specialist area. | CP 3.2 Work with learners to address particular individual learning needs and overcome identified barriers to learning. |
| CK 4.2 Potential transferable skills and employment opportunities relating to own specialist area. | CP 4.2 Work with learners to identify the transferable skills they are developing, and how these might relate to employment opportunities. |

## Domain D: planning for learning

| PROFESSIONAL KNOWLEDGE AND UNDERSTANDING | PROFESSIONAL PRACTICE |
|---|---|
| *Teachers in the lifelong learning sector know and understand:* | *Teachers in the lifelong learning sector:* |
| DK 1.1 How to plan appropriate, effective, coherent and inclusive learning programmes that promote equality and engage with diversity. | DP 1.1 Plan coherent and inclusive learning programmes that meet learners' needs and curriculum requirements, promote equality and engage with diversity effectively. |
| DK 1.3 Strategies for flexibility in planning and delivery. | DP 1.3 Prepare flexible session plans to adjust to the individual needs of learners. |
| DK 2.1 The importance of including learners in the planning process. | DP 2.1 Plan for opportunities for learner feedback to inform planning and practice. |
| DK 3.1 Ways to evaluate own role and performance in planning learning. | DP 3.1 Evaluate the success of planned learning activities. |
| DK 3.2 Ways to evaluate own role and performance as a member of a team in planning learning. | DP 3.2 Evaluate the effectiveness of own contributions to planning as a member of a team. |

## Domain E: assessment for learning

| *PROFESSIONAL KNOWLEDGE AND UNDERSTANDING* | *PROFESSIONAL PRACTICE* |
|---|---|
| *Teachers in the lifelong learning sector know and understand:* | *Teachers in the lifelong learning sector:* |
| EK 1.1 Theories and principles of assessment and the application of different forms of assessment, including initial, formative and summative assessment in teaching and learning. | EP 1.1 Use appropriate forms of assessment and evaluate their effectiveness in producing information useful to the teacher and the learner. |
| EK 4.2 The role of feedback in effective evaluation and improvement of own assessment skills. | EP 4.2 Use feedback to evaluate and improve own skills in assessment. |
| EK 5.1 The role of assessment and associated organizational procedures in relation to the quality cycle. | EP 5.1 Contribute to the organization's quality cycle by producing accurate and standardized assessment information, and keeping appropriate records of assessment decisions and learners' progress. |

## Domain F: access and progression

| *PROFESSIONAL KNOWLEDGE AND UNDERSTANDING* | *PROFESSIONAL PRACTICE* |
|---|---|
| *Teachers in the lifelong learning sector know and understand:* | *Teachers in the lifelong learning sector:* |
| FK 1.1 Sources of information, advice, guidance and support to which learners might be referred. | FP 1.1 Refer learners to information on potential current and future learning opportunities and appropriate specialist support services. |
| FK 1.2 Internal services which learners might access. | FP 1.2 Provide learners with appropriate information about the organization and its facilities, and encourage learners to use the organization's services, as appropriate. |
| FK 3.1 Progression and career opportunities within own specialist area. | FP 3.1 Provide general and current information about potential education, training and/or career opportunities in relation to own specialist area. |

FK 4.1  Professional specialist services available to learners and how to access them.

FK 4.2  Processes for liaison with colleagues and other professionals to provide effective guidance and support for learners.

FP 4.1  Provide general and current information about a range of relevant external services.

FP 4.2  Work with colleagues to provide guidance and support for learners.

# 9
# Developments in post-compulsory education

## 9.1 What is Chapter 9 about?

Teachers and trainers in PCE may teach specialist subjects but they may also see themselves as educators or even educationalists and seek to become knowledgeable about the subject of education. This view is rather unpopular as teaching is seen more and more as a practical activity in which experience is valued over theoretical knowledge. The introduction of competence-based teacher training programmes means that teacher education programmes of the 1970s, built around the study of the subject of education, no longer exist. As we saw in Chapter 1, the new educational thought of that time resulted in ideas, theories and clear distinctions that are now thought to constitute an arid rationalism. It has been argued that too much had been lost in terms of theory, and that this had contributed to the current chaotic state of teaching in the post-compulsory sector. As a way forward the focus was particularly on developing post-compulsory teachers' understanding of the various educational philsophies that influence their professional practice. These views were later related to well-known theories of learning and studies of the curriculum. This chapter complements Chapter 1 and later chapters in a broader way. It provides the post-compulsory teacher with the essential background to begin to examine the contemporary historical development of PCE.

There are pedagogical, professional and theoretical reasons why a chronology is both important and necessary and it may be useful to elaborate these at the outset to avoid any misunderstanding.

In pedagogical terms, a chronology provides a useful starting point for someone new to the study of education or of any subject. It is a pedagogical device. Whatever the reason you want to understand a subject or topic, the essential first step is to develop a chronology of key events. Without this the process of serious study cannot begin. We would argue that if teachers do not have even a familiarity with the barest outline of the history of education they have no real understanding of the subject. If you are a post-compulsory teacher, whatever your academic or vocational background, you should have such a basic knowledge of post-compulsory educational history and also of significant developments in compulsory and higher education.

Trainee teachers in PCE and other sectors often see a chronology as just knowing dates and are uninterested. For very specific historical reasons a certain philistinism is now commonplace about historical events. Eric Hobsbawm has argued that this is because of the collapse of 'social mechanisms', such as the labour movement and trade unions, that linked people's experience to that of previous generations. The result of this collapse is that 'Most young men and women at the century's end grow up in a sort of permanent present lacking any organic relation to the public past of the times they live in' (Hobsbawm 1994: 3). In part, producing a chronology is an attempt to overcome this absence of a historical memory.

In professional terms, teachers sometimes like to think that their academic subject or their vocation is in some way independent of outside influences or broader trends in society. Nothing could be further from the truth. Any consideration of the nature of education or its translation into the sphere of policy is the result of a much more complex set of relations in society. This does not have to be a one-way street from broader social trends to education policy, nor is it a process devoid of contradiction. Serious thinking and passionately held beliefs about education will themselves have an impact on the way that society thinks about itself and there will often be a gap between intention and outcome. Nevertheless the way education is viewed will say a great deal about the society as a whole. This is because it is in the very nature of education that it will be emblematic of how society both would like itself to be and how it hopes and aspires to get there. In general then, it should be no surprise that discussion about education often preoccupies discussion about issues as apparently wide-ranging as economic performance and moral rectitude. The significance of the discussion for us is not at this level of generality but in the specific combination of political consensus and conflict, the identification of new problems and challenges and the shifts in policy that characterize the recent development of PCE in Britain.

We would argue that any professional practitioner must have this 'historical' knowledge if they are to be purposeful and active participants in their own professional development and the development of their profession. Otherwise those that do have that knowledge will merely direct them without them having the benefit of the informed discussion and debate that is essential to the practice of education. Part of the rationale for this chronology is that we recognize that many post-compulsory teachers will not have the background in educational history, social policy or related studies to give them a sufficient knowledge base to make a conscious contribution to debate. If approached studiously the chronology can, along with the associated activities, present opposing views and interpretations that, we believe, uncover the issues at the heart of contemporary debates and will provide clear critical guidelines for further discussion.

As far as theory is concerned, we can illustrate the possibilities of chronological thinking and show its importance by reference to the concept of the 'third way'. This new political idea has general application as well as a specific application to PCE. It is fashionable to talk of the 'third way' but hardly any one asks what was the 'second way' or, indeed, the 'first way'? If we do not know the answer, the 'third way' is a meaningless label. Broadly, we can characterize the 'first way' as the period of political consensus after World War 2 that resulted in the welfare state. The 'second way' is the relatively short period of Thatcherism that undid this consensus as Thatcher set out to destroy what she saw as 'socialism', a process that was entirely negative in social terms. The 'third way' is an attempt to produce policies which do not return to the welfare state or the market-place but allow government to have an impact through its policies on the global market to which 'there is no alternative' (TINA). There are various characterizations, of course, but most see the 'third way' as an attempt to find an alternative between the 'neoliberalism' of the Thatcherite sort and the 'social capitalism' adopted by those European governments that maintain a strong centralized welfare state (see Blair 1998; Giddens 1998; Hodgson and Spours 1999; Hayes and Hudson 2001). The 'third way' in PCE as in all policy-making arenas is a contested road and all that can be predicted is frequent policy changes. One assessment of Labour's first term in office concluded: 'Every day without a new education headline was regarded as a day wasted . . .' (Smithers 2001: 425).

Reading the chronology, it will be easy to see the relevance of developments in PCE to such a broad analysis. Since 2003, when the second edition of this book appeared, more and more reviews and reports have looked at the PCE, and in particular the 14–19, phase (Working Group on 14–19 Reform 2004; Foster 2005; Leitch Review of Skills 2006; DfES 2007a, b). It almost seems that any day without a new PCE headline is a day wasted! We do not draw any conclusions or do the work of interpreting any aspect of this chronology for our readers. Our purpose is to encourage teachers and trainers to think for themselves about the history of PCE and to develop their understanding of events. Suggestions and activities are given about how to think about the historical periods covered. We have also been involved in a small study of PCET student responses to the chronology and some of the activities set out here, that readers may find interesting (Hayes et al 2007).

As well as being important as a vehicle for developing our understanding, it is also true that a chronology is a very useful work of reference for PCE teachers.

Section 9.2 introduces the chronology of PCE in England and Wales presented in Section 9.3 which gives the reader a broad survey of major developments. Even readers familiar with PCE and its history might like to skim-read this chronology before reading later sections. Section 9.4 introduces readers to the possibility of developing useful comparative chronologies and presents several reasons why the USA is the place to start.

## 9.2 The purpose of the chronology

What follows is an overview of major government reports, Education Acts and important developments relating to PCE which provide the essential historical background to the analysis of the issues discussed in previous chapters. Emphasis is given to developments in the post-World War 2 period, although major developments relating to education since the industrial revolution are also summarized. The purpose is to provide the reader with basic factual information in a concise and accessible form. Authorial commentary and discussion has been largely omitted but the selection has a deliberate focus on developments in FE and youth training. We do not hide the fact that it is a central part of our argument that developments in this latter area are now influencing education at all levels. Developments in the general educational sphere, in AE, HE and in special education are also listed if these are essential to the identification of educational trends.

## Reading the chronology

A chronology is often seen as just a list of events in date order. We are using the term to describe a carefully selected list that gives the reader an overview of key events, reports, Acts and writings in the history of PCE. The best way to approach the chronology is to skim-read the dates and headings in bold. Then go back through the whole document reading complete sections or entries of interest. The tasks are in the form of questions to guide your thinking about historical periods.

## Reflecting on the chronology

To make sense of the chronology we suggest two methods of reflection. The first is to think in terms of what different generations of young people might have expected or experienced of PCET in any specific historical period. The second approach is to step back from the details of the particular discussion or development in PCE and attempt to locate young people's expectations in the wider context of social policy and political and economic events.

Boxes within the text contain relevant political and economic facts to remind the reader of the historical context of the events listed. The interaction between these three activities (getting familiar with particular events, imagining the expectations of generations of young people and locating these in a wider social context) are essential to understanding.

## 9.3  A chronology of post-compulsory education

**1563: Statute of Artificers**. This statute established the seven-year apprenticeship as the basic form of training in England. A further Act, the Poor Law of 1601, allowed for the forcible apprenticeship of pauper children. Craft apprenticeship was the form of technical training up to the time of the industrial revolution. Arguably, it remained the dominant form of work-related training up to the 1960s when the Industrial Training Act (1964) was passed.

**1823: Mechanics' Institutes established**. Mechanics' Institutes were set up in Chester in 1810, Perth in 1814, Edinburgh in 1821 (actually a 'school of arts') and most famously in Glasgow in 1823. George Birkbeck taught at what was to become the Glasgow Mechanics' Institute but left to practise as a physician in London. He helped establish a similar institute there in 1823 which was to become Birkbeck College. The movement grew and had its own publication *The Mechanics Magazine*. By 1826 there were 110 institutes and by 1850 some 600,000 people were attending classes in one of 610 institutes.

**1846: pupil–teacher system introduced**. Bright pupils were apprenticed at 13 years of age to head teachers for a period of five years.

**1856: Royal Society of Arts (RSA) founds first national examining board**.

**1856: Education Department formed**. Robert Lowe became vice-president in 1859 and introduced the system of 'payment by results' which lasted until 1900. Grants were given on the basis of school attendance, which was revealed to be low by the Newcastle Commission Report of 1861, and on the results of an examination in the 'three Rs'.

**1864: Clarendon Commission Report**. The commission suggested that the classical curriculum of the public schools be supplemented by instruction in subjects such as mathematics and science.

**1868: Taunton Commission Report**. The commission emphasized the importance of natural science as a subject because it was seen as of value in 'occupations'. The commissioners outlined various 'grades' of education ending respectively at 14 (Grade 3), 16 (Grade 2), and 18 (Grade 1), meeting the needs of the various social classes.

**1870: Elementary Education Act (Forster Act)**. The Great Education Act introduced a national system of elementary education for children up to 13 years of age replacing the previous system based on 'voluntary schools'. School boards became responsible for the running of the new 'Board Schools' and pupil attendance was at their discretion. Fees were charged. The Education Act of 1880 had to be passed to attempt to make elementary education compulsory by requiring school boards to enact by-laws to this effect. Employment of children under 10 was made illegal under the Factory and Workshops Act of 1878. Introducing the Act, Forster told the Commons: 'Upon the speedy provision of elementary education depends our industrial prosperity' (Maclure 1965: 104).

---

**Task 9.1**

Consider what sort of education a young person would receive at this time. Why should an educational debate about the suitability of an education based upon the classics or one extended to include more relevant subjects such as mathematics or science arise in the 1860s? Why should there be only an 'elementary' education Act passed at this time and why one that provided an education which was neither universal nor free?

---

**Education in context: 1868–1922**

*Prime ministers*: 1868 Disraeli (Conservative); 1868–74 Gladstone (Liberal); 1874–80 Disraeli II (Conservative); 1880–85 Gladstone (Liberal); 1885–86 Gascoyne-Cecil, 3rd Marquis of Salisbury (Conservative); 1886 Gladstone (Liberal); 1886–92 Gascoyne-Cecil, 3rd Marquis of Salisbury (Conservative); 1892–94 Gladstone (Liberal); 1894–95 Primrose, 5th Earl of Rosebery (Liberal); 1895–1902 Gascoyne-Cecil, 3rd Marquis of Salisbury (Conservative); 1902–05 Balfour (Conservative); 1905–08 Campbell Bannerman (Liberal); 1908–16 Asquith (Liberal/coalition); 1916–22 Lloyd George (Liberal/coalition).

*Presidents of the Board of Education*: from January 1900, Duke of Devonshire; from August 1902, Marquis of Londonderry; from December 1905, A. Birrell; from January

1907, R. McKenna; from April 1908, W. Runciman; from October 1911, J. Pease; from May 1915, A. Henderson; from August 1916, Marquis of Crewe; from December 1916, H. Fisher.

*Key political and economic events*: 1851 Great Exhibition; 1867 Paris Exhibition, Reform Act; 1868 Trades Union Congress formed; 1870–71 Franco-Prussian War; 1873 'Great Depression'; 1883 Depression, Fabian Society formed; 1887 Jubilee; 1889 first skyscraper in Chicago; 1897 Diamond Jubilee; 1898 Spanish American War, match girls strike; 1889 London dock strike; 1899–1902 Second Boer War; 1903 Ford Motor Company founded; 1914–18 World War 1; 1917 Russian Revolution.

**1879: the City & Guilds of London Institute (CGLI), founded in 1878, is given the responsibility for technical examining from the RSA.**

**1880: the famous Regent Street Polytechnic founded,** one of many polytechnics that developed out of the Mechanics' Institutes in different parts of Britain.

**1882–84: Samuelson Committee.** The committee made recommendations about the need for scientific and technical instruction of the sort that was already available to workers in America and many European countries.

**1889: Technical Instruction Act.** This enabled the new counties and county councils to provide technical education. A transfer of tax reserves popularly known as 'whisky money' was used mostly to provide science education.

**1890: day training colleges for teachers are introduced.**

**1902: Education Act (Balfour Act).** When introducing his bill in the house Balfour stressed the need for a sound general education. There was already a single supervisory body for education in existence at a national level. This was the Board of Education that had been formed by an Act of 1899. Actual provision of education at a local level became the responsibility of local education authorities (LEAs) which took over the powers of the school boards. They were required to form education committees. Pupils could now stay on in an elementary school up to 16 years of age and beyond. LEAs had powers to train teachers.

**1903: the Association for the Higher Education of Working Men founded.** It became the Workers' Educational Association (WEA) in 1905. By 1968 the WEA was catering for 150,000 students and had 85 full-time staff (WEA evidence to the Russell Report 1973).

**1906: Haldane Committee Report on technical education.** The report called for the establishment of a group of colleges of science and technology where the highest specialized instruction could be given. The result was the founding of Imperial College in 1907.

**1907: Ruskin Hall (1899) became Ruskin College, Oxford.** Its founding document states that the college is 'designed to equip the workers for the struggle against capitalism and capitalist ideology'.

---

**Education in context: 1922–45**

---

*Prime ministers*: 1922–23 Bonar Law (Conservative); 1923–24 Baldwin (Conservative); 1924 MacDonald (Labour); 1924–29 Baldwin (Conservative); 1929–35 MacDonald (Labour/coalition); 1935–37 Baldwin (National); 1937–40 Chamberlain (National); 1940–45 Churchill (coalition).

*Presidents of the Board of Education*: from October 1922, E. Wood; from January 1924, C. Trevelyan; from November 1924, Lord Percy; from June 1929, Sir C. Trevelyan; from March 1931, H. Lees Smih; from August 1931, Sir D. Maclean; from June 1932, Lord Irwin (Viscount Halifax); from June 1935, O. Stanley; from May 1937, Earl Stanhope; from October 1938, Earl De La Warr; from April 1940, H. Ramsbotham; from July 1941, R. Butler.

*Ministers of education*: from August 1944, R. Butler; from May 1945, R. Law.

*Key political and economic events*: 1924 first Labour government; 1926 General Strike; 1929 Wall Street crash, Depression; 1931 Empire State Building completed; 1933 Hitler becomes chancellor of Germany; 1936–39 Spanish Civil War; 1939–45 World War 2.

---

**1917: School Certificate introduced**.

**1918: Education Act (Fisher Act)**. This Act raised the school leaving age to 14 with most pupils staying in all-age elementary schools. Other key actions were: abolition of fees; the requirement that central government met not less than half the costs of educational provision; and that young workers should have a right to day release. Many other things 'allowed' but not compelled by the Act fell when funding was cut by one-third in 1922 ('Geddes Axe'). Introducing his Education Bill on 10 August 1917, H.A.L. Fisher, the architect of the 1918 Act, argued that 'education is one of the good things of life' and that the 'principles upon which well-to-do parents proceed in the education of their families are valid; also *mutatis mutandis* for the families of the poor' (Maclure 1965: 175).

**1922: R.H. Tawney's *Secondary Education for All* published**.

**1926: Evening Institutes established**. The precursors of AE institutes and colleges, they, along with the technical schools, provided most of the technical education available in the inter-war period.

**1926: Hadow Report *The Education of the Adolescent***. The Hadow Committee recommended a broad and balanced secondary school curriculum which prepared students for diverse occupational groups. It called for the establishment of 'modern' or 'central' schools and 'grammar' schools for pupils with different gifts. Hadow subsequently headed committees that reported on the primary school (1931) and the nursery and infant school (1933).

**1938: Spens Report**. The *Report of the Consultative Committee on Secondary Education* was strongly supportive of the idea of 'technical high schools' which would not be narrowly vocational but equal in status to grammar schools. The basis for the post-war tripartite system was now set. Spens also suggested changes to the curriculum, the School Certificate and the matriculation system.

**1939–45: day release expands from 42,000 to 150,000 during the World War 2.**

**1940: the Department of Education publishes its 'Green Book'** *Education after the War*.

**1942: Beveridge Report**. This set out plans for a comprehensive system of social security 'from the cradle to the grave'.

**1943:** *Educational Reconstruction*. This White Paper set out a vision of an educational system after the war which would provide for diversity while ensuring equality of educational opportunity.

**1943: Norwood Report**. In a report about examinations appeared proposals for a system of selection through intelligence testing for entry into a tripartite secondary education system made up of modern, technical and grammar secondary schools.

**1944: McNair Report**. McNair proposed three-year training courses for teachers. The report suggested that training for technical teachers should commence after, rather than before, they started to practise as teachers.

**1944: Education Act (Butler Act)**. This Act made provision of primary, secondary and FE a duty. A clause allowed for the possibility of compulsory (part-time) FE for all young people up to the age of 18. It was, however, only to become compulsory on a day to be decided. The school leaving age was to be raised to 15.

---

**Task 9.2**

This task should be in written form, either as short essays or as a group activity using flip charts. Discuss the period from 1870–1945 with your fellow students. What would school leavers expect to receive in terms of PCE during this period? Construct brief educational biographies of people who would have been in their late teens in, for example, 1880, 1910 and 1930. Having done this identify the key characteristics of British education over the period from 1870 to 1913 and between the two world wars (1918–39). Comment on how you think this reflects the position of Britain in the world and its economic situation during the two periods. You might like to consider why 1870 is considered to be an economic turning point for Britain.

---

**Education in context: 1945–51**

*Prime minister*: 1945–51 Clement Attlee (Labour).

*Ministers of education*: from August 1945, Ellen Wilkinson; from February 1947, George Tomlinson.

*Key political and economic events*: 1945 United Nations established; 1947 European reconstruction (Marshall Plan); 1950–53 Korean War; 1950 Britain is the economic leader in Europe; 1951 Festival of Britain.

**1945: Percy Report**. *Higher Technological Education*, the report looked at how universities were responding to the needs of industry.

**1945: Emergency Training Scheme introduced**. The aim of this scheme was to increase the supply of teachers in the aftermath of war. After much criticism, it ended in 1951.

---

**Education in context: 1951–64**

*Prime ministers*: 1951–55 Winston Churchill (Conservative); 1955–57 Sir Anthony Eden (Conservative); 1957–63 Harold Macmillan (Conservative); 1963–64 Sir Alec Douglas-Home (Conservative).

*Ministers of education*: from November 1951, Florence Horsburgh; from October 1954, Sir David Eccles; from January 1957, Viscount Hailsham; from September 1957, Geoffrey Lloyd; from October 1959, Sir David Eccles; from July 1962, Sir Edward Boyle. The Ministry of Education became the Department of Education and Science (DES) in April 1964 with Quintin Hogg as secretary of state for education and science.

*Key political and economic events*: the post-war economic boom; the Cold War; anti-colonial struggles in the Third World; 1952 Mau Mau rebellion in Kenya; 1953 Organization of African Unity formed; 1956 Hungarian Revolution; 1956 Suez crisis, Vietnam War begins; 1957 Treaty of Rome, European Economic Community (EEC) formed; 1961 Berlin Wall; 1962 Cuban missile crisis.

---

**1951: General Certificate of Education (GCE) introduced**. The GCE replaced the much criticized School Certificate.

**1956: White Paper** *Technical Education*.

**1957: Willis Jackson Report** *The Training of Technical Teachers*.

**1959: Crowther Report** *15–18*. The report looked at the different educational needs of a technological age. It noted that over 40 per cent of LEAs had no technical schools. For those who got 'incurably tired of school' the report argued for a 'fresh start in a technical college or some other quasi-adult institution' (HMSO 1959: 412). Specialization in-depth was necessary in the sixth form but not on the basis of vocational usefulness. Crowther recommended that the school leaving age be raised to 16. By 1980 it was hoped that half of 16–18-year-olds should be in full-time FE.

**1960: the Further Education Staff College founded at Coombe Lodge, Blagdon, near Bristol**.

**1963: 'University of the Air' called for in a speech by Harold Wilson**. Wilson told his biographer that this was what he wanted to be remembered for 'above almost anything else in his career' (Timmins 1996: 300).

**1963: Robbins Report** *Higher Education*. 'Throughout our report we have assumed as an axiom that courses of higher education should be available for all who are qualified by ability and attainment to pursue them and who wish to do so' (Maclure 1965: 297). Robbins set out a vision of how HE could expand. He suggested an increase from 8 per cent of the school leaving population to 17 per cent by 1980. The report resulted in the setting up of the Council for National Academic Awards (CNAA) and made the training of teachers a responsibility of HE. Teacher training colleges were renamed Colleges of Education. Colleges of advanced technology (CATs) became university institutions.

---

**Task 9.3**

The 1960s was a decade of influential reports. Two others of note are the Newsom Report *Half Our Future* (1963) which suggested that schools should offer a more modern education relevant to the experiences of pupils of below average ability, and the Plowden Report *Children and their Primary Schools* (1967) which put the case for child-centred education. A reaction came at the end of the decade with the publication of the *Black Papers* on education in 1969 and 1975 which argued for a return to formal methods of teaching, grammar schooling and hard-working academic students at university level. Consider what PCE would be available to young people in the latter half of the decade. What is special about the 1960s that made it a decade of political and educational consensus?

---

---

**Education in context: 1964–70**

*Prime minister*: 1964–70 Harold Wilson (Labour).

*Secretaries of state for education and science*: from October 1964, Michael Stewart; from January 1965, Anthony Crosland; from August 1967, Patrick Gordon Walker; from April 1968, Edward Short.

*Key political and economic events*: post-war political consensus: economic and industrial 'modernization' becomes a theme; The Beatles; Vietnam War; 1964 (USA) Civil Rights Bill; 1968 student protests, Organization of Arab Petroleum Exporting Countries (OAPEC) formed; 1969 first man on the moon.

---

**1964: Certificate of Secondary Education (CSE) introduced.** CNAA established.

**1964: Industrial Training Boards (ITBs)** established by the minister of labour as a consequence of the Industrial Training Act of the same year. The ITBs were meant to improve the quality of training and thus tackle the problem of real craft skill shortages. Administered by employers and trade union representatives the ITBs covered most of the large industrial employment sectors. Within seven years there were '27 ITBs covering employers with some 15 million workers' (Finn 1987: 56).

**1969: Open University founded.**

---

**Education in context: 1970–4**

*Prime minister*: 1970–74 Edward Heath (Conservative).

*Secretary of state for education and science*: from June 1970, Margaret Thatcher.

---

> *Key political and economic events*: 1971 collapse of the Bretton Woods agreement, President Nixon formally ended convertibility of gold 'on demand' with the dollar; 1973 miners' strike, oil crisis, three-day week, Britain joins the EEC; 1974–75 world economic recession.

**1970: Education (Handicapped Children) Act**. A hundred years after the great Elementary Education Act, children categorized as 'severely subnormal' and considered 'ineducable' were brought out of junior training schools and into the education system.

**1970: first tertiary college founded in Devon**. The development of tertiary colleges had been argued for by several influential figures, including Tessa Blackstone.

**1971: Open University** enrolled its first students.

**1972: James Report**. This report suggested three stages of teacher training. A two-year diploma in higher education followed by a year of professional studies based in school. This would lead to the award of the BA (Ed.).

**1972: ROSLA**. The school leaving age was raised to 16 from September.

**1972: *Training for the Future* (DE)**. This White Paper highlighted failures in the 1964 Industrial Training Act and called for the phasing out of the training levy and for a new role for ITBs. It set up the Training Opportunities Scheme (TOPS).

**1973: Technician Education Council (TEC) and Business Education Council (BEC) set up**. This was as a result of the 1969 Haslegrave Report proposals to plan, coordinate and administer technical courses and examinations.

**1973: Russell Report *Adult Education: A Plan for Development***. As the title suggests, Russell argued for an expansion of non-vocational AE, particularly because of the unmet needs of 'school-leavers and young adults, older adults, the handicapped and "the disadvantaged" '. Russell set the tone for much of the subsequent debate about AE.

**1973: Manpower Services Commission (MSC)**. The MSC was set up under the Employment and Training Act 1973 to supervise employment and with sufficient powers to plan training at national level. The MSC assumed its responsibilities on 1 January 1974.

**1973: Haycocks Report (Haycocks I) on the training of full-time FE teachers**. This report made major recommendations for improved training. The government, in Circular 11/77, welcomed the proposals and supported the in-service training of 3 per cent of staff at any one time. The report was followed in March 1978 by Haycocks II on AE and part-time teachers and in August 1978 by Haycocks III on the training of FE teachers for 'education management'.

---

**Education in context: 1974–79**

*Prime ministers*: 1974–76 Harold Wilson (Labour); 1976–79 James Callaghan (Labour).

*Secretaries of state for education and science*: from March 1994, Reg Prentice; from June 1975, Fred Mulley; from September 1976, Shirley Williams.

*Key political and economic events*: sterling crisis, IMF intervention, stagflation (inflation and high unemployment); 1975 Vietnam War ends, civil war in the Lebanon; 1978 Egypt and Israel sign the Camp David Treaty; 1979 Islamic Republic established in Iran, 'winter of discontent' in Britain.

---

**1976: the Great Debate**. Prime minister James Callaghan delivered a speech 'Towards a national debate' on 18 October 1976 at Ruskin College, Oxford. This speech has been described as 'a beacon in the history of post-war education. It brought education into the full light of public debate, giving education a position of prominence on public agendas where it has remained ever since' (Williams 1992: 1–2). One question that Callaghan was addressing had been set for him by Fred Mulley (secretary of state for education and science from June 1975): what was available for the 16–19-year-olds? One concern was the overspecialization at A level. In the speech the goal of education was said to be 'to equip children to the best of their ability for a lively constructive place in society and also to fit them to do a job of work'. Emphasis must be given to 'not one or the other, but both'. One passage is worth quoting as it could have been a statement made by any education minister, secretary of state for education, prime minister or member of the opposition since then:

> Let me repeat some of the fields that need study because they cause concern. There are the methods and aims of informal instruction: the strong case for the so-called 'core curriculum' of basic knowledge; next, what is the proper way of monitoring the use of resources in order to maintain a proper national standard of performance; then there is the role of the Inspectorate in relation to national standards; and there is the need to improve relations between industry and education.
>
> (Maclure 1988: 169)

The Great Debate itself centred around eight days of debate organized at a regional level and led by the DES. A White Paper *Education for Schools* published in 1977 summarized the debate.

---

**Task 9.4**

Claims about the importance of historical figures and their speeches are often made. To understand why Callaghan's speech is held to be exceptional the economic context must be examined. Some thinkers argue that the reasons for the revival of vocationalism since the 1970s are 'primarily economic' (Skilbeck et al. 1994: 1). Try to identify these economic factors. Begin by asking what educational opportunities would young people expect in the middle and late 1970s.

**1977: the Holland Report** *Young People and Work* **(MSC).** The Holland Report proposed 'building a better workforce more adapted to the needs of the eighties'. It proposed work experience and work preparation courses for unemployed young people. They would be paid a weekly allowance. It proposed the setting up of the YOP which began in 1978.

**1977: the FEU set up as a curriculum development and dissemination body for FE.** It was originally called the Further Education Curriculum Review and Development Unit. Although it was a quasi-autonomous body, the FEU was funded by the DES.

**1978: the Warnock Report** *Special Educational Needs.* Warnock abolished the various categories of handicap then in use and suggested a wider more individualized concept of special needs which was to be enshrined in the 1981 Education Act.

---

**Education in context: 1979–90**

---

*Prime minister*: 1979–90 Margaret Thatcher (Conservative).

*Secretaries of state for education and science*: from May 1979, Mark Carlisle; from September 1981, Sir Keith Joseph; from May 1986, Kenneth Baker; from July 1989, John MacGregor.

*Key political and economic events*: monetarism (controlling inflation by controlling the money supply), Thatcherism (the manifestation of this in the Thatcher government), privatization (denationalization of industry and government); 1982 Falklands War; 1984 miners' strike; 1987 stock market crash, 'There is no such thing as society' (Margaret Thatcher); 1989 fall of Berlin Wall, collapse of Communist regimes in Eastern Europe.

---

**1979:** *A Basis for Choice* **(FEU).** This report stressed the need for a 'common core' curriculum which emphasized transferable skills and flexibility through participating in 'learning experiences' rather than narrow skills-based teaching.

**1981:** *A New Training Initiative* **(NTI).** The MSC produced two documents: *A New Training Initiative: A Consultative Document* in May 1981 and later in December *A New Training Initiative: An Agenda for Action*. These documents set the training agenda for the decade. Skills training for young people and adults was covered.

**1982:** *17+ A New Qualification* **(DES).** This document set out the basis for the introduction of the CPVE for students who had not yet chosen their vocation.

**1983: TVEI starts.** Announced by Mrs Thatcher in November 1982, TVEI was to be the largest curriculum intervention ever by a government. The scheme was under the control of the MSC. It was a broad and experimental scheme aimed at preparing 14–18-year-olds for the world of work and developing personal qualities such as enterprise and 'problem solving' skills.

**1983: YTS.** YTS replaced YOP. In 1988 there were over half a million contracted YTS places and an average of 370,000 students in training.

**1983: Business and Technology Education Council (BTEC) formed through the merger of BEC and TEC.**

**1984:** *Training for Jobs.* This White Paper made clear the government's intention to make the MSC the 'national training authority'. Another report, *Competence and Competition* by the National Economic Development Office (NEDO)/MSC saw the competitive success of Japan, Germany and the USA as being related to their investment in education.

**1984: The 'Great Training Robbery' begins.** The lecturers' union NATFHE's label for the way in which private agencies milked the cash cow of MSC money aimed at the new YTS initiative.

**1985: Further Education Act.** This Act allowed colleges to engage in commercial activities related to areas of expertise and generate more funding. Governors were made responsible for the college budgets.

**1985: CPVE introduced.** It was never successful, even with less able pupils, and take-up was poor.

**1986: NCVQ was established on 1 October.** Only 40 per cent of the workforce held relevant qualifications. Despite the 'tremendous expansion in training', this was still a much lower proportion than in other countries. NCVQ's primary task was 'to reform and rationalise the provision of vocational qualifications through the creation of the National Vocational Qualification Framework' (NCVQ 1988: 1). The NCVQ introduced through the awarding bodies (RSA, CGLI, etc.) competence-based NVQs that were based in the workplace and not just work-related.

**1987: Enterprise in Higher Education Initiative (EHEI).** Seen as the HE equivalent of the TVEI this initiative had a budget of £100 million. The aim was to see every person in HE developing 'competencies and aptitudes relevant to enterprise'.

**1988: the General Certificate of Secondary Education (GCSE) replaces the GCE and CSE.**

**1988: Education Reform Act (ERA).** This Act, which followed from Kenneth Baker's so-called Great Education Reform Bill sought to revitalize the 'producer dominated' education system (Maclure 1988: iv). ERA brought in the National Curriculum for schools with core subjects (English, mathematics, science and religious education) to be learned by all. Several cross-curriculum themes were also identified: environmental education; education for citizenship; careers education and guidance; health education; and economic and industrial understanding. It also had a strong emphasis on moral renewal seeking to promote 'the spiritual, moral, cultural, mental and physical development of pupils at the school and of society' (Maclure 1988: 1). The Act delegated financial responsibilities from local authorities to schools. It took polytechnics out of local authority control and replaced the National Advisory Body for Public Sector Higher Education with the Polytechnics and Colleges Funding Council. It required that half of the membership of the governing bodies of FE colleges represented employment interests.

**1988: the MSC is absorbed into the Department of Employment (DoE),** becoming the Training Commission for a short time and then the Training Agency.

**1989: the Confederation of British Industry (CBI) publishes** *Towards a Skills Revolution*, which advocated common learning outcomes for all students over 16. This document set out the employers agenda for LLL.

**1989: in a speech at Lancaster University, Kenneth Baker calls for a doubling of the numbers of students entering HE.** The number of students attending should increase to 30 per cent. This was achieved by the mid-1990s.

**1989: YTS replaced by Youth Training (YT).**

---

**Task 9.5**

Discussions of the YTS and the role of the MSC dominated educational thought during the 1980s. Why was this? Again, it might be useful to construct an educational biography of a young person brought up in the time of the first Thatcher government.

---

**Education in context: 1990–2001**

*Prime ministers*: 1990–97 John Major (Conservative); 1997–2001 Tony Blair (Labour).

*Secretary of state for education and science*: from November 1990, Kenneth Clarke.

*Secretaries of state for education*: from April 1992, John Patten; from July 1994, Gillian Shepherd.

*Secretaries of state for education and employment*: from July 1995, Gillian Shepherd; from May 1997 David Blunkett.

*Secretaries of state for education and skills*: from June 2001, Estelle Morris.

*Key political and economic events*: economic recession, Citizens' Charter, social authoritarianism, globalization, risk aversion; 1991 the Gulf War, civil war in Yugoslavia; 1992 United Nations (UN) intervention in Somalia and Bosnia; 31 August 1997, death of Diana, Princess of Wales; 11 September 2001, World Trade Center towers destroyed.

---

**1990:** *Core Skills 16–19* **published by National Curriculum Council (NCC), after consultation with the FEU, School Examinations and Assessment Council (SEAC), NCVQ and the Training Agency (TA).** It proposed six core skills in two groups:

- Group 1: 1. Communication; 2. Problem solving; 3. Personal skills;
- Group 2: 4. Numeracy; 5. IT; 6. Competence in a modern language.

The first group was to be developed in all post-16 programmes and in every A and AS level syllabus. It also recommended the use of Individual Action Plans (IAPs) and the incorporation of national curriculum themes in the post-16 curriculum with the addition of scientific and technological understanding and aesthetic and creative understanding.

**1990:** *A British Baccalaureate: Ending the Division Between Education and Training* **published by the Institute for Public Policy Research (IPPR)**. This proposed a unitary 'advanced diploma' delivered through a tertiary college system.

**1991: Training and Enterprise Councils (TECs) established**. There were 82 TECs. They were limited companies governed by local industrialists and charged with identifying local training needs and organizing training to meet these needs. They also operated government training schemes such as YT. They were first announced by the Government in 1988.

**1991:** *Education and Training for the 21st Century*. This White Paper was a review of the education and training system for 16–19-year-olds in which equal status was demanded for academic and vocational qualifications. Young people 'should not have their opportunities limited by out of date distinctions between qualifications and institutions' (DES 1991: 58). The DES argued that:

> Colleges lack the full freedom which we gave to the polytechnic and higher education colleges in 1989 to respond to the demands of students and the labour market. The Government intend to legislate to remove all colleges of further education . . . and sixth form colleges . . . from local authority control . . . Our policies over the last decade have not done much to enrich that preparation – for life and work.
>
> (DES 1991: 64–5)

**1991: National Education and Training Targets (NETTs) set by the government but recommended by the CBI in** *World Class Targets* **(1991)**. There was a major review of the targets in 1995 and another in 1998.

**1992: Further and Higher Education Act**. The polytechnics were granted university status and the 'binary division' was subsequently ended when polytechnics became universities in 1993. The CNAA was abolished and separate funding councils set up for FE and HE.

**1992: Education (Schools) Act created Ofsted**.

**1992: Colleges' Employers' Forum** (CEF) was established. It became the Association of Colleges (AoC) in 1996.

**1992: GNVQs introduced**. Unlike NVQs, these qualifications would be based in schools and colleges rather than the workplace. Level 3 (later 'Advanced') GNVQ was to be 'equivalent' or 'comparable' to A levels. By 1997 students with GNVQs had a greater chance of obtaining a university place than A level students.

**1993: the Department for Education's (DfE)** *Charter for Further Education*. The Charter set out rights and expectations and ended with information on how to complain about 'courses, qualifications and results' (pp. 24–9 gives 23 addresses and telephone numbers to complain to). All colleges were required to produce their own charters.

**1993: incorporation of colleges**. The 1992 Further and Higher Education Act was implemented on 1 April 1993. Colleges were taken out of the control of the LEAs and became independent business corporations. Some had turnovers which put them in the *Financial Times* list of big companies. One college had a turnover of almost £50 million.

**1993: Modern Apprenticeships announced**. The first apprentices started on this initiative to revive apprenticeships. Modern Apprenticeships were based on specific occupations and developed by NTOs (National Training Organizations). They consisted of a minimum of an NVQ Level 3 qualification supplemented by GNVQ Core Skills qualifications and sometimes by qualifications outside of the scheme. They were open to both young men and young women aged between 16 and 24.

**1994: *Competitiveness: Helping Business to Win***. Michael Heseltine sets out the theme of national competitiveness and calls for improved careers guidance for young people in this influential White Paper.

**1994: Teacher Training Agency (TTA)**. The Agency was established in September under the directorship of chief executive Anthea Millett 'to improve the quality of teaching, to raise the standards of teacher education and training, and to promote teaching as a profession, in order to improve the standards of pupils' achievement and the quality of their learning' (TTA 1995: 7).

**1994: new contracts dispute at its height**. The FE colleges experienced over three years of action over the introduction of new contracts for lecturers and the abandonment of the so-called 'Silver Book' which set out conditions of service.

**1994: report of the Commission on Social Justice**. This report contains the genesis of what would become the 1997 Labour government's views on education and social policy for the 1990s and beyond.

**1995: Further Education Development Agency (FEDA) formed**. Launched on 7 April, FEDA inherited the staff of the FEU and the Further Education Staff College at Blagdon. Its main function was to 'help FE institutions provide what their student and other customers want and need'. As 'an independent body promoting quality in FE', FEDA intended 'not just to promote best practice but also embody it' (FEDA 1995: 1). Its key aims were to promote quality in teaching and learning, to provide leadership in curriculum design and development, and to ensure effective management.

**1995: the Department for Education and Department for Employment merged in July to become the DfEE (Department for Education and Employment)**.

**1996: Dearing's *Review of Qualifications for 16–19 Year Olds***. This is Dearing's second much publicized report (Dearing II). Dearing II went for stability and did not recommend a unified system to replace the three existing tertiary qualifications NVQs, GNVQs, and A levels. It did suggest the incorporation of 'key skills' in all three qualifications and the relaunch of YT, Modern Apprenticeships and the National Record of Achievement. It also suggested that Advanced GNVQs be renamed Applied A levels. Dearing's first report (Dearing I) *The National Curriculum and its Assessment* (1994) was a response to industrial action by teachers throughout the country concerned about the burden of assessment and the narrowness of the national curriculum. Dearing I reduced time spent on the national curriculum by 20 per cent and reduced the number of attainment targets and their related statements (SATs). It included a vocational option at Key Stage 4.

**1996: the European 'Year of Lifelong Learning'.**

**1996:** *Lifetime Learning* **(DfEE).** A consultation document drawing on previously published work including *Competitiveness: Forging Ahead: Education and Training* (DfEE 1995a). The Labour Party published *Lifelong Learning*, a consultative document (1996).

**1996: awarding bodies combine.** In 1996, BTEC and London Examinations formed Edexcel. In 1998 C&G, the Associated Examining Board and the Northern Examinations and Assessment Board formed the Assessment and Qualifications Alliance (AQA).

**1996:** *Inclusive Learning* **(Tomlinson Report).** This FEFC report called for colleges to embrace the idea of 'inclusive learning'. It wanted every member of staff to consider the individual needs of all learners rather than just those previously categorized as having 'special needs'.

**1996: Labour leader Tony Blair's 'Education, Education and Education' speech to the Labour Party conference on 1 October, 20 years after Callaghan's Ruskin College speech**. The speech was published in the *Times Educational Supplement* of 4 October (p. 6) and some extracts follow.

> Ask me my three main priorities for Government, and I tell you: education, education and education . . . At every level we need radical improvement and reform. A teaching profession trained and able to stand alongside the best in the world and valued as such . . . There should be zero tolerance of failure in Britain's schools. The Age of Achievement will be built on new technology. Our aim is for every school to have access to the superhighway, the computers to deliver it and the education programmes to go on it. With the University for Industry for adult skills, this adds up to a national grid for learning for Britain. Britain the skill superpower of the world.

**1996: Hello DOLLY**.

> . . . what ought to matter most, in my view, to a learning prime minister is that there should be a powerful Whitehall department responsible for promoting learning across society. This department should be a great office of state on a par with the Foreign Office or the Home Office. If the learning society is to be a reality, nothing else will do. I would want to see the DfEE remain one department,

but to change its name – symbolically but importantly – to the Department of Lifelong Learning. It could even be called DOLLY for short. Goodbye DfEE, as it were, Hello . . .

(Barber 1996: 296)

---

**Task 9.6**

Lifelong or lifetime learning, the learning society; these phrases became pre-millennial buzz-words. Can we give them more than rhetorical substance? In what sense is LLL going to be a reality for young people? What features of British society support the claim that we are, or are becoming a 'learning society' (see Field 2000: 35)?

---

**1997: Report of Helena Kennedy's committee of inquiry into widening participation in education *Learning Works*.** Kennedy initially suggested redistributing resources and removing the bias towards undergraduates and school sixth forms. Seventy-five per cent of the 5 million students in England are supported by £3.5 billion of funding through the 'Cinderella' service of FE colleges, whereas the university sector with 25 per cent of the student population receives 75 per cent of the available funding. The shocking fact is that 'Sixty-four per cent of university students come from social classes 1 and 2. One per cent come from social class 5' (Kennedy 1997a). The general direction of the many recommendations of the report is a lifetime entitlement to education up to A level standard, with free teaching for people from deprived backgrounds or with no previous qualifications: 'The government should . . . give priority in public funding within post-16 learning to general education and transferable vocational learning, including key skills, at and leading to level 3: the costs of ensuring that all can succeed to [NVQ] level 3 must be recognised' (Kennedy 1997b: 43).

**1997: publication of the Dearing Report *Higher Education in the Learning Society, National Committee Inquiry into Higher Education*.** One of the nine 'principles' governing the report (Dearing III, Dearing 1997) was that: 'Learning should be increasingly responsive to employment needs and include the development of general skills, widely valued in employment' (Summary Report, p. 5). Dearing III was hailed as the most comprehensive review of HE since the Robbins Report. Dearing III made 93 recommendations. These include: a system by which students pay fees covering up to 25 per cent of the cost of tuition (ch. 20); the establishment of an Institute for Learning and Teaching (ILT) in higher education to accredit training programmes for HE staff and to look at computer-based learning (ch. 8); the promotion of student learning as a high priority (ch. 8); and a review of research which may allow some institutions to opt out of the competitive funding system based on the Research Assessment Exercise (RAE). In his introduction Dearing sees 'historic boundaries between vocational and academic education breaking down, with increasingly active partnerships between higher education institutions and the worlds of industry, commerce and public service' (Summary Report, p. 2).

**1997: the government announced the abolition of student grants and the introduction of fee payments of up to £1000 per annum**. The power to do this is given through the Teaching and Higher Education Bill (see below).

**1997:** *Qualifying for Success: A Consultation Paper on the Future of Post-16 Qualifications*. Key changes suggested in this paper were: new AS levels to encourage take-up of more subjects in the first year of study; modular A levels with synoptic testing at the end of all courses; upgraded and more flexible GNVQs; a new key skills qualification to enhance skills in communication, IT and number after the age of 16.

**1997: NCVQ/SCAA merge to form a new national curriculum advisory body, the Qualifications and Curriculum Authority (QCA)**. Its powers are a cause of concern to the awarding bodies.

**1997:** *Learning for the Twenty-First Century*. In November, Professor Bob Fryer produced the report for the National Advisory Group for Continuing Education and Lifelong Learning. This report consolidates much of the thinking about LLL that has appeared since the Report of the Commission on Social Justice.

**1997: Teaching and Higher Education Bill**. This bill was the first of a series of responses by the government to Dearing III. It gave the secretary of state powers to interfere in university affairs and is seen by some as a major attack on academic autonomy.

**1998: New Deal programme introduced in January as the flagship of the Labour government's 'Welfare to Work' strategy**. It required every young person between the ages of 18 and 24 who had been unemployed for more than six months to take a subsidized job, take up some form of education or training, take part in an Environmental Task Force, or do voluntary work. There was also a *25 Plus New Deal* that came on stream quickly due to the fall in numbers of the 18–24 age cohort.

**1998: National Learning Targets for 2002** were 85 per cent of 19-year-olds to have (NVQ) Level 2 qualifications; 60 per cent of 21-year-olds to have (NVQ) Level 3; 50 per cent of adults to have the same level; and 28 per cent of adults to have (NVQ) Level 4 qualifications. They also sought a 7 per cent reduction in the number of non-learners.

**1998: formation of a General Teaching Council (GTC)**. A GTC was established in Scotland as a result of the Wheatley Report (1963). A voluntary GTC (England and Wales) has been in existence since 1988 and has sought support from the various professional bodies and attempted to secure legislation. The Teaching and Higher Education Bill (1997) established a statutory GTC which will not be a 'teachers' GTC but will have a broad membership. Teachers in schools could now register with the GTC.

**1998:** *The Learning Age: a Renaissance for a new Britain* (**DfEE**). The expected White Paper on LLL appeared as a Green Paper. It promised to bring learning into the home and workplace.

**1998:** *Higher Education for the Twenty-First Century: Response to the Dearing Report.* This response set out the priority of reaching out to groups under-represented in HE. It argued for a better balance between teaching, research and scholarship and for an Institute for Learning and Teaching in Higher Education to be established to accredit programmes of training for HE teachers. Work experience to become a feature of HE courses and the aim of employability stressed.

**1998: FENTO** (Further Education National Training Organisation) approved to operate as an NTO. One of its aims was to be held responsible for assessing the skill needs of all staff (employed) within the post-16 sector. FENTO's first major project was to produce a set of national standards for supporting learning in further education in England and Wales (October 1998).

**1998: a University for Industry (learndirect)** was established after discussions with 'learning organizations' such as Ford, Unipart and Anglian Water. This is not a physical but a virtual university, a network providing access to training.

**1999:** *A Fresh Start: Improving Literacy and Numeracy* (**Moser Report**). Moser reported that one in five adults in the UK has significant literacy or numeracy problems and that 7 million people have no formal qualifications. One of the report's recommendations was that all basic skills teachers should have a basic skills teaching qualification.

**1999:** *Learning to Succeed: A New Framework for Post-16 Learning* (**DfEE 1999**). This White Paper set out the case for and functions of the LSC. There are six reasons given: there is too much duplication, confusion and bureaucracy in the current system; too little money actually reaches learners and employers; there is an absence of effective coordination or strategic planning; the system has insufficient focus on skills and employer needs at national, regional and local levels; the system lacks innovation and flexibility; there is a need to exploit the potential of the new technology in the delivery and planning of provision (s2.11: 27). The report also announces the Connexions strategy 'for making sure that far more young people continue in education and training until they are at least 19' (s6.7: 50).

**1999:** *Bridging the Gap: New Opportunities for 16–18-Year-Olds not in Education, Employment or Training.* This report by the Social Exclusion Unit (1999) proposed that instead of a fragmented approach involving youth, careers and guidance workers there should be a unified service with the task of 'Providing a network of Personal Advisors to provide a single point of contact for each young person and ensure that someone has an overview of each young person's ambitions and needs' (p. 81).

**1999:** *Curriculum Guidance for 2000: Implementing the Changes to 16–19 Qualifications* (**QCA**).

**1999: ILT** (Institute for Learning Teaching in Higher Education) launched. The ILT mission was to enhance the professionalism of teaching and the support for learning. It was absorbed in to the Higher Education Academy (HEA) in 2004.

**2000: foundation degrees announced by David Blunkett, Secretary of State for Education and Employment, at the University of Greenwich New Campus on 15 February**. These degrees stressed innovation in content and delivery and could be achieved, in part, through accrediting workplace learning. They would take two years full-time rather than three. Flexible and part-time delivery was held to be very important. Foundation degrees were considered by some to be a move towards an American-style 'community college' system. By March 2002, 4229 students had enrolled on work-based foundation degrees.

**2000: *Connexions: The Best Start in Life for Every Young Person*.** This government strategy paper outlined their aim of ensuring that all young people had the opportunity to learn the skills they needed to make a success of their adult lives. It was hoped that 50 per cent would later go to university. Personal advisers became a reality within the Connexions framework in April 2002.

**2000: Curriculum 2000 begins in September**. It is announced by the DfEE as introducing 'the most significant changes to post-sixteen curriculum for 50 years'. These included the new AS qualification representing the first half of an A level; a choice of linear or modular assessment; the replacement of Advanced GNVQs with vocational A levels and the introduction of a new key skills qualification.

**2000: new DfEE policy on qualifications and development for further education teachers and college principals**. The government issued a statement on 2 November introducing mandatory teaching qualifications for all new staff in FE from September 2001. New full-time staff will have two years to gain a Certificate in Education following appointment (for fractional and part-time staff a longer period is envisaged depending on the hours worked). The DfEE also made it a requirement that all courses leading to an FE teaching qualification be based on FENTO standards and be endorsed by FENTO as doing so. One of several estimates suggested that 43 per cent of part-time staff and 40 per cent of full-time staff have no 'high level' teaching qualification.

**2000: the LSDA (Learning and Skills Development Agency) launched on 27 November, replacing FEDA**. It seeks a clearer focus on policy development and intends to play a leading role in research through the Learning and Skills Research Network (LSRN).

**2001: an Institute for Learning (IfL) is launched**. Supported by various organizations, this is a complementary body to the GTC and ILT, and parallels their objectives by promoting the professional standing of FE teaching.

**2001: the LSC (Learning and Skills Council) replaces the TECs and the FEFC on 1 April**. The LSC became responsible from that date for funding and planning all post-16 education and training except for HE. With a budget of £5.5 billion, the council operated through 47 local LSCs.

**2001: the DfEE became the Department for Education and Skills (DfES) after the general election in June 2001**. There was a pre-election consensus that 'A basic skills revolution will be at the heart of Labour's education policy if it wins a second term' (FE Focus, *TES*, 23 February 2001).

**2001: Individual Learning Accounts (ILAs) suspended from 7 December**. The cornerstone of the government's LLL strategy, ILAs were reportedly taken up by 2.5 million people. There were some 6000 complaints about the scheme and 279 providers were thought to be suspect and many were investigated, some by the police.

---

**Education in context: 2002–present**

*Prime ministers:* 1997–2007 (resigned) Tony Blair (Labour); 2007– Gordon Brown (Labour).

*Secretaries of state for education and skills:* from October 2002, Charles Clarke; from December 2004, Ruth Kelly; from May 2005, Alan Johnston.

*Secretary of State for Children, Schools and Families:* from June 2007: Ed Balls.

*Ministers of state for lifelong learning, further and higher education:* from September 2004, Kim Howells; from May 2005, Bill Rammell; Skills minister from May 2005, Phil Hope. Secretary of state for innovation, universities and skills from June 2007: John Denham.

*Key political and economic events:* 20 March 2003, invasion of Iraq; 6–8 July 2003, climate change declared by Tony Blair, during his UK presidency of the G8, as 'probably, long-term the single most important issue we face as a global community'; 7 July 2005, bombings in London; 2005–, rise of China as a world economic superpower with exports totalling over $1 trillion.

---

**2002:** *14–19: Extending Opportunities, Raising Standards*. The key proposals of this controversial and 'very green Green Paper' were: to introduce a matriculation diploma that recognizes achievement at 19 across a range of disciplines; to free up the curriculum so that students aged 14 can follow relevant work-related courses; increased flexibility so that students can learn at a pace that is right for them, with a 'fast track to success' option for the more able; an individualized curriculum with all students having an ILP developed with the help of the personal adviser from the Connexions service. 'Vocational' as a term was also to be written out of qualification terminology in an attempt to challenge prejudice. Vocational A levels were just to be called A levels. The Green Paper also proposed that the study of a modern foreign language should no longer be compulsory for the 14+. This ambitious programme of radical reform is due to be in place by 2006.

**2002: the New Deal for Young People**. The first National Audit Office report on the New Deal. The programme promised jobs for 250,000 young people but the study showed that it has resulted in increasing jobs by only 20,000 in its first two years of operation. The National Audit Office suggested that many of the young people on the programme would have found jobs anyway and those that did, did not stay in work for long. Government figures showed that 700,000 young people had participated in the programme and 339,000 had been helped to find jobs.

**2002: the Sector Skills Development Agency (SSDA) takes responsibility for the new Sector Skills Councils (SSCs)**. Along with all other NTOs, FENTO was scheduled to become part of a new SSC. The rationale for the changes was set out in a policy statement: *Meeting the Sector Skills and Productivity Challenge* (DfES 2001). Each SSC had the broad aim of tackling the skills and productivity needs of their sector throughout the UK. To do this they gave responsibility to employers to provide leadership for strategic targeted action to meet their sector's skills and business needs. The first SSDA director was Margaret Salmon, a non-executive director with Kingfisher plc. There were to be some 35 SSCs, less than half the number of NTOs.

**2002: *Success for All*** outlined the reform strategy of the Learning and Skills Council which aimed to bring the FE sector into the mainstream of the education system and to ensure that 14–19-year-old learners have 'greater choice and higher standards'.

**2003: *21st Century Skills: Realising Our Potential*.** This White Paper set out a 'skills strategy' from the DfES (with the DTI and DWP) that sought to ensure that 'employers have the right skills to support the success of their businesses, and individuals have the skills they need to be both employable and personally fulfilled' (Summary: Paragraph 1). E-learning and ICT skills are stressed along with free learning for all adults to enable them to achieve a Level 2 qualification.

**2003: first Ofsted and ALI inspections of FE colleges using their Common Inspection Framework (Ofsted/ALI 2000).**

**2003: the IfL held its first AGM** on 16 June 2003 as a nascent professional body for the sector.

**2003: *Every Child Matters*.** The ECM report formed the basis of the Children Act 2004. It was produced in response to the Victoria Climbie inquiry. The report puts child protection concerns central to the teacher's role.

**2003: the Centre for Excellence in Leadership (CEL)** launched in October. Its aim was to develop world class leadership within the learning and skills sector. CEL training programmes are for governors, principals and advanced teachers.

**2003: *14–19 Opportunity and Excellence*,** published in November, a year after *Success for All*, proposed the creation of a more coherent 14–19 phase with greater flexibility and choice and an increase in vocational learning to tackle the number of learners leaving full-time education at 16 and create a parity of esteem between academic and vocational education.

**2003: Ofsted's report,** *The Initial Teacher Training of Further Education Teachers*, issued on 11 November, declared FE teacher training to be unsatisfactory. The DfES response, which came out on the same day, *The Future of Initial Teacher Education for the Learning and Skills Sector*, set out an agenda for reform.

**2004: Higher Education Academy (HEA) was formed in May**, absorbing the ILT (HE) and other professional and staff develop bodies in higher education.

**2004: *Children Act*.** The Children Act focused the work of the teachers, and what soon became known as the 'wider workforce', including classroom assistants, social workers and police officers, on the ECM outcomes to improve children's well-being in five areas: (a) physical and mental health and emotional well-being; (b) protection from harm and neglect; (c) education, training and recreation; (d) the contribution made by them to society; (e) social and economic well-being.

**2004: Tomlinson Report:** *14–19 Curriculum and Qualifications Reform*. After a lengthy period of consultation, the working party on 14–19 reform's much heralded final report appeared on 18 October. It proposed incorporating and ultimately replacing GCSEs and A levels in favour of a diploma as part of a continuous curriculum for 14–19-year-olds. Diplomas would cover both vocational and academic disciplines, combining them wherever appropriate to overcome the academic/vocational divide.

**2004: QTLS** The award of 'Qualified Teacher Learning and Skills' was announced on 2 November 2004 by Minister of State Kim Howells. It is described in *Equipping our Teachers for the Future: Reforming Initial Teacher Training for the Learning and Skills Sector* which named the IfL as the professional body for the sector.

**2005:** *14–19 Education and Skills*. A White Paper, published in February, was the government's response to the Tomlinson Report of 2004. It aimed to ensure that every young person masters functional English and maths before they leave full-time education, that vocational options are improved, that academic qualifications offer a suitable 'stretch' to motivate disengaged learners.

**2005: Foster Report –** *Realising the Potential: A Review of the Future Role of Further Education*. Foster's review, published on 15 November, argued the need for a clearly recognized and shared core purpose among FE colleges that focuses on the needs of both learners and business. The Review made it clear that the purpose of post-compulsory education is directly linked to the needs of the economy but also describes as 'appalling' the number of young people who lack basic literacy and numeracy skills and which 'suggest great reservoirs of disappointment and poor self esteem' (Foster 2005: 9).

**2005:** *Youth Matters*. This Green Paper proposed an overhaul of youth services on the basis of *Every Child Matters*. To many it implied that the days of informal work with young people were numbered.

**2006:** *Further Education: Raising Skills, Improving Life Chances*. A White Paper proposing reforms in the skills and qualifications in post-16 education, for customized and individualized provision for learners, and diversification of education providers.

**2006: University and College Union (UCU)** formed on 1 June from the merger of the AUT and NATFHE was the largest post-compulsory union in the world.

**2006: LLUK revised the teacher training standards** for FE and consulted on Standards for Teacher Trainers in FE.

**2006: Train to Gain (T2G)** rolled out as a national project to fund adult training. Colleges have to bid for up to three-quarters of their funding in competition with private providers.

**2006: the Further Education and Training Bill** proposed to streamline the LSC so it operates on a regional basis. It focused on learner and employee consultation. In a fundamental change to the FHE sector it announced that the Privy Council will be enabled to grant FE colleges the power to award Foundation Degrees.

**2006: Leitch Review of Skills**. The final report of the Leitch Review was published on 5 December with the title *Prosperity for All in the Global Economy – World Class Skills*. Lord Sandy Leitch's report aimed to 'Strengthen the Employer Voice' and increase employers' engagement and investment in skills. His recommendations included an employer 'Pledge' to commit to train, awareness programmes teaching people the value of skills, and a universal adult careers service.

**2006: ALI released its final report** before becoming part of Ofsted.

**2007: the '157 Group' of FE colleges** held its launch event on 15 January. The 157 Group was named after paragraph 157 of the Foster Review that suggested that the most successful colleges have a bigger role in policy making. It declared that it had 22 members at the time of its launch.

**2007:** *2020 Vision: Report of the Teaching and Learning in 2020 Review Group*. This report, published on 4 January, from the review group headed by Christine Gilbert (Her Majesty's Chief Inspector for Schools) set out 'personalization' or 'personalized learning' as a central focus of education policy.

**2007: ROSLA to 18?** The Green Paper *Raising Expectations: Staying in Education and Training Post-16*, launched on 22 March, proposed the introduction of measures that have the effect of raising the school leaving age to 18 by 2015. Any young person starting work must have training, and prison sentences are the ultimate deterrent for those refusing education and training.

**2007:** The Department for Children, Schools and Families (DCSF) and the Department for Innovation, Universities and Skills (DIUS) replace the DfES and DTI in new Prime Minister Gordon Brown's reorganization on the 28 June.

**2007: the IfL became the gatekeeper to QTLS**. The IfL, from September 2007, was to register all teachers in the learning and skills sector and seeks to provide coherence across sectors. From that date, all new entrants to FE teaching must complete a 30 hour induction course leading to an Initial Teaching Award Learning and Skills (ITALS). A new system of registration of teachers through a 'Licence to Practise' was introduced. The IfL also took responsibility for overseeing the introduction and monitoring of mandatory CPD across the sector.

---

**Task 9.7**

'Third way' policies and practice in PCE since the first election victory of Labour in 1997 have been described as 'weak' because they are marked by a 'pervasive voluntarism' (Hodgson and Spours 1999: 146). 'Voluntarism' is held to be an inadequate basis for real change as it leaves too much up to individuals and institutions. PCE policy can seem directionless and in need of a 'strong' approach requiring structural change through social partnerships, even if this means introducing an element of compulsion, for example, obliging employers to train.

Others have argued that 'third way' policies of the 'weak' or 'strong' sort are inevitably fragile as they are often over-complex and bureaucratic ways of attempting to overcome the disconnectedness and apathy of young people and adults, in what can be described as 'depoliticized' times, through strategies such as 'joined up thinking' (Hayes and Hudson 2001: 63–8). There is some hint now that a new 'strong' approach to discon-nectedness is appearing, taking the form of a *moral* authoritarianism, telling young people what to think and how to behave (Hayes 2007).

Reviewing the policy initiatives and changes in the chronology since the mid–1990s, and from your own knowledge and experience of PCE, consider what might constitute a 'third way' approach and whether it is successful in meeting what you would see as the educational aspirations of young people and adults. Remember that the key ideas in third way approaches are social inclusion, economic competitiveness, (local) community and (individual) choice.

### Task 9.8

Having read the chronology, use your general knowledge of history, and the outlines given in the boxed sections, to connect major historical events with particular pieces of legislation and their associated developments in the educational sphere. If you do this, patterns emerge. For example, the three historical periods, 1870–1902, 1902–45, 1945–present, can be seen as illustrating an almost seamless development in which elementary, then secondary, then further or higher education became a reality for many people. However, also taking 1870 as a starting point we can identify three historical periods: 1870–1914, 1914–39 and 1939–present, that are sometimes seen as key periods in Britain's relative decline (Sked 1987; Gamble 1990).

Historical periods showing the general developments in PCE can also be identified. Draw up a chart showing the broad changes in this area over the last 100 years. To do this, identify clearly the different forms of PCE that were provided, the social policy behind that provision and the relevant dates. This will be easier if the tasks of describ-ing the education and training opportunities available to a young person at a given historical moment have been completed. Compare your chart with Table 9.1.

**Table 9.1** Developments in PCE

| Period | Social policy | Educational provision |
|---|---|---|
| Nineteenth century | Little state intervention | Mechanics' Institutes |
| 1900–45 | Training through 'stop gap' measures | Evening institutes, technical schools |
| 1945–76 | Stop gap measures, social orientation, consensus | Day release, technical colleges |
| 1976–97 | Crisis, vocationalism, the new vocationalism | FE colleges, training schemes |
| 1997–the present | The third way, social inclusion, therapeutic education | Expansion of FE and HE; new 14–19 provision |

**Task 9.9**

Draw up a brief chronology of key events and reports in your own area of subject or professional expertise. This need not be very detailed. How do key developments correlate with those outlined in the chronology?

**Task 9.10**

Your chronology is not fixed and should be kept up to date and extended. Indeed, we have changed this chronology in each edition of this book. Further historical details can be added or deleted as your interests, understanding and ideas develop. Add major events and developments as they occur.

## 9.4  A note on comparative chronologies

Comparative studies of any country might be of academic interest but they usually reflect broader concerns. Traditionally, comparisons were made with imperial powers such as Germany, the USA and Japan. Between the two world wars and during the cold war period comparisons with the Soviet education system were common. Recently, relatively affluent countries such as Finland and Sweden are popular comparators from within the European Union. It might be fashionable to look at countries with more dynamic economies and promote aspects of their education. However, the USA in the 1990s was the model for a country attempting to combat its relative economic decline and, at that time, having some success with a 'Goldilocks' economic strategy: not too hot and not too cold, but, like her porridge, 'just right'. That is why government officials and ministers flocked to study American policy developments in every sphere. We believe that educational developments in the USA are worthy of study because what happens there usually intimates what will happen in British education at all levels. For example, the 'No Child Left Behind' (NCLB) policies directly influenced the *Every Child Matters* policies of the third term of the Blair government. Therefore, it is useful to watch developments that might influence the post-compulsory sector. A short survey of the training and skills initiatives developed from the Carl D. Perkins Vocational Education Act 1984 through various revisions up to the Carl D. Perkins Career and Technical Education Act 2006 shows many parallels with developments in Britain.

It is not just government but radical thinkers who are inspired by the American vocational education system. Some would actively promote the American 'community college' system as a model for Britain. Models from other countries are also promoted, in particular the French baccalaureate (BAC) because of its breadth. The French education system has had more extensive and systematic state involvement and direction than the British system traditionally had and is therefore a model for those looking for centralized guidance within a dirigiste philosophy. However informative such a comparison might be in the context of a united Europe, we argue that developments in the USA are more likely to indicate the direction of British educational thinking. A caveat might be necessary in areas such as further and higher education, where a process of rationalization, sometimes called 'McDonaldization' appears to be more advanced here than in the USA (Hayes and Wynyard 2002a). Task 9.11 has been designed to test this assumption.

There is a comprehensive chronology of federal education legislation and other data on the US Department of Education Digest of Education Statistics website at: http://nces.ed.gov/programs/digest/d05_tf.asp. For discussions of these initiatives, *The Education Gadfly* is a useful resource, and a weekly email newsletter is available: at www.fordhaminstitute.org

**Task 9.11**

Readers who have looked at the on-line chronology of education in the USA will be able to detect many parallels with historical developments in Britain. There is an important difference in that there is a recent trend which appears to be a move away from vocationalism to an emphasis on 'new basics' which seem to reflect traditional education values. One writer has gone so far as to say that all the interesting curricular challenges of vocationalism have been lost because 'advocates of vocational education in the USA have so completely capitulated in the face of perceived threats to their existence based on current demands for basics in education' (Lewis 1991: 106). This trend towards the 'basics' is not as simple as it might seem. American education has been criticized as failing at the highest levels. Allan Bloom's *The Closing of the American Mind: How Higher Education has Failed Democracy and Impoverished the Souls of Today's Students* (1987) says everything in its title. The return to basics is sometimes seen as an attempt to rebuild a liberal education of the sort defended by Bloom, but the 'basics' are not straightforwardly academic or vocational 'skills' in the way we might think. James L. Nolan, in *The Therapeutic State: Justifying Government at Century's End* (1998: ch. 5), shows how an education in 'self-esteem' dominates public education and how this has as its natural predecessor John Dewey's experimental pragmatism. The 'basics' now sought are often more to do with developing attitudes rather than abilities.

To examine this new mix of 'skill' and 'therapeutic' or emotional education and to gain an insight into whether these developments will filter through to Britain, follow articles on current issues in American education in magazines such as *Time* and *Newsweek*. These may help identify general concerns that might be applicable to debates in Britain.

There are some useful websites with regularly updated reports and discussions that can be accessed, for example the US government's Office of Vocational and Adult Education (at: www.ed.gov/about/offices/list/ovae/index.html), the National Dissemination Center for Career and Technical Education and the National Center for Research in Career and Technical Education (at: http://www.nccte.org), which replaced the National Center for Research in Vocational Education (http://ncrve.berkeley.edu); and the American Council on Education (www.acenet.edu). There is also the equivalent of the *TES*, *Education Week*, which offers a regular email newsletter: www.edweek.org.

### Task 9.12: A note on further reading

It is useful to read texts written in different decades to get a flavour of the time. This runs counter to the fashionable desire to have only the most up-to-date texts in an academic reading list. The result is a loss of any sense of history. Here is a very limited selection.

For a historical review of Government reports and Acts, J. Stuart Maclure's *Educational Documents: England and Wales*, was first published in 1965, is an excellent source. For the period up to 1945 H.C. Barnard's *A History of English Education* (1969) and W.H.G. Armytage's *Four Hundred Years of English Education* (1970) are full of detail. They need some supplementing, as they are general histories of education and education policy (see also Coffey 1992; Skilbeck et al. 1994: 156–62).

The key resources for Government policy documents and commentaries are web-sites such as *Every Child Matters* (www.everychildmatters.gov.uk); *14–19 Education and Skills* (www.dfes.gov.uk/14–19/); the Leitch Review of Skills (http://www.hm-treasury.gov.uk/independent_reviews/leitch_review/review_leitch_index.cfm). Some useful surveys of literature and materials can be found on the *Teacher Training Resource Bank* (TTRB) website, although coverage of post-16 issues is limited (www.ttrb.ac.uk/). The DfES also has a further education website (www.dfes.gov.uk/furthereducation). There are many more.

W.O. Lester Smith's *Education* (1957) provides some clear thinking and an interesting comparison with today's debates on education, industry and citizenship. It is available in most Oxfam and secondhand bookshops.

For an understanding of how the new vocationalism was created and contested, Dan Finn's *Training Without Jobs* (1987) is good, as is Cynthia Cockburn's *Two Track Training* (1987) which looks at sex inequalities in the YTS.

For a more recent discussion of policy issues, Ann Hodgson and Ken Spours in *New Labour's Educational Agenda* (1999) provide a useful critical evaluation of government policy for 14+ education and produce their own argument for a 'strong third way'

Analysis of current developments requires reading relevant magazines and news-papers. One very useful source is the journal *Post–16 Educator* (formerly *General Educator*). Each edition contains a detailed summary, by FE lecturer Colin Waugh, of litera-ture and events and discussions of the conflicts and disputes that are written out of most books (www.post16educator.org.uk). *FE Focus*, which appears weekly with the *Times Educational Supplement* (TES) is the key professional PCE newspaper. The arch-ive of *TES* articles on-line goes back to 1994 (www.tes.co.uk/). The *Education Guardian* offers the best source of PCE discussion in the daily papers. All articles are available free on-line (http://education.guardian.co.uk). *Adults Learning*, published by NIACE is useful for adult educators (www.niace.org.uk/Publications/Periodicals/AdultsLearning).

A sound critique of competence-based training is Terry Hyland's *Competence Education and NVQs: Dissenting Perspectives* (1994).

To start you thinking about issues in the 1990s such as postmodernism and globaliza-tion as they are believed to affect PCE, a good book is James Avis and his colleagues' *Knowledge and Nationhood: Education, Politics and Work* (1996).

Tom Bentley, former director of the think-tank DEMOS, has produced an original book: *Learning Beyond the Classroom: Education for a Changing World* (1998). Bentley examines the tension between decades-old educational infrastructures and the new institutions needed to respond to the challenges of lifelong learning.

For a readable account of the changing ideologies that lie behind the current interest in LLL we recommend John Field's *Lifelong Learning and the New Educational Order* (2000).

Those interested in further reading about contemporary issues in PCE will find a stimulating set of papers in the companion to this book, John Lea et al., *Working in Post-Compulsory Education* (2003).

## Related new professional standards for teachers and trainers in the lifelong learning sector

### Domain A: professional values and practice

| PROFESSIONAL KNOWLEDGE AND UNDERSTANDING | PROFESSIONAL PRACTICE |
|---|---|
| *Teachers in the lifelong learning sector know and understand:* | *Teachers in the lifelong learning sector:* |
| AK 2.1 Ways in which learning has the potential to change lives. | AP 2.1 Use opportunities to highlight the potential for learning to positively transform lives and contribute to effective citizenship. |
| AK 2.2 Ways in which learning promotes the emotional, intellectual, social and economic well-being of individuals and the population as a whole. | AP 2.2 Encourage learners to recognize and reflect on ways in which learning can empower them as individuals and make a difference in their communities. |
| AK 3.1 Issues of equality, diversity and inclusion. | AP 3.1 Apply principles to evaluate and develop own practice in promoting equality and inclusive learning and engaging with diversity. |
| AK 4.1 Principles, frameworks and theories which underpin good practice in learning and teaching. | AP 4.1 Use relevant theories of learning to support the development of practice in learning and teaching. |
| AK 6.1 Relevant statutory requirements and codes of practice. | AP 6.1 Conform to statutory requirements and apply codes of practice. |
| AK 6.2 Ways to apply relevant statutory requirements and the underpinning principles. | AP 6.2 Demonstrate good practice through maintaining a learning environment which conforms to statutory requirements and promotes equality, including appropriate consideration of the needs of children, young people and vulnerable adults. |

## Domain C: specialist learning and teaching

| PROFESSIONAL KNOWLEDGE AND UNDERSTANDING | PROFESSIONAL PRACTICE |
|---|---|
| *Teachers in the lifelong learning sector know and understand:* | *Teachers in the lifelong learning sector:* |
| CK 1.2  Ways in which own specialism relates to the wider social, economic and environmental context. | CP 1.2  Provide opportunities for learners to understand how the specialist area relates to the wider social, economic and environmental context. |
| CK 4.1  Ways to keep up to date with developments in teaching in own specialist area. | CP 4.1  Access sources for professional development in own specialist area. |

# BIBLIOGRAPHY

Ahier, J. and Ross, A. (1995) *The Social Subjects Within the Curriculum*. London: Falmer Press.

Ainley, P. (1988) *From School to YTS: Education and Training in England and Wales 1944–1987*. Milton Keynes: Open University Press.

Ainley, P. (1990) *Vocational Education and Training*. London: Cassell.

Ainley, P. (1993) *Class and Skill: Changing Divisions of Knowledge and Labour*. London: Cassell.

Ainley, P. (1994) *Degrees of Difference: Higher Education in the 1990s*. London: Lawrence and Wishart.

Ainley, P. (1999) *Learning Policy: Towards the Certified Society*. London: Macmillan.

Ainscow, M. and Tweddle, D. (1988) *Preventing Classroom Failure*. London: David Fulton Publishers Ltd.

Alexander, T. (1997) *Family Learning: Foundation of Effective Learning*. London: Demos.

Alexander, T. and Clyne, P. (1995) *Riches Beyond Price: Making the Most of Family Learning*. Leicester: NIACE.

Anderson, J. (1980a) Socrates as educator, in D.Z. Phillips (ed.) *Education and Inquiry*. London: Basil Blackwell, pp. 64–80.

Anderson, J. (1980b) Lectures on the educational theories of Spencer and Dewey, in D.Z. Phillips (ed.) *Education and Inquiry*. London: Basil Blackwell, pp. 81–141.

Anderson, J. (1980c) Education and practicality, in D.Z. Phillips (ed.) *Education and Inquiry*. London: Basil Blackwell, pp. 153–8.

Annan, N. (1990) *Our Age: The Generation That Made Post-war Britain*. London: Fontana.

Aristotle (1904) *The Politics, Book VIII*, trans. T.A. Sinclair. Harmondsworth: Penguin.

Armytage, W.H.G. (1970) *Four Hundred Years of English Education*. Cambridge: Cambridge University Press.

AQA (Assessment and Qualification Alliance) (2002) *Media: Communication and Production*. Guildford: AQA.

Association of Colleges (2001) *The Teaching Pay Initiative Guidance*. London: AoC.

AUT (Association of University Teachers) (1997) *AUT Bulletin*, April.

Avis, J., Bloomer, M., Esland, G., Gleeson, D. and Hodkinson, P. (1996) *Knowledge and Nationhood: Education, Politics and Work*. London: Cassell.

Ball, S. (1987) *The Micro-Politics of the School*. London: Methuen.

Ball, S.J., Maguire, M. and Macrae, S. (1998) *Choice Pathways and Transitions Post-16. New Youth, New Economies in the Global City*. London and New York: RoutledgeFalmer.

Barber, M. (1996) *The Learning Game*. London: Victor Gollancz.

Barnard, H.C. (1969) *A History of English Education from 1760*, 2nd edn. London: University of London Press.

Barnes, D. (1982) *Practical Curriculum Study*. London: Routledge and Kegan Paul.

Barrow, R. (1984) *Giving Teaching Back to Teachers: A Critical Introduction to Curriculum Theory*. Brighton: Wheatsheaf.

Beaumont, G. (1995) *Review of 100 NVQs and SVQs*. London: DfEE.

BECTA (2006) *ICT and E-learning in FE*. Coventry: BECTA. Available at: http://publications.becta.org.uk/display.cfm?resID=28534 (accessed January 2007).

Bell, J. (2005) *Doing your Research Project*, 4th edn. Maidenhead: Open University Press.

Benn, C. and Chitty, C. (1997) *Thirty Years On: Is Comprehensive Education Alive and Well or Struggling to Survive?* Harmondsworth: Penguin.

Benn, C. and Fairley, J. (eds) (1986) *Challenging the MSC on Jobs, Training and Education*. London: Pluto Press.

Bennett, N. and McNamara, D. (1979) *Focus on Teaching*. London: Longman.

Bentley, T. (1998) *Learning Beyond the Classroom: Education for a Changing World*. London: Routledge/DEMOS.

Bills, D. (1988) Credentials and Capacities: Employers' Perceptions of the Acquisition of Skill. *The Sociological Quarterly*, 29(3): 439–49.

Black, P. and Wiliam, D. (1998) *Inside the Black Box: Raising Standards Through Classroom Assessment*. London: School of Education, King's College.

Black, P., Harrison, C., Lee, C., Marshall, B. and Wiliam, D. (2002) *Working Inside the Black Box: Assessment for Learning in the Classroom*. London: nferNelson.

Blair, T. (1998) *The Third Way: Politics for of the New Century*. London: Fabian Society.

Bloom, B.S. (1964) *Taxonomy of Educational Objectives: Handbook 1/Cognitive Domain*. London: Longman.

Bloom, A. (1987) *The Closing of the American Mind: How Higher Education Has Failed Democracy and Impoverished the Souls of Today's Students*. Harmondsworh: Penguin.

Bloom, A. (1991) Introduction, in Rousseau's *Émile or On Education*. Harmondsworth: Penguin.

Bloomer, M. (1996) Education for Studentship, in J. Avis et al. (eds) *Knowledge and Nationhood: Education, Politics and Work*. London: Cassell, pp. 140–163.

Bloomer, M. (1997) *Curriculum Making in Post-16 Education – The Social Conditions of Studentship*. London: Routledge.

Boden, M.A. (1994) *Piaget*. London: Fontana.

Bottery, M. (2000) *Education, Policy and Ethics*. London: Continuum.

Bourdieu (1986) The forms of capital, in J.E. Richardson (ed.) *Handbook of Theory of Research for the Sociology of Education*. Westport, CT: Greenwood Press, pp. 241–58 (reprinted in Halsey, A.H. et al. (1997) *Education: Culture, Economy, and Society*. Oxford: Oxford University Press, pp. 46–58).

Boyd, W. (1956) *Émile for Today: The Émile of Jean-Jacques Rousseau*, selected, translated and interpreted by William Boyd. London: Heinemann.

Brookfield, S. (1986) *Understanding and Facilitating Learning*. Milton Keynes: Open University Press.

Brooks, R. (1991) *Contemporary Debates in Education: An Historical Perspective*. London: Longman.

Brown, S., Jones, G. and Rawnsley, S. (eds) (1993) *Observing Teaching*. Birmingham: Staff and Educational Development Association.

Bruner, J. (1990) *Acts of Meaning*. London: Harvard University Press.

Bryan, J. (1998) Review of F. Reeves (ed.) (1997) *Further Education as Economic Regeneration: The Starting Point*. Bilston: Bilston Community College and Education Now Books (pp. 99–101 in *Youth and Policy*, Issue 61, Autumn 1998).

Buchanan, S. (ed.) (1982) Introduction, in *The Portable Plato*. Harmondsworth: Penguin.

Burnyeat, M. (1990) *The Theatetus of Plato*, trans. M.J. Levett. Cambridge: Hackett Publishing.

Butler, R. (1988) Enhancing and undermining intrinsic motivation: the effects of task-involving and ego-involving evaluation on interest and performance, *British Journal of Educational Psychology*, 58: 1–14.

Calderhead, J. (1987) *Exploring Teachers' Thinking*. London: Cassell.

Capey, J. (1995) *GNVQ Assessment Review: Final Report of the Review Group*. London: NCVQ.

CBI (Confederation of British Industry) (1991) *World Class Targets: A Joint Initiative to Achieve Britain's Skill Revolution*. London: CBI.

Chickering, A.W. and Havighurst, R. (1981) The life cycle, in A.W. Chickering (ed.) *The Modern American College*. San Francisco, CA: Jossey-Bass.

Child, D. (1993) *Psychology and the Teacher*. London: Cassell.

Cockburn, C. (1987) *Two Track Training: Sex Inequalities and the YTS*. London: Macmillan.

Coffey, D. (1992) *Schools and Work*. London: Cassell.

Coffield, F. (1997) Prophets of the true god, *Times Educational Supplement*, 24 January.

Cohen, L. and Manion, L. (1989) *Research Methods in Education*. London: Routledge.

Corbett, J. and Barton, L. (1992) *A Struggle for Choice*. London: Routledge.

Cornwall, J. (1996) *Choice, Opportunity and Learning*. London: Fulton.

Corson, D. (ed.) (1991) *Education for Work*. Clevedon, Avon: Multilingual Matters Ltd.

Cottrell, S. (1999) *The Study Skills Handbook*. Basingstoke: Macmillan

Coulby, D. and Jones, C. (1995) *Postmodernity and European Education Systems*. Stoke-on-Trent: Trentham Books.

Cronbach, L.J. (1980) *Toward Reform of Program Evaluation*. San Francisco: Jossey-Bass.

CSJ (Commission on Social Justice) (1994) *Social Justice: Strategies for National Renewal*. London: Vintage.

Cuban, L. (2001) *Oversold and Underused: Computers in the Classroom*. London: Harvard University Press.

Curzon, L.B. (ed.) (1990) *Teaching in Further Education*, 4th edn. London: Cassell.

Daunt, P. (1991) *Meeting Disability: A European Response*. London: Cassell.

Davies, W.J.K. (1975) *Learning Resources*. London: Council for Educational Technology.

Dearing, R. (1994) *The National Curriculum and its Assessment* (Dearing I). London: SCAA.

Dearing, R. (1996) *Review of Qualifications for 16–19 Year Olds* (Dearing II). Hayes: SCAA.

Dearing, R. (1997) *Higher Education in the Learning Society: Report of the National Committee of Inquiry into Higher Education* (Dearing III). London: HMSO.

DES (Department of Education and Science) (1991) *Education and Training for the 21st Century*, Cmnd. 1536. London: HMSO.

Dewey, J. (1915) *The School and Society*. Chicago: University of Chicago Press.

Dewey, J. ([1916] 1966) *Democracy and Education*. New York: Macmillan/The Free Press.

Dewey, J. ([1938] 1971) *Experience and Education*. New York: Collier Books.

DfEE (Department for Education and Employment) (1995a) *Competitiveness: Forging Ahead, Education and Training*. London: HMSO.

DfEE (Department for Education and Employment) (1995b) *Lifetime Learning: A Consultation Document*. London: HMSO.

DfEE (Department for Education and Employment) (Department for Education and Employment) (1997) *Qualifying for Success*. London: DfEE.

DfEE (Department for Education and Employment) (1998a) *Higher Education for the 21st Century: Response to the Dearing Report*. London: DfEE.

DfEE (Department for Education and Employment) (1998b) *The Learning Age: A Renaissance for a New Britain*. London: DfEE.

DfEE (Department for Education and Employment) (1999) *Learning to Succeed a New Framework for Post-16 Learning*. White Paper. London: The Stationery Office.

DfES (Department for Education and Skills) (2001) *Meeting the Sector Skills and Productivity Challenge*. London: HMSO.

DfES (Department for Education and Skills) (2002a) *14–19: Extending Opportunities, Raising Standards*. London: The Stationery Office.

DfES (2002b) *Success for All*. London: HMSO

DfES (2003a) *21st Century Skills: Realising our Potential*. London: DfES.

DfES (2003b) *14–19 Opportunities and Excellence*. London: DfES.

DfES (2003c) *The Future of Initial Teacher Education for the Learning and Skills Sector*. Sheffield: Standards Unit.

DfES (2004a) *Children Act 2004*. London: Stationery Office.

DFES (2004b) *14–19 Curriculum and Qualifications Reform* (Tomlinson Report). London: DfES.

DfES (2004c) *Equipping our Teachers for the Future: Reforming Initial Teaching Training for the Learning and Skills*. London: HMSO.

DfES (2004d) *Every Child Matters*. London: The Stationery Office.

DfES (2005a) *14–19 Education and Skills*. London: The Stationery Office.

DfES (2005b) *Harnessing Technology: Transforming Learning and Children's Services*. Available at: www.dfes.gov.uk/publications/e-strategy/ (accessed: February 2007).

DfES (2005c) *Youth Matters*. London: The Stationery Office.

DfES (2005d) *Realising the Potential: A Review of the Future Role of Further Education Colleges*. (Foster Report) Nottingham: DfES.

DfES (2006a) *Further Education: Raising Skills, Improving Life Chances*. London: The Stationery Office.

DfES (2006b) *Specialised Diplomas – Your Questions Answered*. London: DfES.

DfES (2006c) *Further Education and Training Bill [HL]*. Norwich: DfES.

DfES (2007a) *2020 Vision: Report of the Teaching and Learning in 2020 Review Group*. Nottingham: DfES. Available at: www.teachernet.gov.uk/docbank/index.cfm?id=10783

DfES (2007b) *Raising Expectations: Staying in Education and Training Post 16*. Available at: www.dfes.gov.uk/publications/raisingexpectations/

Dickinson, L. (1992) *Learner Autonomy*. Dublin: Authentik.

DoH (Department of Health) (1999) *Making a Difference: Strengthening the Nursing, Midwifery and Health Visiting Contributions to Health and Healthcare*. London: DoH.

Donald, J. (1992) *Sentimental Education*. London: Verso.

Dunnill, R., Nakarada, S. and Raffo, C. (1995) An approach to the revised Advanced Business GNVQ, *Economics and Business Education*, 3(11): 135.

Ecclestone, K. and Hayes, D. (2007) *The Dangerous Rise of Therapeutic Education*. London: Routledge.

*Economist* (1996) Training and jobs: what works? 6 April.

Egan, G. (1994) *The Skilled Helper*. Pacific Grove, CA: Brooks/Cole Publishing Co.

Eisner, E.W. (1985) *The Educational Imagination: On the Design and Evaluation of School Programs*. New York: Macmillan.

Ellington, H. and Race, P. (1993) *Producing Teaching Materials*, 2nd edn. London: Kogan Page.

Ellington, H., Percival, F. and Race, P. (1993) *Handbook of Educational Technology*, 3rd edn. London: Kogan Page.

Elliott, J. (1993) Introduction, in J. Elliott (ed.) *Reconstructing Teacher Education*. London: Falmer Press.

Engels, F. ([1878] 1975) *Anti-Duhring*. London: Lawrence and Wishart.

Farish, M., McPake, J., Powney, J. and Weiner, G. (1996) *Equal Opportunities in Colleges and*

*Universities*. Buckingham: The Society for Research into Higher Education and Open University Press.

FEDA (Further Education Development Agency) (1995) *Launch Newsletter*, May.

FEFC (Further Education Development Agency) (1996) *Quality and Standards in Further Education in England: Chief Inspector's Annual Report 1995–96*. Coventry: FEFC.

FENTO (2001) *Governors and Clerks in Further Education Benchmark Standards*. London: FENTO.

FEU (Further Education Unit) (1987) *Marketing Adult and Continuing Education: A Project Report*. London: FEU.

Field, J. (2000) *Lifelong Learning and the New Educational Order*. Stoke on Trent: Trentham Books.

Finegold, D.N. and Soskice, D. (1988) The failure of training in Britain: analysis and prescription, *Oxford Review of Economic Policy*, 4(3): 21–53.

Finegold, D.N., Keep, E., Miliband, D. et al. (1990) *A British Baccalaureate*. London: IPPR.

Finlayson, H. et al. (2006) *e-learning in Further Education: The Impact and End-point outcomes*. Sheffield: Sheffield Hallam University School of Education.

Finn, D. (1986) YTS: the jewel in the MSC's crown?, in C. Benn and J. Fairley (eds) *Challenging the MSC on Jobs, Training and Education*. London: Pluto Press.

Finn, D. (1987) *Training Without Jobs: New Deals and Broken Promises*. London: Macmillan.

Foster, A. (2005) *(The Foster Report) Realising the Potential: A Review of the Future Role of Further Education Colleges*. London: DfES.

Francis, D. and Young, D. (1979) *Improving Working Groups*. London: University Association.

Fryer, R.H. (1997) *Learning for the 21st Century: First Report of the National Advisory Group for Continuing Education and Lifelong Learning*. London: NAGCELL.

Füredi, F. (1997) *Culture of Fear*. London: Cassell.

Füredi, F. (2004) *Therapy Culture: Cultivating Vulnerability in an Uncertain Age*. London: Routledge.

Gagné, R. (1977) *Conditions of Learning*. New York: Holt, Rinehart and Winston.

Gamble, A. (1990) *Britain in Decline: Economic Policy, Political Strategy and the British State*, 3rd edn. London: Macmillan.

Gardner, H. (1983) *Frames of Mind: The Theory of Multiple Intelligences*. New York: Basic Books.

Gardner, H. (1993) *Multiple Intelligences*. New York: Basic Books.

Gibbs, G. and Habeshaw, T. (1989) *Preparing to Teach*. Bristol: Technical and Educational Services Ltd.

Gibbs, G., Habeshaw, S. and Habeshaw, T. (1988) *53 Interesting Ways to Appraise Your Teaching*. Bristol: Technical and Educational Services Ltd.

Gibbs, G. and Parsons, C. (1994) *Course Design for Resource Based Learning*. Oxford: Oxford Centre for Staff Development.

Giddens, A. (1998) *The Third Way: The Renewal of Social Democracy*. Cambridge: Polity Press.

Giddens, A. (1999) *Runaway World*. London: Profile Books.

Gilbert, C. et al. (2006) *2020 Vision: Report of the Teaching and Learning in 2020 Review Group*. London: DfES. Available at: www.teachernet.gov.uk/docbank/index.cfm?id=10783

Gilroy, P. (1993) Reflections on Schön, in P. Gilroy and M. Smith (eds) *International Analyses of Teacher Education*. Abingdon: Carfax, Journal of Education and Training Papers 1.

Glennerster, N. (1995) *British Social Policy Since 1945*. London: Basil Blackwell.

Golden, S. et al. (2006) *Impact of e-learning in Further Education: Survey of Scale and Breadth*. London: DfES.

Goleman, D. (1995) *Emotional Intelligence*. London: Bloomsbury.

Goodson, I.F. (1994) *Studying Curriculum: Cases and Methods*. Buckingham: Open University Press.

Goodson, I.F. and Hargreaves, A. (eds) (1996) *Teachers' Professional Lives*. London: Falmer Press.

Grenfell, M. and James, D. (1998) *Bourdieu and Education: Acts of Practical Theory*. London: Falmer Press.

Hall, V. (1994) *Further Education in the UK*, 2nd edn. London and Bristol: Collins Educational and the Staff College.

Hamilton, D. (1976) *Curriculum Evaluation*. London: Open Books.

Hargreaves, A. (1994) *Changing Teachers, Changing Times: Teachers' Work and Culture in a Postmodern Age*. London: Cassell.

Harkin, J., Turner, G. and Dawn, T. (2001) *Teaching Young Adults: A Handbook for Teachers in Post-compulsory Education*. London: Routledge/Falmer.

Hayes, D. (2002) Taking the hemlock: the new sophistry of teacher training for higher education, in D. Hayes and R. Wynyard (eds) *The McDonaldization of Higher Education*. Westport, CT: Bergin and Garvey.

Hayes, D. (2002) New Labour: new professionalism, a paper presented at the Discourse, Power and Resistance in Post-Compulsory Education and Training Conference, Plymouth University, 12–14 April.

Hayes, D. (2003a) New Labour: new professionalism, in J. Satterthwaite, E. Atkinson and K. Gale (eds) *Discourse, Power, Resistance: Challenging the Rhetoric of Contemporary Education*. Stoke-on-Trent: Trentham.

Hayes, D. (2003b) The changed nexus between education and work, in J. Lea, D. Hayes, A. Armitage, L. Lomas and S. Markless (eds) *Working in Post-Compulsory Education*. Maidenhead: Open University Press, pp. 43–55.

Hayes, D. (2003c) Managerialism and professionalism in post-compulsory education, in J. Lea, D. Hayes, A. Armitage, L. Lomas and S. Markless (eds) *Working in Post-Compulsory Education*. Maidenhead: Open University Press, pp. 87–100.

Hayes, D. (2004) The therapeutic turn in teacher education, in D. Hayes (ed.) *The Routledge Falmer Guide to Key Debates in Education*. London: Routledge, pp. 180–5.

Hayes, D. (2005) Theoretically, how are you feeling? *FE Focus, TES*, 29 April.

Hayes, D. (2006) Rehumanising education, in D. Cummings (ed.) *Debating Humanism*. Exeter: Imprint Academic/Societas, pp. 84–92.

Hayes, D. (2007) Past caring about history, *FE Focus, TES*, 2 February.

Hayes, D. and Hudson, A. (2001) *Basildon: The Mood of the Nation*. London: Demos.

Hayes, D. and Wynyard, R. (2002a) Resisting McUniversity, in D. Hayes and R. Wynyard (eds) *The McDonaldization of Higher Education*. Westport, CT: Bergin and Garvey.

Hayes, D. and Wynyard, R. (2002b) Whimpering into the good night: resisting McUniversity, in G. Ritzer (ed.) *The McDonaldization Reader*. Thousand Oaks, CA: Sage Publications.

Hayes, D., Marshall, T. and Turner, A. (2007) *A Lecturer's Guide to Further Education*. Maidenhead: Open University Press.

Hayes, D., Browne, E. and Simmons, J. (2007) *An Evaluation of the Pedagogical Uses and Cognitive Applications to Subject Specialism Teaching in Post-compulsory Education of the 'Chronological' Approach Described in the Best Selling Text Book Teaching & Training in Post-Compulsory Education*. Bristol: Escalate.

Hearnshaw, L.S. (1979) *Cyril Burt, Psychologist*. London: Hodder and Stoughton.

HEFCE (2005) *HEFCE Strategy for E- Learning*. Available at: www.hefce.ac.uk/pubs/hefce/2005/05_12/05_12.pdf (accessed January 2007).

Hickox, M. (1995) Situating vocationalism, *British Journal of Sociology of Education*, 16(2): 153–62.

Higham, J., Sharp, P. and Yeomans, D. (1996) *The Emerging 16–19 Curriculum*. London: Fulton.

Hillier Y (2005) *Reflective Teaching in Further and Adult Education*, 2nd edn. London: Continuum

Hirst, P.H. ([1965] 1973) Liberal education and the nature of knowledge, in R.S. Peters (ed.) *The Philosophy of Education*. Oxford: Oxford University Press.

Hirst, P.H. (1974) *Knowledge and the Curriculum*. London: Routledge and Kegan Paul.

Hirst, P.H. (1993) Education, knowledge and practices, in R. Barrow and P. White (eds) *Beyond Liberal Education: Essays in Honour of Paul H. Hirst*. London: Routledge, pp. 184–99.

HMSO (1959) *15–18: A Report of the Central Advisory Council for Education/England* (Crowther Report). London: HMSO.

HMSO (1986) *The National Council for Vocational Qualifications: Its Purposes and Aims*. London: HMSO.

Hobsbawm, E. (1994) *Age of Extremes. The Short Twentieth Century 1914–1991*. London: Michael Joseph.

Hodgson, A. and Spours, K. (ed.) (1997) *Dearing and Beyond 14–19: Qualifications and Frameworks*. London: Kogan Page.

Hodgson, A. and Spours, K. (ed.) (1999) *New Labour's Educational Agenda. Issues and Policies for Education and Training from 14*. London: Kogan Page.

Hodgson, A. and Spours, K. (2000) *Institutional Responses to Curriculum 2000*. London: Institute of Education.

Hodgson, A. and Spours, K. (2001) *Evaluating Stage 1 of the Hargreaves Review of Curriculum 2000*. London: Institute of Education.

Hodgson, A. and Spours, K. (2003) *Beyond A-levels: Curriculum 2000 and the Reform of 14–19 Qualifications*. London: RoutledgeFalmer.

Hodgson, A., Savory, C. and Spours, K. (2001a) *Planning and Implementing Curriculum 2000: Different Institutional Approaches*. London: Institute of Education.

Hodgson, A., Savory, C. and Spours (2001b) *Improving the 'Use' and 'Exchange' Value of Key Skills*. London: Institute of Education.

Hoggart, R. (1996) *The Way We Live Now*. London: Pimlico.

Holland, R.F. (1980) *Against Empiricism: On Education, Epistemology and Value*. London: Basil Blackwell, pp. 2–25.

Hopkins, D. (1989) *Evaluation for School Development*. Milton Keynes: Open University Press.

Houle, C.O. (1961) *The Enquiring Mind*. Madison: University of Wisconsin Press.

Houle, C.O. (1972) *The Design of Education*. San Francisco: Jossey-Bass.

Huddleston, P. and Unwin, L. (1997) *Teaching and Learning in Further Education: Diversity and Change*. London: Routledge.

Hudson, A., Hayes, D. and Andrew, T. (1996) *Working Lives in the 1990s*. London: Global Futures.

Hudson, L. (1966) *Contrary Imaginations*. London: Methuen.

Hyland, T. (1994) *Competence, Education and NVQs: Dissenting Perspectives*. London: Cassell.

Hyland, T. (2005) Learning and therapy – oppositional or complementary processes? *Adults Learning*, January: 16–17.

Hyland, T. (2006) Vocational education and training and the therapeutic turn, *Educational Studies*, Sept., 32(3): 299–306.

IfL (2006a) *Towards a Code of Good Environmental Practice*. Available at: www.ifl.ac.uk/ members_area/code_environ.html

IfL (2006b) *Towards a Code of Professional Practice*. Available at: www.ifl.ac.uk/members_area/ code_prof.html

IfL (2006c) *Towards a Code of Ethics*. Available at: www.ifl.ac.uk/members_area/code_ethics.html

IiP (Investors in People UK) (2006) *The Investors in People Standard*, 2nd edn. London: IiP.

IRDAC (Industrial Research and Development Advisory Committee) (1990) *Skills Shortages in Europe*. Brussels: IRDAC.

Jackson, P.W. (1968) *Life in Classrooms*. New York: Holt, Rinehart and Winston.

Jarvis, P. (1995) *Adult and Continuing Education Theory and Practice*. London: Routledge.

Jeffries, A. et al. (2004) Introducing web-based learning: an investigation into its impact on university lecturers and their pedagogy, *Journal of Information Technology Impact*, 4(2): 91–8. Available at: http://www.jiti.com/ (accessed March 2007).

JISC *E-learning Programme*. Available at: www.jisc.ac.uk/whatwedo/themes/elearning/programme_elearning.aspx (accessed March 2007).

JISC (2007) *The Learners' Voice*. Available at: www.jisc.ac.uk/whatwedo/programmes/elearning_pedagogy/elp_learneroutcomes/elp_learnervoices.aspx (accessed March 2007).

JISC (2006) *Designing Spaces for Effective Learning*. Available at: www.jisc.ac.uk/uploaded_documents/JISC%20learning%20spaces.acc.pdf (accessed February 2007).

Johnson, H. (2004) *Personalised Learning: An Emperor's Outfit?* London: ippr.

Kennedy, H. (1997a) *Guardian*, 27 May.

Kennedy, H. (1997b) *Learning Works: Widening Participation in Further Education*. Coventry: FEFC.

Knowles, M. (1984) *The Adult Learner: A Neglected Species*, 3rd edn. Houston, TX: Gulf Publishing Company.

Kolb, D. (1984) *Experiential Learning: Experience as a Source of Learning and Development*. New York: Prentice Hall.

Korndörffer, W. (1991) Vocational skills training in transition education, in D. Corson (ed.) *Education for Work*. Clevedon, Avon: Multilingual Matters Ltd, pp. 220–31.

Krol, E. (1994) *The Whole Internet*. Sebastopol, CA: O'Reilly and Associates.

Labour Party (1996) *Road to the Manifesto: Lifelong Learning*. London: Labour Party.

Langenbach, M. (1988) *Curriculum Models in Adult Education*. Malabar, FL: Krieger Publishing.

Langford, G. (1985) *Education, Persons and Society: A Philosophical Enquiry*. Basingstoke: Macmillan.

Laurillard, D. (2002) *Rethinking University Teaching: A Framework for the Effective Use of Educational Technology*, 2nd edn. London: Routledge.

Lave, J. and Wenger, E. (1991) *Situated Learning: Legitimate Peripheral Participation*, Cambridge: Cambridge University Press.

Lawton, D. (1983) *Curriculum Studies and Educational Planning*. London: Hodder and Stoughton.

Lea, J., Armitage, A., Hayes, D., Lomas, L. and Markless, S. (2003) *Working in Post-Compulsory Education*. Milton Keynes: Open University Press.

Leadbeater, C. (2004a) *Learning about Personalisation*. London: Demos.

Leadbeater, C. (2004b) *Personalisation through Participation*. London: Demos.

Learning and Skills Council (LSC) (2001) *Circular 01/02: Quality Improvement Standards Fund 2001/02*. Coventry: LSC.

Leicester, M. (1994) Competence, knowledge and education: reply to Hyland, *Journal of Philosophy of Education*, 28(1): 113–18.

Leitch Review of Skills (2006) *Prosperity For All in the Global Economy – World Class Skills* (Final Report). London: HM Treasury. Available at: www.dfes.gov.uk/skillsstrategy/uploads/documents/Leitch%20Review.pdf

Lewis, T. (1991) Difficulties attending the new vocationalism in the USA, *Journal of the Philosophy of Education*, 25(1): 95–108.

Lewis, T. (1997) Towards a liberal education, *Journal of the Philosophy of Education*, 3(3): 477–90.

LLUK (2005) *National Occupational Standards for Leadership and Management in the Post Compulsory Learning and Skills*. London: LLUK.

LLUK/FENTO (2005) *E-learning Standards for E-Learning Context – Application of ICT to Teaching and Supporting Learning*. London: LLUK.

LLUK (2006) *New Overarching Professional Standards for Teachers, Tutors and Trainers in the Lifelong Learning Sector*. London: LLUK.

Locke, J. ([1693] 1989) *Some Thoughts Concerning Education*. Oxford: Clarendon Press.

Lovell, R.B. (1980) *Adult Learning*. London: Croom Helm.

Lukás, G. (1968) *History and Class Consciousness*. London: Merlin Press.

Maclure, J.S. (1965) *Educational Documents: England and Wales*. London: Chapman and Hall.

Maclure, S. (1988) *Education Reformed: A Guide to the Education Reform Act*. London: Hodder and Stoughton.

McGivney, V. (1990) *Access to Education for Non-Participating Adults*. Leicester: NIACE.

McIntyre, D., Hagger, H. and Wilkin, M. (eds) *Mentoring: Perspectives on School-Based Teacher Education*. London: Kogan Page.

McNamara, B. (1979) *Focus on Teaching*. London: Longman.

McNiff, J. (2003) *How Do We Develop a Twenty-First Century Knowledge Base for the Teaching Profession in South Africa? How Do We Communicate Our Passion for Learning?* Available at: www.jeanmcniff.com/21.html

McNiff, J. with Whitehead, J. (2002) *Action Research: Principles and Practice*. London: RoutledgeFalmer.

Mortiboys, A (2005) *Teaching with Emotional Intelligence: A Step-by-Step Guide for Further and Higher Education Professionals*. London: RoutledgeFalmer.

Malik, K. (2001) *What is it to be Human?* London: The Institute of Ideas.

Martinez, P. (1999) *Learning from Continuing Professional Development*. London: FEDA.

Marx, K. ([1867] 1974) *Capital*, vol. 1. London: Lawrence and Wishart.

Marx, K. ([1875] 1968) Critique of the Gotha Programme, in K. Marx and F. Engels, *Selected Works*. London: Lawrence and Wishart.

Maslow, A.H. (1970) *Motivation and Personality*. New York: Harper and Row.

Maynard, T. and Furlong, J. (1993) Learning to teach and models of mentoring, in D. McIntyre, H. Hagger and M. Wilkin (eds) *Mentoring: Perspectives on School-based Teacher Education*. London: Kogan Page.

Millerson, G. (1964) *The Qualifying Associations: A Study in Professionalism*. London: Routledge.

Minton, D. (1991) *Teaching Skills in Further and Adult Education*. Basingstoke: City and Guilds/Macmillan.

Moore, M. (1983) On a theory of independent study, in D. Sewart, D. Keegan and B. Holmberg (eds) *Distance Education: International Perspectives*. London: Croom Helm, pp. 68–94.

Muttona, T., Mills, B.G. and McNicholls, J. (2006) Mentor skills in a new context: working with trainee teachers to develop the use of information and communications technology in their subject teaching, *Technology, Pedagogy and Education*, October, 15(3): 337–52.

Napier, R.W. and Gershenfeld, M.K. (1989) *Groups, Theory and Experience*, 4th edn. Boston: Houghton Mifflin.

National Commission on Education (1993) *Learning to Succeed: Report of the Peter Hamlyn Foundation*. London: Heinemann.

NCVQ (National Council for Vocational Qualifications) (1988) *Information Leaflet Number 1*. London: NCVQ.

Nolan, J.L. (1998) *The Therapeutic State: Justifying Government at Century's End*. New York: New York University Press.

Nuttall, L. (1988) Transmitted, caught or taught? A whole school approach to personal and social education, *Pastoral Care*, March.

Ofsted (Office for Standards in Education) (2001a) *Handbook for Inspecting Colleges*. London: Ofsted.

Ofsted (Office for Standards in Education) (2001b) *Curriculum 2000: The First Year of Implementation*. London: Ofsted.

Ofsted (Office for Standards in Education)/ALI (Adult Learning Inspectorate) (2001c) *A Common Inspection Framework for Post-16 Education and Training*. London: The Stationery Office.

Ofsted (2003) *The Initial Training of Further Education Teachers: A Survey*, HMI 1762. Available at: www.ofsted.gov.uk/publications/index.cfm?fuseaction=pubs.summary&id=3425

O'Reilly, T. (2005) *What is Web 2.0?* Available at: www.oreillynet.com/pub/a/oreilly/tim/news/2005/09/30/what-is-web-20.html (accessed March 2007).

Passmore, J. (1973) On teaching to be critical, in R.S. Peters (ed.) *The Concept of Education*. London: Routledge and Kegan Paul, pp. 192–211.

Perkinson, H.J. (1980) *Since Socrates: Studies in the History of Western Educational Thought*. London: Longman.

Peters, J. M. (1994), Instructors as researchers and theorists: faculty development in a community college, in R. Benn and R. Fieldhouse (eds) *Training and Professional Development in Adult and Community Education*. Exeter: CRCE.

Petty, G. (2004) *Teaching Today: A Practical Guide*, 3rd edn. Cheltenham: Stanley Thornes.

Phillips, M. (1996) *All Must Have Prizes*. London: Little, Brown and Company.

Pincas, A. (1997) IT Focus, *Guardian*, 27 May.

Plato (1993) *The Apology*, in H. Tarrant (ed.) *The Last Days of Socrates*. Harmondsworth: Penguin.

Plato (1956) *Protagoras and Meno*, trans. W.K.C. Guthrie. Harmondsworth: Penguin.

Plato (1982) *Republic*, in *The Portable Plato*, edited with an introduction by Scott Buchanan. Harmondsworth: Penguin.

Pollard, A. and James, M. (eds) (2004) *Personalised Learning: A Commentary by the Teaching and Learning Research Programme*. London: ESRC

Powell, R. (1991) *Resources for Flexible Learning*. Stafford: Network Education Press.

Poynter, G. (2000) *Restructuring in the Service Industries*. London: Mansell.

Preedy, M. (1989) *Approaches to Curriculum Management*. Milton Keynes: Open University Press.

Prensky, M. (2001) Digital natives, *On the Horizon*, 9(5). Available at: www.marcprensky.com/writing/Prensky%20-%20Digital%20Natives,%20Digital%20Immigrants%20-%20Part1.pdf (accessed February 2007).

Priestley, M. (2003) Curriculum 2000: a broader view of A levels? *Cambridge Journal of Education*, 33(2): 237–55.

Pring, R. (1992) Liberal education and vocational preparation, in M. Williams, R. Daugherty and F. Banks (eds) *Continuing the Education Debate*. London: Cassell, pp. 54–64.

Pring, R. (1993) Liberal education and vocational preparation, in R. Barrow and P. White (eds) *Beyond Liberal Education: Essays in Honour of Paul H. Hirst*. London: Routledge, pp. 49–78.

Pring, R. (1995) *Closing the Gap: Liberal Education and Vocational Preparation*. London: Hodder and Stoughton.

Quality Assurance Agency (1999) *Guidelines on the Quality Assurance of Higher Education*. Gloucester: QAA.

QCA (Qualifications and Curriculum Authority) (2001a) *Review of Curriculum 2000: Report on Phase 1*. London: QCA.

QCA (Qualifications and Curriculum Authority) (2001b) *Review of Curriculum 2000: Report on Phase 2*. London: QCA.

Race, P. (1992) *53 Interesting Ways to Write Open Learning Materials*. Bristol: Technical and Educational Services Ltd.

Raffe, D. (2005) Learning from 'Home International' comparisons: *14–19 Curriculum and Qualifications Reform in England, Scotland and Wales*, Joint seminar of Education and Youth Transitions Project and Nuffield Review, 15 March. Available at: www.nuffield14-19review.org.uk/cgi/documents/documents.cgi?a=117&t=template.htm

Raggatt, P., Edwards, R. and Small, N. (eds) (1966) *The Learning Society, Challenges and Trends*. London: Routledge in association with the Open University.

Reece, I. and Walker, S. (1994) *A Practical Guide to Teaching, Training and Learning*. Sunderland: Business Educational Publishing.

Reece, I. and Walker, S. (2003) *Teaching Training and Learning*. Sunderland: Business Educational Publishing.

Reeves, F. (ed.) (1997) *Further Education as Economic Regeneration: The Starting Point*. Bilston: Bilston Community College and Education Now Books.

Reigeluth, C. M. (1999) *Instructional-design theories and models*. Mahwah, NJ: Lawrence Erlbaum Associates.

Riley, P. (1985) *Discourse and Learning*. London: Longman.

Robbins, Lord L.C. (1963) *Higher Education: Report of the Committee on Higher Education*, Cmnd 2154. London: HMSO.

Roberts, K., Blunden, G. and Ruseborough, G. (1994) Review symposium: class and skill, *British Journal of Sociology of Education*, 15(1): 119–27.

Robertson, J. (1989) *Effective Classroom Control*. London: Hodder and Stoughton.

Robertson, J. (2001) *Teaching Young Adults*. London: Hodder and Stoughton.

Rogers, C. (1983) *Freedom to Learn for the '80s*. Columbus, OH: Merrill.

Rogers, A. (1996) *Teaching Adults*. Buckingham: Open University Press.

Rousseau, J.J. ([1762] 1991) *Émile*. Harmondsworth: Penguin.

Rowe, M.B. (1974) Wait time and rewards as instructional variables, their influences on language, logic and fate control, *Journal of Research in Science Teaching*, 11: 81–4.

Rowntree, D. (1987) *Assessing Students: How Shall We Know Them?* London: Kogan Page.

Russell, B. ([1959] 1989) *Wisdom of the West*. London: Bloomsbury.

Ryan, A. (1995) *John Dewey and the High Tide of American Liberalism*. New York: W.W. Norton.

Ryle, G. (1973) Teaching and training, in R.S. Peters (ed.) *The Concept of Education*. London: Routledge and Kegan Paul, pp. 105–19.

Satterly, D. (1990) *Assessment in Schools*. London: Basil Blackwell.

Salmon, G. (2002) *E-tivities: The Key to Active Online Learning*. London: Kogan.

Schön, D.A. (1982) *The Reflective Practitioner: How Professionals Think in Action*. New York: Harper Collins.

Scrimshaw, P. (1983) *Purpose and Planning in the Classroom*. Milton Keynes: Open University Press.

Simon, B. (1985) Marx and the crisis in education, *Does Education Matter?*. London: Lawrence and Wishart, pp. 173–96.

Sked, A. (1987) *Britain's Decline: Problems and Perspectives*. London: Basil Blackwell.

Skilbeck, M. (1976) *Curriculum Design and Development.* Milton Keynes: Open University Press.

Skilbeck, M., Connell, H., Lowe, N. and Tait, K. (1994) *The Vocational Quest: New Directions in Education and Training.* London: Routledge.

Skinner, B.F. (1938) *The Behaviour of Organisms: An Experimental Analysis.* New York: Appleton-Century-Croft.

Skuse, P. (1997) Evidence from Turner's Syndrome of an imprinted X-linked locus affecting cognitive functioning, *Nature,* 387: 705–8.

Smith, W.O. Lester (1957) *Education.* Harmondsworth: Penguin.

Smithers, A. (2001) Education policy, in A. Seldon (ed.) *The Blair Effect.* London: Little, Brown and Company, pp. 405–26.

Smyth, J. (1989) Developing and sustaining critical reflection in teacher education, *Journal of Teacher Education,* 40(2): 2–9.

Social Exclusion Unit (1999) *Bridging the Gap: New Opportunities for 16–18 Year Olds Not in Education, Employment or Training.* London: The Stationery Office.

Stenhouse, L. (1975) *An Introduction to Curriculum Research and Development.* London: Heinemann.

Stanton, G. (2005) *The Proposals for a New System of Specialist (Vocational) Diplomas,* Nuffield Review of 14–19 Education and Training Working Paper 32. Available at: www.nuffield14-19review.org.uk/cgi/documents/documents.cgi?a=117&t=template.htm

Stothart, C. (2006) Do the iPod shuffle, but don't miss the lecture, *Times Higher Education Supplement.* Available at: www.thes.co.uk/search/story.aspx?story_id=2030201 (accessed March 2007).

Sutcliffe, J. (1990) *Adults with Learning Difficulties.* Leicester: NIACE.

Taba, H. (1962) *Curriculum Development: Theory and Practice.* New York: Harcourt Brace.

Tanner, D. and Tanner, L.M. (1980) *Curriculum Development: Theory Into Practice.* New York: Macmillan.

Tarrant, H. (ed.) (1993) *The Last Days of Socrates.* Harmondsworth: Penguin.

Tawney, R.H. ([1922] 1988) *Secondary Education for All.* London: The Hambledon Press.

Taylor, P.H. and Richards, C.M. (1985) *An Introduction to Curriculum Studies.* Windsor: NFER/Nelson.

Tennant, M. (1988) *Psychology and Adult Learning.* London: Routledge.

Tennant, M. (2002) *Learning and Change in the Adult Years: A Developmental Perspective.* San Francisco: Josscy-Bass.

Tennant, M. and Pogson, P. (1995) *Learning and Change in the Adult Years. A Developmental Perspective.* San Francisco: Jossey-Bass.

Therborn, G. (1978) The Frankfurt School, in New Left Review (ed.) *Western Marxism: A Critical Reader.* London: Verso, pp. 83–139.

Thorndike, E.L. (1912) *Education: A First Book.* New York: Macmillan.

Tight, M. (ed.) (1983) *Adult Learning and Education.* London: Routledge.

Tight, M. (1996) *Key Concepts in Adult Education and Training.* London: Routledge.

Timmins, N. (1996) *The Five Giants: A Biography of the Welfare State.* London: Fontana.

Tomlinson, S. (2001) *Education in a Post-welfare Society.* Buckingham: Open University Press.

Tough, A. (1979) *The Adult's Learning Projects: A Fresh Approach to Theory and Practice in Adult Learning.* Toronto: Ontario Institute for Studies in Education.

TTA (Teacher Training Agency) (1995) *Corporate Plan 1995: Promoting High Quality Teaching and Teacher Education.* London: TTA.

Tyler, R. (1971) *Basic Principles for Curriculum and Instruction.* Chicago: University of Chicago Press.

Usher, R. and Edwards, R. (1994) *Postmodernism and Education.* London: Routledge.

Wake, G. (2005) *Functional Mathematics: More Than 'Back To Basics'*, Nuffield Review of 14–19 Education and Training Aims, Learning and Curriculum Series, Discussion Paper 17. Available at: www.nuffield14-19review.org.uk/cgi/documents/documents.cgi?a=117&t=template.htm

Wallace, S. (2005) *Teaching and Supporting Learning in Further Education*, 2nd edn. Exeter: Learning Matters.

Walker, D.F. and Soltis, J.F. (1997) *Curriculum and Aims*. London: Teachers College Press.

Walklin, L. (1990) *Teaching and Learning in Further Education*. Cheltenham: Stanley Thornes.

Waugh, C. (2000) Learning policy: a powerful indictment – but what role has the working class to play? *General Educator*, Jan.–Feb., 62: 13–16.

Wenger, E. (1998) *Communities of Practice: Learning, Meaning, and Identity*. Cambridge: Cambridge University Press.

Williams, M. (1992) Ruskin in context, in M. Williams, R. Daugherty and F. Burns (eds) *Continuing the Education Debate*. London: Cassell.

Williams, K. (1994) Vocationalism and liberal education: exploring the tensions, *Journal of Philosophy of Education*, 28(1): 89–100.

Williams, M., Daugherty, R. and Burns, F. (eds) (1992) *Continuing the Education Debate*. London: Cassell.

Willis, P. (1987) Foreword, in D. Finn (ed.) *Training Without Jobs: New Deals and Broken Promises*. London: Macmillan.

Winch, C. (2003) *Some Philosophical and Policy Considerations Concerning Vocational and Prevocational Education*, Nuffield Review of 14–19 Education and Training Working Paper 1. Available at: www.nuffield14-19review.org.uk/cgi/documents/documents.cgi?a=117&t=template.htm

Wolf, A. (1993) *Assessment Issues and Problems in a Criterion-based System*. London: FEU.

Wolf, A. and Black, H. (1990) *Knowledge and Competence: Current Issues in Training and Education*. Sheffield: Careers and Occupational Information Centre.

Working Group on 14–19 Reform (2004) *The Final Report on 14–19 Curriculum and Qualifications Reform* (The Tomlinson Report) London: Working Group on 14–19 Reform.

Woudhuysen, J. (1997) Before we rush to declare a new era, in G. Mulgan (ed.) *Life After Politics*. London: Fontana, pp. 352–9.

Woudhuysen, J. (1999) *Cult IT*. London: ICA.

Wragg, E. C. (1999) *An Introduction to Classroom Observation*, 2nd edn. London: Routledge.

Yaffe, D. (1978) *The State and the Capitalist Crisis*. London: Mimeo.

Young, M.F.D. (1998) *The Curriculum of the Future: From the New Sociology of Education to a Critical Theory of Learning*. London: Falmer Press.

Youngman, M.B. (1986) *Analysing Questionnaires*. Nottingham: University of Nottingham School of Education, Trentham Books.

# INDEX